1952

7/6

ZEUS CASTING HIS THUNDERBOLT.

(*See* p. xi.)

(V)

# MAN AND DEITY

## An Outline of the Origin and Development of Religion

With Extracts from Sacred Books

by

## A. C. BOUQUET, D.D.

*Stanton Lecturer in the Philosophy of Religion*
*in the University of Cambridge;*
*Hulsean Lecturer, 1923-24*

CAMBRIDGE
W. HEFFER & SONS LTD.
1933

LONDON AGENTS
SIMPKIN MARSHALL LTD.

PRINTED IN ENGLAND

To Francis Crawford Burkitt

# Foreword

I suppose that this essay might be described as a detailed examination of the argument "from universal consent" for the nature of Deity. A young (rather unorthodox) biologist remarked to me the other day that he thought the "consensus claim" could fairly be used in more than one way. With this I am bound to agree. There is a "consensus infidelium" as well as a "consensus fidelium." "Universal need" is a much better phrase than "universal consent." There is no real "consensus" except upon the need for a unification of life by purpose related to the Whole; and not every sort of unification is equally good or valid.

This book has been planned to meet the requirements of the general reader and at the same time to supply the needs of those students in both universities and theological colleges who, in the course of their training, are approaching the study of religion comparatively and without *parti pris*. I hope that the avoidance of undue technicalities will satisfy the former, and that the provision of a narrative illustrated by original texts will be of assistance to the latter; for I am given to understand that such a book is in request. Parts of the work have been delivered as lectures under the auspices of the Stanton Foundation.

Number 6 of this series, in which the Christian religion is considered, will be found to form a sequel to the present volume.

v

I wish to express my gratitude to my wife and two or three other persons for their secretarial aid, and especially to the Rev. J. O. Cobham, Vice-Principal of Westcott House, and to Mr. Miles Burkitt for reading nearly the whole of the MS. and making a number of valuable criticisms and suggestions. To the Rev. Professor A. C. Moule I am indebted for advice regarding the section upon Chinese religion. For the opinions expressed in the books of this series I of course alone am responsible. I desire to record my gratitude to the following publishing firms for permissions to make extracts from their editions of sacred texts and other publications: The Trustees of the British Museum (Egyptian and Babylonian texts); The Society for Promoting Christian Knowledge (Babylonian texts); The Oxford University Press and The Clarendon Press (Sacred Books of the East, Sikh literature, Upanishads, Gita, etc., the writings of Mr. C. L. Woolley, Prof. J. H. Moulton); The Cambridge University Press (Prof. Adam's translation of the Hymn of Cleanthes); Messrs. Charles Scribner's Sons (Peruvian hymns, and the writings of Prof. Breasted); The Hakluyt Society (Fr. Acosta's works); Messrs. Hodder & Stoughton, Ltd. (Egyptian texts); Messrs. J. M. Dent & Sons (The Koran). I am also indebted to the Trustees of the British Museum for permission to reproduce the photographs of Ishtar and Amenhotep III, to the Syndics of the Cambridge University Press for blocks of illustrations (Plates 1 and 7, Zeus and Apollo), to Mr. T. Fall for permission to reproduce his photograph of the Bodhisattva statue in the Fitzwilliam Museum, to the United Council of Missionary Education for permission to reproduce the illustration of the Pearl Mosque at Agra, and to the Oxford University Press for permission to reproduce the photograph of the bronze statuette of Siva, from Vincent Smith's *History of Fine Art in India and Ceylon*.

I should also like to record my appreciation of the pains and courtesy displayed by Messrs. Heffer & Sons, Ltd., and to thank Mr. J. H. Bullock, and Mr. P. W. Bavey, of University College, Durham, for reading the proofs. To Mr. R. J. C. Gutteridge, of Trinity Hall, I am indebted for secretarial aid with the bibliography, and to Miss Vreena Lea for help with the index.

A. C. BOUQUET.

GILLING HOUSE,
    CAMBRIDGE,
      *September, 1933.*

# Contents

# NOTES ON THE ILLUSTRATIONS

The importance of religious symbolism is now so much recognised that the illustrations of this book need little justification.

(1) Frontispiece.

> *Zeus Casting his Thunderbolt*, a picture of a small bronze image, (reproduced by kind permission of the Syndics of the Cambridge University Press), shows the typical male deity of the Nordic races, the personification of the warrior-king, patriarch sky-god and old-man-of-the-tribe combined, and equally the projection of the idea of the ruthless autocracy of nature. The original is of the colour of lapis lazuli, and is from Dodona (date c. 490 B.C.).

(2) To face p. 76.

> *The Long Stone, Chapman Barrows, Exmoor*, is a typical English example of a primitive sacred stone, of phallic pattern. It stands on high ground near the source of the Heddon at the north-west edge of the great moor, and in damp weather is almost inaccessible, being surrounded by bog (note the cotton grass). Mr. Chanter records (*Devon Archæological Collections*, Vol. 38), that it was formerly central in relation to a number of smaller stones which formed a rectangle. It is characteristic that the stone should be surrounded by long barrows (see page 354). The spot is evidently a very sacred one, and it is significant that the further away one gets from it, the fewer are the burials. Upright phallic obelisks of this kind are found at a certain phase of human civilisation nearly all over the world, and in Yorkshire at any rate are (perhaps unknowingly now) connected with the fertility of cattle, and known as "rubbing stones," implying that female cattle rubbing against a phallic object may the more easily conceive. (Photographs by author).

(3) To face p. 120.

> *Ishtar*. A very early representation of the great mother goddess. A Sumerian statuette, dated approximately 3000 B.C. (Reproduced by kind permission of the British Museum Trustees).

(4) To face page 145.

> *Amenhotep III and his Queen*. The inscription upon the pedestal gives full explanation of this. (Reproduced by kind permission of the British Museum Trustees).

(5) To face p. 213.

Siva Dancing. A typical Hindu symbolic representation of the Divine Life-Force dancing with zest surrounded by a circle of flames. (Reproduced by kind permission of the Clarendon Press from Vincent Smith's *History of Fine Art in India and Ceylon* : the original image is in Colombo Museum).

(6) To face page 243.

*A Bodhisattva.* The photograph (reproduced by kind permission of Mr. T. Fall of 22, Baker Street, W.), is of a large fifteenth-century Chinese wooden statue in the Marlay Gallery of the Fitzwilliam Museum at Cambridge. The conception of dignified compassion is well expressed, and the artist has admirably succeeded in conveying the impression of a human being in whom is specially incarnate the Divine Purusha.

(7) To face page 300.

*Apollo.* An early example (dated approximately middle fifth century B.C.) of a colossal statue representing this god (reproduced by kind permission of the Syndics of the Cambridge University Press, from a photograph of a cast in the Cambridge University Museum of Classical Archæology). The original is part of the western pediment of the temple of Zeus at Olympia. Note the representation of the Divine as best symbolised in the form of the most perfect human beauty, and the "self-contained power and majesty" shown in the attitude of the god, with arm outstretched. (See Walston, *Alcamenes*).

(8) To face page 383.

*The Pearl Mosque at Agra* (*interior*). This Moslem building has often been photographed, and the present view well illustrates the dominant features of Islamic belief and worship, *i.e.* the total submission implied in the attitude of the worshipper; the spacious dignity of the temple; and the entire absence of imagery in the symbolism—only geometrical patterns being tolerated.

It is worth observing that the tendency to represent a high and super-sensible deity by a symbol other than human is very wide-spread, and that failure to understand it may involve us in a complete mis-apprehension of much symbolism, primitive and otherwise. We have no actual justification for assuming that because a symbolic object of a crude or simple nature is in common use, therefore the conception of deity which lies behind it is equally crude or debased. Even in Buddhism it is said that it was not until nearly 400 years after the time of Gautama, when India had absorbed the artistic traditions of Greece, that the Buddha was represented in Indian art otherwise than by a symbol. So also in the art of the Maya, it was not until Toltec influence made itself felt in Yucatan that the High god of the Maya, Kukulkan, who had become the tribal god of the Toltec, Quetzalcoatl (and in the process had lost a good deal of his mystery) was depicted in anthropomorphic manner. Actually Kukulkan is described in one legend current in a Maya tribe in the peculiar terms of "the feathered snake which goes in the waters." This must surely mean the wind, which produces the ripple or catspaw upon the water, suggesting motion involving elements of both bird and reptile. Kukulkan is therefore in essence none other than the familiar Pneuma, which "bloweth where it listeth, and thou hearest the sound thereof, but canst not tell whence it cometh and whither it goeth." Yet Kukulkan's symbol in such places as Chichén-Itzá and Palenque is a feathered snake. Even in Dürer's famous "Adoration" painting the glorified and spiritual Jesus, in accordance with the language of the Apocalypse, is represented as a "Lamb, as it had been slain." These considerations may lead to a more temperate estimate of the symbolism of primitive peoples, as well as of that of the more highly developed polytheisms.

B

"We limit not the truth of God
    To our poor reach of mind,
By notions of our day and sect,
    Crude, partial, and confined.

Darkling our great forefathers went
    The first steps of the way:
Theirs but the dawning, yet to grow
    Into the perfect day.

O Father of our spirits, send
    Thine increase from above;
Enlarge, renew all Christian souls
    To comprehend thy love.

To hear thy voice, to learn thy will
    Be nobler powers conferred;
For thou hast yet more light and truth
    To break forth from thy word."

                G. RAWSON, 1807–89.

----

"Science is the great clarifier of thought. It renders impossible any religion except the highest."—AN ANGLICAN BISHOP.

----

"Adoration is the contemplative surrender to a supreme good."—HEILER: *Das Gebet* (Eng. trans.).

----

"Religion is not in itself divine, it is the human reference to the divine. From man's nature rises up this thing called religion, like exhalation. It rises up because God's sun is in the heavens."—F. W. CAMFIELD.

# MAN AND DEITY

## GENERAL INTRODUCTION

WE have had many outlines in recent years, both at home and abroad, notably outlines of History, of Science, of Natural History, of Literature and Art, and of Knowledge taken in all its branches synoptically: we have also had an outline of Christianity, attempted in a number of volumes. We have not yet, however, had an outline of Religion taken as a whole. The time has surely come when someone should attempt this.

It does not follow (nor is it the case) that in writing such a history of religon one can never come to traditional conclusions, but, as one certainly cannot in every instance, it is undesirable to give the appearance of having made up one's mind beforehand that one is going to write one's history in the interests of establishing moderate orthodoxy. Moreover the generation of teachers and students which is now growing up regards truth as a quest to be sought with honesty. Truth is, of course, an inheritance as well as a quest, but it is essential that in stating the nature of the inheritance there should be a careful avoidance of any real or apparent attempt to include in it elements of which the truth is debatable, or at any rate to include them without appending a note stating that they are open to question. I intend to try, therefore, to write a systematic

outline of religion in as straightforward and scientific
a manner as possible.[1]

My readers will not find that I am out to establish or
to attack a series of traditional dogmas, but that if any
such still claim to be true, they must and will take care
of themselves and establish themselves by their own
truth. My business is simply to state facts and
describe beliefs, indicating probabilities. I believe
that there is a very considerable demand for an account
of the way of religion which tries to be honest, constructive and impartial, and that many persons are ready
to welcome any attempt at providing them with such.

In dealing with so vast a subject the selection of
matter must needs be an anxious task, but I have tried
to observe a due proportion in regard to this, and also
to avoid using such technical phraseology that the
account would be intelligible only to pure specialists.

It has recently been asserted that we theologians
have in many cases lost the ear of our own people. So
far as educated lay folk are concerned, the books in this
series are written in the hope that they will read them.

[1] Such outlines are appearing in continental countries, and
typical of them are: *Allgemeine Religionsgeschichte*, by Dr. A.
Jeremias, Münich, 1924, and a similar treatise by Professor Karl
Clemen of Bonn, 1930. In a sense Bishop Gore's Trilogy taken
together with his Gifford Lectures forms one; but it is obviously
written with the intention of establishing a particular sort of conservative position. Dr. Cave's admirable book, *Living Religions
of the East*, and the larger work by Dr. A. S. Geden on a similar
subject are limited in scope by their titles, while others merely give
an historical account of the greater positive religions without any
attempt at putting them in their setting. The late lamented
Archbishop Söderblom's Gifford Lectures, *The Living God*, published
since this book was written, stand by themselves. Composed by
a Swede in English, they are as much a literary *tour de force* as the
novels of Joseph Conrad; and their treatment of the subject displays
not only immense learning but deep insight.

But here a warning must be interposed. We can hardly expect to arrive at an apologetic which will rehabilitate everything in the old scheme of traditional Christian theology, and I am afraid that if any persons of ability employ their wits to produce one, it will, in spite of its probable ingenuity, find few purchasers and still fewer readers outside the circle of those who wish to discover deft excuses for religious conservatism. Such a book will, for example, be received with distrust by nearly all modern students. At the same time, in writing about religion, the absolute impartiality of the complete outsider is a serious handicap to him. It has been well said that to be an honorary member of all religions is to understand none of them, and he who at least believes in one may find it less difficult to be fair to the others. There is thus a perfectly good case to be made out for writing a general treatise from the point of view of an Anglican. Anglicanism is no longer the religion of a tight little island, but as an expression and developing interpretation of Christianity it has extended its roots over a large part of the globe, and while it does not turn its back upon the ancient strongholds of Catholic piety, it has also points of possible contact with vast masses of Protestants who have come to look wistfully to it for leadership. It has a gigantic if not very efficient *diaspora*, and it may easily, on account of its roominess and tolerance, determine the nature of the common world-religion of the future.

Yet although the word "apologetics" has a perfectly proper technical meaning, it unfortunately resembles only too closely the word "apology," and suggests that the cause of religion is perpetually on the defensive.

It is difficult to imagine a treatise on medical or biological apologetics.    Medical and biological science are
rightly held to need no defence.    It is unfortunate
(to say the least), if the impression gains ground that
religion is somehow in an uncomfortable position, not
sure of itself, and finding a measure of difficulty in
establishing its right to exist as a proper sphere of
human activity.    Now the more religion allows itself
to seem to be on the defensive, the worse it is for
religion, since any one who is inside a working scheme
of religion is well aware that to deprive him of that
scheme is to a large extent, so to speak, to disembowel
his life.    The enormous accumulation of buildings,
institutions, literature and social welfare movements
associated with religion is in itself enough to establish
the certainty that religion of some kind has certainly
hitherto been a genuine form of human activity, and
is so still.    On the other hand, mankind, as far as we
can judge, has never before witnessed such wide-
spread anti-religious propaganda as has appeared
during the last two hundred years, and especially in
eastern Europe since 1918.    Nor can we ignore the
rather frequent denials made by a certain type of
educated philosopher or scientist that there is for him
any evidence which convinces him that a Being really
exists such as he conceives to be the Personal God
spoken of by religious persons.    Never before perhaps
has the great mass of civilised mankind been tempted
to indulge in religious doubt and uncertainty as it is
to-day.

It therefore appears to be almost the minimum duty
of any one whom the community recognises as an

official exponent of religion to deal frankly and firmly with this abnormal situation, and to state his position without panic or hysteria. Instead of writing a defence, I have come to the conclusion that it is better to tell a plain tale.

The strange decline at the present time in any belief in spiritual authority renders our own age an abnormal one. It has been well observed that this decline is no temporary disorder such as may have occurred at previous epochs, but a real fundamental change of outlook. Many doubt whether there has ever before been so complete a transformation of the habits of humanity. A better knowledge of history is likely to modify this doubt, yet it is probable that those who feel it are not far from the truth. In certain pockets of population the disturbance is less apparent than in others, but it is nevertheless so wide-spread that it is difficult to believe that these pockets will not sooner or later be invaded by it. The best remedy is to remain calm, and to take long views, much longer and much better proportioned ones than are usually taken. When we consider (as we shall in these pages) the ultimate destiny of our planetary system, the complete collapse of past human cultures, the precariousness of our own, and the characteristics of other periods of decadence—consider in fact that decadence is a real thing even recognisable by decadents themselves, we shall perhaps come to lay less emphasis upon the vagaries and wilfulness of much modern thought.[1]

---

[1] At the same time it is difficult to believe that a nation should suddenly enact anti-religious laws without grave reason, even if the enactment be due to error or misunderstanding.

See Govt. White paper, Russia, No. 2 (1930), *Certain legislation*

We certainly need to keep our heads. The popular view at any time is not necessarily the true view. Human beings in the mass have sometimes a strange way of doing things for which they are afterwards heartily ashamed. Lunacy and neurasthenia can attack communities as well as individuals, and we have only to consider European history in the past and present, with its epidemics of witch-burning, Jew-baiting, war-fever and dancing-mania, to be convinced of this. A mere epidemic of anti-god propaganda would in itself furnish but shoddy evidence for the bankruptcy of so ancient and majestic a thing as the spiritual experience of the race.

But the matter cannot be quite so easily dismissed. It may turn out to be the case on investigation that anti-god propaganda (so-called) is an honest and sincere revolt against an inadequate or unworthy representation of the nature of Deity, and is therefore a sort of rough preliminary to a new and higher type of religion altogether, compared with which some past types will appear much as ancient alchemy does in comparison with modern chemistry. Eastern Europe is hardly the place in which to seek the best and most enlightened expression of spiritual truth, and pity for the victims of alleged persecution should not blind us to the fact that the Christianity of Eastern Europe, if of no other area, has strangely failed to express itself in such a way as to commend iself to the modern educated

---

*respecting religion in force in the U.S.S.R.*; also the statement made in August, 1930, by M. Bubnov, Minister of Education in the U.S.S.R.: "We intend to banish all mysticism and metaphysical rubbish from our new primary schools."

mind, or to secure the best general education for its adherents.[1]

Prof. Julius Hecker records that "religion" such as is stigmatised by the Bolsheviks means something quite different from what it does (let us say) to the people who forgather at Swanwick for conference each year. Much Russian religion actually spelt evasion of life, death rather than fuller and richer existence. (The subject recurs in Chapter II of this book.) An excess of mysticism quite as much as an excess of institutionalism may do serious harm, especially if it should seem to breed an indifference to the reasonable well-being of mankind in the mass.

Moreover no religious belief can endure which is only "a decent formula wherewith to embellish a comfortable life" or "an embroidery on the margin of a life devoted to other interests." Such trivialities are doomed. Religion is either something to grip and transmute the whole individual or it is worthless. Critical as is the present situation, there is less danger to be feared in the face of it from those people who are in earnest than from those who have lost their earnestness. The fact of our conditioned freedom (which I

[1] The following extracts from a not unsympathetic survey of recent events in Russia will serve to illustrate what is meant:—

"Our Church has striven after external gorgeousness at the expense of inner virtue, after showy splendour at the cost of spiritual perfection. It acquired pomp, power, rites, but lost its soul." —Abp. Wedensky.

"The ministration of the Orthodox Church had a sterilising effect on the spiritual life of the peasant. It depended for its appeal not on living sentiment, not on understanding of the real purpose of faith and the meaning of service, but on miracle, magic, ceremonial." —Maurice Hindus.

But what of some of our organised Christianity in the west end of London or among the plutocracies of New York or Stockholm?

shall be at pains to maintain) enables the trifler to thwart and set back the purposes of life even for generations.

May I express the slender hope that at least a few professedly atheistic communists will encounter these pages, and that such will believe that, however deeply my conclusions may seem to differ from theirs, I have tried to win them by fair argument to a better communism. It must prejudice them from the start that the bulk of books upon religion are in their eyes the works of persons who spring from the bourgeois class, and therefore infected with the point of view belonging to those who are inside a particular frame of reference. I am sorry. Will they take it from me that my own early life was lived among the humble surroundings of what they call the proletariat, that I know what it feels like to be poor, and that whatever my own stock, I have never known the security of belonging to a class wielding extensive economic power? I have therefore tried to write in a detached spirit, and I do not believe that the concept of Deity has any *necessary* connection with a particular economic structure of society, however much that structure may afterwards limit and modify its expression, but that it derives in any social group from a direct apprehension of the world of nature and the mind and consciousness of man. I regard as a mésalliance of the worst sort a marriage between a doctrine of anti-theistic hatred and any serious attempt at the construction of a society which shall aim at giving greater security to the average man, at eliminating wasteful competition and at removing an unhealthy emphasis on the money motive.

This book then, whatever its sequel, does not set out with the primary object of proving that religion in general or Christianity in particular is true, but with the telling of a plain tale. If the inevitable truth of religion or of any expression of Christianity should happen to emerge in the course of its pages, it will only do so because the facts appear to justify it, and because, if they do, it is just as well that such a conclusion should be as widely known as possible. It will probably be found, however, that some expressions of Christianity cannot be justified by the facts, and again that some non-Christian systems of belief are inferior to some expression or expressions of Christianity, while others are good enough to be regarded as actually roads which lead to Christ; and I repeat, that if this should turn out to be the case it is just as well that such facts should be as widely known as possible. There can be no imaginable advantage in suppressing them. On the other hand, a conclusion may emerge from our survey that no existing form of Christianity is, as it stands to-day, final, but that finality only exists in the whole process or movement taken as trending in a certain direction, and this will lead us either to a free liberal or liberal Christian position, according to the view we take regarding the career of the historical Jesus, whether as incidental to or normative for that whole process.

I readily admit the reasonableness of the objection which some may urge, that the period in which these pages are written is one which is in such a high degree transitional that any hope of a lasting synthesis may well seem premature, and that one can only try to achieve the provisional, not the permanent. If we take a world-view, (which it is fairly easy to do) we must be conscious that a vast number of the old nuances and differentiations hitherto prevailing among the races and peoples of the planet are fast disappearing. Many must regret their disappearance, and the science of anthropology is busily engaged (not a moment too soon) in constructing a permanent record of them. Thus (to take an example) except in so far as differences of temperature exercise control, the pattern of human clothing is rapidly losing local and national variations and is tending towards standardisation. Machinery again, in spite of the varieties of pattern as yet prevalent, seems likely also to increase in standardisation, for the simple reason that renewal and repair of parts is more difficult if there are too many local peculiarities. The last century has seen a remarkable disappearance of local customs and crafts, and the replacement of regional industries by the importation of goods of a fixed pattern made by a limited number of associated factories. It would be easy to multiply instances of this gradual elimination of local types. When we come to the sphere of religion we find similar factors at work, and a slow but sure elimination, not only of the many varieties of animism and polytheism, but even of some of the greater faiths as well. The increase of communication by aeroplane and motor-coach, and of mental interchange by radio and cinema, renders it probable that we of this generation are only at the beginning of a process which in the course of a few thousand years (perhaps a few hundred) will have transformed the erstwhile rich variety of human cultures and beliefs into, I will not go so far as to say a monotonous uniformity, but at least into a federated system in which variety will be much less prominent. To that extent our age is transitional. Whatever form religious belief and practice may assume in ten thousand years time, of this we may feel tolerably certain, that it will have passed far beyond the phase of conflicting beliefs, and will have approached much nearer to the possession of a common mind. We who live to-day can, I venture to think, do a good deal more than perhaps we realise to help to determine what that common mind shall be; for it is not impossible for it to be an agreed but a misinformed mind, and it may be that, unless we do our part. Standing as we do betwixt the old and the new worlds, in an age in which the motor lorry and the bullock waggon, the aeroplane and the dug-out canoe, antiseptic surgery and primitive witch-doctoring, modernist theology and primitive fetichism, classical and scientific studies still co-exist, we, it seems, are better fitted than the dwellers in an age which has banished for ever this co-existence of incongruous types, to determine prudently what kind of common belief in the mutual relations of Deity and humanity should govern the future of mankind. It would be presumptuous to suppose that we can guarantee every detail of our synthesis, or put the final touches to it, but, inexpert though we may be, we are at least a generation before which, while it is still able to remember and appreciate the past, the curtain veiling the future has been strangely uplifted.

The peculiar and distinctive features of the culture which is now developing are familiar to all, and need only be briefly enumerated. They comprise a discovery of new sorts of fuel and new sources of energy, and the rapid depletion of natural resources as compared with the relatively slow consumption which has taken place in the past; the construction of intricate and precise machinery which enlarges and extends the operation of man's limbs, quickens his movements and multiplies his creative acts; enormously increased density of population and its concentration into huge urban areas; increased expectation of life, together with possibilities of greatly improved health and added vitality on the one hand, and the limitation and eugenic control of breeding upon the other; a general unsettlement of beliefs about ultimate things, together with optimistic and daring speculations regarding the future, and an equal condemnation of *all* religious institutions, balanced by the alternative conception of an ethical state based upon a natural theology, in which theocratic ideas and the notion of a supernaturally revealed religion are just barely tolerated.

The contents of this book and its companion (No. 6) must not be taken as representing anything more than a guide to knowledge. They strive to indicate how others have sought and found it, how it has grown through misunderstanding and controversy to clearer vision, and how it may still be sought. Yet at their best these chapters will seem to the reader who seeks immediate contact with Deity, but second-hand goods. There is knowledge by inference and deduction, dealt with briefly in No. 1 of this series, and there is knowledge gained by study, dealt with here and in No. 4, and these two are knowledge *about* what is studied.

Knowledge of the thing itself is direct, and however much it may be amplified by inference, deduction, or study, nothing can ever take the place of immediate apprehension.

I earnestly hope that no one will set aside what I have written because I have tried in it to do justice and to be fair to the beliefs of what will be called old-fashioned people, even where I am compelled to disagree with them: and equally, that no one will impatiently dismiss the author as a "modernist."

Let me try to explain the policy I have adopted in this series of books, and my reasons therefor.

Certain facts have become known to the world of our day which we can only manage to ignore by, as it were, putting blinkers on to ourselves, and a blinker doesn't destroy a fact; it only stops you from seeing it. The fact is there behind the blinker all the time. So far then as certain new facts are well-attested by the same sort of evidence that has led us to accept the old and well-worn facts of life, so far we simply cannot refuse to accept those facts, unless we are prepared to act contrary to the ordinary rules of reason. It may be that we have not as complete a knowledge of all the facts of life as will be possible in two thousand years time or even two hundred, though in many cases it would seem as though our generation has been favoured with a knowledge of the universe so extensive as to be decisive even if it be not exhaustive.

It is otherwise when we leave facts and come to opinions. Of course an opinion about the relation of facts to one another will be of value in so far as it recognises all the facts instead of only some of them, and recognises them in due proportion. An opinion based upon modern knowledge may in this way claim to be of more value than an opinion held by someone who lived at a time when the facts, now accessible to all, were either not known or imperfectly known. At the same time such an opinion may be dependent for its validity upon facts which were as easily ascertainable a thousand years ago as they are to-day, and so the opinion is just as good now as it was then. So far from having become obsolete, it is what we should call a piece of ancient wisdom which time has not been able to invalidate.

Again there are modern opinions which are based upon a hasty reading of the facts, or upon prejudice or exaggerated emphasis, and these must always be regarded with suspicion. There is no reason for regarding them as correct merely because they are modern. It is true that an opinion which has been held for many centuries may in the end prove erroneous. On the other hand, an opinion which has been justified in the experience of centuries cannot be wholly erroneous. It must correspond in some way or other to experience. There must be a substantial part of it which is correct, so far as the latter is a qualitative valuation of fact. It is with the above principles in mind that I propose to approach my subject.

In making this attempt I shall assume certain axioms:

(1) That reality is one thing and our sense-perceptions are another, and that whatever the nature of reality, it must always be distinguished from our human picture of it.

(2) That nevertheless, since our sense-perceptions seem in the main to be of a similar character, there is no reason why we should not use them as data in constructing that picture.

(3) That among these perceptions are some which are evidently caused by reality apprehended as a whole, rather than by pieces of it.

(4) That whatever the destiny of the *individuality* which we find in living creatures, part of our data is a sense that in each one of us there is to a varying degree an element which is not subject to dissolution and decay, and which may either be a temporary kink or discontinuity in the indestructible substance of an Eternal Being, or a permanent differentiation of that Being.    (It will be part of our task of investigation to enquire as to the status and prospects of that element.

(5) To these I must add, at the risk of putting it out of order, the consciousness of duality between self and the sacred, however either of these may be defined.

A well known divine once remarked that somewhere about the beginning of the nineteenth century there was still in existence a kind of general scheme of belief which might have been called "the Protestant religion," that is to say, that although there might be differences as to the relative merits (for example) of establishment and nonconformity and as to the practical value of infant baptism, there was at any rate a good deal of theological principle which was common to all the reformed churches.    On the whole, they all agreed in accepting the Old Testament cosmogony, justification by faith, the declaratory nature of sacraments, and the right of private judgment.    That general point of view has gone, and at present no agreed scheme has come to take its place.   Some of the elements in the old scheme have given way before the flood of new knowledge, others have actually turned out to be less defensible or at any rate no more defensible than those held by Catholics.   I believe that the time has now come when it is possible to see a new general outlook in process of arriving and establishing itself, an outlook conditioned and created by the spirit of the new learning.   I wish to try to set down a description of it, so that it may be studied, discussed, modified and perhaps adopted. That is the position with which this book and its companions in the series set out to deal, and now without further ado let us ring up the curtain.

# CHAPTER I

## OF THE NATURE AND ALLEGED NECESSITY OF RELIGION IN HUMAN AFFAIRS

ALL sentient creatures must sooner or later attempt to organise their lives with some purpose in view. Certainly no human being can pass through this world without asking the question: "Why am I here, what does it mean, and what is my particular function in the whole scheme?" The policy of drift may satisfy for a time, but as soon as the novelty of life begins to wear off a feeling of emptiness ensues, and nothing can be more dangerous than for men and women to find themselves past the age of forty-five with the sensation that their appetite for new enterprises is declining, and their opportunity for new sensations diminishing, and then suddenly to wake up to the fact that they have not only put less into the world than they have taken out of it, but have actually no very definite idea as to the nature of their ultimate aims, or whether those aims are worth while. We may in fact enlarge the well-known assertion of Plato, and say that the *unorganised* life is not livable by any human being worthy of the name. Sooner or later, and sooner rather than later, each individual must adopt a world-view, and must organise his or her life in harmony with the same.[1] The possibility of the successful achievement of this is

[1] Gordon, *Personality*, ch. xvii. (Inter. Lib. of Psychology.)

17

greater to-day than hitherto, since, as those who have read the preceding volume in this series[1] will realise, we are presented to-day with a picture of the universe vaster and more complete than any which lay before the eyes of our ancestors; so that encouragement is given to the tendency of modern thinkers to deal as much as possible with all subjects from a universal standpoint. Things are no longer in water-tight compartments. To-day we are being pressed on all sides to take long views of life, and extend our outlook to the fringes of an expanding Universe; and the pressure of this appeal is coming down upon the "dim common populations" of our planet with a force which will take no denial. One inference which has been drawn from the present passion for sport and pleasure is that mankind has for the time being lost its way, and having no serious sense of purpose, or of the worth-whileness of life, is drugging its senses by a frenzied round of frivolity. But this loss of orientation is also partly due to bewilderment at the enormous mass of highly technical information with which our systems of higher education are crowded, to the extent to which material has out-stripped moral progress, and to the artificial and morbid lives of our vast urban populations. A busy and bustling life full of diversion may seem to carry its own weight and to be self-explanatory. So it may, as long as the whirl lasts: but once let the dancers stop and think, and they will realise that it is by itself as mere motion, meaningless.

Possibly there may be some who are sufficiently contented with the fact that they are in motion, and

[1] No. 4, "The World We Live In."

care nothing that they have no sense of direction, so long as they are able to join with a certain Yorkshire comedian in singing: "Ah doant knaw wheer Ahm goan, but still Ahm on ma way!" I cannot, however, believe that such a mental attitude is worthy of our race.

Increasing secularity, in whatever way we interpret it, is a lesser menance than the absence of seriousness. The eighteenth-century evangelicals were sometimes described as "serious men." A lack of seriousness is much more dangerous than unorthodoxy. The age of the cinema has led to the development of much short-sighted frivolity. It is far more important to study our human objective and to devote ourselves to that, than to be concerned in mere amusement.[1]

That the problem of what is worth while in life is beginning to be seriously debated is sufficiently evident. The mere challenging of the ideals of the last hundred years is a symptom. Younger persons question the validity of the code of competitive industry, "of running endless races for bread and butter against someone else." They seem to present a lack of ambition, but this appearance is due to a secret doubt

[1] The basis of so-called Sunday neglect is really to be found in this lack of seriousness. It appears to be maintained by many that no part of the weekly rest day should be spent in reflection. I hold no brief for the Sabbatarian fundamentalist, or for those heavy persons whose seriousness is entirely unrelieved by a sense of humour, and I fully recognise the necessity of rhythms in life, whereby work and recreation are made to alternate. But recreation in the true sense cannot all be of the lighter sort. Let those who do not wish to attend a Christian church at least substitute something else of equal weight for its worship, and if they are religious persons, but dissatisfied with the provision which their National Church makes for them, let them aid in reforming it and in helping it to meet their needs.

as to whether the competitive system, if they venture
to let themselves get entangled in it, will not enslave
them and use them for its own impersonal ends.   They
are not lazy, but they fail to see how hard work which is
competition in acquisitiveness rather than in the service
of the community can be a proper *telos* for man.
Certainly the communist dialectician is a "serious man,"
and takes himself and expects us to take him very
seriously.

The situation may be summed up in a few sentences
from a modern writer who is extremely sensitive to the
movements of his age.  "Nearly all of us," he says,
"want something to hold us together, something to
dominate this swarming confusion and save us from
the black misery of wounded and exploded pride, of
thwarted desire, of futile conclusions. . . . We want
more oneness, some steadying thing that will afford an
escape from fluctuations. . .  It seems to me that this
desire to get the confused complex of life simplified is
essentially what has been called the religious motive,
and the manner in which a man achieves that simplification, if he does achieve it, and imposes an order upon
his life, is his religion."[1]

Now it will be noted that I have myself carefully
refrained, in beginning this chapter, from using the
word religion at all, except in the title.   It is a word
which has been so much misunderstood, cheapened,
and misused, that I felt I wanted to keep away from it.
It seemed better to get the thing itself clear without
using the name, and to let the name be introduced by
someone of whom it could not be said that he had a

[1] H. G. Wells, *First and Last Things.*

special prejudice in its favour; and this I have tried to do. It may be said, then, that to avoid futility *we must have as true and accurate as possible a general knowledge of the nature of reality taken in its entirety and of the proper reaction of the human species towards it.* Such a definition of religion, however, will to some seem inadequate, and they will say that it is only philosophy. It will be well to anticipate their objection by granting that to many persons any description of the nature of reality will be found incomplete which does not place in the forefront the prophetic intuition that there is an element in reality which is responsive. Philosophy concerns itself with a systematic understanding of reality, and it might therefore be said that a philosophy of life is what everyone needs; but (1) some philosophy assumes no necessary activity or responsiveness on the part of that which is contemplated, but regards it as passive, static, or neutral. (2) All persons are not by nature philosophers. *With regard to the first objection,* it may be answered that the genuinely religious view of life begins with twofold intuition that there is an essence to the universe which forbids relationships beyond itself, and that between that essence and the individual self there is capable of being developed a quasi-personal relationship which would be impossible unless this essence were discovered to possess the quality of responsiveness. The allegation is made that this ultimate essence of Being exhibits responsiveness in that it submits itself and its activities to enquiry and investigation. It is willing to be known; and whatever its nature, it is not hostile to our desire to understand and to obtain truth, however partial, imperfect and

symbolic our understanding; while in certain circumstances we may speak of its exhibiting initiative. A
really synthetic philosophy of life will therefore seem
bound to include within its universal scheme the
observed facts of intuitive as well as of rational
experience; it will in fact be philosophical theology.
while the application of such a philosophy to daily
affairs will necessarily involve the practice of this
quasi-personal relationship as a habit, and will be
philosophical religion, based on a determined attempt
to think things together. The responsive element in
reality, or rather self-existent Being in its aspect as
responsive, we propose to call *Deity*, since that is the
term which from its general character and associations
seems most proper to be used. To call one's self an
atheist and to deny the existence of Deity in the sense
of denying the existence of this responsive element in
the universe is to confess to considerable shallowness
of outlook. At the same time to affirm the existence of
Deity in this sense does not commit one to any so-called
superstitions or even "over-beliefs." The word, it
must be pointed out, is almost a blank cheque. It is a
colourless term, involving no moral or spiritual
assumptions as to quality. This is hardly a dis-
advantage. Until we have built up by a survey of
experience a secure balance of divine attributes, it is
best to confine ourselves to the use of a term which is,
as far as possible, non-committal. We need, however, to
observe as a preliminary caution that if the universe is
one, then a complete and adequate system of philosophy
will be that only which views the universe from the
stand-point of Deity, and since this can only be possible

to Deity Itself, the human race will only approximate
to a complete and adequate view of the universe in
proportion as it endeavours to harmonise itself with
Deity. Hence true religion, as a quasi-personal
relationship with responsive Deity, is indispensable to
the very existence of any philosophy which claims to
approximate to a synthesis of truth. We may well
accept as valid the weighty asseveration of one of our
finest modern philosophers: "There is nothing more
real than what comes in religion. To compare facts
such as these with what is given to us in outward
existence would be to trifle with the subject. The man
who demands a reality more solid than that of the
religious consciousness seeks he knows not what."[1] We
may add to this another assertion made still more
recently:[2] "The fact of religious vision and its history
of persistent expansion is our one ground for optimism.
Apart from it, human life is a flash of occasional
enjoyment lighting up a mass of pain and misery, a
bagatelle of transient experiences." The contention
of this chapter then is that religion cannot wisely or
safely be ignored and neglected as it is by so many
frivolous persons to-day. Even a defective or obsolete
scheme of religion will serve the individual better than
none at all. This is why so many old-fashioned persons
possess, in spite of their defective views on some topics,
a wholeness and completeness of character which is
absent from the young ultra-moderns.

*With regard to the second objection,* I do not mean to
suggest that every human being must necessarily be in
conscious possession of a system of philosophical

[1] F. H. Bradley.        [2] A. N. Whitehead.

theology.  Far from it.  What I do affirm is that the
religious practices, ritual, or whatever term is used to
express the habitual organisation of the life of each
human individual as related to Deity, must be based
upon a sound system of philosophical theology which
at least a few competent persons consciously hold and
understand, and which others can therefore take for
granted.  The superiority of Catholicism to most forms
of Protestantism lies in its possession of such a system—
the scholastic; and the weakness of Catholicism lies in
its having attached itself too securely to a static
philosophy, which, whatever its many merits, was
framed at a time when the data accessible were
obviously fewer and less well-known than at the present
time.  Scholasticism, taken as it stands, is inadequate;
though we concede that it may be capable of reform
and renewal.  This, however, does not remove the fact
that an evangelical Protestant with no general world-
outlook is in a much more precarious position than the
Catholic with a partly obsolete one.  Hence Volumes
1 and 4 of this series.

It is suggested by some persons that the reign of the
religious outlook may be merely a phase and no more,
a phase due to the varying prevalence of a naïve
personalism, and that it may be succeeded by a phase
of philosophy based upon scientific observation; in
which case it may well be asked: "Would not a
philosophy based upon science serve well instead of a
naïve religion?  Would it not *be*, indeed is it not
already, in a sense religion, and very good religion at
that?"

To this a threefold answer may be given.  First, we

may concede that though the mere mental accumulation of knowledge does not in itself constitute the possessor of that knowledge a religious person, it may lead him to a coherent and consistent world-view, expressing itself in an habitual attitude; and the latter, as I shall presently urge again, constitutes the essence of a religion.

Secondly, however, it must be pointed out that the worth of such an attitude depends upon its being based upon a truly comprehensive world-view. If the latter is constructed by a deliberate exclusion of certain phenomena,—if, for example, it takes no account of the course of events in human history, or only does so at the cost of ignoring or explaining away religious events in the sense that it excludes the critical biographies of individuals or groups of individuals who have experienced and communicated alleged spiritual experiences and perceptions of divine guidance—such a world-view can only be a false and distorted one, and can result in no sound scheme of philosophy, and issue in no proper religious attitude.

And thirdly, it may be questioned whether a world-view expressing itself in an habitual attitude can be deduced from scientific enquiry as commonly conceived; for science is not concerned with values but with phenomena irrespective of quality. Its processes are those of classification and analysis, or of construction as a result of the latter. Thus it analyses the workings of the body-machine, with results which are of interest for the chemist and the engineer. But the bodies of the sane man, the criminal, the lunatic, the genius and the prophet, are all equally matter for scientific analysis, and scientific research does not pronounce any qualitative judgment upon their respective brains. It merely says that they differ, and indicates the nature of the difference. Things which the human mind classifies as "good" and "bad" are equally matter for the observation of the scientist. He cannot afford to show moral passion, to exhibit disgust, or betray preference, when dealing with the object he is studying. If he does, he will be in danger of warping his judgment and of marring his conclusions. It is his business to be descriptive, even in the interests of synthesis or invention. It is not his business, when showing how a particular gas is made, to say whether it is right or wrong to use it for killing members of another nation, or when aiding in the improved construction of motor-car engines to stipulate that they shall not be employed by bandits. Hence a world-view on a *purely* scientific basis would seem to be impossible, unless by science we mean more than physical science, and make it embrace an impartial observation of human *thought*, with deductions therefrom.

There are those who deny that the whole of Reality is more than an aggregate of an infinite number of primary parts, "full of spots and jumps"—not a Universe at all. Such atomistic scepticism defeats itself. If there is nothing in existence which remotely resembles a Whole, where do I get my idea of a Whole from? The question seems to be a form of the ontological argument: yet it is not mere sophistry, since it must be admitted that without the idea of a Whole being present to me I can have no conception of what that is like which is *not* a Whole, and again if the Whole is a mere aggregate of an infinite number of primary parts, how can I know anything about those parts if they have no common characteristics? Without these characteristics I should need as many symbols as there were primary parts with which to designate those parts, and since each symbol would be unique it would not be a description any more than a picture of the primary part it represented. In fact it would have to be a photographic ideogram of that individual primary part, and even then it would belong to the *class* "ideogram." It seems then that I cannot divest myself of the concept Whole or Class.

Again there are others who say that they see no positive value in religion. My reply must be that if any religion be false, it is certainly valueless. But if any religion were capable of being true, as a sufficient description of the Whole and of the proper relations between us and it, then the mere fact of its truth would make it positively valuable. Religion has ever approximated to being of positive value in proportion as it has succeeded in making man at home in the universe. The nearer it has come to being a true description, the more it has provided this solution for human uneasiness. Personally I think it is arguable that no one has ever been so much at home in the universe as a certain active type of Christian saint. But that is another matter, and is a question not merely of the validity of religious experience in general but of the Christian experience in particular.

There are those who do not want religion at all, but rather a practical organisation of life—efficiency—

"the cult of the one best way," as it has been called. This gospel is presented to us by writers on both sides of the Atlantic, and it has affinities with the organisation of the collective man which we see going on in Russia. It is the theory which lies behind all mechanisation and all standardisation of production. Yet it is a gospel which immediately raises the question; "efficiency for what?" and therefore shirks the ultimate issue. One can imagine a philosopher some thousands of years hence pondering over the reasons which made it worth while for his remote ancestors to search for the one best way of making Mills bombs or of rolling cigarettes. Mechanisation profits nothing without a selective principle, by which we may be enabled to judge what sort of efficient actions are worth while and what sort are not. Without subscribing to the whole of Mr. Gandhi's opinion about the simple life it is quite clear that what he has called Satanism and what its own supporters call industrial efficiency may lead to the total sterilisation of creative thought and so to a barren stability of society.

There is one further view of religion which (although I profoundly disagree with it) I cannot ignore. It is that which says that nothing worth while can be found out about Deity through studying the world. Deity exists, but our world is clean cut off from Him. Creation itself is a catastrophe; a fall from eternity into time, the great negative in the life of Deity; and the whole of what happens in the cosmos so created is from top to bottom alienated from Him. The religions of the world, being activities within the cosmos, are as such tainted with the defects of their origin. There is no denying that this picture exhibits certain plausible features; and a learned Irish Jesuit has summed up the sequences in the modern world as: belief in God < disbelief in God < belief in man < disbelief in man; so bringing us round in a circle to where we started.

Yet I cannot help feeling that this interpretation is deeply subjective, and is the fruit not of a more than usually clear vision, but of a more than usually serious failure of nerve. Are we really to say that human life throughout the centuries is so perverse that not a crumb of knowledge that is worth anything about the mystery behind it can be picked up from its activities? Or may we say that the race is struggling upwards slowly and painfully, guided, lovingly watched over, inspired, stooped down to and rescued as it stumbles, but ever continually being lifted by a supreme and mighty Source of life?

I should proceed no further with this book if I felt in doubt about the answer to such questions. Doubtless the poor reach of our minds is totally inadequate for the task of acquiring an exhaustive knowledge of the Divine Majesty, but that is no argument for not doing the best that we can, and even if there be a severe contrast between our meagre investigations and the rich response of Deity, both are within the one totality of our experience, and must be treated as such. It is only our experience that can interpret what theologians have called revelation, and test its validity. Much as we may wish to, we can no more eliminate experience than we can jump out of our own skins; and although we may come to disbelieve in man's capacity to make the best of himself by himself alone, yet it must be obvious to any one who tries to think clearly that even the mere acceptance of Divine aid is impossible without some preliminary stirring of himself on man's part, even if it be no more than a decision passively to accept that aid, since such a decision involves an act of conscious will.

It will not suffice, however, to leave the account of the nature of religion at this point without further consideration. To do so would be to ignore the many attempts which have in the past been made to provide definitions, and so leave this chapter incomplete. We shall obtain a broader and more solid basis for the remainder of our study if we take into account these various attempts and try to summarise them. The results, even if they lack originality, will provide us with something like a tradition, which, having the authority of collective experience, should at least claim our respectful notice. I will give, then, a number of definitions, selected in part from the famous appendix to a well-known American book.[1] It opens with the much criticised statement of *Max Müller*. "Religion is a mental faculty or disposition, which, independent of (nay in spite of) sense and reason, enables man to apprehend the Infinite under different names and under varying disguises." The obvious objection to this is that it is bound up with the fortunes of the now obsolete faculty of psychology.

This definition is followed by *Herbert Spencer's* "Religion has from the beginning dimly discerned the ultimate verity, and has never ceased to insist upon this

[1] Leuba, *A Psychological Study of Religion.*

truth that all things are manifestations of a Power that transcends our knowledge."

*James Martineau* understands by religion "the belief in an ever-living divine mind and will ruling the universe and holding moral relations with mankind."

According to *G. J. Romanes*, "Religion is a department of thought, having for its object a self-conscious and intelligent Being."

*F. B. Jevons* gives as his definition: "Religion as a form of thought is the perception of the invisible things of Him through the things that are made."

*Kant* declared that religion was "the recognition of all our duties as divine commands."

*Schleiermacher*, as is well-known, decided that the essence of true religion consisted in "the feeling of an absolute dependence upon the Infinite," in describing which he began by using impersonal terms and ended by using the word "God."

*Tiele* said that in religious emotion we have the awakening rather than the origin of religion, and this emotion he defined as "the consciousness that we are in the power of a Being whom we revere as the highest, and to whom we feel attracted and related, a consciousness which issues in adoration impelling us to dedicate ourselves to the adored object, yet also to possess it and to be in union with it."

*Warde Fowler*, the great authority on Roman religion, defines thus: "Religion is the effective desire to be in right relationship to the power manifesting itself in the Universe."

*Brightman*, an American writer upon philosophy,

D

proposes another inclusive definition: "The total attitude of man towards what he considers to be superhuman and worthy of worship, devotion, propitiation, or at least reverence. It ought to be characterised by the feeling of dependence upon or responsibility to a superpersonal Deity, and dominated by the will to co-operate with Deity in the conservation and increase of values."

To these may be added two quite recent definitions, the first that of Professor *Pratt*, the American psychologist, who says that religion is "the serious and social attitude of individuals or communities towards the Power or Powers which they conceive as having ultimate control over their interests and destinies"; the second that of *Dr. Thouless* of Glasgow, who defines it as "a felt practical relationship towards a superhuman Being or Beings."

All the above definitions have a certain transcendental flavour about them. We will now take some of an immanental or pantheistic type. *Hegel*, for instance, defines religion as "the knowledge possessed by the finite mind of its nature as absolute mind," and he expands this in one place by saying that religion is "the realm where all enigmatical problems of the world are solved, where all contradictions of deep musing thoughts are unveiled, all pangs of feelings soothed . . . the whole manifold of human relations, activities, joys, everything that man values and esteems, wherein he seeks his happiness, his glory, and his pride—all find their final middle point in religion, in the thought, consciousness, and feeling of Deity. Deity is therefore the beginning and the end of

everything. . . . By means of religion man is placed
in relation to this centre, in which all his other relations
converge, and is elevated to the realm of highest
freedom, which is its own end and aim. This relation
of freedom on the side of feeling is joy, which we call
beatitude; . . . on the side of activity its sole office is to
manifest the honour and to reveal the glory of Deity,
so that man in this relation is no longer chiefly concerned with himself, his own interests and vanity, but
rather with the absolute end and aim."

*McTaggart*, as is well-known, described religion as
"a state of consciousness resting upon conviction of a
harmony between ourselves and the universe at large."
Again, *Simmel* said that the religious life was "the
whole of existence pitched in a certain key." *Josiah
Royce*, the American, has declared that religion is
"the consciousness of our practical relation to an
invisible spiritual order," and *Wundt* says that "all
ideas and feeling are religious which refer to an ideal
existence, an existence which fully corresponds with
the wishes and requirements of the human mind";
while a modern British biologist has defined religion
as "our total reaction to our total experience of the
universe;" in which statement everything of course
depends upon what is signified by the term "universe."
One considerable group of thinkers emphasises the
social character or group-character of religion and
suggests that the latter consists in being in harmony
with one's group, which is, as it were, objectified and
elevated to the position of deity. An enlargement of
this view may also be found in the original doctrine of
the Buddha, where a very definite and earnest attitude

is inculcated towards the Universe, which by its inexorable law of Karma determines our destiny.

Is it possible to bring these two seemingly very different groups of definitions within the embrace of a larger unity?

The task, though difficult, does not seem impossible. As we shall see when we come to our more detailed study, a complete transcendence satisfies neither the conceptions of the modern scientific philosopher nor the intuitions of the mystic, while on the other hand a pure pantheism (using the term to describe that conception of the universe which makes deity to be equally manifest qualitatively in all its events)—pantheism is of such unstable equilibrium, that it cannot avoid falling either into acosmism or into monism, and in any case shirks facing dualisms which are fundamental in human experience, the dualisms of one's self and the sacred, of the finite and the infinite, and of good and evil.

We will therefore propose the following inclusive definition, i.e. *Religion is an harmonious and disinterested relationship maintaining itself between the One and the many, between the Whole and the parts.*[1] There

---

[1] The reader may like to compare with this what is I believe the most recent definition arrived at on the Continent, propounded by a brilliant Swiss scholar, Oskar Bauhofer (and which I had not seen when I wrote the above). [The italics are my own.]

Alle Strukturformen des religiösen Bewusstseins sind charakterisiert durch das, was wir *die religiöse Grundattitude* nennen wollen . . . . Alle Religion ist ihrer Intention nach dual, zweisam, dialogisch. Das ist das durchgehende, *vielmehr das einzige durchgehende Merkmal* . . . . Jede Religion neben den Menschen stellt das göttliche Du . . . . Mit dieser polaren Dualität: Ich — Über-Ich; Kreatur — Schöpfer; Zeit — Ewigkeit; . . . . manifestiert sich Religion als Religion. Religion ist immer der Wille oder die Not

may be (probably there is) a religious attitude on the
part of stones and zoophytes, electrons and elephants.
Here, however, we are concerned with *human* religion
only, and indeed this is all that religion usually means
in common parlance, *i.e.* the relation existing between
human beings and the Whole of which they feel themselves to be members.  This is practically the same
as Professor Pratt's definition, but it differs from it in
this one respect that his explanation of the word
"relationship" is conditioned by the phrase "controlling their destinies," and suggests that in all religion
the answer expected by the individual to the quest is an
answer to the enquiry: "what is going to happen to me
or to us?"  Now there can be no doubt that very
much popular religion is of this sort; but a definition
which would seek to embrace the whole of religious
activity is also bound to take into account the not
inconsiderable section of humanity which instead of
asking "what is to become of me?" says that religion
consists in trying to understand the universe and to
identify one's self with its aims, and therefore enquires
"what is the meaning and purpose of the Power in
question, and how can I absorb myself in it?"  By
trying to answer this question mankind also indirectly
obtains the answer to the other, but it does not appear
that any religious answer except the Christian has

zu einem göttlichen Du, die Überwindung oder das Überwinden-
wollen, der Einsamkeit des Ich *in der Begegnung mit einer dem
Menschen gegenüber irgendwie* (durch Stärke, Wissen, Güte, oder
auch Schrechlichkeit) *qualifizierten Macht* . . . . Die im Kult, im
Opfer, Gebet, und religiösen Mythos sich realisierende Dualitäts-
verstellung ist das konstituierende Moment jenes komplexen
geschichtlichen Phänomens, das wir Religion nennen.
                        *Das Metareligiöse.*  Genf, 1930.

effectively succeeded in persuading people actively
rather than passively to absorb themselves in the
purpose of the controlling power, while at the same
time quieting their misgivings as to the ultimate lot of
their own little individualities.  That they ought not
to be unduly obsessed with the latter problem may
be quite true, but I think it will appear arguable, as we
proceed, that whatever may happen in the future,
hitherto no one but Jesus has been able with equal
success to persuade mankind to abandon the problem,
because He has with complete effectiveness persuaded
a large part of mankind that the Power controlling
their destinies is of the nature of a trustworthy Parent,
kindly, wise and benevolent, and that therefore the
future may be left entirely in His hands.  (This last
sentence of course is an anticipation, but it seemed
better to insert it here.  It is another way of saying
what I said a page or two back, about the Christian
saint being most of all completely at home in the
universe).  Meanwhile, I will conclude this chapter by
urging that the antithesis between the two types of
definition ought not to be pressed.  What if they be
just two different ways of regarding the same reality?
We have lately been reminded, and this will be the last
definition which I shall quote) that the religious
interest is a disinterested delight in the *sacred* or
supernatural, "the numinous," wheresoever it may be
discoverable—perhaps everywhere—as a quality resident in, permeating and running through, and destined
to emerge in complete perfection from the whole.
Whether then we find our interest to lie in regarding
the sacred as transcendent or immanent will depend

upon whether we are concerned with it as (*a*) prior to the process of the universe, (*b*) resident in the process, or (*c*) emerging in perfection from the process, or perhaps as all three. At all events, whichever way we look at it, religion is an inescapable factor in human life, and there is still an obstinate dualism which refuses to resolve itself, since not everything is sacred.[1] What we call the religious quest and religious experience do not disappear. The old patterns of religion were really forms of translating that experience and the results of that quest into symbols. Those who claim to possess the experience but discard the old symbolic patterns are obviously ill at ease. If they suppress the experience, or ignore it because of its association with the old symbolic patterns which they deem obsolete, they are left with what has been called "a god-shaped blank" in their lives. Their efforts at the creation of new patterns do not so far seem to have been very successful, and it is not unfair to suggest that the wisdom of the past might after all have been more worth their attention than they thought, since their so-called novelties are usually revivals of previously invented systems.[1]

We may sum up this chapter by saying that

(1) Whatever absolute or final truth there may or may not be in any system or systems of religion which have hitherto existed or may in the future exist, the most general and inclusive account which we are able

---

[1] The *sacred* has been further defined as that which is wholly transcendent and unoriginate, appearing as immanent at a point or points within the world. As such it emerges from within, and does not enter *ab extra*, in the sense of getting in by a sudden intrusion.

to get as to the nature of religion fully justifies the assertion that in some form or other it has hitherto been regarded both as a legitimate and a necessary activity of the human race.

(2) That whatever conclusions we may reach concerning individual religious systems, the necessity of such a unifying principle as they claim to apply is evident.

(3) That two main types of system claim to supply this unifying principle, and that of these the first stresses the idea of quasi-personal transcendence, while the second in its extremest forms seems to dispense entirely with the idea of a personal God, and substitutes for it an eternal order.

(4) That probably there is no real discordance between the two.

The nature and necessity of religion having been thus indicated, it follows as a consequence that it is the duty of every human being, not only towards himself, but towards society in general, to acquire and practise this correct religious relationship; and further that every human being as such has equally the right to demand of the society in which he dwells fulness of opportunity both to acquire and to practise that correct relationship. This right is as much his possession as any right he may possess to a fair wage, or to equality of educational opportunity, or physical maintenance. It may not be treated as the monopoly or concern of a particular class. The state must secure this right for all its citizens, and must endeavour to give facilities for the promotion of true religion, and for the banishment of false. It is impossible for a state to have no concern with true religion, as though it were an optional affair like the drinking of Chartreuse or the breeding of pheasants. True and correct religion is everyone's affair and is as indispensable as an adequate supply of pure milk.

It follows further that if any religion be good and true, it will provide, in proportion to its truth and adequacy, a means of release for the aesthetic impulses of those who profess it, and will issue in forms of art, whether pictorial or acoustic, or just the art of living a beautiful life.

## NOTE TO CHAPTER I

(A) Some may wonder that although I have quoted F. H. Bradley on page 23 I have made no comment upon his definition of religion.   Bradley of course agrees that religion involves a relation between the human species and Deity But Deity for him is only an *aspect* of the Absolute and not identical with it, and since the human species desires to apprehend the Absolute, it would seem that it must pass beyond religion, and that Deity must "pass beyond himself" and give place to the Absolute. And when this has happened, Deity has become all in all, and man is nought. And Deity under such conditions is something different from the Deity of religion, who is in relation to and therefore distinct from that which is in relation to Him.   I cannot help feeling, however, that there is a contradiction here due to the somewhat rigid use of the word "relation."   Of course "to live in God" is not the same as "to live apart from God."   But the whole notion of the balanced system to which I believe we shall be led by our studies is that to live in God is possible without losing one's identity, and that God, though including within Himself all that is, does not thereby annihilate the many and reduce them to a bleak and featureless unity. While, therefore, religion in the sense of the proper reaction of the human species towards Reality under their present circumstances cannot be the same as religion in the future when the circumstances may be wholly different, I cannot see that this involves the disappearance of that element which makes religion distinct from other occupations of the finite self.

(B) The now much canvassed saying of Karl Marx: "Philosophers have only explained the world; the task is to change it." seems to illustrate very well the difference between religion (whether or not it be based upon a philosophical theology) and philosophy in isolation from religion. But it was probably a saying which could only have come from the lips of a Jew. To him to understand the universe is not to pardon it, or to be content with its imperfections, but to become possessed in true prophetic fashion with a longing for a Day of the Lord, a vast Divine Initiative, which shall create a new heaven and a new earth wherein dwelleth righteousness. It is significant that the followers of Marx now claim his thought to be the lineal descendant of that of Spinoza—another Jew—, and that to both men Deity is presented in terms of anti-anthropomorphic negation, like the Mâkom of the Rabbis of old.

# Chapter II

## OF GOOD AND BAD RELIGION

An impartial observer acquainting himself for the first time with the institutions prevailing upon our planet would, I think, be puzzled at the prevalence of what might seem to him contradictory views regarding the value of religion. He would find a number of persons using as testimony to the good character of an individual the phrase: "He or she is very religious." The character of such an individual might, however, appear on closer observation to be less attractive than the testimony had led one to expect, and in some cases a person described as very religious might even turn out to be a rogue. Nevertheless the fact that a number of people were in the habit of using this phrase "very religious" as a sign of virtue would seem to indicate that as a rule it was a safe guide regarding the nature of the character of the person to whom it was applied. Our observer would therefore be still more puzzled to find another section of the community holding diametrically opposite views, and regarding anyone who professed the slightest interest in religion as self-condemned; and it would be natural to enquire how such a contradictory state of affairs could possibly have come to exist. I propose therefore, in this chapter, to try to offer some explanation.

A religion in the sense of a system of theory and practice which sets out to explain the nature of reality as responsive and to indicate and foster a proper reaction towards it, on the assumption that there should be an harmonious and disinterested attitude which we should maintain towards whatever power controls our destinies,—such a system may be of several kinds.

(1) It may give an inadequate account of reality, but may nevertheless incite persons to make a proper reaction towards it. In this case the system will be sound as to its values, but unsound as to its facts, and those who insist upon accuracy in matters of fact will condemn it as bad, and may be tempted in consequence to draw the sweeping conclusion that all religion is faulty as to matters of fact, and that it always will be so.

(2) It may be unsound both in its description of reality and also in the reaction which it prescribes. It will then unquestionably be bad all through.

(3) It may be correct as to its description of reality but faulty in the reaction which it prescribes. It may then be regarded as the wrong way of reaching the goal in question.

(4) It may give as good as possible an account and prescribe what appears to be a proper reaction in view of our present circumstances, though in neither case the best conceivable; since even if reality be responsive, our beliefs about it will only be human images, and thus liable to be limited by the knowledge and outlook of our own generation.

The general conclusion to be drawn from the above analysis is that it is unwise to assume that because a religion exists or is believed in by certain persons it must therefore necessarily be good or true or even the best. The usual reason why it is assumed to be good is that over a very large part of the planet it has hitherto been taken for granted that the normal human being will instinctively possess some kind of wholeness of view with regard to the universe, involving an emotional reaction towards a superpersonal reality. Not to possess this in any form is therefore regarded as the equivalent of being abnormal, and the abnormal person or social group, if not regarded as actually evil, is at any rate and not without justification looked upon with suspicion.

Observation of human affairs however leads us inevitably to the conclusion that many of the practices associated in the past with religion can only be described by the unqualified use of the word "bad." They appear at the very mildest to be often stupid, and at the worst to be hideous. I recognise, of course, that there might be a totally different reason for characterising a religion as bad. If that religion were to condemn as evil certain practices which a large number of human beings (whether rightly or wrongly we will not for the moment consider) held to be pleasant and desirable, then it would not be surprising if that large section of mankind stigmatised the religion in question as bad, since it would be opposing itself as an obstruction to that section of mankind in the satisfaction of its desires. But this kind of objection I am for the present leaving on one side. What I am concerned with is the fact that a very large amount of the religious belief and practice recorded, let us say, in the pages of an eminent exponent of the comparative method[1] strikes us as definitely repulsive. Now this,

[1] Meaning, of course, Sir James Frazer.

of course, might be due to the bias of the author, and in certain cases this may be so, but only in certain cases. As a general rule he is impartial, and sticks to the recording of facts, and it is just this accumulation of facts which produces such an impressive panorama of stupidity, cruelty and wrong-headedness. There is, however, something to be said on the other side. We shall have occasion presently to indicate the way in which the path of human progress forks into the two broad highways of religion and science, but it will suffice for the moment to remind the reader that in the beginning there was but one track in which religion and science were confused; although, as the idea of the nature of Deity developed, man ceased to think of it in terms of food and weather, and came to think of it as concerned with moral values. To put this more simply, primitive man as a two-legged land-animal was (even more than modern man) very largely concerned with keeping himself alive. He wanted to know how to evade the inconveniences of the weather, how to make animals come to be killed, how to cure disease, how to avoid being killed himself by wild animals or by other men, how to be sure that he was conducting the propagation of his species in the right way, and later on how to make the crops grow. So[1] he set to answer a great many questions which we should regard as questions of medical, agricultural or mechanical science as though they were questions of religion. This may seem to us rather odd, but we must reflect that it was due to his interpretation of the external world as made up of a plurality of spirits which

[1] As we shall show in detail in our third chapter.

inhabited material objects. As he found that most of the things in the external world were not uniformly friendly or tractable to mankind, but caused him a good deal of trouble in handling and controlling them, he came to the conclusion that the great bulk of these spirits were hostile to him, and that in order to achieve his end he must do something to secure their neutrality even if he could not capture their good will. Some of these spirits came to be regarded as rather important, and finally assumed the rôle of greater deities, but they were still regarded as hostile, capricious or indifferent so far as man was concerned. Looking back, it is surely hard to blame the human race in its primitive infancy for coming to such conclusions. It surely matters little whether nature be conceived as "the one" or "the many," if she be thought hostile, capricious, or indifferent, as far as man is concerned. Science to-day, as we shall see, strongly insists upon the unity of structure in reality, but scientists either tell us nothing about the moral quality of reality, or else, when they venture to desert for a time their scientific impartiality, say that the universe is hostile or indifferent to all that is going on upon our little planet, and that the latter with all its complex activities is doomed to perish and to become as though it had never been. The improbability that this doom will overtake our earth next year, and its corresponding (possible) postponement for a million million years may furnish some consolation to ourselves who are now living, since we may thus be spared the discomfort of it: but the final certainty obviously lowers the worth of every human activity, unless there be some compensating factor yet to be taken into account. We cannot fall back on the idea of racial immortality, and even the postponement of the final débâcle does not abate the bitterness of individual death-beds. It seems, therefore, rather foolish to condemn our ancestors for holding the same view of the universe as some of our modern pessimistic philosopher-scientists, merely because our ancestors expressed themselves in terms of a crude animism. On the contrary, it would seem that we have only a right to call their religion bad if we hold one of two convictions. We must either hold that they were wrong in their pessimism, and that the ultimate power behind the universe, in spite of the disharmonies and shadows of nature, is really good in all that we human beings can mean by the term good; or, on the other hand, we must hold the conviction that although the universe is hostile to us it is idle to try to propitiate it, whether it be one or many, and that therefore when our ancestors sacrificed human beings in order to secure the favour of the spirits of the Rain, the Wind, or the unconquerable Sun, they were merely wasting their time.

Of course it is just possible that in the face of a desperate situation it is worth trying any desperate remedy, but our modern pessimistic philosopher (Lord Russell) does not seem inclined to inculcate a return to the sacrificial system; but rather paradoxically to the practice of the highest moral virtues as a sort of dignified but despairing protest against the blind crudity of the universe, which intends in any case to destroy the society of beings practising these moral virtues. This view may possibly satisfy the minds of a small minority, but it seems hardly possible that it can ever come to be endorsed by the common judgment of mankind. It leaves the problem of the "good" isolated, as though it were unrelated to anything else in reality. (I must be careful not to enlarge here any further upon this point, since it will come up for detailed consideration in other chapters, but it was impossible to avoid mentioning it here.)

We have seen, then, that some of the badness in religion is due to a sombre view of the nature of reality, and can only be called bad if one does not believe that reality is sombre, or that the sombre element is being misrepresented. We have also seen that a good deal of what is bad in religion ought not to be called bad religion at all, but bad science, and then only bad in the sense of being obsolete.

There are, however, a few other reasons for the condemnation of the religious attitude. The first of these, though rather curious, is perfectly genuine, and was crystallised in one single sentence by an eminent anthropologist when he said:—"I have known some extremely religious fellows who were terrible blackguards." He happened, I fancy, to be thinking more particularly of primitive savages, but that matters little. The fact which we have to face is that a certain wholeness of view, or, if the phrase is preferred, a kind of cosmic emotion, may and does exist, quite in detachment from a strict sense of morality. There are many parallel cases to this. A talented poet, musician, or painter, may have undeniable genius associated with a moral character which seems objectively bad or unpleasant. We do not say in this case

E

that his particular genius is of the highest rank, but we cannot refuse to call it genius. It is the odd experience of all ministers of religion that in the course of their pastoral duties they come across individuals who have a very strong sense of the reality of Deity, coupled with an equally poor capacity for performing their duty to their neighbour. The poor devils believe, though they do not invariably tremble.

The impartial observer to whom we referred at the beginning of this chapter need not therefore, I think, long remain puzzled as to the contradictory views prevailing upon the value of religion. I think that he might, however, take some other matters into account also. He might consider whether in almost every department of human activity it would not be possible to find bad exponents of those activities, bad traditions, bad and obsolete lines of development.[1]

Perhaps the most obvious example which he might take is that of art. Although there may be difference of opinion in matters of detail, there can be no question as to the existence of goodness and badness in the expressions of art produced by the human race. A picture, a statue, or a building is not necessarily good because somebody has made it, nor is it good as a picture or statue merely because it obeys the laws of perspective and is correct in the same way that a photographic print is correct. A building is not necessarily good because its designer and builder have obeyed the laws of building construction, so that the

[1] Thus I note Dr. Needham ironically invites the Soviet to abolish the printing-press because of its misuse by the bourgeois governing class.

building does not fall down, but is capable of being
inhabited and used. All this is obvious, and yet the
undisputed fact remains that pictures, statues, and
buildings, which have a certain survival value because
they comply with certain conditions in matters of
measurement, are capable of being described as ugly,
decadent, inartistic, meretricious. It is true that in
these matters standards of judgment are somewhat
relative, so that one generation will throw on to the
rubbish heap that which a previous generation has
regarded as full of beauty, while some future generation
may disinter it from the rubbish heap and set it up
once again as an object of admiration.

I am not going to allow myself to be diverted into
writing a treatise on aesthetics. All I wish to do
(and I think that the above remarks will suffice to that
end) is to make the point that the existence of a system
of religion no more guarantees its goodness than the
fact that certain people hang in their houses the
paintings executed by some particular artist guarantees
that these paintings judged by the best standards are
specimens of good art. The paintings to a subsequent
generation may have a certain historical or antiquarian
value as showing what people of a certain class in a
certain period liked to hang up in their houses and to
look at. The paintings will thus show something of
the mentality of their former possessors, but the
result may be unfavourable so far as our judgment
upon the taste of their possessors is concerned. Even
then, we shall not be wise in deducing from the existence of a large number of bad pictures or of admirers
of bad pictures, that the art galleries of the world

should all be pulled down or converted into factories
for petrol-engines. The real remedy would seem to be
(1) a proper theory of aesthetics and (2) an improvement
of the public taste. The elimination of art as a pernicious element from life will only lead to a violent
reaction against the would-be eliminators. Of course
it is possible to proceed on the lines adopted by educational propagandists in certain countries and to
issue an order from a government office that all pictures
and decorations are to be removed from the schools,
that no school building is to be erected except of a
standardised box-pattern, and that children are to be
taught that it is wrong to draw and paint, or to use
pen or pencil for anything except writing in notebooks
(anyone found using them for another purpose to be
punished); while parents are to be prohibited from
dressing their children in anything except the school
uniform, which is to be as drab and utilitarian as
possible. The absurdity of such proposals is patent,
and they seem revolting to most of us, yet they are
perfectly logical if art in any sense is a bad thing, and
as such only fit to be eliminated from life. Now we
can all see what would be the result of such proposals;
"Naturam expellas furca, tamen usque recurret" gives
the best summary of what will probably happen. Yet
it need not happen at once. Human nature is a
curiously pliable thing, and it is possible to mould it
in such a way as to deprive it for a time, at any rate,
of even some of its characteristic features. That this
will make it poorer and meaner may be quite reasonably maintained, and most of us would admit the force
of the argument, but to say that the quality of the race

is incapable of deliberate attenuation is to ignore the evidence before our eyes in the older quarters of any industrial town.

A modern observer has made the somewhat depressing assertion that the mass of humanity tends to adopt a religious belief which suits it, rather than a belief which is true, and he infers that a decadent race will therefore have a decadent religion.[1] It is difficult to dispute this, however unwelcome it may be. The sting lies in the words "which suits it." We should naturally expect mankind to desire that which was intellectually true and morally bracing. Strange to say, however, this is not the case. A desire for that to which one is accustomed, or for that which flatters one's vanity or soothes one's fears, is in most persons stronger than the desire for truth. The causes for this are largely physiological, and may often be sought in loyalty to a beloved relative or in some variation or other of the sex-impulse. Obviously conservatism tends to grow as age creeps on and vitality declines. Fear of disturbance is a sentiment prevalent among those who live with small margins and who are therefore likely to be deeply affected by any sort of revolution. These tendencies have a slight value in holding men back from hastily adopting ill-considered opinions, but if yielded to in excess they hamper sincerity of thought and so blunt the mind, besides pandering to a craven spirit which will take no risks, but desires safety first. There is also an element of laziness in the make-up of many persons, and the female sex (whatever it may do in the future) has in the past almost always defended established institutions, even when

[1] W. R. Inge.

unsatisfactory, since without them it feels that there is little security for the birth and rearing of the family.

Stranger still, mankind is subject to fits of perversity which make it react more strongly in some cases against a religion which is good and true than against one which is patently trivial or false. Such reaction is, however, not the reaction of a higher religion against a lower, but of wicked and rebellious persons against a truth which interferes too much with their inclinations. A clergyman who preaches a sane modernism, or social righteousness, will sometimes prove much more of an offence to those of his parishioners who are inclined to be worldly and corrupt than one whose doctrines are so foolish that no thinking man can seriously believe in them, or who is content to keep religion in a separate department from daily conduct. Similarly, it has been pointed out that to those who desire a materialistic organisation of society, a sound intellectual presentation of the claims of religion is offensive, because it has to be taken seriously, and is therefore an obstacle to the realisation of the ends they have in view. Indeed, cynics have been heard to remark that the prosperity of atheistic communism, or the promotion of the aims of the rationalist press association might well be furthered by judicious subscriptions to the work of fundamentalists.

I do not propose to commit the indiscretion of overstating my case, and I shall not therefore maintain that all good religion at all times will produce or does produce a state of pleasure. It must be obvious that such a claim is not made even by those persons who assert that good religion is a good thing and that that good thing is in their possession. If the business of religion be to explain the nature of reality as responsive, and to indicate and foster our proper reaction towards it, then, assuming that such an explanation is possible, the first demand which we need to make is that we should be offered an explanation which is true. And if such an explanation can be offered, it is obvious that it will be more satisfactory for us to be in possession of that explanation than to be ignorant of it, even though the knowledge of that explanation may be productive of pain at certain points and under certain circumstances, since knowledge is always a more satisfactory state than ignorance, and is therefore to be preferred, for it will in the long run produce a state of tranquillity and acquiescent harmony, of stable joy transcending temporary pain. The first question then to be asked is, Can any religion be true? or rather, Can any explanation of the universe, which regards reality as responsive, and which prescribes a reaction towards it upon the part of human beings, possibly be true? If the answer to this be a negative one, then no amount of pleasure on the part of individuals can possibly be justified as the result of religion, since that pleasure being the result of believing something which is not true is consequent upon falsehood, and therefore to be deprecated. If, however, we are able as the result of a survey of the situation to answer this first question in the affirmative, we can then go on to ask a second question concerning the various religious systems brought before our notice: Which of these is good and which is bad? Is there one which is better than the others? Or do they all contain elements which are good? Is there one which contains a maximum of these good elements? And having asked, and as far as possible answered such a group of questions, we may then take the third step and ask: Is the best religion which we can find in any sense absolute and final, or are we justified in supposing that the future will produce something better still, in the sense of a religion which still more accurately than any religion of the past explains the nature of reality taken as a whole and indicates and fosters our proper reaction towards it?

So far the contention has been that if any religion can be true, no religion can be called good which is not true, and no religion can be called the best possible, unless it appear to provide mankind with the most accurate and complete and correct account possible of the nature of reality and our proper reaction towards it. If, therefore, any religion be true in this sense, it will not be proper to ask whether or no it produces or can produce states of pleasure in individuals. If it is true, we shall be bound to accept it, whether to do so gives pleasure or not. Of course if anyone can be found who is able to say that this particular religious system has afforded him pleasure as the result of his believing it, we shall not and we cannot refuse to take note of his evidence and to regard it as perhaps an item standing to the credit of the system in question, but we cannot regard the provision of pleasure unqualified as the main object of any religion.

Pleasure, however, may be of different kinds. There may be pleasure produced by indulgence or possibly over-indulgence in some appetite or other, where the indulgence, or at any rate the over-indulgence, is anti-social and therefore to be condemned. Any religion which produces pleasurable sensations in us by encouraging a propensity to indulge a weakness must be pronounced a bad religion. If it be wrong for any one who is young and vigorous to desire to live in safety and self-indulgence and to be freed from all risks, then obviously any religious belief which creates the presumption that a young man or woman is right to desire safety is a vicious belief. Similarly any belief which creates the presumption that persons who have borne the burden and heat of the day bravely and without complaint, or who have uncomplainingly suffered bodily ill-health or the frustration of their good desires or the defeating of their good purposes, or perhaps the destruction of good and useful work to which they have given their best efforts, that such persons have no refuge or remedy, but that the Being Who controls the universe is either indifferent to their sufferings or actually the cause of them—such a belief will commonly be called bad. It may maintain that it is true, but its discordance with rationality must render it severely suspect.

We shall require, therefore, of any religious belief to be regarded as true, that it shall harmonise with the conditions of human life by providing at once both stimulus and confidence. Not to hold such a belief is to regard what appears to be a universe as four-fifths rational and one-fifth irrational, and this combination of incompatible elements is impossible in a universe. But since the system with which we are dealing bears, as we shall see, indications of being a universe, it seems that there should be some way of explaining the discordance without breaking up the unity.

The allegation that religion is opium for the people, though it may be true of some forms of religion, is most emphatically false with regard to others, since it is plain that certain types of it seek to foster such an habitual reaction towards a responsive reality that they are a perpetual goad and stimulus for those who believe in them, and indeed an actual deterrent hindering those who desire to live in a state of somnolence and self-indulgence from accepting their tenets. The confidence in a rational and benevolent influence guiding the universe is not only an incentive to useful and productive work, but is also a justifiable confidence, if the experience of long lives be taken into account, and has a steadying effect upon those who find that the experience of living in the world is a strain and an anxiety, or who have had to endure some kind of acute suffering. Such persons often exhibit as the result of their religious beliefs a quiet joy and a serene happiness which render them infinitely more useful and satisfactory members of society than those who hold no such beliefs. Since results of this kind cannot proceed from a wholly false and irrational conception of the nature of reality, it is legitimate to assume that the beliefs producing them are not merely useful, but contain some underlying basis of truth, expressed it may be in terms of $\mu\hat{v}\theta os$, but qualitatively factual, and not pure delusion.

Much has been made of the harm wrought by religious controversies, and the advocates of secularism point to the European wars of religion in the sixteenth and seventeenth centuries, and to the bitter fruits of Hindu-Moslem animosity in India, as well as to the clash between Catholic and Protestant in Ireland, quoting at once the old Lucretian tag

"tantum relligio potuit suadere malorum."

This however, is hardly fair. We may well ask whether it is likely to be possible for human beings ever to avoid acute cleavage of opinion over any of the deeper problems and issues of life. No one troubles to quarrel over trivialities, or to kick a dead horse. Questions affecting matters of life and death in the literal sense are certain to cause animosity. If we disagree on these we are sure to disagree fiercely; and if we have any liking for a fight, we shall not improbably make difference of view upon such questions an excuse for fighting. But further, we may well ask, in addition, how far racial differences and fear of economic rivalry, or pressure of a competing population with a high-birth rate, rather than mere religious beliefs, are responsible for these warlike clashes. It seems very hard to get the Nordic and Mediterranean natures to agree. Sooner or later they get on one another's nerves, if not over religion, at any rate over politics. One of the future tasks of religion may well be that of trying to bring together these discordant elements, and trying to make them exercise patience in understanding one another. It will be a hard task, and hitherto it has never seriously been attempted.

The objection to religion as the promoter of ugliness is not often made by outsiders, but is more often the complaint of religious persons themselves. Yet it would be fair to say that new religion, whether Christian or non-Christian, is prone to adopt and consecrate the art-forms of its adherents, without elevating them, and that real beauty is in consequence as rare in religion as goodness and truth.   The problem is an intricate one, but it is plain that aesthetic splendour is not necessarily the zenith of religious art.   King's College Chapel, glorious as it is, is inferior to the white austerity of a thirteenth-century nave, while the architecture of nineteenth-century bourgeois Puritanism is so ugly that it makes one feel sure there must have been some flaw in the theory of the religion which produced it.

## NOTE TO CHAPTER II

The answer to the militant "gottlos" which I propose when he asks: "show me that religion is necessary" must run as follows:

(1) Religion in the past has proved a unifying and organising centre for human life.

(2) Such a centre is necessary—you yourself admit it, by your adoption of a restricted form of positivism of a proletarian colour as your point of organisation.

(3) I admit that all religion is not a good thing.

(4) You say that no form of theism can be good, and that yours is the better point of organisation.

(5) It remains for you to prove the latter proposition— the *onus probandi* rests with you, because you must show why something already established in large areas should be abandoned.

(6) The actual number of persons (large or small) among your opponents who hold any form of theism to be good is irrelevant to the truth of the belief, since many indisputable truths are not held by a majority of persons at some time or other.

(7) Our contention will be:

    (*a*) that a form of theism is the most satisfactory explanation of the total number of data available for observation.

    (*b*) that therefore it is necessary if life is to be duly organised.

    (*c*) that it is not inevitably connected with those features of organised society which many of us, in common with you, regard as either evil, obsolete, or irrelevant to the true expression of religion.

I fancy however that the "gottlos" is himself on trek, and that his mind is divided between loyalty to his past leaders and heroes who held a form of positivism, and the consciousness that there is more to be known and said about religion than those leaders were acquainted with. He is pledged to a liquidation of religion, but at the same time he does not really know what religion can be, but is only acquainted with certain forms of it obtaining in his own area.

Whatever may be said about other forms of religious belief, the Christian religion is not tied to any political system. It can exist, though not necessarily flourish, under any system of government. Its natural tendency, however, is to resist any organisation of society which joints the individual on to his fellow so as to leave no elbow-room. It recognises functional, though not property, differences in mankind, and is definitely opposed to the class-spirit with its denial of human brotherhood. In so far as communism seeks to eliminate competitive and predatory struggles of individuals against one another, private gain in business with its appeal to cupidity rather than service, and the money-motive as distinct from work for the common good, the Christian religion is wholly on the side of communism.

But, as has been said above, it regards the marriage of idealistic communism with atheistic materialism as a mésalliance. No communist who thinks sanely can evade the notion of Self-Existent Being. Sooner or later he is bound to come up against it. All that the Christian does is to declare prophetically the truth regarding the *nature* of that Self-Existent Being, and so to declare the true and proper character for all dependent and contingent beings. "Ye shall be perfect even as your Heavenly Father is perfect." The problems of religion and its tasks begin just where the secularist (of any sort) stops short.

The real political difference between communism and Christianity is that the former relies on coercion, the latter on persuasion. We Christians maintain, therefore, that ours is the more durable method. We desire to replace predatory individualism by a fellowship of love and service, but we are determined not to be misled, as Mohammed was centuries ago, into supposing that a spiritual creed can really be effectively propagated or maintained by blood and iron. Pure Christianity is no opium, no superstition, but a creed in harmony with the high scientific prosecution of the search for truth. It can therefore dispense with coercion and bribery as a means of propagation, and it is only a debased form of it which uses either.[1] The above remarks about the use of force and coercion apply equally in the case of fascism.

---

[1] Cf. Lippmann (*A Preface to Morals*) who says quite truly:

"Institutional Christianity, as a popular religion, is suited to the capacities of the unconverted. The majority of its adherents can understand nothing except a simple scheme of rewards and punishments, and this is what the Churches, which are really secular institutions, provide. The fact that they use rewards and punishments, and appeal even to Caesar to execute them, proves that they are dealing with the unconverted. For the few who are converted, goodness is pleasant and needs no sanctions. When men have to be coerced into goodness it is plain that they do not care for it for its own sake."

# Chapter III

# OF THE ORIGINS OF RELIGION, AND ITS EARLIER DEVELOPMENTS

After a long period of half-animal existence the age of reflection dawned and man entered upon a new phase of mental life.[1] His times of creative thought were neither continuous nor consistent and were sometimes followed by periods which were unfavourable both to reason and devotion.

It is important, however, to recognise the fact that he did reflect. Those who have taken the trouble to

---

[1] I do not wish to imply that animals do not think. Some of them certainly do, and are capable of forming and indicating preferential judgments. The Adélie penguins have expressed preferences for certain coloured stones. Cats and dogs watching from the windows of houses are often obviously seen to be using their wits. A horse has been known to appreciate scenery, and a dog to discriminate between certain kinds of music; while the researches into the mentality of apes undertaken by Köhler and others show an advanced if still rudimentary stage of animal cerebration. The essential difference between the thought of the higher animals and that of the lowest human beings known to us is in their twofold consciousness (a) of self as something containing a permanent as distinct from a transitory element (hence ceremonial burial). (b) of something "sacred" which is even more important than self. No animals appear to have ever buried one another ceremonially. No animals appear to have ever set the value of sacredness upon anything. In their nests or lairs they have no "sacred objects" or symbols.

The whole subject is usefully dealt with in Sir J. A. Thomson's Gifford Lectures, Vol. II, Lect. xvi, and his main conclusions may be summarised as follows: Behaviour in living organisms evolves through the stages of tentative movement (in free-swimming organisms), leading on to occasional new departures and experiments, with answers to stimuli, and then, by trial and error, through perseverance to the discovery of a response which meets the situation and relieves the creature from further stimulation. With the establishment of a nervous system these responses are organised into live intimately for a protracted period with savage peoples report that they have the same kind of mental activity as ourselves. They are observant, they take note of natural phenomena, they draw inferences, and within the limits of their small experience they arrive at serviceable conclusions. Their powers of observation may be relatively undeveloped, but in such matters as making and handling tools and canoes, building huts, or tracking game, they show a remarkable aptitude for putting two and two together, and not only for drawing a conclusion, but for remembering it and passing it on.

hereditable automatisms, known as reflexes and tropisms, but the main-line of development still continues, with the beginnings of inference, learning, and memorising. With the improvement of the brain comes instinctive behaviour, another and still higher hereditable form of organisation, and then intelligent behaviour, which implies more difficult processes of trial and error, and the power to profit by experiences derived from them. The climax, so far as we are concerned, is the rational conduct of our own species. Behaviourists so-called are inclined to treat all this organisation as complete in itself, but they contradict their own assertions, since (1) they admit the fabrication of *thought* as among the functions of the mechanical system of organic life; (2) they overlook the fact that the progressive automatisation is only of value in so far as it saves time and worry and sets "mind" free for further adventures: it is in fact a device for the emancipation of mind; (3) they wrongly assume that what is now automatic never required mental control; since, however certainly habituation may lead to automatisation, merely learning to swim or to drive a car will convince us that (in the beginning) to make a new movement demands attention, thought, and concentration of will; (4) Some reflexes are still under control of a psychic factor; (5) we can be conscious of our behaviour; (6) in a mental process as distinct from a reflex action pure and simple there is always an element of what has been called "pre-awareness" which forestalls, and is anticipatory.

Thomson concludes that in the face of the stories connected with many of the more highly developed birds and animals we are led to regard the psychic theory of the laboratory-naturalists and behaviourists as outrageous superstition. How much more then must it be the case with man!

It is therefore not surprising that we should find evidence that even primitive man concerned himself not merely with tool and canoe-making, hut building, and hunting, but with theorising about the totality of his environment and his proper relation to it, in other words with religion, science, and philosophy.

We arrive at a knowledge of the religion of primitive man by several means:

(a) By studying the data unearthed and sorted by archaeologists. This specially comprises the palaeolithic carvings and paintings and ceremonial burials found in different parts of the world. (b) By a study of religious practices among still existing or recently existing primitive races, or by survivals among ourselves. (c) By the study of the habits of children.

Putting together the evidence and probabilities which we derive from these three sources, we may say that on the whole there is a remarkable unanimity about the beliefs and practices of the more primitive peoples and of the votaries of what are commonly called the nature-religions, and that the beliefs and practices so much resemble one another that it is often hard to believe that (as is often the case) they are concurrent independent developments, and not invariably genetically related to one another. Beneath the rich variety of outward expression and ceremonial there is great and almost monotonous uniformity. Actually however, since nature herself is one and the same all the world over, it is hardly surprising that the different races of mankind should react to her phenomena in a similar fashion, and indeed this leads us on to the conclusion that should any one chance to

F

hit upon the right answer to the question "What is the proper relation of mankind towards the whole of Reality?" it ought to prove acceptable to these various races, in spite of their many differences of custom.

Much religious practice and ceremonial is obviously man-centred rather than God-centred and cannot therefore be described as disinterested; but whether it be the one or the other it arises undoubtedly from a vague sense *of two things*:

(1) *Of an element commonly called the sacred, where "sacred" means "abnormal," "unusual" or "extraordinary," and therefore outside common experience, or reserved or separated off from profane or common uses.* ("Sacred" to the primitive does not necessarily mean "good," since there may be for the savage both friendly and unfriendly objects among the abnormal or unusual and therefore both good and bad "sacred.")

(2) *Of dependence upon some power or powers dimly conceived, whose presence invokes a feeling of awe, and whose activities may be of singular or plural expression, and not being wholly understood are thought to be capricious.* We can perhaps distinguish a so-called pre-animistic stage in which the power, called by various names, is an element possessed by different objects in common, like an electric charge, vague, potent, and terrifying. Gradually, however, by analogy from primitive man's own observation of himself in dream states, in trances and in dying, the power or powers, as being possessed of a detachable soul, are in fact regarded as in substance "soul-like." This is the animistic stage of belief. Unfortunately the consciousness of dependence may affect man in two different ways

It may either lead him to try to utilise the vague sacred force or "soul-like" powers for the realisation of his own private ends, or it may lead him to surrender himself into their hands, in the assurance that he will only in this way be able to realise the true end of his being. Now it must be admitted that the great bulk of primitive religious practice shows the influence of the sense of dependence acting in the first way rather than in the second. Indeed it is difficult to deny that this self-centred attitude shamelessly survives in the cultus of not a few modern Christians. The object of such persons is to get the sacred on to their side, rather than themselves on to the side of the sacred.

Dependence in the selfish sense necessarily diminishes, in proportion as pre-animistic and animistic views of the universe are superseded by a scientific one: and it has been pointed out that strangely enough the affirmations contained in the teaching of Jesus actually prepared the way not only for better religion, but also for the rebirth of science, by freeing the general mentality of mankind from belief in divine caprice. It is only when one has confidence that Nature is trustworthy, and desirous that we should discover her secrets, that science is at all possible. In a world where cabbage-leaves can turn into apple-pies or croquet-balls intermittently come to life and walk about, and where all natural objects are believed to be peopled with tricksy spirits, one can never know what is going to happen next, so that science is impossible, and fear of the unpredictable[1] dogs one's footsteps.

[1] It may be questioned whether an excessive re-affirmation of the unpredictable would not lead to a revival of this fear.

Such a universe is not the universe as represented and strongly affirmed by Jesus. The universe to Him is under unitary control, and the Controller is the embodiment of wisdom and benevolence; henceforward science is possible, and by obeying the laws of the Wise Controller man himself has learned to control a large part of Nature. This has inevitably produced in mankind a sense of self-dependence. How should it not? If you know that the sacred is benevolent, you take less trouble to get it on your side.

In spite of the sure expectation of the death of the individual and the apparently distant death of the planet, it can hardly surprise us that many have come to feel as though human skill, ingenuity, perseverance and goodwill ought to be able, independently, to solve all problems and supply all needs.

But this is just where the sense of dependence in its other interpretation enters in. If Deity were only a Being needed by man when his own efforts were failing, religion would be reduced to a position little short of ludicrous. The reader is reminded of an amusing passage at the beginning of Plato's *Republic*, where Socrates asks Polemarchus, (who is not a particularly profound thinker), in what special department of life justice is needed. Polemarchus falls into the trap and is made to admit that on his definition of justice there is no place for it in any particular department except "in relation to goods left in safe custody"; whereupon Socrates remarks, "Then justice is only useful for what is out of use." A somewhat similar nemesis is bound to overtake anyone who defines religion as based upon a sense of dependence, without saying what he means by it, since religion, like justice, is of no use if it is merely a departmental affair, or one in which the intervention of Deity is desired merely for the private satisfaction of man. It may be said that sacrifices were offered by the ancient farmer for much the same object that the modern one employs chemical manures. It is precisely for this reason that in another famous Platonic dialogue Euthyphro finds it so difficult to answer Socrates when he asks "What is the good of the cultus?" because Socrates has already cut away the connection between the gods and natural phenomena, as conceived on a basis of miraculous intervention, or on that of bargaining with and propitiating powerful and capricious spirits.

Thus the prophet and the philosopher clearly perceive that any dependence upon a superhuman power which is worth preserving must not mean dependence so much in the sense, let us say, in which a traveller in a motor car in China is dependent upon a particular oil company controlled by brigands or by officials who have to be bribed for supplying him with fuel for his engine at stations dotted along the points of his journey, as in the sense in which one man is dependent upon another who besides being his parent, employer, leader, and guide, is also his gracious friend and companion (a very *dimidium animae suae*) in the direction and orientation of his whole life.

In the history of early religion the two elements of science and worship are intertwined and confused. Science itself is there seen to be of two kinds, (1) science proper, and (2) magical science, and mingled with these there also occurs an element of what may be called wistful disinterestedness, in which man ceases to think of his own selfish advantage, and does not even bargain with the powers of the world beyond, but somehow dimly conceives of them as desiring a response from him.

Science proper may be of two kinds, applied and theoretical; and although the latter is the basis for the former, and only ceases to be anthropocentric when its aim becomes the increase of human efficiency for ideal ends, yet it is found capable of standing in its own rights, as in sober fact one aspect of religion, *i.e.* the disinterested delight in the discovery of true facts about the universe. In this way the physicist, chemist, mathematician and archaeologist may be said to have a real sense of dependence upon the sacred, in that they are devoted to the cause of truth and accuracy, which uses them for its own purpose, *i.e.* that of getting itself proclaimed.

Pure religion and undefiled is thus from its very crudest beginnings the devotion to a "sacred" (whether a gross material object or a taboo), which is felt to be more important than one's own personal and private convenience, and ultimately more important even than human life itself. Hence human sacrifice, self-surrender, self-immolation, and martyrdom. It may well be enquired whether the sacred even in its crudest form is not identical with the Self-Existent Being of the religious philosopher. Primitive man is not conscious of this identity, but the awesome Holy may well be the first step in the direction of sensing The Impassible Whole, and by the latter is not meant that which is without sympathy or feeling, but That Which is Container rather than Contained, That Which *is* in Its own right, and is incapable except by Its own permission of suffering any action upon Itself, That Which is the logical Ground and Basis of all that comes into existence, and upon Which all things depend. Such a Being may be sensed by the savage as a vague, impersonal, and terrifying power, but the vagueness is a prelude to the greater precision of the concepts framed later on by civilised man. It is not in opposition to them.

The sacred is certainly no illusion, but a desperately real thing, however varied in scale its definition; and if man projects onto it his highest ideals, he is thereby building no phantasy, but investing the sacred reality with an ascending scale of attributes.

Considerable difference of opinion still obtains as to the prevalence of an early belief in a single spiritual deity. If such could be established, it would obviously much strengthen the so-called argument "from general consent," to which we have elsewhere referred.[1] There are those apologists who declare that the evidence still supports a belief in the former prevalence of a primitive monotheism, afterwards overlaid and corrupted, as primitive man degenerated into the modern degraded savage. The evidence for this primitive monotheism as a universal feature is precarious. Where traces of it are believed to have been found they have sometimes proved to be the relics of a prophetic religion

[1] In No. 1 of the Series.

introduced from elsewhere, occasionally by Christian missionaries.[1]

What we actually find most widely in primitive circles is that of which we have already spoken, the vague sense of a power, sometimes described by the Polynesian word "mana," sometimes as "orenda" or "wakonda." the sacred or the numinous, a dynamic force whose being is never doubted, but whose nature remains undefined. The sacred is everywhere, the gods or God in the strict sense as yet nowhere.

The possibility of a monotheistic belief developing early even among primitive peoples cannot of course be denied; but so far as we are able to depend upon observed fact it would seem that such a monotheism is usually not an early development, and that when it occurs it has to struggle for existence in the face of a tendency upon the part of the majority of the population to prefer a form of pluralism, which for some reason or other seems to it more attractive and easier to understand. Thus we have in Egypt the failure of the temporary spiritual reformation initiated by Amenhotep IV, the gradual decline of the monotheistic ideas connected in China with the worship at the so-called altar of Heaven, and the inability of Hebrew prophetic religion, of prophetic Christianity and of Islam, to capture more than a proportion of the populations which have come under their influence. In all cases there is a marked tendency on the part of the great mass of mankind to revert to some form or other of pluralistic animism. In Egypt polytheism

[1] Notice must be taken however of an important survey of this problem by various experts which is given later in this chapter.

soon reasserted itself. In China the popular cults are those of daemons and ancestors. In India, beside the higher Hinduism and a certain amount of pseudo-monotheism, we have the enormous development of polytheistic cults, the worship of local and mostly female nature-divinities, and the wide-spread vulgar belief in more or less dangerous and capricious spirits of minor importance. Buddhism in Ceylon is influenced by animism, and in Japan and Tibet by polytheism and animism. Christians in spite of their inheritance have tended to fall back upon devotion to madonnas and saints, or if they are Protestants upon ancestor-worship performed either in graveyards or before the statues of eminent persons or dead heroes. There are considerable animistic elements in popular Islam, and there is also a cultus of saints. Secularist materialism develops a cult of heroes; atheistic philosophy a doctrine of pre-existent and immortal "selves."

To make a survey of the religious beliefs and practices of the various nations of the world or of the various ancient races or primitive tribes, however necessary it might be if we were engaged upon a text-book of anthropology or an extremely detailed treatise on comparative religion, would be in the present instance to inflict upon the reader a large mass of information which is already accessible to him in works devoted to the subject, and which by reason of its monotony of detail would inevitably weary him. A full description for instance of the polytheism of the northern Celts, of the Mayas of Central America, of the Babylonians or Egyptians, or of the Dravidians of Southern India, would largely consist in recounting the strange

names by which each group designated the daemons
presiding over the different departments of natural
life.   In practically all such cases there will be found
to be a sun-god, a god of fertility, a god of war, a god
of spring-time, and a god of wind and rain.   There
will also be deities depicted as men and women of a
larger growth, with strange and wonderful stories
attached to them, each perhaps presiding over one
of the previously named departments of life and
associated with it.   It is believed that these polytheistic groups derive their existence from two main
sources.

(1) The animistic personification of natural objects
and forces, such as mountains, winds, rivers and
heavenly bodies.

(2) The cultus of dead men and women of striking
personality.

It seems clear that whatever contribution the worship
of natural forces and objects may make to the development of a rich and complex pluralistic religion, a great
deal also depends upon the veneration given to the
departed spirits of kings, queens, chiefs, ancestors,
medicine men, warriors and persons of striking beauty.
So much is known about the anniversary com-
memorations of such persons, and of the dramatic
ceremonies which were held in connection with them,
that it is difficult not to believe that the major element
in the developed polytheism of the planet is the
reverence for great human beings.[1]   Once male or
female leaders came to be reverenced in this way, it
was not difficult to associate them with the operations

[1] See *Dramas and Dramatic Dances*, Sir Wm. Ridgeway, C.U. Press.

of nature, and to believe that they were in some way after their decease active through the forces of nature, perhaps in the same way as they had been prior to their birth. Polytheistic thought is very loose in its employment of words signifying "deity" and "divine." It will apply such words with the slightest provocation not only to human beings, but also to moments of emotional disturbance or spiritual exaltation, to accidents and disasters, and to strange and awe-inspiring objects.

Whether a monotheistic belief could develop or ever has developed directly in the human mind without any intervening pluralistic phase cannot yet, as we have said, be definitely ascertained from the evidence at our disposal. The importance of our obtaining such evidence has probably been exaggerated, since, although it would no doubt be extremely interesting to find that some race of brutish savages had directly and immediately arrived at the belief in the existence of a single great benevolent creator Spirit (assuming this to be the true belief about God), yet in reality, so long as the belief is reached, the route of arrival must surely be a matter of secondary importance. Apart from the possibility of a sudden prophetic interpretation of the data, it seems probable that the normal way of arriving at monotheism is along the lines of what is called *theocrasia*; that is to say by a process of fusion resulting from the recognition that the different divinities are not different beings, but aspects of one and the same deity: there is evidence that this operated in ancient Mesopotamia and in India: and a familiar exposition is to be found in the writings of Plutarch

(98 A.D.) who explains that Isis and Osiris are the same as other gods and goddesses worshipped in other parts of the empire, though under different names, Osiris being identical with Dionysus; while there is a famous passage in the *Golden Ass* of Apuleius, in which Isis is made to declare:

"The primal Phrygians call me at Pessinus the mother of the Gods; hence the Athenians . . . name me Cecropian Minerva, the wave-beat Cyprians Paphian Venus, the archer Cretans Dictymnan Diana, the Sicilians Stygian Proserpina, the people of Eleusis ancient Ceres, others Juno, others Bellona, some Hecate, others again Rhamnusia, but the Aethiopians and the Egyptians . . . Queen Isis."

Similar ideas occur to-day among educated Hindus in India, and it seems as though the craving for a variety of cults suited to the respective temperaments of different worshippers is to-day satisfied within the confines of Christianity by the existence of different denominations or sects, each of which tends to emphasise some aspect in the character of Deity, although from the nature of the case Christians are precluded from holding an avowedly pluralistic view of the Godhead. It remains to point out that the tritheistic interpretation of the triune Godhead and the thinly veiled polytheism provided by the Roman and Eastern cultus of saints and martyrs furnish outlets for the discharge of an instinctive sentiment which is not easily banished.

Perhaps the most important feature of primitive religion is its conception of what is a sacred object. It is inaccurate to say that this is in all cases immediately connected with a doctrine of universal vitality. A well-known expert[1] deems it important to draw a distinction between what may be precisely called animism and animatism, the former referring to the possession of spiritual personality by some striking or peculiar object, the other the notion of a general animation of nature. The widespread existence of the latter is just one of those things that is open to doubt. Some of us moderns hold it of course in a manner resembling that in which it was held by the eighteenth-century thinker Leibnitz, with his doctrine of monads. It is doubtful, however, whether the ordinary savage, while be believes either in a vague impersonal potency or a plurality of powerful spirits, does not distinguish in the world of his ordinary work-a-day experience between *things* and *persons*. As there is a good deal of loose generalisation on this matter it is important to press the point. An observer who knows Australian natives intimately, and can tell truly how their minds work, says that to the ordinary blackfellow his club and his spear are tools connected with his ordinary daily life which in themselves contain no supernatural potency. If they are to receive it, they must be specially charmed. It is quite otherwise with his spear-thrower or his bull-roarer. The former for no obvious reason enables him to throw his spear extra-ordinarily far. The latter, though a mere chip of wood on the end of a string, emits the noise of thunder. Both these, then, being things out of the ordinary, contain some kind of virtue. Whether this virtue is thought of as alive or as in any way personal is another matter. Here again there is evidence that a generalisation

[1] Dr. R. R. Marett.

in favour of the latter opinion would be an over-
statement. The savage sometimes seems to describe
the mysterious $x$ resident in such things as the bull-
roarer or spear-thrower as power, sometimes as vitality
sometimes as spirit. He draws no fine distinctions. All
he can say is that in his experience some things in the
world are ordinary, and you can say beforehand how
they are going to behave, and there are other things
which are extraordinary, and whose behaviour is unpredictable, for the simple reason that you cannot
explain the why or the wherefore of it. Again, of the
latter class of things some are obviously friendly and
some are hostile, and for the savage, at any rate, part of
the function of religion is to get the friendly things (the
good sacred) on his side so as to enable him to overcome the hostile (the bad sacred). This, however, can
hardly be described as the best element in savage
culture, and we must revert to the point that there
is also in it an element from time to time which can
only be dignified with the epithet "disinterested."
As the story of religion proceeds, this disinterested
element slowly disentangles itself from that of self-
interest, grows somewhat purer, and takes a line
of its own. Science succeeds to sympathetic magic,
and along the path of applied science proceeds an
ever increasing multitude of those who seek the
satisfaction of their own desires, and the preservation
of their own interests. There is nothing shameful
about this, the only discreditable feature being the
confusion of the element of self-interest with that of
true religion. Religion in its true and best form is not
a mere prop for our weakness, nor a means of safety,

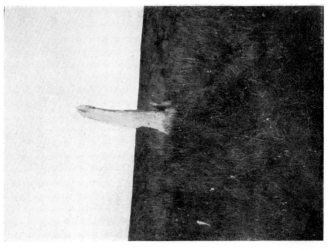

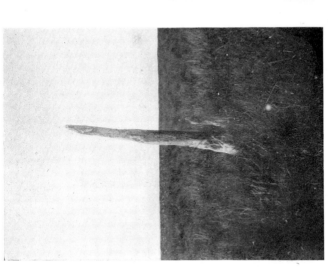

THE LONG STONE, CHAPMAN BARROWS, EXMOOR.

(*See* p. xi.)

nor a kind of universal provision for our necessities, nor yet simply "a very present help in time of trouble." Religion may be incidentally one or more of these things, but they cannot be regarded as the full measure of it. Religion at its highest is that which gives us a sense of being part of a larger whole in which our co-operation is both needed and desired. It is religion which needs us rather than we who need religion. Deity exists, not as a convenience for our use; we exist in order that we may co-operate with Deity, and find our true métier in being absorbed in the pursuit of His great purposes. We are not necessary to Him in the sense that He is incapable of dispensing with our aid even by His own choice. He has Himself chosen to be dependent on our free decision to co-operate with Him, having Himself bestowed on us as a gift that freedom, which is thus a part of Himself.

The consequence of such a belief as this will be that we seek the fellowship of Deity in our moments of strength, when we feel the creative impulse to be strong within us, and not merely as many in the past have been inclined to do only in moments of weakness, when we seemed unequal to our task. It is true that our best talents need to be transfigured and transmuted by the Divine fire if they are to achieve their full excellence, but the Divine fire quickens and does not consume. If we may change the metaphor, we may say that there exists an apparently inexhaustible reservoir of Divine energy ready to flow through us, and to be released upon the world. In relation to this store of energy our wills are of the nature of switches or sluices, whereby the flow of that energy can be either obstructed and checked, or released and directed. Whenever we consciously place ourselves in harmony with Deity as the prelude to engaging in any constructive or creative work, great or small, we may justly regard ourselves as releasing Divine energy and positively carrying out the Divine purpose; and although this is but an expression in symbolic terms of what really happens, rather than an exact description of the process, it is near enough to the truth for all practical purposes, and its importance can hardly be exaggerated.

No one can doubt that such a high view of the spirit of religion comes but slowly among primitive men, or indeed for that matter among civilised men too. Hence, as we have seen, the need for distinction between good and bad, superior and inferior, religion. The relation between child and father does not cease to exist, even when the child's conception of the function of the father is purely utilitarian, as the provider of sixpences or treats, of food or protection. The child, we may almost say, is justified in looking to its father to provide such things, but wrong if it limits the relationship between itself and its father to the expectation of such benefits. Even so, mankind in its ages of immaturity may justly stress its sense of dependence upon Deity. But it will be wrong if it limits the possibilities of relationship to a mere position of dependence. Primitive man, as we have said, is very largely concerned with the promotion of fertility and the conservation of food values, and his cere- monies are to a great extent connected with what he believes will secure for him from the unseen power or powers a sufficiency of milk or corn, fruit or vegetables, children, or animals to be killed. As his civilisation develops, the values which he seeks to conserve come to be less crude and simple, but strange to say he almost always recognises that their conservation may only be attainable at the expense of a life. The values are actually greater than his own personal safety or protection, and compared with them, the physical death of an animal, of himself, or of his nearest and dearest seems to be a secondary affair. The Source of Life seems prodigal of His children, and in thus imitating the behaviour of the Source of Life, man experiences a sense of exaltation which makes him feel superior to the changes, chances, and buffets of this fleeting world.

The offering of a life in order to secure rain, a good crop, the cessation of a famine, or the lifting of an epidemic is intelligible. It is less obvious on a materialistic interpretation of phenomena why the ideal values should come to be thought worthy of conservation at the expense of a life. Of the whole vast mass of religious belief and practice which has existed up to the present upon the planet it will, we fear, be generally agreed that a relatively small proportion has reached that high and noble level, and where it has done so it may in general be said that the advance has been due less to a slow process of evolution of thought, or to the collective thinking of groups or communities of average persons, than to a more or less sudden and discontinuous advance resulting from the creative energy of inspired individuals.

G

Some description should be given of five special institutions of primitive religion to which reference is frequently made. These are (1) sacred men, (2) totemism, (3) taboo, (4) initiation, and (5) sacrifice.

(1) The words of a Red Indian,[1] if we are justified in regarding them as independent of any influence exercised by a Christian missionary, are of decisive importance: "No man can succeed in life alone, and he cannot get the help he needs from men." This is certainly the belief of primitive peoples, that there is a generally unseen and mostly invisible world, which is related to the world of outward appearances, and that some individuals more than others are in contact with this unseen world, possibly through superior intelligence, but more commonly through trances or dreams or other psycho-physical phenomena. Such persons come to be held as themselves sacred and important, because it is thought that they are able to exercise influence upon the unseen world for the profit, protection and advantage of their fellows. They may not all, it is true, be of the same quality. Some may be really outstanding personalities, others mere tricksters and charlatans, men or women of unstable personality, and even criminal neurotics, and unfortunately with the credulous multitude these latter will have as much influence as the genuine seers and mystics. It is along these lines that there develops the class of sacred men, and the linking up of these exceptional people with the impersonators of the totem-object finally produces the typical magician (or Shaman as he is called in Siberia). There

---

[1] Quoted by Mr. C. Dawson, *Religion and Progress*, p. 97, cheap edition.

is much more to be said for the view that the vital
change in primitive culture is less from magic to
religion than from Shamanism to priesthood. As one
writer has said, a Shaman may be a veritable idiot,
but a priest must be a man of intellect. This is true,
yet there are often elements in priesthood which are
survivals of Shamanism. Priest is sometimes Shaman
writ in other letters and glorified, though this need
not be so. Under prophetic leadership, a priest may
be no mere conjurer, but the representative leader of
his people in the godward movement, sacred not to
their exclusion, but only in his special task to bear
his people in his heart, to love the souls whom God
Himself loves, and to lift them to the full realisation
of the common sanctity which they all are intended
to share. Meanwhile we shall see, in the course of
our studies, that different groups have very different
estimates of the office and functions of sacred men,
and in any case that there develops in time a broad
distinction between the priest and the prophet. The
function of the prophet is to speak as the interpreter
of the Divine, to act as God's spokesman, and to show
the meaning of life and its successive events. A
prophet *may* be a priest as well, but a priest need not
necessarily prophesy. The prophet is exceptional in
his ecstatic endowment, but the priest is exceptional,
chiefly because he has to see that the correct ceremonies
are performed. He deals in sacred actions—the ritual
whereby the sacred is approached and rendered
favourable to the values which the community desires
to preserve. Thus among the Todas of South India the
priest is the keeper of the sacred dairy, and knows the
ceremonies for securing the milk supply. The mediaeval

Christian priest was primarily the person who knew how to say Mass, and so to secure for the quick and dead the benefits of the vicarious and expiatory death of the historical Jesus upon Calvary.[1]

(2) *Totemism* is an explanation of life, the significance of which has been very much over-estimated. It is much less a matter of religion than of primitive natural history. Wherever human beings found themselves associated with certain animals, birds, or other living creatures of importance, they came to invent somewhat similar theories about their relations to them, so that in a sense the archetypal animal of a particular genus seems to have been regarded as a sort of ancestor or source of life for one particular group of persons. The Algonkin Indian name for this class of creatures, "totem," has been taken as the universal technical term. As a result, individual specimens of the totem creature were treated by such a group with reverence, and contradictory regulations came into existence with regard to it; so that the members of a particular totem were strictly enjoined either not to eat their totem animal or to eat no other meat than that of their totem animal, to marry only members of their own totem, or conversely to avoid all such marriages. The connection of totemism with religion involves the casting of the mantle of sacredness over these various regulations, and issues in or is associated with the development of the worship of animals. The most complete example of this is to be found in Egypt, where a very great

[1] Yet in this sense, in spite of the doctrine of the priesthood of all believers, all ministers of religion are in some sense priests and sacred men, whether they will or no, because they have to *lead* their less spiritually agile followers in a godward movement in which collective as well as individual action is necessary, because man is a social being.

variety of animals, including the cat, the baboon, the ibis, the hawk, the bull, and the dung-beetle were held sacred; but other instances are easy to quote, such as the cult of the horse among the horse-breeding tribes of ancient Britain, and the cults of various prairie animals among the north American Indians. "Cow-protection" in India may be ultimately connected with totemism. It is important to recognise a distinction between totemism and theriolatry. Though the one may involve the other or derive from it, they are not to be regarded as the same thing.

(3) *Taboo* is a Polynesian word and means "forbidden." The institution under other names is found all over the world, and appears to be one at least of the origins of morality, though the connection is not always obvious, and the taboo ordinance is sometimes due to a faulty chain of reasoning. Thus blood is almost invariably taboo. It must not be touched or looked at, and if anyone touches it, he or she in turn becomes untouchable. This is not difficult to understand, since blood is a mysterious substance which is obviously connected with the presence, propagation, or extinction of life. Hence to touch it is both dangerous and possibly irreverent. It seems to be a source of vitality, and it is therefore sacred; perhaps it may hurt one to touch it. By a process of faulty logic this prohibition is extended to include anything which recalls blood, such as red wine or a red blanket, and in the former case the savage mind is confirmed in its logic by the fact that the effects of red wine can be sampled and are found to be potent. Taboo-like institutions are universal and varied. They are by the nature of the case negative and serve a useful purpose in keeping the

ruder elements of human nature in check. Sometimes they contain more reason than at first sight appears, at other times they seem wholly irrational.

To a great extent they are the product of community (one might almost say dormitory or barrack-room) existence. To a great extent also they are the product of numinous fear in the presence of peculiar objects. The taboo-sense is the sense of the Kantian "ought" or "ought not" in embryo, and it can and does sometimes maintain itself in opposition to mass-opinions. There may almost be said to be two sorts of taboo, that which is prohibited by herd-custom, and that which is prohibited by the insight of an exceptional individual, and afterwards imposed more or less successfully upon the human herd.

Taboo extends to the prohibition of business or pleasure on certain days and to forbidding people to look at certain things or to enter certain buildings or to touch certain objects. Sometimes these regulations are mere matters of convenience, but more often than not they are due to the supposition that the functions associated with certain objects or places are manifestations is a special and distinctive way of the sacred or numinous, and therefore "not to be enterprised nor taken in hand unadvisedly, lightly or wantonly, but reverently, discreetly, advisedly, soberly, and in the fear of deity." Thus not only totems but also their models are often surrounded with a variety of taboos. (It is sometimes said that the historical Jesus explicitly abolished prohibitions of this kind. This is only partly true. While substituting a positive for a negative morality as the ultimate ideal, He gives us no warrant for supposing that he undervalued or intended to destroy useful regulations which restrain and discipline human habits or aid in their healthy formation.)

(4) *Initiation* is the generic term for a vast mass of ceremonies associated with the transition of human beings of both sexes from childhood to maturity. Some of these practices are of a more or less crude educational nature, and their purpose is to toughen the individual and make him capable of bearing pain or of enduring hardships; and sometimes they are made the occasion for imparting and handing on traditions of the tribe; but there is also intimately associated with the initiation ceremonies the sense of the mystery and sacredness of life and of the inexplicable and apparently uncontrollable process by which the child is transformed into the adult. The expression given to this awareness of mystery is often in the highest degree grotesque, but it undeniably shows that the transition excites in the savage a sense of numinous awe which he struggles to express. Later, initiation comes to be extended to embrace ceremonies which purged the individual of those elements in himself which he deemed base and perishable, and so assured him of rebirth into a blissful and imperishable existence. This latter type of initiation was obviously open to all persons of whatever age and not merely to those reaching puberty; and it might even be extended to benefit people standing outside the tribe or nation.

(5) Of all religious practices the one which has attracted most attention is what is called *sacrifice*. There are many practices which it is difficult to

consider as merely religious, since they seem to be utilitarian in object,—curious ceremonies performed no one now knows exactly why, but undoubtedly with the idea that they will increase the milk supply, induce animals to come to be killed, or make the crops grow. Other practices seem to be simply an outlet for what we may call numinous emotion. Sacrifice, however, though the ulterior motive of seeking to render Deity propitious may seldom be far absent, is nevertheless more than any other practice animated by disinterested motives. Those who have travelled in the African forests of Mount Elgon relate that the pigmies make little huts in which they place pots of honey as votive offerings to some spirit which is believed to inhabit the forest. No doubt they desire its goodwill, and feel it advisable to treat it with respect, but when one considers without prejudice the way in which peasants and the simpler kind of artisan give little presents to one another and to their superiors it is difficult not to believe that they are actuated by feelings of mingled friendliness, courtesy, and gratitude, in their behaviour towards Deity. When the village postman's wife makes a large twist of bread and offers it in church at harvest time she is probably reproducing in another environment the sacrificial offering of the pigmies and with probably the same motive. The offering of flowers and rice in Hindu temples is an action of the same sort; and is of the nature of a present to the celestial being in question.

Five motives for sacrifice have been suggested:

(1) Adoration or paying one's respects.

(2) Thank-offerings for good received.

(3) Freewill offerings made to obtain some general or particular benefit by procuring the goodwill of the god.

(4) Peace offerings to propitiate an angry god or malevolent spirit.

(5) Sin-offerings for the expiation of guilt.

Offerings of the first sort do not usually involve much of the nature of deprivation, but are merely little compliments. In the other four cases, however, experience shows that there must be a sense of costliness about the offering. It must be the giving up of something which causes the worshipper expense or possibly pain. The second class of sacrifice may contain less of this element than the others, since it may involve merely a *quid pro quo*. In the other three classes, however, the gift offered must be really substantial. The third and fourth classes pre-suppose no very exalted conception of the character of the god concerned. He may be subject to fits of anger, he may be capricious, or he may be cruel. The fifth type of sacrifice on the other hand represents a considerably higher stage of development, for it implies that the relationship with Deity has been marred by the fault of the worshippers themselves, and that they are under a moral obligation to try to mend matters. The god himself is holy and righteous and is in no way to blame for the breach which has occurred.

In propitiatory or expiatory sacrifices there usually appears to be a shedding of blood, either that of a fowl, an animal, or even a human being. The further idea of substitution has here come in; the slaughtering of a living creature being of the nature of a sop to

Cerberus. The deity in question being angry desires to see someone hurt, and it is believed that be will be satisfied if he sees the blood of the sacrifice, and will accordingly turn away his fierce anger.[1] Instances of sacrifices of this kind will naturally occur to any who have read the Old Testament, and it is to be noted that the type of Hebrew religion which they represent must on no account be used to interpret the Christian religion, but rather as an example of precisely the kind of heathen religion from which the greater prophets and finally Jesus Christ Himself sought to deliver mankind.

It is important, however, to recognise that bloody sacrifice seldom, if ever, meant the offering of *death*, but on the contrary the offering of life, of life-force, of the blood in which was believed to reside the principle of life. Hence, however crudely expressed in the first instance, sacrifice could, as time went on, come to have a more deeply ethical significance and so become the offering of personality to the service of an ethically holy spirit.

In provisional classifications of human religious systems a line has often been drawn between those which are regarded as natural growths, and those which seem to be the work of prophetic founders. The line is sometimes artificially drawn, since a prophetically founded faith may come to express itself in connection with the institutions of a nature-religion, while a nature-religion may in the course of its history produce one or

---

[1] It has been suggested that animals were sacrificed *instead* of human beings in the hope that the God would be content with them. The evidence here is not quite convincing.

more prophets, and may even have developed under the influence of exceptional individuals, as it sometimes probably did. The broad distinction, however, is by no means useless, since there is a marked difference between the type of religion which localises the sacred and finds it as the expression of the activity of one or more spiritual beings in definite natural objects or natural phenomena and that which apprehends the sacred through states of consciousness which, although they may not in themselves be permanent and continuous, furnish the worshipper with access to fellowship with a Being whose existence is permanent and unchangeable, and who is equally omnipresent even when he is not being apprehended.

The earliest and simplest mode of classifying religious systems is as (1) *true* and (2) *false*, one single religion being true and the remainder only worthy of rejection. In the last resort there is still something to be said for this, since, as we have already seen, it is possible to distinguish legitimately between good and bad religion.

Tiele, as is well known, first adopted a classification by date and distribution, and then abandoned it for the division into nature-religions and ethical religions. But this does not work very well, for the obvious reason that ethical ideas are found within the sphere of nature-religions, while some less respectable types of alleged prophetic religion have abandoned ethics.

Hegel (and Principal Caird following him) divided the field into Nature Religions or Objective Cults, Religions of Spiritual Individuality or Subjective Religion, and Absolute or Universal Religion.

Another classification is into tribal, national, and universal; while a typical Teutonic analysis is that of Siebeck, *i.e.* into Primitive Religion, Morality Religion, and Redemptive Religion. The modern German school,[1] reverting to the earliest division, puts truth on the side of revelation, and presumptuousness and falsehood on the side of religion, conceiving the whole of the latter as an entirely human and therefore corrupt activity, since there is no way from man up to God, and we are incapable of discovering God for ourselves in this world by any faculty of our own.

One of the first complete scientific attempts at classification was that of Orelli, made in 1899. He divided the religions of the world into seven groups:

A. Turanian; which includes the Chinese, Japanese, Finnish, and Mongol-Tartar.

B. Hamitic, to which he assigns the religion of the ancient Egyptians, and allied peoples.

C. The Semitic, with eight sub-divisions:
   (1) Babylonians and Assyrians (he does not treat the Sumerians as separate).
   (2) Phoenicians, Canaanites and Carthaginians.
   (3) Aramaeans, Ammonites, Moabites, Edomites, Arabians.
   (4) Israel.
   (5) Christendom.
   (6) The Mandaeans.
   (7) The Manichaeans.
   (8) Islam.

[1] *i.e.* the Barthian.

D. Indo-Germanic:
   (1) India.
   (2) Parsism.
   (3) The Greeks.
   (4) The Romans.
   (5) The Celts.
   (6) The Teutons.
   (7) The Slavs.

E. African, including everything which does not come under B or C.

F. American, comprising the Mexicans and Peruvians, and the primitive Indians of the New World.

G. Oceanic, including the Australians and Tasmanians, and the peoples of the smaller Pacific Islands.

This grouping is obviously open to amendment and in its form attempts to be anthropological. It takes no real account of the distinction between natural and prophetic religion, and while it has its uses in making a merely descriptive survey, does not allow for the necessity of grading religions according to their standard of development. A somewhat similar grouping is adopted in the important handbook of Chantepie de la Saussaye, which has been re-edited in its present form by Bertholet and Lehmann. The comparative study of religion is still a young science, and it has entered upon its task as the heir of theories of development and progress associated with the nineteenth century. The result has been the somewhat premature conclusion that the various religious systems can be arranged in a tree rather like the orders of living creatures in a text book of zoology. This is a very risky assumption, and it ought not to be adopted without caution.

Bertholet and Lehmann divide their subject as follows:

1.  The nature-peoples (*i.e.* the primitives, or peoples at the primitive stage of thought.)
2.  The Chinese.
3.  The Japanese.
4.  The Egyptians.
5.  The Semitic peoples of the near and middle East.
    (*a*)  Babylonians and Assyrians.
    (*b*)  Canaanites, Syrians and Phoenicians.
6.  Islam and the Arabs.
7.  The Religions of India.
8.  The Persians.
9.  The Greeks.
10.  The Romans.
11.  The Slavs and Lithuanians.
12.  The Germans.
13.  The Celts.

Alfred Jeremias, in a similar and less important book, issued at München in 1923, makes a still different arrangement.

1.  The Primitives.
2.  The Nearer East:
    (*a*)  Babylonia, from Sumerian days onwards (appendix on the Elamites).
    (*b*)  Egypt.
    (*c*)  Syria.
    (*d*)  Arabia.
    (*e*)  Asia Minor, with special reference to the Hittites and Phrygians.
    (*f*)  Iran, with special reference to Zarathustra and Mani.

3. The Far East:
   (a) India.
   (b) China.
   (c) Japan.

4. America in ancient times (Mexico and Peru).

5. Europe.
   (a) The Greeks.
   (b) The Romans.
   (c) The Celts.
   (d) The Slavs.
   (e) The Germans.

These groupings may be convenient for purposes of study, but if considered as indicating origins, some of them are not even provisionally sound. Thus China and Japan must not only be taken together, but also grouped with Ceylon, Cambodia, and Tibet, as countries exhibiting Buddhist influence. The Maya peoples and those of the Andean area may or may not be genetically related to the Egyptians (as Perry would have us believe), but they are obviously a development of the same stock as the Haida Indians of British Columbia, who, however, have not developed the same elaborate culture. The Semites cannot be split up when we are considering religious origins, but must be taken together. The Celts proper cannot be separated too widely from the Germans, since both are Nordic with Alpine elements; and the Celtic adoption of already existing Iberian language- and religion-forms obscures the fact that these are pre-Celtic. And finally, the distribution of a belt of religious ideas from the Atlantic sea-board of Ireland round the planet to South India may or may not be capable of establishment, and may or may not be due to the spread of a race approximately that which we call the small dark white Neolithic; but at any rate the *appearance* of such a belt is puzzling and perplexing.

A further objection to many of these attempts at grouping (not to all) is that they confuse the natural with the prophetic, the national with the international. It is obviously necessary to take together the various efforts of creative genius, and to group (for example) Zarathustra, Lao-tzŭ, Buddha, the great Greeks, and the Hebrew prophets.

But it is also equally unnecessary to separate the Japanese, Babylonian, Egyptian and Indian and Graeco-Roman polytheists on account of racial difference. We learn much more by putting their various performances side by side.

More recently we have the classification propounded by Dr. Oman, in which he arranges the various types according to the way in which they relate the Natural and the Supernatural. According to him, "when the Supernatural is submerged in the Natural we have idolatry, when the Natural is submerged in the Supernatural we have pantheism, when they are set sharply apart we have deism, when they are related by some kind of moral victory we have at least some kind of theism."

Archbishop Söderblom, in his Gifford Lectures of 1931, after dealing with aspects of religion in its primitive stages and its relation to magic, discusses in turn its greater creative developments:

1. As method. Yoga (the yoking or uniting of the soul with Deity by ascetic discipline).

2. As psychology. Jainism and Hinayana Buddhism. Salvation by insight.

3. As devotion. Bhakti. Theistic salvation religion.

4. As a fight against evil. Zarathustra.

5. As the practice of having a good conscience. (Socrates in particular. Söderblom here says little or nothing about the Hebrew prophets or the Chinese Confucius.)

6. As revelation in history. The Hebrew idea.

7. As culminating in a "once-for-all" incarnation in history.

8. As ever-present and continued revelations, flowing forward from the "once-for-all" incarnation.

I cannot expect to equal the magnificence with which Söderblom has expounded his thesis, but I have the satisfaction of noting that I have been able to expand a little his treatment of the Chinese, and also that his general scheme harmonises with the trend of the 5th and 6th volumes of my series, in that he makes due allowance for the concept of discontinuous revelation, which many writers upon comparative religion have hitherto been reluctant to do.

It is perhaps a fruitless task to distinguish with accuracy between primitive and early civilised peoples, since few if any of those known to us are really primitive. Even the most savage have cultures and traditions, both ancient and elaborate, in which one generation stands upon the shoulders of those who have gone before, so that in no case are we able to say that we are in touch with the beginnings of religion. There must always be a certain area concerning which we are only able to conjecture. At the same time there is a marked difference between village cultures such as

H

may be studied in Papua or Northern Rhodesia, and the cultures of town dwellers, where the handling of stone and metals and the continued elaboration of life develop a public expression of religion on a far grander scale. These urban systems have much in common with one another. Whether we consider the ziggurats of Mesopotamia or the elaborate temples of Egypt and Greece, the great and lavishly ornamented shrines of Southern India, or the teocallis of the Maya civilisation of Central America and the ceremonial connected with them, whether we consider the Jewish temple or the great cathedrals of Catholic Christendom, in every case we find ourselves dealing with centres of a highly complex cultus, which could never have continued to exist apart from the stability provided by that curious thing which we call civilisation, involving the systematic provision and storing of a food-supply and a continuous occupation of permanent dwelling-houses for long periods. This cultus involves the pre-supposition that the temple is objectively the home of the Deity (conceived as the celestial lord of the manor, township, or city-state) who is venerated in its precincts. All that is done in the temple is for His benefit and satisfaction rather than that of the worshippers. It is His house, not theirs, and they are present as suppliants and courtiers.

Omitting from consideration the Temple at Jerusalem and the Catholic cathedrals, all the remaining buildings may be said to have been designed for the worship of a rich variety of Deities. Egypt, Assyria, Babylonia, India and Mexico had each its pantheon. For that matter so also had the Romans, Celts and Teutons, although Rome seems to have elaborated her temples but little, while Celts and Teutons, like the Japanese Shintoists, contented themselves with far less distinctive shrines, such as stone circles, green hillsides, and groves of trees. Economic conditions, as well as the supply of building materials, have always largely determined the character and extent of temple structures and ornamentation.

Beneath these developed polytheistic systems lie the remains of older ones such as we associate with the village cultures of our so-called primitives. Customs often no longer understood are permitted, because of their ancient sanctity, to survive within a system which no longer needs them, or are re-interpreted so as to fit into a system of more recent growth.

The more thoughtful among such peoples sooner or later realised and expressed the truth that there must be some central and supreme authority, and this they visualised, either as the Father of fathers, or as the Father of gods and men, or sometimes as Impersonal Fate, beneath whose sway even the gods and goddesses, though real and powerful, stood subordinated as men and women of a larger growth.

In order to make the situation clearer, it will be well at this point to state as clearly as we can what we mean at the present time by "the primitive peoples." No race exists to-day whose ancestors did not pass through the primitive stage. That is obvious and we need say no more about it. It is equally obvious that of the so-called primitive inhabitants of the world to-day a considerable proportion are passing with varying degrees of rapidity out of that stage. A hundred years

ago almost the whole of the African continent outside
Christian and Moslem areas could have been written
off as primitive. To-day the influences of civilisation
are penetrating almost everywhere, even if they only
take the form of cheap machine-made tools and
utensils. What is true of Africa is true of nearly all
primitive areas in the globe. Swift means of communication, government and mission schools, machinery and colonisation are rapidly transforming the life of
the savage. We can therefore only give an approximate estimate of what ought to be called primitive
areas, and in nearly every case these will be in process
of modification by Christian and secularist influences.
For the purpose of our survey we can write off Africa,
with the exception of Egypt and part of French
territory, as well as a good deal of the areas under
Moslem and Christian influence. We can write off
all the aboriginal tribes and some of the low-caste
peoples of India, Burma, Ceylon, Indo-China Tibet
and the Malay States, the blackfellows of Australia,
and some of the heathen Maoris of New Zealand; the
non-Christian Indians of North and South America; the
non-Christian Eskimos; and the uncivilised tribes of
the Pacific. The inhabitants of the three great islands
of Borneo, Papua and Madagascar should also be
included, though it must be remembered that in
Borneo and Papua there are strong Christian influences
at work, and that in Madagascar the civilisation of the
inhabitants has proceeded on a considerable scale
partly through the work of French secularists, partly
through that of Roman Catholic, Anglican and
Congregationalist missionaries.

In making our preliminary survey, therefore, we must exclude from consideration the above areas, except in so far as Christian, Moslem, Buddhist, Hindu, and other influences have penetrated into them.

## A PRIMITIVE MONOTHEISM

With regard to the origin and progress of theistic ideas, a suggestive explanation has been put forward by a learned American Jew.[1] The gist of this is as follows: Primitive people are not so different from ourselves as we are apt to imagine. They are quite as logical, and even have a truer sense of reality. There is no indication of the existence of any fundamental difference in their emotional nature as compared with ours. There is also ample reason for believing, granted that chance mating has existed right from the first emergence of the *genus humanum*, that the distribution of ability and temperament has never been appreciably different. What has developed has been the size of populations, with its corollary of a larger proportion of men of a certain type of ability and temperament. If this be correct, and if we are right in assuming that in every group of approximately the same size there is to be found the same more or less fixed distribution of ability and temperament, it follows that from such a group no type has ever been totally absent. In all primitive groups of a reasonable size we can on this assumption be certain to find the idealist and the materialist, the dreamer and the realist, the introspective and the non-introspective, the devoutly religious, the intermittently religious and the indifferent. Moreover we shall find that individuals with specific temperaments express themselves in much the same way at all times.

[1] Dr. Paul Radin. (The Arthur Davis Memorial Lecture, 1924.)

Now it is certain that in the midst of polytheistic peoples, whether Jew or Gentile, there have been a certain number of individuals who have given utterance to definitely monotheistic beliefs, and who picture the world as under unitary control. Two theories have hitherto claimed to explain this. The one treats the monotheistic belief as due to a primary revelation, the other treats it as due to a process of evolution.[1] But it is contended that neither is necessary, and neither can be proved to have happened. What has happened is that a certain number of individuals have been born of a certain type. Beside them and vastly in the majority have always been found others with a temperament fundamentally distinct, to whom the world has never appeared as a unified whole, and who have never evinced any marked curiosity as to its origin. All the monotheists, it is claimed, have sprung from the ranks of the eminently religious individuals. Such people are admittedly few in number, for the overwhelming mass belong to the indifferently religious group, materialists or realists to whom a god is simply to be regarded as a convenient source of power. Explicit monotheism, it is true, is rare among primitive peoples, but it is possibly not quite so uncommon as the literal reading of the facts might seem to indicate. The expert in question adds that he is inclined to assume from his own experience that a limited number of explicit monotheists are to be found in every primitive tribe that has at all developed the idea of a creator-god. The problem in short is not the origin of monotheism, but its survival and development as the dominant conception.

The origin of monotheism may go back even to beyond Neanderthal man. The question remains, what made it ultimately the almost exclusively prevailing religious belief? One answer of course is that it does not actually occupy this position, but only seems to do so. This, however,

[1] Thus, *e.g.*, Jevons, Söderblom, Buchanan Gray, and many others.

cannot be regarded as satisfactory. Monotheism possesses somehow or other so subtle an appeal that, in addition to the vast number of its adherents, there are to be found many persons of doubtful belief who yet feel constrained to pay lip-service to it, and also many stubborn polytheists and animists over whose thought it is seen to exercise a definite influence. It is open to the sceptic to attribute this success to an historical accident, or even to economic causes and to the prevalence of a certain type of political theory. Yet such explanations do not go to the root of the problem. It is far more in accordance with the whole of the evidence to say that monotheism is winning and has won its way because it has seemed to the largest number of ordinary thoughtful individuals to be the best theory.

An elaborate attempt has been made by an eminent Roman Catholic anthropologist, Father Schmidt, to establish the general principle that the belief in, and worship of, one supreme Deity is universal among all really primitive peoples. He alleges that an exhaustive survey of all the existing primitives compels us to this conclusion. The "high god" is found among them all, not indeed everywhere in the same form or the same vigour, but still everywhere prominently enough to make his dominant position indubitable. He is by no means a late development, or one traceable to Christian missionary influences. Moreover there is, he says, a distribution of this belief like a girdle around the south central part of at least the old world; while for the new, there is a large group south of the Amazon. There is also a lateral extension reaching to the most distant extremities, north and south of the respective continents. No later culture therefore can boast of a distribution so completely encircling the earth; and if it can be established that wherever remnants of the primitive peoples are discoverable over this wide area they show belief in a supreme Being, then there will be a strong probability that such a belief is an essential property of whatever ancient human culture existed in the very earliest times, before the individual groups had separated from one another. The writer further alleges that this supreme being of the primitive culture is a genuinely monotheistic Deity, that he is universally described as Father, and less widely as Creator, and that a kind of eternity is ascribed to Him, as well as complete beneficence, moral holiness and creative omnipotence.

These are obviously very large claims, and their vindication must depend entirely upon the adequacy of the evidence adduced for them. It is plainly impossible for the present writer to investigate every detail of the evidence, and he must therefore content himself with saying that up to the present expert opinion has not been favourable to the theory above outlined. The handling of the data has been regarded as either tendencious or at any rate lacking in thoroughness. There would appear to be too many exceptions to the rule for it to be possible to accept its universal operation. It is very difficult to determine the extent to which an apparently primitive people reproduces the vestiges of a previous contact with some group of monotheists. The abandonment of a rigid adherence to an evolutionary theory of the origin of religion need not commit us to the adoption of its complete opposite. Much more minute and wholly impartial sifting of the information collected, with a most careful scrutiny of the credentials of the collectors and of those from whom they derived their information, together with a note of the date when it was obtained and the circumstances of the people concerning whom the information was given—all this is indispensable before we can be satisfied that the so-called "high god" theory is firmly established beyond all dispute.

Opinion indeed is much divided upon Father Schmidt's

thesis.  Thus Dr. Lowie of the University of California says that he has no objection to it on the score of logic, but only on the score of facts.  In other words, if all the primitives of the lowest type share the belief in a distinctive hoch-gott, then it must certainly represent an element of archaic culture.  The question remains, however, do they share it?  Lowie shows that for the determination of the points involved in the theory the evidence cited for any of the tribes is inadequate, while, where material is available, as among the Andamanese and the bushmen, it is anything but convincing.  Among the former in addition to a number of lesser spirits there is a character known as Biliku who might be thought to be a monotheistic deity. But Biliku is not universally conceived as beneficent or omniscient, for the natives sometimes try to deceive him (or her) while the common view makes him (or her) hostile to mankind or at best reluctantly benevolent.  The bushmen also furnish contradictory evidence.

Karl Beth of Vienna in the second edition (1927) of his book on Religion and Magic deals fully with the hoch-gott hypothesis (p. 328 ff.), making special reference to the Australians, though he surveys all the different alleged instances.  He is, however, very guarded in his conclusion, *i.e.* that the study of the hoch-gott " opens up an important way of insight into evolution of religious ideas; and even though this hoch-gott may as a rule be less important and more of a deus otiosus, yet he is none the less significant as betokening the attainment of an essentially higher level of belief."  Heiler in his great book on Prayer, p. 129 ff., has an important section on the question of the priority of the belief in a high god, and discusses the whole subject of high gods in a long section previous to this, p. 118 ff. (Engl. trans., O.U.P., p. 488–52).  One cannot help feeling that Heiler is influenced by the general Catholic preference (born of a not unnatural desire) for the theory of a high god,

He says definitely that the belief in a supreme Being arises
(1) out of the question which the primitive is quite ready
to ask: "What is the origin of the world and of mankind?"
(2) Out of the sense of absolute powerlessness and dependence. From these two roots springs the conception of a
supreme Being or All-Father, to whom cultus was offered.
Ancestor-worship followed close upon this, and in time the
cultus of one's forefathers to some extent eclipsed that of
the high god. Then, as a still more secondary consideration,
came the worship of nature-spirits and local divinities.

This is a very pleasing theory, and the existence of a
number of high gods among primitive peoples is indisputable
and lends it plausibility. But we know very little about
the actual priority of the belief in question to another
of a more pluralistic and animistic character, and it is
easy to attribute too spiritual a character to these single
deities, whose characteristics are often very human and
grotesque. If we were able to prove conclusively that
primitive man started everywhere with the thought of a
single supreme spiritual being it would no doubt revolu-
tionise our ideas of the development of religion, but it
would not prove in itself that the thought was more
correct than that of a polytheist. The mere chronological
priority of a belief does not guarantee its correctness.
That must be decided upon other grounds.

The best known exponent in the nineteenth century of
the idea of a primitive monotheism was the Scots archaeologist, Andrew Lang. The late learned Archbishop
Söderblom examined his thesis with some care, and concluded that although modern scientific anthropology will
not always support Lang's interpretation there is still
something to be said for it, and he holds that there were
three original sources of unitary belief, that of a creator
or ancestor, that of an impersonal element, Mana, and that
resulting from a fusion of separate spirits; and he holds

that the real starting point for each is a unity of awareness. This, as will be seen, is not the same as Radin's theory, but a mediating explanation lying between it and that of Father Schmidt. Certain additional points have been stressed by Dr. Stanley Cook: first, the failure of a primitive monotheism, (if such existed), to lift those who believed in it out of their insignificance, or to save them from being pushed out by more advanced and self-confident peoples with keener intellects; second, the importance of recognising varieties and qualities within monotheism itself, instead of talking about it as though it were a complete unity; and thirdly the importance of co-ordinating the phenomena of the more highly developed with those of the earliest religions of which we can find any traces, one result of which will be to enable us to give a proper recognition to the phenomena connected with *deterioration* in religion. Too much has been written with the tacit assumption that the main feature in religion is progress. This is not the case. Over enormous areas there is stagnation, and over equally large areas the melancholy spectacle of the thinning out or even corrupting of some strong and precious prophetic delivery of truth.

We may conclude therefore that the High God is one line of development among primitive peoples, though we shall be cautious about assuming that he in any way foreshadows later developments of monotheism. It is significant that in the vast majority of cases he is a deus otiosus, and does not directly concern the individual, who makes his prayers to lesser beings. Although the ultimate control may be in the hands of the High God, for practical purposes one has to deal with subordinate officials of His Majesty, who at best is rather like the headmaster of a great Public School with whom the rank and file of its members very rarely have an interview except perhaps on entering or leaving it, or on some special and not always

happy occasion. Such a High God hardly differs from the
supreme Being of the eighteenth-century Deists, and it is
obviously absurd to equate Him with the Deity of the
Lord's Prayer. If we are to posit a primitive divine object
for human devotion it seems much more likely that this
was of the female sex, a Great Mother, symbolising the
fecund creative force of nature.

The gap between the emergence of man as a separate
species of animal and the great early civilisations which
we shall presently be considering is most difficult to
bridge, and we can only piece together as well as we
can the various fragments of evidence which we
possess, and avoid unreasonable conjectures. At the
time when history begins, a number of well-defined
species of human beings are already in existence, and
this pre-supposes the settlement of groups in comparative isolation from one another for extremely long
periods. If we accept the chronology offered us, we
must recognise that for a period of well over a hundred
thousand years (that is to say for a period fifty times
the distance between ourselves and Christ) the only
man-like beings in existence were sub-men who were
perhaps most of them capable of making rude flint
tools,[1] and some of whom buried their dead as though
they contemplated a sort of future existence for them.
These were, however, to all appearance lower than the
lowest known existing savages. Again for the next
twenty thousand years (ten times the period between
ourselves and Christ) a rather higher type of man
appeared, whose skeletons suggest that he was much
more like ourselves, both in the size of his brain and the

[1] Apparently *Sinanthropus* did not.

shape of his hand. There is difference of opinion among archaeologists as to the total extermination of the older species. Some say that there was no inter-marriage, and that the older race was completely exterminated; others that the invaders forgot their prejudices and intermarried. Some say that the older race were ape-like monsters, others that they were cousins to the Tasmanian aborigines and the Australian blackfellow. When, however, we are deal-ing with such enormously long periods of time it is only fair to ask "how can we possibly know?" One reflection from a well-known expert on savage races is, however, worth recording because of its extreme probability: "The dim racial remembrance of such ape-like monsters (as the early sub-men) with cunning brains, shambling gait, hairy bodies, strong teeth, and possibly cannibal-istic tendencies, may be the germ of the ogre in folk-lore.[1]

On the whole the new series of human beings was very much like some of the African tribes which still exist to-day. The oldest surviving race in Africa is that of the bushmen, of whom there are still a fair number in the Kalahari desert. Both in the appearance of their women and in the style of their rock-paintings they are obviously much akin to the people who spread over Spain and France and the Southern part of Britain at some time during the 20,000 years we are considering. What was happening at this time in the East we cannot yet tell, although the discovery of the bones of the so-called Peking man and woman and of fragmentary human remains in the South of Britain

[1] Sir H. H. Johnston.

suggest that the range of the sub-men at some time during the whole of the approximate 120,000 years previously referred to, extended at least from China to Sussex (remembering of course that Europe geographically is only a large peninsula projecting from Asia, and that the English Channel did not then exist). It will never do to forget the enormous length of the periods and the scarcity of our information. Hundreds and thousands of migrations and developments may have taken place, of which no traces at all have come down to us. In general we may assume that the movements of man were in periodic waves, times of mutation alternating with times of stability. If we take the great Central Eurasian mountain-belt as (in some form) of primeval antiquity, and also consider the present distribution of races to the north and south of it, we may suppose the human stock to have perhaps arisen somewhere in Asia and to have spread pretty widely before this mountainous belt reached its present proportions. We find, however, that to-day the dark-skinned peoples are confined to the south of it, and the lighter-skinned people to the north.

It used to be thought that there was an actual gap between the end of the Palaeolithic period and the development of the type of human being with whom we are familiar to-day. Indeed, so marked was the seeming disappearance of the Palaeolithic industries and art, that it was actually believed that for a time Europe became deserted, and was re-peopled at a much later date by new invasions of the race of people commonly called Neolithic, who came from the East.

This judgment has been modified by the discovery of at least six cultures (denominated "Mesolithic") lying between the old and the new Stone Ages, some of them resembling the cultures of the former, some those of the latter. Even so there is a great step forward when we come to the true Neolithic; human life changed profoundly, for man found out how to grow food and to store it, how to domesticate animals, how to make pottery, and how to grind and polish tools. He also found out little by little that it was possible to obtain metals (copper and tin) from the rocks, and that these could be melted by fire and so shaped into tools. Beginning with the use of copper, he gradually came to mix it with tin,[1] and so produced bronze.

It may seem that these facts have nothing to do with religion. Directly they may not, but indirectly they are of immense importance. The security which these discoveries gave to men, and the community life which they rendered possible, furnished a condition for existence in which man began to have leisure (a) to reflect on the meaning of life and (b) to form traditions. We need not be surprised to find, therefore, that, with the advent of the so-called true Neolithic age, developments of art, literature, politics and religion come thick and fast.

It will serve to set the various greater developments of the religious spirit in true perspective, if we now briefly describe some of the earlier systems, and indicate their respective contributions. The entire period to be covered in such an outline is more than twice the whole of that contained within the history

[1] The standard mixture being 1 part to 10 parts of each respectively.

of the Christian movement up-to-date. This fact should give food for the reader's reflection. No one can possibly say what developments of the human spirit lie irretrievably hidden in the lost records of these past centuries. Archaeologists may assure us that they are able to reconstruct the essential outlines of the religion and philosophy of these defunct civilisations, and they may be right, for probability is on their side. Yet we can but consider that if we had to reconstruct the history of the Christian Church for let us say half the span of Egyptian history from similar fragmentary materials we should find ourselves deprived of much that we regard as of great importance. In any case the legacy from Sumeria (let alone Egypt and Crete) *via* Israel to Christianity is undeniable; while if we give Christianity at least as long a run of existence as Egyptian religion, what form may we not expect that it will ultimately reach? Certainly something far beyond that with which we are familiar.

The actual division of the subject leads us to put part of the primitive developments in this chapter, and part in the next two. This may seem arbitrary. Yet when we are telling the tale of development, it is difficult to avoid keeping the account of one particular country as a continuous narrative. To put part of it in one place and part in another is to break the chain of events. I have therefore reserved for the first section the story of those peoples where the course of religion stands almost entirely aloof from the achievements of the great creative periods, and for the second the story of those which, although they passed through the customary early stages, crowned their development

by throwing up in flower-like fashion some great prophet or prophets, whose contribution was of a unique
and normative character, deeply influencing the development of the religious systems which stand before us
to-day, though standing out in melancholy splendour
above the feeble and perverse efforts of average men;
since the latter either killed them as heretics, or (worse
still) built tombs for their teaching in the form of
institutional systems.

## NOTE ON THE WORSHIP OF THE PRIMITIVES.

Dr. Marett (Gifford Lectures) rightly observes that the
religious ceremonies of mankind, whether they be ritual
burials, dances, processions, or sacramental meals, are the
deliberate efforts of humanity to create the sensation that
it is stronger than it really is, and by processes of suggestion
to make itself able to overcome fear and weakness. Since,
however, the strength so obtained must come from somewhere, *i.e.* it is superhuman, the release of a hidden store
of "mana" from the secret springs of life, it is fair to assert
that the ceremonies are *effectual*, and in the language of
Christian theology "contain grace," and that they do
actually render the person who participates superior to
the fear of death, brave in danger, and adequate to the
needs of life.

I

# Chapter IV

## OF RELIGION IN MESOPOTAMIA AND EGYPT

### Mesopotamia

RECENT years have brought us a vast mass of information about the religious beliefs and practices of the peoples inhabiting Mesopotamia in ancient times. We are informed that for a period covering many centuries and prior to 3000 B.C. there were in this country a number of small city-states, occupied by a mysterious people known as the Sumerians. Who they were and whence they came we do not certainly know, but there is some reason for thinking that they were dark whites, related to Iberians of south-western Europe on the one hand and Dravidians of South India on the other. It has been suggested indeed that there was a belt of peoples stretching from East to West, with an early type of culture, whose languages form more or less of a group. Perhaps some of these people survive in the Basque country.[1]

We have at any rate reason to believe that there was a vast chain of prehistoric cultures stretching from Central Asia to the plateau of Iran and thence to Syria and Egypt long before 4000 B.C. and that the Sumerians themselves entered Mesopotamia before 5000.[2] It is

[1] This however is not the latest view concerning the Basques.

[2] Owing to the alterations in the area covered by water, we have no Palaeolithic remains in Mesopotamia. The nearest are in the desert to the west of it, and to the north in the mountainous districts.

clear that they had a considerable civilisation of their own, and they were probably the first founders of the city-state as an institution; they had a written language which they inscribed upon thin clay tablets, and each city had its own god and temple, so that the importance of a state or its monarch influenced the status of its god. These gods are mostly nature deities, combined with personifications of the social organism. Thus Enlil the god of the city of Nippur presided over the earth, while the great goddess Ishtar, specially worshipped at Uruk, was the patron of fertility and love. A tendency appears not only to group gods and grade them in hierarchies, but also to fuse them together as far as they resemble one another. The first empire of which we know anything was founded by the high-priest of Uruk, and a merger of city-states was accompanied apparently by a merger of celestial beings.

The Sumerians themselves would seem to have been (in their original state) dwellers in a mountainous district, and their gods were, like the Olympians, mountain deities. Hence when their worshippers settled in a district where there were no hills at all, they made artificial mountains (called ziggurats) on which decently to perform their ceremonies, and of these citadels the temple of the moon-god at Ur (recently excavated) is typical. These temples had external ladder-like stairways, and it has been suggested that their appearance when thronged with sacred ministers in vestments may have been the origin of the symbolism of Jacob's dream.

Mr. Woolley[1] writes of these deities:

"While terrifyingly aloof, the gods were at the same time peculiarly close to man. The religion was anthropomorphic and the gods were but men writ large; the temples were their houses in the city's midst, where they lived a normal human life, eating the meats of sacrifice of which their worshippers also partook, marrying human women and having children by them; their ceremonies symbolized and secured the recurrence of the seasons and the success of the crops in which, as landlords, they were no less interested than were men; they went to battle, and the defeat of an enemy was not complete unless his gods were brought as honoured captives into the palace of the divine lord of the city. In everything they shared the prosperity and the disasters of their worshippers: the embodiment of the State, they rewarded virtue and punished social wrongdoers, but their rewards and their punishments were limited to this world . . . .

". . . The fact is that throughout, the religion of the Sumerians is one not of love but of fear, fear whose limits are confined to this present life, fear of Beings all-powerful, capricious, unmoral. Somehow or other virtue does not appeal to the gods (that this should be so seems to be rather a necessity of human nature than an attribute of the godhead as conceived of in Sumer), but experience shows that mere virtue is not enough to engage and keep their favour; practical religion consists in the sacrifices and the ritual that placate, and in the spells that bind them.

"The daily sacrifices made to the god were in the nature of meals, and were in fact shared by the priests and personnel of the temple; they consisted of beer, wine, milk, bread and dates, and meat of all sorts; in a temple

[1] *The Sumerians.* (Camb. Univ. Press, 1930.)

where there were several hundred persons to be fed the number of animals killed was proportionately great; on feast-days there was a special diet and those who were employed in the preparations for the ceremony were treated to the best portions of the sacrifice. Other rites were of the nature of sympathetic magic, and a symbolic act performed by the priests was intended to prompt the god to exercise his power in some particular direction; thus the libations of pure water poured into a vase containing ears of corn and bunches of dates were meant to procure the due amount of water for the crops. Private sacrifices carried out in the temple were really charms to secure an answer to prayer; bread, sesame, wine, butter and honey and salt were placed before the statue of the god and a beast was killed of which the god's portion was the right leg, the kidneys and a roast, while the rest would be shared amongst the participants in the rite. In these cases the animal stood for the man, as the liturgy was careful to explain—'The lamb is the substitute for humanity; he hath given up a lamb for his life, he hath given up the lamb's head for the man's head'—and we have here a relic of human sacrifice such as was actually found in the graves of the prehistoric kings at Ur. In these sacrifices there was so much magic and so little religion that, in the case of a sick man praying for health, for instance, the carcass of the victim duly dismembered was laid on the body of the offerer in order to purify him of his complaint. Medicine was a well-recognized art, and for every disease there was an appropriate drug to be prescribed; but at the same time all sickness was brought about by the malignant spirits which thronged the universe and preyed on men, and while the doctor might deal with the physical symptoms the demons must also be exorcized. Prominent in the priesthood then were the magicians whose duty it was to conjure away evil when it came; and next to them came the soothsayers who gave warning of its approach and told how it might be avoided."

Much of this is not far removed from the level of religious practice prevailing in Uganda at the time when that African kingdom was discovered in the nineteenth century, though the level of artistic achievement is higher, and the use of the precious metals more frequent.

As far as we can tell, the Sumerians were conquered by a Semitic invader from Arabia, coming from the north-west by way of the Syrian coastlands somewhere about three thousand years before Christ. (The date is uncertain, some placing it earlier and some later). The leader of this invasion was called Sargon, and his subjects were known as Akkadians. He also founded an empire, styled the empire of Sumer and Akkad, which lasted for about two centuries. As often happens on these occasions the conquerors did not impose a new culture, but adopted that of the people they defeated. Thus they took over the Sumerian language and probably many Sumerian beliefs. A second wave of Semites at the end of the period came along and made their headquarters at a small town called Babylon, and after another century, under the great king Hammurabi, became masters of the whole country. A third wave brought in the Assyrian domination. The Assyrians had settled on the upper waters of the Tigris round a number of cities, including Nineveh, at a period prior to the Akkadian invasion; and after a series of vicissitudes, during which they were temporarily conquered by Sargon and also intrigued with Egypt, they finally conqured Babylon for themselves somewhere about 1100 B.C. For four hundred years their power endured and then in the eighth century B.C. a second Sargon arose, who was probably the monarch responsible for the first great deportation of the Hebrews. The Assyrian empire continued for another one hundred and fifty years, and then a coalition between a new Semitic people (the Chaldeans) and two Aryan nations from the north (the Medes and the Persians) ended in its downfall, with the capture of Nineveh in 606 B.C. The new Chaldean empire, better known as the second Babylonian empire, lasted under Nebuchadnezzar the Great and his descendants until 539 B.C. It was then followed by the conquest achieved by Cyrus the Persian, and after two hundred years of Persian rule by the Greek conquest under Alexander the Great in 330 B.C.

A word should be said about the people called Hittites. They are mentioned frequently in the Hebrew Bible, and the Hebrews seem to have been in close contact with them and to have recognised in addition to the main northern group a further group in the south. The northern Hittites appear to have established a substantial civilisation in the heart of Asia Minor, for the remains of their capital at Boghaz Keui are the centre of an area towards which all the roads in the country converge. As represented in Egyptian paintings, the Hittites are a yellow-faced, black-haired people often apparently wearing pigtails and sharp pointed beards, and characterised by possessing as a rule strikingly aquiline noses having depressed tips and large wings. (The typical modern representatives of this race are the Armenians.) The Hittites were not

Semites, but rather a branch of the great Alpine stock, and it is remarkable that they would appear through intermarriage to have bestowed upon the Hebrews their characteristic nose, which is evidently a dominant, since this feature is not specially marked among the Arabs, who are otherwise typical Semites. It is advisable to mention the point, since the mistake is sometimes made of supposing that the Hittites were related to the Hebrews, which they certainly were not. Indeed the Sumerian people themselves seem to have acquired this Hittite nose in some cases. The Hittites appear to have overthrown the King of Babylon about 1926 B.C.

Another noteworthy race were the Kassites. These were mountaineers who began to invade Mesopotamia about 2072 B.C., and held Babylon itself from about 1746 to 1169, a period as long as that which separates us from the reign of Edward the Third. Although their influence afterwards completely perished, it seems likely that they were an early wave of the Aryans, whose movements, it is necessary to remember, began somewhere about this time. So far as we can judge, the Aryan peoples, when first we are able to glean any information about them, were living a more or less nomadic life in Central Asia in the plains round about the river Oxus. They tamed and bred the horse, and were the first to introduce it into Mesopotamia. Their various contacts with the belt of prehistoric civilisation which we have previously mentioned extended from east to west, and again eastward to India, where the higher caste people are of Aryan descent. The Mitanni, who are also prominent at this period, were probably, like the Hittites, Armenoid peoples, but even they were ruled by an Aryan aristocracy, who tamed and bred the horse and had religious beliefs of an Aryan type. It is probable that the Mitanni developed an ethical conception of a universal Deity. Little is known of them, but we have reason to think that it was to peoples of their sort, coming from the northern plains, that the conception is to be traced of a great sky-god ruling over all other gods, and that the fusion of hierarchies under the presidency of one supreme Deity was helped on by their influence.

It is said that the story of the siege of Troy is based upon an early account of a nomadic people much excited at coming in contact with the settled civilisation of an early Mediterranean city state; and we can well imagine something of the same excitement filling the Kassites when they came down into the Mesopotamian area with its wonderful cities. Other Aryan waves followed them, notably, as we have already said, those of the Medes and the Persians.

This all-too-brief historical outline is necessary, if we are to understand the developments of religion in and from Mesopotamia. What we have first to realise, however, is that there is as great a distance chronologically between Sargon the First and Alexander the Great as there is between Alexander the Great and the present day, and that long before the empire of Sargon was established, people had been living in cities under Sumerian rule practising religion and cultivating the soil for perhaps as long again. It has been well said that half the duration of human civilisation and the keys to all its chief institutions

are to be found before Sargon the First. The excava-
tions and discoveries of recent years have only tended
to confirm this judgment.

It is therefore necessary at this point to reaffirm
the conclusions which have of late been reached with
regard to the influence of the Sumerians. What we
have to remember is that these people by their ability
developed a civilisation which lasted for nearly fifteen
hundred years after the disappearance of its authors,
and the main treasures of which were passed on directly
or indirectly to nations which had never heard of
Sumer.[1] Thus the political changes which we have
related made little or no difference to law, art and
religion. It has been pointed out[2] that the old Sumerian
laws, slightly adapted, became the code of Babylon,
and influenced the great code of Hammurabi and
ultimately the Hebrew legal system. The stories of
the creation and the flood which were taken over and
purified by the Hebrews were adopted from those
who had already inherited them from a still more ancient
people. Hence it is no exaggeration to say that
Christians owe some of the deepest ideas in the dogmas
which they have erected upon the basis of scripture to
a people far more ancient than the Hebrews or even
the Babylonians; and further, that from these same

[1] I am indebted to the Rev. J. Newton Flew for the following
interesting parallel. In Rome there is a church of Sta Maria del
Parto (child-birth) which is frequented by expectant mothers, and
on the walls of which are to be seen little votive-tablets recording
gratitude to the Virgin Mother for safe delivery. The Church is
thus the centre of a Christianised fertility cultus. But what is
rather startling is that similar votive-tablets, dedicated to the
Sumerian goddess Ishtar, and dating from several thousand years
B.C. have been discovered in Mesopotamia.

[2] C. L. Woolley, *The Sumerians*.

ISHTAR.

(*See* p. xi.)

people are derived ideals of social life and justice which
have been regarded by Christian races, in theory if
not in practice, as criteria for their own customs and
enactments. It may be that in time we shall find the
Sumerians in their turn dependent (as they very
likely were) upon some still older civilisation, perhaps
that of the Indus Valley. It is certainly thought that
these people came from the east, and it has been said
that the ancient Sumerian face can still be seen among
the inhabitants of Afghanistan and Baluchistan until
the Valley of the Indus is reached; while certain
archaeological pieces of evidence seem to show that
there was a primitive culture in Mesopotamia prior
to the incoming of the Sumerians.

We can only conjecture what were the origin and
early history of the religious beliefs inherited by the
inhabitants of Mesopotamia. They were already in the
time of Hammurabi most ancient and most venerable,
and may well have received some of their best features
from the minds of great thinkers of a prehistoric age,
whose names have not been handed down to us. These
thinkers, whoever they were, seem to have seen in the
vast world of the heavens the source of all knowledge,
and to have believed that the fundamental law of the
world consisted in the harmony between heavenly and
earthly events. The secret knowledge of this relationship might appear irrational to the untutored consciousness of man, but it was regarded as a revelation
by which humanity was placed in a position to understand the order of the world, to discover the Will of
God, and to bring all thought and action under a single
scheme. The obvious consequence of this general

outlook was the concentration of attention upon the study of the heavenly bodies, with whom the oldest divinities of the Babylonian pantheon were associated. Thus we are told that the Annunaki and the Igigi, who are bodies of deified spirits, were identified with the stars of the northern and southern heavens respectively. Shamash was the sun, Ishtar the moon, and so on. It was believed that the will of the gods was made known to men by the motions of the planets, and that careful observation of them would enable the skilled seer to recognise in the stars favourable and unfavourable portents. Observations were carefully recorded and in this way a considerable literature accumulated, in which was embedded a certain amount of genuine astronomical fact, for we find that at any rate as early as 2000 B.C., and probably much earlier, the Mesopotamians were able to calculate astronomical events with considerable accuracy.

The literature in question consists chiefly of inscriptions on baked clay cylinders, seals and pieces of stone. There are no papyri and the writing was drawn on the surface of the wet clay or cut in a stone or jewel with a sharp instrument. The inscriptions have not all been translated and of some of those which have, the meaning is still doubtful. We are also uncertain as to the precise significance of all of the figures which appear in wall carvings and on seals and tablets. Many of them represent composite animals, such as lions with eagles' wings or human beings with birds' heads. In the latter instance it seems hazardous to label the individual as a representation of a god. In some cases, if not in all, it is quite likely that the being so represented is a priest wearing a mask. Primitive peoples, as we know, often dressed their witch-doctors or even their chiefs ceremonially for special occasions by making them wear the skin or the head of a totem animal, and the survival of this in more highly developed polytheism can hardly be doubted. Hence a composite creature with human lower limbs may well represent a priest performing rites addressed to a deity who is believed to be connected with, if not identified with, a sacred animal, bird, fish or reptile. It will not serve our purpose to give a detailed account of the legends connected with the Mesopotamian gods, or with the practices prevailing in their temples. To do so would make this book too unwieldy. Information on such subjects is easily accessible, and may be found by the reader in the books to which be is referred at the end of this volume. It may be pointed out, however, that there are certain family resemblances between the names given to Semitic nature-deities, and that Babylonian cosmogony undoubtedly influenced to a certain extent the form of the Hebrew cosmogony recorded in Genesis, although in the latter the stories are much spiritualised.[1] There is also a certain superficial resemblance between the Babylonian and Hebrew penitential psalms, while the code of laws connected with the name of King Hammurabi of Babylon, who flourished about 1950 B.C., bears a certain affinity to the decalogue. In these cases, however, the important question is less: "what did Hebrew religion evolve from?" than "what did it develop into?" No one doubts the influence of ancient forms in the expression of Hebrew religious and ethical ideas, any more than

[1] Especially in the so-called Elohist source.

one doubts the influence of pre-Christian terminology in the names of the days of the week, the selection of sites for Christian churches, or even the vestments and ceremonial used within them; yet the full significance of any development is not necessarily to be determined by merely tracking it back to its source.[1]

European versions of some of the principal passages in Babylonian literature are now available, especially those which record the legends of the Creation and the Flood, and the conflict between the god Marduk and the monster called Tiamat, which may be a personification of the conflict between light and darkness, or a kind of prehistoric combat with a dragon. Tiamat is sometimes represented as a great serpent, sometimes as a monster with wings, claws and horns. The general impression created by a perusal of these various fragments is their extraordinary inferiority in every way to the corresponding type of literature which we get in the Hebrew Bible. They are polytheistic, curiously antique and primitive, and yet the ancestors of the later literature, perhaps, in somewhat the same way that the primeval horse-like animal of the steppes is the ancestor of the arab thoroughbred.

The following extract gives the account of the conflict between Marduk and Tiamat.

93.   Tiamat and Marduk, the envoy of the gods, roused themselves,
94.   They advanced to fight each other, they drew nigh in battle.
95.   The Lord cast his net and made it to enclose her,
96.   The evil wind that had its place behind him he let out in her face.
97.   Tiamat opened her mouth to its greatest extent,

---

[1] See Lehmann and Haas. Also S.P.C.K. pamphlets.

98. Marduk made the evil wind to enter (it) whilst her lips were unclosed.
99. The raging winds filled out her belly,
100. Her heart was gripped, she opened wide her mouth (panting).
101. Marduk grasped the spear, he split up her belly,
102. He clave open her bowels, he pierced (her) heart,
103. He brought her to nought, he destroyed her life.
104. He cast down her carcase, he took up his stand upon it.
105. After Marduk had slain Tiamat the chief,
106. Her host was scattered, her levies became fugitives
107. And the gods, her allies, who had marched at her side
108. Quaked with terror, and broke and ran
109. And betook themselves to flight to save their lives.
110. But they found themselves hemmed in, they could not escape.
111. Marduk tied them up, he smashed their weapons.
112. They were cast into the net, and they were caught in the snare,
113. The . . . of the world they filled with (their) cries of grief.
114. They received (Marduk's) chastisement, they were confined in restraint,
115. And (on) the Eleven Creatures which Tiamat had filled with awfulness,
116. The company of the devils that marched at her . . .
117. He threw fetters, he . . . their sides.
118. They and their resistance he trod under his feet.
119. The god Kingu who had been magnified over them
120. He crushed, he esteemed him (as little worth) as the god Dugga (as a dead god?).
121. Marduk took from him the TABLET OF DESTINIES, which should never have been his,
122. He sealed it with a seal and fastened it on his breast
123. After he had crushed and overthrown his enemies,
124. He made the haughty enemy to be like the dust underfoot.
125. He established completely Anshar's victory over the enemy,
126. The valiant Marduk achieved the object of Nudimmud (Ea),
127. He imposed strict restraint on the gods whom he had made captive.
128. He turned back to Tiamat whom he had defeated.
129. The Lord (Marduk) trampled on the rump of Tiamat,
130. With his unsparing club he clave her skull.
131. He slit open the channels (i.e., arteries) of her blood.
132. He caused the North Wind to carry it away to a place underground.
133. His fathers (i.e., the gods) looked on, they rejoiced, they were glad.
134. They brought under him offerings of triumph and peace,
135. The Lord (Marduk) paused, he examined Tiamat's carcase.
136. He separated flesh (from) hair, he worked cunningly.
137. He slit Tiamat open like a flat (?) fish (cut into) two pieces,

138. The one half he raised up and shaded the heavens therewith,
139. He pulled the bolt, he posted a guard,
140. He ordered them not to let her water escape.
141. He crossed heaven, he contemplated the regions thereof.
142. He betook himself to the abode of Nudimmud (Ea) that is opposite to the Deep (Apsu),
143. The Lord Marduk measured the dimensions of the Deep,
144. He founded E-Sharra, a place like unto it,
145. The abode E-Sharra, which he made to be heaven.
146. He made the gods Anu, Bel and Ea to inhabit their (own) cities.

The following extract gives an account of the Flood as conceived by the Sumerians.

Ut-Napishtim saith to him, even to Gilgamesh
Let me unfold to thee, Gilgamesh, a secret story,
And the decree of the gods let me tell thee!
Shurippak, a city thou knowest—
On the bank of Euphrates it lieth;
That city was very old, and the gods within it—
To make a flood their heart urged them, even the mighty gods.
. . . . . Their father was Anu.
Their counseller the warrior Enlil.
Their messenger Ninib,
Their prince Ennugi.
Nin-igi-azag, the god Ea, sat in counsel with them
And their word he repeated to the reed-house:
"Reed-house, Reed-house! Wall, Wall!
Reed-house, hearken! O Wall, give heed!
Man of Shurippak, son of Ubara-Tutu,
Pull down thy house, build a ship!
Leave wealth, seek life!
Property forsake, and life preserve!
Cause seed of life of every sort to go up into the ship!
The ship which thou shalt build,
Let her proportions be (well) measured!
Its breadth and length correspond!
On the ocean launch it!"
I understood, and said unto Ea, my lord:—
"The command, my lord, which thou spakest thus,
I honour, I will execute,
But what shall I say to the city, the people and the elders?"
Ea opened his mouth and spake.
He said unto me his servant:—
"Thou shalt thus say unto them:—
'Enlil hateth me, and

I may no longer dwell in your city, and towards Enlil's ground no
    longer may I turn my face,
I will go down to the ocean, and with Ea, my lord, will I dwell!'
Upon you will he then rain fullness!
(A catch) of birds, a catch of fish
(. . .) harvest
(. . .) the ruler of the darkness (?)
Shall rain upon you a mighty rain-storm"
As soon as the morning glow appeared

*(Some ten lines broken or gone altogether.)*

On the fifth day, I drew its design.
In its (plan) 120 cubits high on each of its sides.
By 120 cubits it corresponded on each edge of its roof.
I laid down its form, I enclosed it.
I constructed it in six stories,
Dividing it into seven parts.
Its interior I divided into nine parts,
Water-plugs I fastened within it.
I prepared a rudder, and supplied what was necessary,
Three *sars* of bitumen I poured over the outside,
Three *sars* of bitumen I poured over the inside,
While the basket-bearers were carrying three *sars* of oil aboard,
Besides a *sar* of oil which men use as a libation,
The skipper stowed away two *sars* of oil,
For the . . . I slaughtered oxen;
I slew lambs every day.
Of must, sesame-wine, oil and wine,
I gave the people to drink like water from the river
A feast (I made), like that of a festival day.
I opened a box of ointment; I put it in my hand.
(At the rising) of the great Shamash, the ship was completed,
. . . was difficult,
. . . above and below,
. . . two thirds.
With all that I had, I freighted it.
With all that I had of silver, I freighted it.
With all that I had of gold, I freighted it.
With all that I had of living things, I freighted it.
I put on board all my family and relatives,
The cattle of the field, the beasts of the field,
Craftsmen all of them, I put on board.
A fixed time had Shamash appointed (saying):—
"When the ruler of darkness (?) sends a heavy rain in the evening,
Then enter into the ship, and shut thy door."
The appointed time arrived,
The ruler of darkness at eventide sent a heavy rain.

The appearance of the weather I observed,
I feared to behold the weather,
I entered the ship and shut my door.
To the ship's master, to Puzur-Amurri, the sailor,
The great building (*i.e.* the ship) I handed over with its goods.
When the first light of dawn appeared
There came up from the horizon a black cloud,
Adad in the midst thereof thundered,
While Nabu and Sharru (*i.e.* Marduk) went before.
They passed like messengers over mountain and plain,
Nergal tore away the anchor-cable (?),
Ninib goes on, the storm he makes to descend,
The Anunnaki lifted up their torches,
And with their brightness they lit up the land.
The raging of Adad reached into heaven,
All light was turned into darkness.
It (flooded) the land like . . .
One day the tempest . . .
Hard it blew and . . .
Like an onslaught in battle it rushed in on the people.
No man beheld his fellow,
No longer could men know each other.   In heaven
The gods were dismayed at the flood,
They retreated, they went up to the heaven of Anu.
The gods cowered like dogs, they crouched by the walls.
Then Ishtar cried aloud, like a woman in travail,
Belit-ili lamented with a loud voice:—
"Yon generation is turned again to clay
Because I gave the word for an evil thing in the council of the gods,
Since I gave the word for an evil thing in the council of the gods,
For the destruction of my people, I gave the word for an onslaught!
I alone bore my people.
(Now) like the spawn of fish they fill the sea!"
The gods of the Anunnaki wept with her,
The gods were bowed down, they sat a-weeping,
Closed were their lips . . .
For six days and nights
The wind blew, the flood, the tempest overwhelmed the land.
When the seventh day drew near, the tempest, the flood, ceased
    from the battle in which it had fought like a host.
Then the sea rested and was still, and the wind-storm and the
    flood ceased.
When I looked upon the sea, the uproar had ceased,
And all mankind was turned to clay.
The tilled land was become like a swamp,
I opened the window and daylight fell upon my face,
I bowed myself down and sat a-weeping;
Over my face flowed my tears.

I gazed upon the quarters (of the world)—terrible (?) was the sea,
After twelve days, an island arose,
To the land of Nisir the ship took its course,
The mountain of the land of Nisir held fast the ship, and suffered
it not to stir.
One day, a second day, did the mountain of the land of Nisir hold
it fast and suffered it not to stir,
A third day, a fourth day, did the mountain of the land of Nisir
hold it fast and suffered it not to stir.
A fifth day, a sixth day, did the mountain of the land of Nisir hold
it fast and suffer it not to stir.
When the seventh day drew nigh,
I sent forth a dove and let her go,
The dove went to and fro,
But there was no resting-place, and she returned.
Then I sent forth a swallow and let her go,
The swallow went to and fro,
But there was no resting-place and she returned.
Then I sent forth a raven and let her go,
The raven flew away, she beheld the abatement of the waters,
And she came near, wading and croaking, but did not return.
Then I sent everything forth to the four quarters of heaven, I
offered sacrifice,
I made a libation on the peak of the mountain.
By sevens I set out the vessels,
Under them I heaped up reed and cedar-wood and myrtle,
The gods smelt the savour,
The gods smelt the sweet savour,
The gods gathered like flies about him that offered up the sacrifice.
When at length Belit-ilani drew near,
She raised the great jewel which Anu had made according to her
wish (and said):—
"These gods—by the lapis-lazuli upon my neck—I will not forget!
These days will I bear in mind, and never more forget!
Let the gods come to the offering,
But let not Enlil come to the offering,
Forasmuch as he took no counsel, but caused the flood,
And delivered my people to destruction."
But when Enlil drew nigh,
He saw the ship, and Enlil was filled with wrath,
He was consumed with anger against the gods, the Igigi
(saying):—
"Who then has escaped with his life?
No man must live through the destruction!"
Then Ninib opened his mouth and spake,
He said to the warrior Enlil,
"Who then but Ea could have done this thing,
For Ea knoweth every matter?"

Then Ea opened his mouth and spake,
He said to the warrior Enlil,
"Thou art the sage of the gods, O warrior, Enlil,
But thou wouldst not take counsel and hast sent the flood!
On the sinner visit his sin,
On the transgressor lay his transgression;
But forbear, let not (all) be destroyed, have mercy . . .
Instead of thy sending a flood,
A lion might have come and diminished mankind.
Instead of thy sending a flood,
A leopard might have come and diminished mankind.
Instead of thy sending a flood,
A famine might have come and (laid waste) the land.
Instead of thy sending a flood,
Urra (*i.e.*, Pestilence) might have come and (slain) mankind.
I have not disclosed the decree of the great gods.
I made Atrahasis see a dream, and thus he heard the decree of the
     gods.
Now take counsel for him."
Then Ea went up into the ship;
He took me by the hand and led me forth.
He brought out my wife, and made her kneel at my side,
He turned us face to face, standing between us and blessing us
     (saying):—
"Formerly was Ut-napishtim of mankind,
But now let Ut-napishtim and his wife be like the gods, even us!
And let Ut-napishtim dwell afar off at the mouth of the rivers!"
Then they took me and afar off, at the mouth of the rivers, they
     made me to dwell."

From an inspection of Babylonian tablets it is fairly
clear that the hymn is already well-established as a
part of religion, and the best examples of it to be
found are addressed to Shamash. Three extracts may
here be given, the first showing the tendency to
conceive the sun-god as certainly the king of the gods
and almost the sole divinity, the second as illustrating
the development of ethical ideas in connection with
his rule, the third a penitential psalm addressed to
a pair of divinities. To those who regard the Hebrew
Yahweh as the sole source of ancient pre-Christian
morality the second of these will come as a surprise.

(1)

"O lord, illuminator of darkness, who reveals the face [of heaven?] . . .
Merciful god, who lifts up the lowly, protects the weak,
To thy light all the great gods look up.
All the Annunaki look up to thee.
All mankind thou guidest like a single being.
Expectantly with raised head they look up to the sunlight.
When thou dost appear, they rejoice and exult,
Thou art the light for the most distant ends of the heavens,
The standard for the wide earth.
The multitudes look up to thee with joy."

(2)

"Who plans evil—his horn then thou dost destroy,
Who in fixing boundaries annuls rights,
The unjust judge thou restrainest with force.
Who accepts a bribe, who does not judge justly—on him thou
   imposest sin.
But he who does not accept a bribe, who has a care for the oppressed,
To him Shamash is gracious, his life he prolongs.
The judge who renders a just decision
Shall end in a palace, the place of princes shall be his dwelling.

.        .        .        .        .        .

The seed of those who act unjustly shall not flourish.
What their mouth declares in thy presence wilt thou destroy;
   what they purpose thou wilt annul.
Thou knowest their transgressions; the declaration of the wicked
   thou dost cast aside.
Every one wherever he may be is in thy care.
Thou directest their judgments, the imprisoned dost thou liberate.
Thou hearest, O Shamash, petition, prayer and appeal,
Humility, prostration, petitioning, and reverence.
With loud voice the unfortunate one cries to thee.
The weak, the exhausted, the oppressed, the lowly,
The one removed from his family, the one dwelling afar from his
   city.
The peasant when he gathers in his harvest appeals to thee."[1]

(3)

O my god, who art angry with me, turn (thy face?) towards me!
O my goddess, who viewest me with displeasure, receive my prayers!
Receive my prayer! Let thy soul be pacified!
O my lord, forgiving and merciful,
Who guidest the span of life and softenest death, receive my
   supplication!

[1] See C. D. Gray, *Shamash Religious Texts*.  Chicago, 1901.

O my goddess, look favourably upon me, accept my prayer!
May my sins be absolved, and my misdeeds forgotten!
May the evil spell be broken and the fetters loosened!
May my sighing be carried away by the seven winds!
Let me rend asunder the evil, let the bird take it away to heaven!
May the fish take off my trouble, let the stream bear it away!
May the beasts of the field carry it away from me, and wash it
    away in flowing water!
Make me bright like a golden cord (?)!
As the brilliance of a — stone may I be of value before thee!
Remove the evil, protect my life, so shall I protect thy forecourt,
    and set up the image (?).
Let the evil depart from me, so that I may be preserved with thee!
Let me have a propitious dream,
The dream which I dream, may be propitious, yea, established be
    the dream which I dream!
The dream which I dream, turn it to good.
May the god Mahir, the god of dreams, stand at my head!
Let me enter E-sagila, the temple of the gods, the house of life!
To Marduk, the merciful and compassionate, into his merciful
    hands deliver me!
So shall I do homage to thy greatness and extol thy godhead!
May the dwellers in my city glorify thy might
. . . may mankind extol thee!

An attempt has sometimes been made to refer back
the greater part of religious mythology to the astral
beliefs of Mesopotamia. This, however, is an exaggeration. Astral observation certainly plays a substantial
part in the formation of early religious belief, but
when all is said and done it is not the only formative
element. The usual varied sources must be looked to
for the development of belief in superhuman beings.

At the end of the code of Hammurabi (c. 2300 B.C.)
are a number of anathemas, and in these eleven
separate deities are mentioned: Enlil, "the lord who
determines destinies," Marduk, "my lord," Belit, "the
august mother," Ea, "the great prince," Shamash,
"great judge of heaven and earth," Sur, "lord of
heaven, my divine creator," Adad, "lord of abundance,"

Zamama, "the great warrior," Ishtar, "goddess of battle and conflict," Nergal, "the warrior without an equal," Nintu, "the exalted mistress of the lands, the mother who bore me," Ninkarrasa, "the daughter of Anu," and in addition, "the great gods of heaven and earth, the Annunaki in their assembly, whose King is Anu." (Nergal seems to have been the god of scorching heat and therefore of plague. Hence he was also the god of the dead.) Yet in spite of all this, it is remarkable that Hammurabi is pictorially represented as receiving his code from Shamash the sun-god, as though the latter were the chief over all the other divine beings.

On the boundary stones of property we get anathemas against removal or defacement in which as many as twenty-three gods are invoked, but Assurbanipal (B.C. 668–626) never invoked more than eleven, though these are not the same as in the code of Hammurabi. The variations are generally due to the introduction of the names of local divinities.

It appears that besides these numerous more or less propitiable deities there were also a number of evil spirits whom the Sumerians (strangely to our minds) regarded as sons of the gods, and who were seven in number—these were the "bad sacred," ghost-devils, or daemons, and they figure very largely in Sumerian sculptures.

It is regarded as certain that Sumerian religion and culture had established themselves in Palestine before the Hebrew invasion, which has thus been compared to the Anglo-Saxon invasion of Roman Britain. Jerusalem was an ancient stronghold of sun-worship, and it is possible by a careful scrutiny to detect many references to Sumerian religious ideas in Hebrew literature.

## EGYPT.

The story of Egypt is not unlike that of Mesopotamia. There is the same great river valley, affording food to a large population, and there is the same blending of species, caused by very early pre-dynastic incursions from the south-west, and later influences coming in from the north. The peoples of Egypt are, as far back as we are able to trace, a section of the great brown Mediterranean race, blended with immigrants of Armenoid, Semitic, and even negro stock. We find the usual stone age remains, both Palaeolithic and Neolithic. About 5000 B.C. there is a change from primitive Neolithic to Neolithic of a higher type, and what are called the true Egyptians begin to appear. Whether they were the products of a migration from Mesopotamia followed by intermarriage we do not know, but it is difficult to see any very close connection between them and the Sumerians.[1] Their writing is quite different, and their gods are not by any means the same, though this may have been due to their taking over totem-divinities from the people they conquered. From the time when what is called the dynastic period begins, to the conquest of Egypt by Alexander the Great in 332 B.C., there are thirty-one dynasties, and just before Alexander there was a conquest by the Persians. The period covered is about four thousand years, again a much longer period

[1] It is suggested that the pyramid is a development of the ziggurat, and another instance of an artificial mountain.

than that which separates us from Alexander the Great, and if we include the Roman occupation, the history may be divided into nine phases.

(1) The old kingdom, which came to a head in the fourth dynasty, and the rulers of which were responsible for the great Pyramids, 3315 to 2540 B.C.

(2) A conquest of Semites (who founded an alien dynasty probably contemporary with the empire of Hammurabi), followed by a war of liberation in which the native Egyptians ultimately expelled foreign rulers, 2540 to 1580 B.C. This was followed by

(3) The new empire, a time of great prosperity under Egyptian rulers, in which military undertakings extended as far as the Euphrates, 1580 to 1100 B.C.

(4) The so-called Libyan period, 1100–670 B.C., in which the country suffered conquest by an Ethiopian dynasty which was overthrown in 670 B.C. by the Assyrians, (5) who in turn were overthrown (605) by the Babylonians and they (6) by the Persians (525).

(7) In 332 there was a Greek conquest by Alexander, followed by (8) the so-called Ptolemaic period, which ended with (9) the Roman conquest in 30 B.C.

Egyptian religion before the Greek and Roman invasions is not a single faith, but a group or loose federation of different cults. This group derives from four main sources: (a) the primitive Libyan inhabitants; (b) the conquering reddish-brown (or venetian red) race, akin to the mysterious Etruscans; (c) Semitic immigrants; (d) negroid intermarriage; and it is in consequence not at all homogeneous.

It may be that the importance of Egyptian religion

and civilisation has been over-estimated, for our early
knowledge of Egyptian antiquities was on the whole
greater and more detailed than in the case of Mesopotamia; and at a time when the inherited wisdom of
Egypt was influencing the Graeco-Roman world, little
or nothing was known of the great religions and rich
cultures of ancient India. To-day we see the facts more
in proportion; and yet we cannot deny the immense
influence of the temples of Egypt and their priesthoods.
We have already remarked that in Mesopotamia
considerable attention was given to the movements of
the heavenly bodies. We find the same attention in
Egypt. It appears that as early as 3000 B.C. the
Egyptian priests had divided the stars into constellations, and were familiar with what we call the
twleve signs of the zodiac. Again, it is very difficult
to define any limit to, or to assign any single origin
for, the tendency in various countries to treat the king
with divine honours. Certainly it did not begin with
the Emperor of Rome. It has been pointed out that
the kings of Mesopotamia were secularised priests,
that is to say, priests who became kings and were
afterwards deified. But the kings of Egypt, as far
back as we can explore, were more than that. They
were incarnations of a god. This divine origin of
kings had an extraordinary influence upon Western
thought and it is safe to say that not even Christianity
has been able to sweep it away. Perhaps one ought
not to say "even Christianity," for not only does the
Christian faith centre round the idea of an incarnation,
but it has actually encouraged at times the bestowal
of semi-divine honours upon secular rulers. The

chronicler of the Council of Nicaea says that Constantine there "spoke like a god,"[1] while European monarchy in general, like the Byzantine, and the Egyptian before it, has been accompanied by ceremonies in which the monarch is solemnly invested with robes of a priestly character and receives homage from his people as though he were a divine being.

Unlike India, Egypt has no ancient philosophy. There is nothing prior to the Greek conquest to compare with the Upanishads. Even after 332 B.C. it was the Greeks and not the Egyptians who founded the Alexandrian school of philosophy. Egypt herself remains polytheistic and at different cities different gods were worshipped. Gradually the patient studies of the Egyptologists have furnished us with a sort of general view of the progress of thought and worship in the Nile valley. It is said that the earliest Egyptian thought is revealed in mortuary practices, and the elaborate burial customs of the Egyptians have for long been familiar to the public. Nowhere else has the practice of embalming the dead been so greatly elaborated, and nowhere else have such magnificent tombs as the great Pyramids been erected. The costly furnishing of these tombs has been well-illustrated by the discoveries of recent years. At the same time it appears that from the thirtieth to the twenty-second century B.C. the idea of a glorious personal immortality seems to have been exclusively reserved for kings and possibly nobles.

---

[1] It is true that at first Christianity resisted the prevailing tendency, which came in strongly with Augustus, of treating the Emperor as divine. Constantine, however, seems to have overcome the scruples of the bishops !

It has been suggested that the idea of embalming, as distinct from cremation or burial in barrows, may have sprung from the discovery made by the Egyptians that corpses when laid in the dry warm sand of the desert did not putrefy but remained in a state of comparative preservation. The possibility of preserving the body may then have led to more or less elaborate speculations about the soul. Certainly Egyptian thought on the subject of the unseen world has special features of its own, among which we find the conception of the Ka, who is a kind of genius or guardian angel and who protected the soul in life and in death. At first the Ka seems to have been exclusively possessed by kings, and it was only after slow development that the possession of a Ka by ordinary people came to be believed in. The progress of the soul after death seems to have been connected with current Mediterranean ideas about a god of the underworld, who sat in judgment on the departed spirits and apportioned them bliss or torment.

Apart from these speculations, and from the common stock of primitive religious and magical ideas, it is natural to find two main sources for early Egyptian religious belief and practice, the sun and the river Nile. This is hardly surprising, since the Nile flood and the warmth of the sun were obviously the very means of life to the inhabitants of the country, and the source of their food supply. Gradually Re, the sun-god, from the twenty-eighth century B.C. came to be regarded as the father of the king of Egypt, and even as a former king—"a kind of celestial reflection of the earthly sovereign." The origin of the god Osiris is peculiar, because in the first place he appears to be the personification of the Nile-water, then (from some of the early representations), of the soil and even of the vegetation. On other occasions, however, he figures as a subterranean or earth-spirit, the god of the underworld, and so the ruler of the realms of the dead. At the same time he greatly resembles a genuinely historical hero-king, and it seems as though the story of some such hero has been fused with a picture of the cycle of Nature, and the story of the waxing and waning fertility of the earth. Osiris is reputed to have had for his wife and queen his sister Isis. He was slain by a conspiracy and his body dismembered, but afterwards, through the pious search of the queen, recovered and restored to life. It is note-worthy that upon this Osiris-legend was concentrated very much of the national idealism of the Egyptian people. Isis, like her counterpart Sita in India, was the embodiment of wifely fidelity and affection, while her little son Horus personified filial piety. It was natural to exalt Isis in worship as the queen of heaven, and her representation as seated with the boy Horus on her knee not only reminds us of the commonest representations of the Christian Madonna and Child, which may well owe to it their origin, but also of certain bronze Hittite images of mother and infant, and of the curious Japanese representations of the goddess Kwannon and her little son, which is of course pre-Buddhist in origin, and has also no con-nection whatever with Egypt or Asia Minor, but is merely an instance of the manner in which human fancy has all the world over dwelt fondly upon the

sacred element in maternity. Complicating this
scheme of supernatural beings we have the large
number of Egyptian divinities of more or less totem
character, to which reference has already more than
once been made, and which seem to imply the fusion
of several cults into one system. The feature is
not of course peculiar to Egypt, but occurs also in
India, where, for example, we find Hanuman the
monkey-god and Ganesha the elephant-headed god
among the minor divinities of Hinduism. We can
indeed help ourselves to think sympathetically about
the great Egyptian system from a consideration of
the rich polytheism of India. To western Christians
the whole outlook seems unfamiliar and unreal. We
have grown so much accustomed to thinking in terms
of monotheism that we cannot easily conceive of life
going on century after century in which the objects of
human devotion are plural instead of singular. It is
less difficult for persons of Catholic antecedents to do
so, since the cultus of saints allows them large liberty
in paying their devotions sometimes to one holy person
and sometimes to another. Reformed Christianity,
however, has cut itself completely off from this tradition,
and through its patient adherence to the stern monotheism of the later prophetic writings of the Hebrew
Bible has come to take its stand virtually on the
same side as Islam, where there is but one God
who has no fellow, and where to say that he begets
or is begotten or that there are any others like him
is deadly sin.

The Egyptian pantheon comprised, then, the following
beings, among others of less importance: Re the

sun-god, who is the most universally and generally
worshipped, Joh the moon-god, Nut the sky, Geb the
earth, and Hapi the Nile; but these universal beings
were then identified with local divinities whose cultus
could hardly be regarded as properly extending outside
the boundaries of Egypt.   Thus Re was identified with
Horus, Joh with Thoth, Nut with Hathor, Hapi or
Apis with Osiris;  and these, as well as other local
divinities, have often animal representations.   Thus
Hathor figures as a cow, Apis as a bull, Seth or Seti as
a crocodile, Nechebit as a vulture, Ta-Urt as a female
hippopotamus, Anubis as a jackal, Bes as a baboon,
Thoth as an ibis-headed man.   The Sphinx itself is
only a colossal instance of an extremely common cat-
or lion-like image of a divine being.

It is curious to note that, contrary to the practice
of other peoples, the Egyptians regarded the heaven
as female and the earth as male.   Later the heaven
was itself partitioned, and regarded as bisexual, the
lower part, next to the earth, being still female, and
procreative activity being conceived as the result of
the embrace of the male earth, and the lower heaven:
but the teaching was current that prior to creation
there was only one deity, who called into existence
from Nu or primeval chaos the world that was to be.
There was a certain amount of theologising, as time
went on.   The priestly codifiers sought to arrange
their numerous divinities in some sort of grouping.
They began to deal with them as though they were
aspects of one god rather than independent sacred
individuals, and where this was not done to arrange
them in triads or even enneads, or in the form of a

genealogical table, so as to subordinate them to one another.

As in Mesopotamia, there appears an ethical element in the relation of the worshipper to his gods; and it is evident that, from whatever source they derived it, the Egyptians came to hold the idea of a divine inquisition into the works of each individual, conducted by Osiris, seated upon his judgment throne. The representation of this in the papyrus of Ani (where Osiris presides over the weighing of the soul, which is performed by Thoth and his associate Anpu (Anubis) in the presence of a sort of divine jury composed of the twelve Great Gods of Heliopolis) is familiar to all who have visited the British Museum. The following Hymn to Osiris, however, is probably not so familiar. It occurs in the same papyrus of Ani, and has been translated by Sir E. A. Wallis Budge as follows:

"Homage to thee, O Great God, Lord of Maāti; I have come to thee, O my Lord, that I may behold thy beneficence. I know thee, and I know thy name, and the names of the Forty-two who live with thee in the Hall of Maāti, who keep ward over sinners, and feed upon their blood on the day of estimating characters before Un-Nefer .... Behold, I have come to thee, and I have brought *maāt* (*i.e.* truth, integrity) to thee. I have destroyed sin for thee. I have not sinned against men. I have not oppressed [my] kinsfolk. I have done no wrong in the place of truth. I have not known worthless folk. I have not wrought evil. I have not defrauded the oppressed one of his goods. I have not done the things that the gods abominate. I have not vilified a servant to his master. I have not caused pain. I have not let any man hunger. I have made no one to weep. I have not committed murder. I have not commanded any to commit murder for me. I have inflicted pain on no man. I have not defrauded the temples of their oblations. I have not purloined the cakes of the gods. I have not stolen the offerings to the spirits (*i.e.* the dead). I have not committed fornication. I have not polluted myself in the holy places of the god of my city. I have not diminished from the bushel. I did not take from or add to the acre-measure. I did not encroach on the fields [of others]. I have not added to the weights of the scales. I have not misread the pointer of the scales. I have not taken milk from the mouths of children. I have not driven cattle from their pastures. I have not snared the birds of the gods. I have not caught fish with fish of their kind. I have not stopped water [when it should flow]. I have not cut the dam of a canal. I have not extinguished a fire when it should burn. I have not altered the times of the chosen meat offerings. I have not turned away the cattle [intended for] offerings. I have not repulsed the god at his appearances. I am pure. I am pure. I am pure. I am pure . . . ."

It is startling to find that the Byzantine Christian school of painting, which prescribed the correct form for the representation of the doctrines of the Faith of the Christian Church throughout Europe, preserved this conception of the weighing of the soul, substituting Christ for Osiris, Michael the Archangel for Anpu, the recording angel for Thoth, and the devils of hell for the monster Amemit, the eater of the dead. One of these representations of the weighing of the soul is to be seen in Barton Church near Cambridge, where the Virgin Mother, who is substituted for the goddess Meskhenet, puts a rosary into the balance to weight it in favour of the soul's acquittal.

The discovery of such parallels does not of course invalidate the Christian ethical idea of personal responsibility; but it makes its origin far older than the time of Jesus, who gave new form and significance to it. In any case

L

the contrast between the address to Osiris and the 51st
Psalm is sufficiently striking.  Ani is concerned not to
confess his shortcomings, but to affirm his innocence before
the celestial jury.  If we seek a parallel to this we shall
find it perhaps in the 26th Psalm.

Egyptian polytheism (and probably the other polytheisms as well) had a curiously dualistic tinge, in
that the deities were classified into those mainly
beneficent, "the great gods," and those (mainly malevolent) strange powers which infested the path through
which the dead must travel in passing from this world
to the next.  Even the sun was menaced each morning
by a monster known as Anpep, who was conceived in
the form of a great serpent.  This is the contrast once
again between the good sacred and the bad sacred.
The great gods were believed to be afraid of the powers
of evil, and even compelled to protect themselves
against them by the use of spells and magical words of
power.  Thus Re, the sun-god, was believed to owe
his daily preservation to the possession of a secret
spell by which he was able to paralyse the malignant
Anpep.  These spells and powerful sentences were
believed to have been provided for the rest of the
gods by Thoth (or Tat as he appears in later times).
The actual origin of Thoth himself as the chief medicine-
man is obscure.  Sometimes he is the moon-god, and
it might almost seem as though the whole scheme
had arisen out of a myth purporting to describe the
relations of the earth, clouds, sun and moon.  At other
times he is the witch-doctor wearing a bird-like head-
dress and mask.  It seems probable, however, that there
is an element of hero-worship involved, and that

[57399]

STELE SHEWING THE DEAD KING AMENHOTEP III & HIS QUEEN, TEIE,
SEATED BEFORE A STAND OF OFFERINGS AND RECEIVING THE SYMBOL OF LIFE
FROM THE ATEN OR SOLAR DISK.

FOUND IN A HOUSE OF THE TIME OF AKHENATEN AT TELL EL-AMARNA.    [XVIIIᵗʰ Dynasty, about 1370 B.C.]

*Given by the Egypt Exploration Society, 1924.*

The figure of the queen is much destroyed, but that of the king is perfect, and is a remarkable instance
of the realistic style of Akhenaten's time. The face is obviously meant for a faithful portrait of the king
and the careless attitude of the figure is unique.

AMENHOTEP III BEFORE THE SYMBOL OF ATEN.

(*See* p. xi.)

Thoth's attributes are largely those of a cunning fellow,
a kind of celestial magician.   At any rate, the striking
feature is the limited power of the good gods.   The
great world of the Egyptians is no unitary system,
but full of conflicting powers which administer check
and counter-check to one another.   It is more like a
huge game of chess, except that at present there
are no players, but only self-determining pieces of
varying magnitudes which move about of their own
initiative.

The deification of abstract qualities, which, as we
shall see, is so marked a feature of Roman religion,
appears here also, and we find Eternity, Stability, Joy,
Speech, Taste treated with Divine honours, and
represented by more or less human figures bearing
appropriate labels.

With the growth of an Egyptian empire a wider
outlook came to the national religion.   Hitherto the
sun-god had ruled only Egypt, and it has been pointed
out that in the texts carved on the pyramids he is
represented as guarding the Egyptian frontiers.   The
first tendency to expansion appears in his gradual
absorption of the other gods of the country, a process
of *theocrasia* which again is typical of developments
taking place elsewhere, in Mesopotamia and India
alike: but in the period 1580 to 1350 B.C. the imperial
expansion of Egyptian to north and south gave her
undisputed supremacy from Asia Minor to the Sudan,
and made a corresponding expansion of religious
thought inevitable.   It has been said that monotheism
is only imperialism in religion.   About 1400 B.C. in
the reign of Amenhotep III, the greatest of the

Egyptian emperors, we have the following hymn of the sun, written apparently at Thebes.

"Hail to thee, beautiful god of every day!
Rising in the morning without ceasing,
(Not) wearied in labour.
When thy rays are visible,
Gold is not considered,
It is not like thy brilliance.
Thou art a craftsman shaping thine own limbs;
Fashioner without being fashioned;
Unique in his qualities, traversing eternity;
Over ways (with) millions under his guidance.
Thy brilliance is like the brilliance of the sky,
Thy colours gleam more than the hues of it.
When thou sailest across the sky all men behold thee,
(Though) thy going is hidden from their sight.
When thou showest thyself at morning every day,
. . . under thy majesty, though the day be brief,
Thou traversest a journey of leagues,
Even millions and hundred-thousands of time.
Every day is under thee.
When thy setting (comes),
The hours of the night hearken to thee likewise.
When thou hast traversed it
There comes no ending to thy labours.
All men, they see by means of thee.
Nor do they finish when thy majesty sets,
(For) thou wakest to rise in the morning,
And thy radiance, it opens the eyes (again).
When thou settest in Manu,
Then they sleep like the dead.
Hail to thee! O disk of day,
Creator of all and giver of their substance,
Great Falcon, brilliantly plumaged,
Brought forth to raise himself on high of himself,
Self-generator, without being born.
First-born Falcon in the midst of the sky,
To whom jubilation is made at his rising and his setting likewise.
Fashioner of the produce of the soil,
.   .   .   .   .   .   .   .   .
Taking possession of the Two Lands (Egypt), from great to small,
A mother, profitable to gods and men,
A craftsman of experience, . . .
Valiant herdman who drives his cattle,
Their refuge and giver of their sustenance,
Who passes by, running the course of Khepri (the Sun-god),

Who determines his own birth,
Exalting his beauty in the body of Nut,
Illuminating the Two Lands (Egypt) with his disk,
The primordial being, who himself made himself;
Who beholds that which he had made,
Sole lord taking captive all lands every day,
As one beholding them that walk therein;
Shining in the sky 'a being as the sun.'
He makes the seasons by the months,
Heat when he desires,
Cold when he desires,
He makes the limbs to languish
When he enfolds them,
Every land is in rejoicing
At his rising every day, in order to praise him."

This hymn is addressed to Amon or Amen, who was originally the local god of Thebes, but had come to be identified with Re, the sun-god, and it appears that at Thebes was the centre of the Egyptian priesthood, the high priest of Amen-Ra being the head of the national organisation of the priesthood. The tone of the utterances suggests a greatly widened outlook, not far removed from monotheism.

In 1375 B.C. under the next emperor, Amenhotep IV, comes the most important of all developments. The young king devoted himself to the pursuit of a kind of religious reformation, and the sun-god under his auspices was called by an old name, Aton, specially revived for the purpose. This word represents the solar emblem, and a new symbol was invented, that of a disk with rays radiating from it and terminating in a human hand. So far it is difficult to see what changes were really involved. It appears, however, that Amenhotep IV held that even the most highly developed worship of the traditional type was too deeply connected with primitive conceptions of a less satisfactory and less exalted nature to be adequate, and that a fresh start must be made, accompanied by a new and different set of symbols. The centre of this reformation was Heliopolis, which had previously been the centre of the old worship of Re, and it was introduced deliberately into Thebes, where Amenhotep at his own expense built a new sun temple, but did not succeed in overcoming the opposition of the priesthood. Finally the king built himself a new capital midway between Thebes and the sea, at the place which is now known as Tell el-Amarna.

The following hymn is attributed to Amenhotep IV, and represents his outlook:

### UNIVERSAL SPLENDOR AND POWER OF ATON

"Thy dawning is beautiful in the horizon of the sky,
O living Aton, Beginning of life!
When thou risest in the eastern horizon,
Thou fillest every land with thy beauty.
Thou art beautiful, great, glittering, high above every land,
Thy rays, they encompass the lands, even all that thou hast made.
Thou art Re, and thou carriest them all away captive;
Thou bindest them by thy love.
Though thou art far away, thy rays are upon earth;
Though thou art on high, thy 'footprints are the day.'

### NIGHT

"When thou settest in the western horizon of the sky,
The earth is in darkness like the dead;
They sleep in their chambers,
Their heads are wrapped up,
Their nostrils are stopped,
And none seeth the other,
While all their things are stolen
Which are under their heads,
And they know it not.
Every lion cometh forth from his den,
All serpents, they sting.
Darkness . . .
The world is in silence,
He that made them resteth in his horizon.

## DAY AND MAN

"Bright is the earth when thou risest in the horizon.
When thou shinest at Aton by day
Thou drivest away the darkness.
When thou sendest forth thy rays,
The Two Lands (Egypt) are in daily festivity,
Awake and standing upon their feet
When thou hast raised them up.
Their limbs bathed, they take their clothing,
Their arms uplifted in adoration to thy dawning.
(Then) in all the world they do their work.

## DAY AND THE ANIMALS AND PLANTS

"All cattle rest upon their pasturage,
The trees and the plants flourish,
The birds flutter in their marshes,
Their wings uplifted in adoration to thee.
All the sheep dance upon their feet,
All winged things fly,
They live when thou has shone upon them.

## DAY AND THE WATERS

"The barques sail up-stream and down-stream alike.
Every highway is open because thou dawnest.
The fish in the river leap up before thee.
Thy rays are in the midst of the great green sea.

## CREATION OF MAN

"Creator of the germ in woman,
Maker of seed in man,
Giving life to the son in the body of his mother,
Soothing him that he may not weep,
Nurse (even) in the womb,
Giver of breath to animate every one that he maketh!
When he cometh forth from the body . . . on the day of his birth,
Thou openest his mouth in speech,
Thou suppliest his necessities.

## CREATION OF ANIMALS

"When the fledgling in the egg chirps in the shell.
Thou givest him breath therein to preserve him alive.
When thou hast 'brought him together,'
To (the point of) bursting it in the egg,
He cometh forth from the egg
To chirp 'with all his might.'
He goeth about upon his two feet
When he hath come forth therefrom.

## THE WHOLE CREATION

"How manifold are thy works!
They are hidden from before (us),
O sole God, whose powers no other possesseth.
Thou didst create the earth according to thy heart
While thou wast alone:
Men, all cattle large and small,
All that are upon the earth,
That go about upon their feet;
(All) that are on high,
That fly with their wings.
The foreign countries, Syria and Kush,
The land of Egypt;
Thou settest every man into his place,
Thou suppliest their necessities.
Every one has his possessions,
And his days are reckoned.
The tongues are divers in speech,
Their forms likewise and their skins are distinguished.
(For) thou makest different the strangers.

## WATERING THE EARTH IN EGYPT AND ABROAD

"Thou makest the Nile in the Nether World,
Thou bringest it as thou desirest,
To preserve alive the people,
For thou hast made them for thyself,
The lord of them all, resting among them;
Thou lord of every land, who risest for them,
Thou Sun of day, great in majesty.
All the distant countries,
Thou makest (also) their life,
Thou hast set a Nile in the sky:
When it falleth for them,
It maketh waves upon the mountains,
Like the great green sea,
Watering their fields in their towns.
"How excellent are thy designs, O lord of eternity!
There is a Nile in the sky for the strangers
And for the cattle of every country that go upon their feet.
(But) the Nile, it cometh from the Nether World for Egypt.

## THE SEASONS

"Thy rays nourish every garden;
When thou risest they live,
They grow by thee.
Thou makest the seasons
In order to create all thy work:
Winter to bring them coolness,
And heat that 'they may taste' thee.

Thou didst make the distant sky to rise therein,
In order to behold all that thou hast made.
Thou alone, shining in thy form as living Aton,
Dawning, glittering, going afar and returning.
Thou makest millions of forms
Through thyself alone:
Cities, towns, and tribes, highways and rivers.
All eyes see thee before them,
For thou art Aton of the day over the earth.

.    .    .    .    .    .    .    .    .

### REVELATION TO THE KING

"Thou art in my heart,
There is no other that knoweth thee
Save thy son Ikhnaton.
Thou hast made him wise
In thy designs and in thy might.
The world is in thy hand,
Even as thou hast made them,
When thou hast risen they live,
When thou settest thy die;
For thou art length of life of thyself,
Men live through thee,
While (their) eyes are upon thy beauty
Until thou settest
All labor is put away
When thou settest in the west.

.    .    .    .    .    .    .    .

Thou didst establish the world,
And raise them up for thy son,
Who came forth from thy limbs,
The king of Upper and Lower Egypt,
Living in Truth, Lord of the Two Lands,
Nefer-khepru-Re, Wan-Re (Ikhnaton),
Son of Re, living in Truth, lord of diadems,
Ikhnaton, whose life is long;
(And for) the chief royal wife, his beloved,
Mistress of Two Lands, Nefer-nefru-Aton, Nofretete,
Living and flourishing for ever and ever."[1]

With the Persian and Greek conquests, Egyptian
religious history loses its independent features, and
becomes merged in the general life of the Hellenistic

[1] I owe these passages to Prof. Breasted's work, *The Development
of Religious Thought in Ancient Egypt.*

world; but even under Alexander and his successors Egypt remained the land of ancient culture and occult wisdom, and her divinities were popularised for the benefit of the whole of the Mediterranean, so that the cult of Isis is to be found in many spots outside the country of its origin, while Sarapis from the fourth century B.C. absorbs the interest hitherto shown in Osiris: indeed Sarapis is identified (by *theocrasia*) with Zeus and Helios, as the sole male divinity in the world.

We have said that there was no native philosophy in Egypt. This perhaps needs qualification. Though there remains nothing to equal the literatures of Greece, India, or China, there were certainly maxims current among the Egyptians regarding the path of virtue. The Hebrew book of Proverbs has been shown to depend in part upon a treatise composed by one Amen-em-ope, approximately dating from the twenty-fifth dynasty, and contemporary with Hezekiah king of Judah; but both treatises may of course represent selections from a common stock of proverbial philosophy current throughout the East in early times. A few extracts from Amen-em-ope will perhaps prove interesting:

"The beginning of teaching how to live, guidance for welfare . . . to direct a man in the path of life and make him prosper upon earth.

Beware of robbing a poor man, of being valorous against the man who has a broken arm.

Give way unto him that attacketh; sleep a night before speaking; leave the passionate man to his own devices. God will know how to reply to him.

The truly tranquil man . . . is like a tree grown in a plot (?): it grows green, it doubles its yield, its fruit is sweet, its shade is pleasant.

Remove not the landmark on the boundaries of the sown fields, nor shift the position of the measuring-rod . . . mark well him who hath done this on earth, for he is an oppressor of the weak.  (But)

his goods are taken out of the hand of his children and his property
is given to another. . . . A man propitiates God by the power of the
Lord (Aten), when he defines the boundaries. Desire then to make
thine own self prosperous; beware of the Universal Lord. Better is a
bushel that God giveth thee, than five thousand (obtained) by force.
Better is poverty at the hand of God than riches in the storehouse;
better is bread with a happy heart than riches with vexation.

Labour not to seek increase, (then) thy needs shall be secure for
thee; if riches be brought to thee by robbery, they shall not stay
the night with thee. They have made themselves wings like geese.
The boat of the covetous is left in the mud, while the bark of the
tranquil sails free. Thou shalt pray to the Aten when he rises,
saying, 'Give me prosperity and health,' and he will give thee thy
needs in life, and thou wilt be safe from fear.

Speak not to a man in falsehood, the abomination of God.

If thou find a large debt against a poor man, make it into three
parts: forgive two, let one remain; thou wilt find it a path of life.

Justice is a great gift of God; He will give it to him whom He
will . . . . Sit thee down at the hands of God; thy tranquillity will
overthrow (thine adversaries).

Empty not thine inmost soul to everybody . . . nor associate
thyself with one who lays bare his heart.

Verily man is clay and straw; God is his fashioner. Happy is
he who hath reached the West, where he is safe in the hand of God.

God loves the happiness of the humble more than that the noble
be honoured.

(In the ferry boat) take the fare from the man of wealth, and
welcome also him who has nothing."[1]

When we consider the span of Egyptian history we
are well able to understand that there was time within
it for the accumulation of such and similar experience,
and that even in this respect "the wisdom of the
Egyptians" is no empty phrase.

Perhaps the best summary of this section is to be
found in the reflection *that for a period exceeding that
which separates us from the reign of Alexander the
Great polytheism reigned almost unquestioned.* To
say, therefore, that Christian monotheism is incapable
of supersession because it has been unquestionably

[1] *J.E.A.*, Vol. XII, Oct., 1926. (F. H. Griffith.) Cf. also the
wisdom of Ptah-hotep, quoted by Breasted, *op. cit.*, pages 231 ff.

accepted for some two thousand years is to employ a
not very strong argument. Other grounds than those
of a *consensus saeculorum* must be found, if we are to
satisfy ourselves that it is a permanently tenable belief.

Further comment upon the merits or demerits of
these Egyptian interpretations of the universe may
be reserved until we have surveyed several other
types of the same. Meanwhile let it suffice to point
out a fact of which a visit to the British Museum or the
Louvre should be enough to convince anyone, namely,
that the most striking feature of polytheism, whether in
Egypt or Mesopotamia, is its profuse and often magnificent symbolism. We shall see, as we go on, the reason
for this feature, and how it was designed to preserve,
reawaken, and intensify the feelings of numinous awe
and sense of Presence produced by the sight of some
fierce, beautiful, or grotesque animal, or of a priest-
king decked in the splendour of his vestments as the
representative of Deity. It matters little that some
of the sacred objects are queer and gross, since animal
life itself is both gross and queer. If physical existence
be steeped in mystery, then it is no wonder that bull
and eagle, cat, jackal, ibis, and scarab alike should be
able to awaken consciousness of it, and their models
to possess a sacramental value;[1] but since solar heat
is the most potent agency in promoting growth,
stimulating fertility, and causing pestilence and
death, it is least strange of all that the solar disk and
its daily appearance and disappearance should have
become the central object of mystery and adoration.

[1] It may be recalled that the writer of the final portion of the book
of Job describes the hippopotamus as "the chief of the ways of God"!
See note on symbolism appended to description of plates (p. xii).

## CHAPTER V

# OF THE GREAT CREATIVE PERIOD IN
# RELIGION

### INTRODUCTION

IT seems probable that somewhere within the region of 800 B.C. there began a new and special series of questionings and enquiries in a number of different spots on the earth's surface, and that three main aims became clearly defined, to know the world, to know ourselves, and to know the meaning and purpose of the Whole. The attempt at a solution of these problems was at once a source of pleasure and of pain, of pleasure in achievement, and of pain in the consciousness of failure to reach complete and immediate harmony with the whole of reality. We may classify these problems briefly by saying they are problems of science, problems of society, and problems of spirit.

Strangely enough, it is the last of the three to which man applied himself most eagerly in the period indicated. It is true that he did not neglect the others, and problems of science certainly from the very first perplexed all primitive human beings, while Greek free thought for a time busied itself quite as much with the question of the best way to organise human society as with investigations into the nature of matter. Nevertheless, it is the third class of problems with which we chiefly associate the names

which will be given below, with their approximate
dates. The period, as we have said, is one beginning
roughly about 800 B.C. and extending down to 300 A.D.
and it is surprising how little by way of enrichment
has been added since then to the results achieved
within it. We might suppose that the devotion to
problems of the first class which has been the con-
spicuous feature of the past one hundred and fifty
years would have seriously altered the conclusions of
this earlier period, but strangely enough this is not the
case, as we shall try to show.

The world of antiquity in which there grew up the
great creative systems of religion and philosophy,
believed itself to be almost, if not quite, the final age
of the planet. The golden period of the earth's
history lay in the dim past, and in the main the thinkers
of Christian and non-Christian antiquity alike did not
look to the future for the achievement of perfection.
"The world is perishing and running down and reaching
its last end" said Eusebius of Caesarea about the year
318 A.D., and it is doubtful whether the view of the
Buddha was really very different, because, although
like most Indians he had little or no idea of the
significance of history except as cycles of divine
activity devoid of any serious purpose, nevertheless
he did definitely affirm (what it was difficult to deny)
that all human existence was subject to decay and
death. Now the primary effect of the age of science
which dawned about three hundred years ago and to
some extent of the age of European renaissance which
preceded it was to stimulate a belief in progress, and
to popularise the notion of a state of terrestrial bliss

to be reached by the human race, somewhere in the not very distant future. The worthiest expression of this is to be found in the well-known poem by John Addington Symonds:

These things shall be! A loftier race
  Than e'er the world hath known, shall rise
With flame of freedom in their souls
  And light of science in their eyes.

They shall be gentle, brave, and strong
  To spill no drop of blood, but dare
All that may plant man's lordship firm
  On earth and fire and sea and air.

They shall be simple in their homes
  And splendid in their public ways,
Filling the mansions of the state
  With music and with hymns of praise.

Nation with nation, land with land,
  Inarmed shall live as comrades free;
In every heart and brain shall throb
  The pulse of one fraternity.

Woman shall be man's mate and peer
  In all things strong and fair and good,
Still wearing on her brows the crown
  Of sinless, sacred motherhood.

New arts shall bloom of loftier mould,
  And mightier music thrill the skies,
And every life shall be a song,
  When all the earth is paradise.

The first blow to the security of this notion has come from the discovery that such an ideal civilisation, though possible, might and probably would be extremely vulnerable to changes of climate, so that the shifting of the rain-belt might dry it up, or the swooping down of an ice-age freeze it into extinction. In the past many civilisations may have come to sudden disaster through the spread of the anopheles or malaria-carrying mosquito, or through the ravages of pneumonic or bubonic plague, or even through a series of earthquakes. We to-day recognise that economic crises are not easy to control and may speedily ruin a continent, while a new menace to stability is found in the weapons of destruction which science has put into the hands of passionate mankind. And further, even though new cultures may arise upon the ruins of the old, still better and still nobler, and so on for a million million years, yet the whole of these will still (as we have seen in No. 4 of this series) be bound to come to an end when radiation has proceeded so far that this planet can no longer support life. Of course it makes some difference to a child of ten as to whether it will die to-morrow or live sixty years, and it makes some difference to a race in its infancy whether it will be exterminated next year by sword or pestilence or live on for five hundred years to develop a noble and complex civilisation; but in these two cases the chance of making a mature contribution only matters if there is some future to which the contribution can be handed on, and it would seem that although the natural sciences have presented us with a descriptive account of the contents of the universe and of the so-called laws according to which these various items which it contains have arrived at their present condition (so that we are able to make a tolerable forecast as to the direction in which they will continue to develop if undisturbed during the more immediate future), yet these sciences have not been able to show us that apart from the qualitative conceptions of religion the whole process has any meaning which makes it worth while. The prospect of planetary death, so long as we believe in nothing else, lowers indeed the worth of every human activity.

We are to-day, therefore, as has been said, back again at the period of problems of spirit, which was really more like our own than, let us say, the middle of the nineteenth century. It is significant that during that remoter period occur practically all the main attempts to answer questions about the ultimate meaning of life. With these attempts we must therefore next occupy ourselves.[1]

We have first the vague figure of Zarathustra the Persian, who probably in the seventh century B.C. sought for unity in existence. Somewhere about the same time we have the appearance of Lao-tzŭ in China, whose birth is given approximately as 604 B.C. In the next century we have a series of great names, Mahavira in India (599–529), Pythagoras in Greece (580–500), Kung-fu-tzŭ (more recognisable as Confucius) in China (551–479) and Gautama in India (563–483). Simultaneously with these, though beginning a little earlier, we have the wonderful series of Hebrew prophets, and during the latter period, parallel with these, we have Greek free thought, and especially the

[1] I ought to observe that this chapter was in type six months before I had seen or read Bp. Gore's Gifford Lectures. The similarity between my argument and his at this point is therefore only a coincidence.

M

figures of Socrates, Plato and Aristotle. China again gives us between the years 372 to 289 the honoured names of Mêng-tzŭ and Chuang-tzŭ. Then comes the movement which centres around Jesus of Nazareth and springs forth from Him, and this establishes at first a kind of relationship with various elements in the preceding systems, and then has its development checked by what are commonly known as the Dark Ages. As Europe gradually emerges from this period of obscurity the task of adjustment is again taken up and continued, and the period of the last one hundred and fifty years has to some extent again interrupted that adjustment, because attention for the time being has been diverted to the natural sciences, while the new development of communication between different parts of the planet has brought east and west, north and south, into such bewilderingly close contact, that a re-statement of the position in which their respective thinkers stood to one another has become absolutely necessary. We are therefore now in a better position than the human race has been for centuries to form a calm and balanced view as to the meaning of life, but the curious fact stands out that qualitatively we have no new data to guide us. We are still in regard to the problems of the spirit very much where our ancestors were some 2500 years ago. At the risk of repetition I will try to express this more clearly.

The background against which the teaching of Jesus stands out is well recognised as that of a world awaiting judgment. It is true that in the actual teaching of Christ Himself there occur many principles which depend for their exercise upon the continuance of an organised society, *e.g.* the right use of money. It is also clear that the authority of Christ as teacher survived the collapse of the expectation of the speedy end of the world. Nevertheless teaching such as we get in the twenty-sixth chapter of St. Matthew or II Peter took shape after the time of Jesus himself, at a time when many of the surrounding population believed literally that within the lifetime of those who were then active there would be a sudden visitation of judgment, swift and unexpected as a thief in the night, in which the heavens would pass away with a great noise and the elements melt with fervent heat, so that the earth and all its contents would be burned up. The early Christian writer who expresses this, graphically continues: "Seeing then that all these things shall be dissolved, what manner of persons ought ye to be in all holy living and godliness?" It is true that he goes on to say that there is a prospect (according to the divine promise) of the reconstruction of a new heaven and a new earth wherein dwelleth righteousness, but in order to qualify for citizenship in this new commonwealth it is necessary to be found "in peace, without spot, and blameless." Otherwise presumably one will be condemned to destruction along with the earth.

If we compare this with the position to-day, we find that as a race of beings we may expect a much longer run of activity, but it does not seem as though that activity has any more serious significance than a dance of gnats in the sun, "a fuss in the mud,"[1]

[1] So H. G. Wells in *The Undying Fire.*

perhaps not even as much as that, since the end of it
appears likely to be both racial and planetary extinction.
It is all very jolly while it lasts, but what is the
permanent use of it, anyway? The answer to that
question looks surprisingly like that offered to the
human race by the early creative religious philosophers.
By a process of foreshortening we are able to con-
template the spectacle of human history unfolding
itself in the future in much the same way as they did,
and the art of living the life that is worth while turns
out to be precisely as they defined it, namely, as the
habitual subordination of body to spirit, of matter to
value, of concrete achievements to character as
estimated by the divine reckoning.

Let it be clearly understood that this art of living
is not in the least what is commonly called other-
worldliness. Other-worldliness in the ordinary sense
is a coarse travesty of it, in which the individual makes
himself miserable, and abstains from ordinary social
joys in the hope of acquiring merit as a sort of accumulated compound interest in the bank of Heaven. What
we are dealing with is something different. Plainly, if
the researches of astronomy speak truly, ninety per
cent. of what happens all over this planet is of very
little permanent importance, taken by itself. It is
both fussy and futile. Yet life for that reason is not
to be abandoned by all for the career of a contemplative
in a cloister or hermitage: nor is its brevity to be
made an excuse for mourning or licentiousness. Rather
it is to be used as a means to an end, the end being
the maximum production of human character on the
basis of the eternal values. That this is the right

way of regarding life has been perceived not once but many times by the more penetrating intelligences upon this planet. Thus, for example, Ignatius Loyola begins his famous spiritual exercises with the assertion that man was made in order to serve the purpose of Deity: and he continues:

"Man was created to praise, do reverence to, and serve God our Lord . . . . And other things on the face of the earth were created for man's sake, and to help him in the following out of the end for which he was created. Hence it follows that man should make use of creatures so far as they do help him towards his end, and withdraw from them so far as they are a hindrance to him in regard of that end. Wherefore it is necessary to make ourselves detached in regard of all created things—in all that is left to the liberty of our free will . . . . So that we, on our part, should not wish for health rather than sickness, for riches rather than poverty, for honour rather than ignominy, for a long life rather than a short life, and so in all matters, solely desiring and choosing those things which may better lead us to the end for which we were created."[1]

The keyword is the word "detachment." It involves a different conception of the external world from that of the eastern pessimists, in the sense that the latter speak of the external world as illusion. Regarded as an end in itself it *is* illusion, in the sense that it is only a means to an end and a means which has apparently only a temporary existence. Regarded, however, as a means to an end, *i.e.* as a means to the development of personality, and personality of a certain quality or character, it has considerable value of a relative sort, and so long as we preserve in regard to it that proper attitude of detachment which we sometimes express by such a phrase as "sitting loose to one's possessions," so long we are entitled to enjoy the form and colour, the rich intricacy and the complex variety of the pageant of life.

[1] From the translation of Fr. Rickaby, S.J.

If the life of the human race be compared to that of an individual, it does not seem unreasonable that the discovery of the vocation of the race and of the proper relation of the evanescent to the eternal should have taken place at a relatively early period in its history. A boy in his teens usually discovers his objective and then proceeds to train for it, occupying the remainder of his life with the fulfilment of the end for which he seems by birth and training to be fitted. It would be unreasonable to expect a true religious outlook to emerge *late* in the history of the race.

After these introductory observations we are now in a position to go back and take the great creative systems of religious thought in turn, noting the main features in their story, and trying, as we go, to form an estimate of the value and position which should be assigned to each. The Christian religion for obvious reasons must be reserved for treatment by itself in the next volume of the series.

## OF ZOROASTRIANISM

The remoteness of Zarathustra is more apparent than real, for his influence outside his own country, although indirect, was so great that he deserves special attention, while the system of faith and practice deriving from him became the national religion of ancient Persia and still persists in that country amid Moslem surroundings. This religion is referred to by Herodotus, who describes it in some detail, and it is also described by Plutarch: its priests are spoken of in both writers as μάγοι, and we also find references to them in Strabo and in Plato. During the residence of the Jews in Babylon they came under the influence of the Persians, who conquered the country from the Babylonians. It is noticeable that in Matthew ii the travellers from the east are described as μάγοι, and the same term is also applied to Bar-Jeshua the Jew in the island of Cyprus in Acts xiii. The religion of Persia influenced Christianity in more ways then one, while the Arabs and especially Mohammed himself borrowed ideas from it. We are able to some extent to acquaint ourselves at first hand with a modified form of it through the surviving communities, num- bering several thousand, which still exist in Yezd and Kirman, and also in Bombay, where under the name of Parsis they number about a hundred thousand, the latter being descended from Persians who migrated to India in the seventh century in the hope of escaping Moslem persecution. What can we discover about the founder of this faith and his teaching? It is dis- appointing to find that biographical details regarding him are almost non-existent.

In a previous section mention has been made of the existence of so-called Aryan peoples in the middle east who moved southward and finally conquered Mesopo- tamia in the sixth century B.C. Among these must be numbered the people whom we call usually by the name by which they are known in the Hebrew Old Testament and to the Greeks, *i.e.* as Persians, but who in early times came to call themselves Iranians and their territory Iran. The root of this name is obviously the same as Arya, and while indicating the genetic relationship between these people and the conquerors of North India, means essentially "noble" or as we should say "aristocratic." It thus expresses the consciousness of these nomadic invaders that they were in some way or other a ruling race, superior in qualities to the peoples they encountered and endowed with special gifts of leadership. It is curious to note in passing the almost uncanny correctness of this self-denomination. The pure Nordic Aryan, wherever present, tends to rise to the top and to be accepted as the natural ruler, even though in the last resort perhaps he rules himself out.

In the north-west of the territory now called Persia the Iranians first become historically known to us in the kingdom of the people called the Medes. It is true that Iranians are referred to in the Tell el-Amarna tablets (approximately 1375 B.C.) in which dynasties of the Mitanni carry Indo-Germanic names. These Indo-Germans may have remained, in their migration, in the neighbourhood of Syria and Mesopotamia, while their companions of the same stock travelled further east in the direction of the river Oxus. From the time of the Assyrian King Shalmaneser III the latter group become known under the name of the Medes. Sargon II fought against them during the last twenty years of the eighth century, and for a time checked their progress, but about a hundred years later they allied themselves with the Babylonians and brought about the conquest of Nineveh. Another group of the same eastern migration of Iranians bore the name of Persians. These were brought under Median rule by a king known as Phraortes, whose son Kyaxares is a contemporary of Nebuchadnezzar and can therefore easily be dated. Although the coalition which finally conquered the

Babylonian empire and controlled the middle west until its overthrow by Alexander is known in the Old Testament as that of the Medes and Persians, in its impact upon Greece it is spoken of as that of the Persians, from which we may reasonably infer that the latter in the end became its dominant element. The religion of these people seems to have been closely akin to that of the Aryans who invaded North India, *i.e.* a polytheism dominated by the personification of the forces of nature, with special emphasis upon the sky-god and upon the numinous aspects of ceremonial intoxication through the imbibing of a sacred alcoholic liquor, Haoma or Soma.

The Parsis say that Zarathustra lived and taught under a king called Vishtaspa, and they identify the latter with Hystaspes, the father of Darius, and so fix his date somewhere about the middle of the fifth century before Christ; but this identification is very doubtful and it may be that the prophet lived rather earlier. His life has been surrounded with legend and fable, and we do not even know his real name, since that applied to him is a Greek corruption of a Persian word which means "high-priest." Actually the religion which bears his name seems to be a reshaping of the much older nature-cult, closely allied to the ancient Vedic religion of India to which we have referred above, and if Zarathustra be an historical character (as seems certain), he probably played the part of a reformer,[1] purifying what already existed and guiding it in a monotheistic direction. Considerable fragments

[1] Söderblom thinks he championed a pastoral community against the oppressive rule of a warrior caste.

of the sacred literature connected with this reforming movement have been preserved, and were first translated for Europeans by a Frenchman, but of these writings only the five Gathas, or songs, claim to have been composed by the founder. The Gathas are written in very early Persian and closely resemble the Sanskrit hymns of the Rigveda: they comprise some prayers and instructions by Zarathustra himself, a number of isolated sayings, some of them claiming only to be the words of the immediate disciples of the prophet, and two fairly complete chapters on the nature and claims of the Supreme Deity. A considerable mass of writings of a later date follows the Gathas, and the whole corpus is to-day known by the name of the Zendavesta. In the Gathas, if anywhere, we may reasonably look for evidence of the original teaching of the founder. As known to the Greeks and as manifested in its later developments Persian religion appears quite definitely as dualistic, and many scholars in the past have treated it as though it had been so from the beginning. It is now generally held, however, that whatever the views of his contemporaries or successors, Zarathustra himself regarded the ultimate power in the universe (which he called Ahura Mazda), as one and benevolent. We will illustrate this by a few passages from different parts of the Gathas:

(i) "Therefore at the first did I conceive of Thee, O Ahura Mazda! as the one to be adored with the mind in the creation as, the Father of the Good Mind within us, when I beheld Thee with my eyes as the veritable maker of our Righteousness, as the Lord of the actions of life."

(ii) "Where are Thine offerers, O Mazda! Thy helpers, who as the enlightened of the Good Mind are producing the doctrines with wide mental light as inherited treasures, in misfortune and in woe?

I know none other than You; then do Ye save us through Your righteousness."

(iii) "So I conceived of Thee as bountiful, O great Giver, Mazda! when I beheld Thee as supreme in the generation of life; when, as rewarding deeds and words, Thou didst establish evil for the evil, and happy blessings for the good, by Thy virtue, in the creation's final change."

(iv) "He who gives to this (good citizen) that which is better than the good; yes, He who bestows on him in accordance with his religious choice is Ahura Mazda. And this will He bestow through His divine Authority, while on the withholder of the sacrifice He will send worse than the evil, in the last turning of the creation in its course."

(v) "So grant me also, O Thou most bountiful Spirit Mazda, Thou who hast made both the Kine and the waters and the plants, both Immortality and Welfare, those two eternal powers, and through Thy Good Mind in the doctrine."

It appears certain from the above passages that at least in some of his writings Zarathustra decided in favour of a Single Supreme Deity, although he probably accepted the existence of a number of subordinate spirits. Even later Zoroastrianism is not dualistic in the sense of teaching that the powers of good and evil are of equivalent authority and status. The evil power, though possessing the ability to create evil and evil beings, is nevertheless strictly limited and is not omniscient or omnipresent. It is in fact doubtful whether real dualism in the strict sense has ever had any wide popular influence, although it may have been the creed of some philosophers. At any rate as a modified dualism Zoroastrianism spread, and the position of the power of evil in it so much resembles that of the personal devil of popular Christianity that it is hard to believe that they are independent of one another. Moreover this later Persian religion also contemplates the coming of a future rescuer who will destroy the power of evil and establish a permanent commonwealth of righteousness. It is difficult to reject the idea that the particular form of the Jewish messianic hope which so greatly influenced the primitive valuation of the person of the historical Jesus was determined in some measure by these beliefs, just as the belief in good and evil spirits influenced the Jewish idea of angels.[1] In the Gathas is to be found the assertion of a future life and of the immortality of the soul. The idea of judgment presented in these writings is interesting. All the thoughts, words and deeds of the individual, both good and bad, are said to be recorded in a book. This after his death is produced as witness, and if good thoughts and deeds are found predominant in the record, favourable sentence is passed and the soul crosses in safety the bridge of Chinvat and enters paradise. If evil predominates, the soul in attempting to cross will fall off the bridge into a place of torment.[2] If the good and the evil works are evenly balanced, the soul will then be dismissed to a kind of intermediate state, there to await the general judgment which will be held by the great prophet who is to appear and inaugurate the kingdom of goodness. In the earlier literature there is no reference to a bodily resurrection, but this appears in the later writings:

Yasht xix. 10. ff.:—Ahura Mazda made the creatures many and good . . . so that they may restore the world which will thenceforth never grow old and never die, never decaying and never

---

[1] Prof. Langdon of Oxford, however, holds the view that the Jewish doctrine of Satan did not come from Persian but from Babylonian sources.

[2] Representations of this bridge occur even in Christian mediaeval paintings, under Byzantine influence., *e.g.* the famous wallpainting at Chaldon in Surrey.

rotting, ever living and ever increasing and master of its wish, when the dead will rise, when life and immortality will come and the world will be restored at its wish; when the creation will grow deathless, the prosperous creation of the Good Spirit, &c."

Two further extracts may be given from the Gathas. The first, in a prose translation, is of the nature of a prayer:

"May the Creator of Vision teach me his ordinances through Good Thought, that my tongue may have a pathway.

For you I will harness the swiftest steeds, stout and strong, by the prompting of your praise, that ye may come hither, O Mazda, Right and Good Thought. May ye be ready for my help.

With verses that are recognised as those of zeal I will come before you with outstretched hands, before thee, O thou Right, with the worship of the faithful man, before thee with the capacity of Good Thought.

With these prayers I would come and praise you, O Mazda and Right, with actions of Good Thought. If I be master of my own destiny as I will, then will I take thought for the portion of the wise in the same.

Those actions that I shall achieve, and those done aforetime, and those, O Good Thought, that are precious in the sight, the rays of the sun, the bright uprisings of the days, all is for your praise, O Right and Mazda Ahura.

Your praiser, Mazda, will I declare myself and be, so long, O Right, as I have strength and power. May the Creator of the world accomplish through Good Thought its fulfilment and all that most perfectly answers to his will."

The second, in a verse translation, runs:—

"This I ask thee—tell me truly, tell me truly, Holy Lord—
How to worship with a service worthy thee, O King adored.
Teach me Wise One, as the heavenly may the earthly, as to friend
Friend may speak—so may the kindly Right his timely succour
    bring,
And with heaven's Good Thought to usward in his gracious power
    descend.

Tell me duly, tell me truly, as I pray, O Holy King—
When the Highest Life is dawning, at thy Kingdom's opening,
Shall the dooms of heaven's tribunal give to every man his due?
Surely he, the holy prophet, to his watchful soul doth lay
All men's sin, yet ever friendly doth the worlds of life renew.

This I ask thee—tell me truly, tell me duly, as I pray:
Who the Sire from whose begetting Right was on Creation Day?
Who their several paths appointed where the Sun and Stars should
    go?
By whose power is yon moon waxing, by that power again to wane?
These things, Wisest, I am yearning, these and more beside to know.

This I ask thee, Lord of Wisdom—truly make the mystery plain:
Who this world, beneath, above us, safe from falling did sustain,
Nether Earth and vault of Heaven?    Who the Waters hath upborne,
Who the Plant world?    Who yoked swiftness to the clouds and to
    the wind,
Who is he, O Wise Creator, from whose soul Good Thought was born?

Tell me truly as I ask thee—Lord, illuminate my mind:
Light and Darkness, who hath made them? who such wondrous
    skill could find?
Who the hours of sleep and waking hath ordained with wisest skill,
Dawn of day and noon's refreshment, and the late approach of eve,
Set to call the man of knowledge hests of duty to fulfil?[1]

We need hardly concern ourselves in a short outline
with the ritual and ceremonial observances of later
Zoroastrianism, nor even perhaps with the very ancient
and interesting reverence shown to the flame of the
sacred fire.[2] It is the resemblance of the moral and
spiritual teaching of this Iranian religion to that of
traditional Christianity which is so startling, and
which compels us to believe not only that the form

[1] Both these translations are by Prof. J. H. Moulton.

[2] The worship of fire is a very ancient and natural practice among
nomadic peoples.  The mysterious character of flames must have
had a strong "numinous" effect upon primitives, and it is not
surprising that songs and dances of a religious character should
have taken place round camp-fires.
    The Aryans, when first we hear of them, were nomads, and it is
noticeable that in the Vedic period in India there was a sacred
ceremony which involved standing round a fire, casting fuel into it,
and chanting.  This ceremony had been revived in India by the
Arya-Samaj.  Its resemblance to ancient Iranian fire-worship is
more than superficial.  But, of course, it would easily be possible
to multiply instances of ceremonies connected with fire, *e.g.* the
Beltane ceremonies in Britain, and the ritual connected with funeral
pyres.

in which Jesus chose to deliver his teaching was to some extent at any rate indirectly influenced by Persian thought, but that apart from his own teaching the development of the latter by his disciples and their immediate successors was partially determined by current ideas derived from Persia and present in the religious world of thought in the midst of which the Christian faith first began its expansion.

On a general view, the message of Zarathustra is of singular importance, especially if its early date be taken into consideration. Without reading into it any interpretation which may seem to belong to a later period, we have in it a prophetic intuition of a high order. Man's life is a good and precious thing, and each human being, man or woman, is responsible for making the most of it. Life is full of temptations and surrounded by perils, but it is nevertheless inspired by a good purpose. Wisdom personified is Lord of all, creator and judge, and will some time in the future triumph over all opposition and reign supreme, giving to each human soul its just due. The object of human life is to work together with this beneficent deity, and to put one's self entirely at his service in the fight against evil; and his character is declared to be one of truth, social righteousness and justice.

It may safely be said that if we had encountered the above statement without knowing the name of the prophet to whom it referred, we should have almost inevitably pronounced it to be a summary of Christian doctrine, and a rather commonplace one at that. The startling fact remains that it is not only pre-Christian by several centuries, but also as far as we can judge an isolated phenomenon. All authorities agree that the teaching attributed to Zarathustra was only a momentary flash of insight, swallowed up almost immediately in a gross return to the darkness of magic and superstition.

It is probable that Zarathustra's teaching emerged in the midst of a simple pastoral community (he frequently refers to the care of the cattle), and that it is really more naïve and primitive than it sounds when we try to paraphrase it. In any case it had no background of a quality capable of maintaining it in stability: hence it perished as a living belief, and only survived in a fragmentary form because the written records of it somehow came to be regarded as powerful charms.

## OF RELIGION IN INDIA

To write an account of the development of religion in India and the Far East is no easy task for a European of Christian antecedents, since he has very little chance of being able to think himself into the position of an oriental. The attempt, however, must be made if this outline is to be in any sense complete. If the writer seems to show signs of unfair bias, it must be remembered that he has done his best to avoid it.

It is commonly supposed that the systems of the East were developed in such complete isolation from those of the West that there cannot possibly be any analogy between them. It will be well, therefore, to begin by setting forth certain points of contact.

We must first remember that the inhabitants of India and the Far East are genuine instances of civilised man, although their civilisation differs widely

from that of the West. Moreover the data with which
they had to work in constructing a world-view were
substantially the same as ours. Their problems were
our problems. They had to deal with the phenomena
of nature, and with the facts of birth and death,
sickness and pain. Like us they had to face the
struggle for existence and maintain the security of
their food supply. Like ourselves, they felt the desire
to live, and yet like us the sensation that life on the
merely animal level was not capable of satisfying the
restless activity of the human mind. And further,
they felt perhaps more acutely than any other race,
except Africans and Papuans, the apparently ruthless
destructiveness of nature, her plagues, famines,
droughts, floods, and disintegrating hordes of bacteria.
In addition to this we may add, when we speak of
India, the further consideration that, except in the
south, great masses of her middle and upper classes
are similar in race to our own. Both are Aryans and
show traces of their common ancestry.

The comparative study of earlier religious systems
reveals, as we have seen, great similarity between the
modes of approach to the problems of life adopted by
primitive and early civilised human beings nearly all
over the planet. It is in detail that variations occur.
Thus a study of Egyptian, Greek and Roman polytheism followed by a similar study of Hindu polytheism
will reveal many points of resemblance between the
two groups. It is in the details that local variations
will be found to occur. Men sometimes say that the
pessimism of thought in India which led to the development of world-renouncing asceticism is a specially

N

Eastern product, but even this must be regarded as at least doubtful. It is true that a steamy climate and pressure of population have something to do with it, but climate, as we now know, is not a fixed and unalterable thing, not even at the poles. We must, I think, give up the idea that a world-renouncing pessimism is likely to be confined to the Indian peninsula. It may arise anywhere, given suitable conditions. The successful development of natural resources, and the application of science to the construction of labour-saving machinery may for a time stave off its approach, and render people less sensitive to the problems of existence by keeping them amused. But this is only the prolongation of an unstable condition of affairs, made possible by living on capital. Already we see in this country the development of a pessimistic philosophy, and it is surely no accident that the contemplation of the Buddhist outlook on life increased in popularity in Germany after the European war of 1914–18. In studying, therefore, the systems of the East we are actually engaged in comparing notes with the thinkers of other branches of the same human species as ourselves, not because they have arrived at a point of view which we under no circumstances can ever reach, but because they have arrived at a point of view which may some day or other make a serious bid for popularity in our own part of the world, even if it is not already beginning to do so.

There is just this difference. So far as we can discover, the kind of civilisation which we associate with the use of electrical power and the full development of mineral resources (including oil) has no parallel, and therefore to many of us the human race would seem to be entering upon a really new phase in its history. It must, however, be remembered that this phase is almost entirely dependent upon the destruction of natural resources without replacement, pursued at so rapid a rate that it can hardly be of as long duration as some of the preceding agricultural phases. When this spendthrift process is through, what is left of mankind will find itself considerably reduced in numbers, and forced to return to a simpler, and probably more leisurely mode of existence. It may well occur that during the decline of a mechanised and industrialised civilisation men will once again be tempted to revert to the less optimistic views of life which have continuously prevailed over the Eastern continent.

The population of India, which at the last census was recorded as 319,000,000, consists in the main of three groups:

(a) The pre-Dravidians, consisting mostly of primitive tribes of a low culture. It is thought that these formerly extended over the greater part of India. Certainly in the Central Provinces they were much more numerous a century ago than they are to-day. Many of them remind us in physical characteristics of the Australoid peoples.

(b) The Dravidians, who possess a general characteristic culture and finer features than those of the primitive tribes. It is believed that these people came into India somewhere before 2000 B.C., whether by sea or land is uncertain. There is a sufficient number of points of resemblance between the Dravidian and Mediterranean peoples to make it probable that there was an ancient connection between the two, and that perhaps they had a common origin. Of these two divisions the higher castes in South India mostly belong to the latter, the lower castes and the outcasts to the former.

(c) It is generally admitted that there was an invasion of Aryans from the north about 1700 B.C., and that they brought with them their women, and so managed to keep their type pure. It is these people who are responsible for the religious group of ideas which we shall presently describe as Vedic, and for the high-caste Brahmins, especially in North India.

In addition to these, there have been many other local invasions, too numerous to be recounted, including the introduction of Mongolians, Arabs and Scythians, the two former resulting from the Moslem occupation, which has left so deep a mark that some sixty millions of the population recorded themselves at the last census as followers of the Prophet.

With these preliminary remarks let us turn to the story of the development of religion in India.

It is said to divide itself into three early periods, first the primitive or Vedic period extending roughly from 1500–800 B.C., a stretch of 700 years; next what is called the Brahmanical epoch, from 800–500 B.C., a period of 300 years, during which we get degeneration and advance combined; thirdly the philosophical period, roughly from 500–100 B.C. Since then what is called Hinduism (*i.e.* the religion of Hind) has shaped itself in the form of a series of quasi-theistic

cults with a background of monistic pantheism, chiefly
dividing into two classes, connected with the worship of
(1) Vishnu, (2) Siva and his female consort, and modified
by external influences proceeding from Islam and
Christianity.

It is not altogether easy to give details of development of the accuracy of which we can be sure, since
our knowledge of early Indian religion is derived almost
entirely from literature, and although the latter is of
enormous extent, it is almost impossible to date it,
and the Indian mind shows but little interest in history
and biography. Numerically the inhabitants of the
Indian Peninsula outnumber the Anglo-Saxons (even
including the entire population of North America) in
the proportion of three to two, and three-quarters of
these (estimated at about 266 millions) claim to be
Hindus.[1] The importance of Hinduism can therefore
hardly be exaggerated, and it is noticeable that many
Indians who visit the West proudly adhere to what
they feel to be a more spiritual reading of the Universe
than that of many Westerners. At the same time it
is necessary to recognise that a certain not inconsiderable proportion of Indians who receive a Western
scientific education abandon Hinduism, and sink into
a state of agnosticism or of naturalistic atheism.
Indeed those who have a right to express an opinion
say that the religious systems of the East are more on
the side of Christianity in the face of modern
materialism than allies of the latter against it. To a
certain extent this is true, in so far as Hinduism in

[1] In 1901 the population of India was $8\frac{1}{2}$ times that of England
and Wales.

its manifold forms encourages the renunciation of
riches, pleasure, comfort and worldly advancement.
It is assumed, indeed, that the man who is striving
towards a goal beyond this world-order is ready to
sacrifice the world without regret, and throughout
India the assumption is justified surprisingly often.
On the other hand the sort of metaphysical pessimism
which seems to emerge in the writings of some
Westerners who are acquainted with the Universe as
physicists and biologists claim to reveal it, bears a
considerable resemblance to theories of life long since
thought out in India. If that Universe is too vast
and too baffling to be controlled by any mind or
purpose of a nature akin to or conceivable by man,
the Indian would say that this did not surprise him.
He regards the ultimate reality as self-existent, omnipresent and superpersonal, and holds it to be not
merely immanent in all things but actually identical
with all things, so that the soul liberated from illusion
can see that it is one with Him and that nothing else
exists, the Universe being rather the outcome of the
zest of life in the Divine Being, and not necessarily
embodying any rational purpose, simple or complex,
since the Divine Being is neither personal nor moral.
The association of Indian thought with the unfamiliar
oriental titles and terminology of a great polytheistic
religion and culture and with alien philosophical
systems is apt to blind us to the affinities between
Indian thought and that of some persons in the West.
It is now widely recognised that the acute intelligences
of Indians anticipated hundreds of years ago much
philosophical speculation which has only just begun

to formulate itself here.  One reason for this is that the Indian thinkers agree with many of our moderns in their endeavour to avoid dualism, and to construct a monistic philosophy.  Recognising the apparently non-moral character of the forces of nature, they have come to the conclusion that the world-process is devoid of significance and is even a vain thing to be fled from, while the Ultimate Reality is beyond good and evil. All choice in religion must ultimately resolve itself into an acceptance or rejection of ethical values.  The Indian, in common with the scientific pessimist of to-day, seems to regard these values as not guaranteed by the Ultimate Reality, and is therefore in no sense an ally of the Christian optimist.

Thus, as a Scots religious thinker has pointed out:

"There are two kinds of patience, one that of faith in the over-coming power of goodness and of God, the patience in which, as Christ says, we win our souls; the other the patience that looks round wearily upon a world that has no purpose or end.  The first of these two alternative kinds of moral attitude is that of the Christian, the second is that of the Hindu.  Between the two and dividing them from each other lies a whole moral universe.

"Not only is this the attitude of the Hindu; it is, in its essentials, that of many of the outstanding figures in the modern Western world.  A. E. Housman, or Thomas Hardy,[1] (or as a type of a less important group, J. Middleton Murry) differ from one another in their personal reactions towards the conclusions that they reach regarding the worth and significance of life, but their conclusions are closely similar.  In one there may be an element of the old Epicureanism, 'Shoulder the sky, my lad, and drink your ale': in another there is the Stoic spirit of Epictetus or Cleanthes, of 'a bird deprived of wings': in a third there is a sense that the inward division is healed, a sense of inward harmony and of liberation.  Acceptance in each case comes from the necessity of things; 'the freedom of the will,' they might say with Mr. Middleton Murry, 'is an adolescent fiction.'  They might all say also, with the same writer, that God has become 'too vast to be their friend, too intimate to be their enemy.'"

---

[1] Though perhaps not his latest mood.  See his hymns in *The Dynasts*.

He concludes:

"Over against this tide of thought which is setting so strongly across the world alike in India and in the lands of the West we have to set the Christian conviction . . . of the Grace of God . . . of the necessity of the surrender of a free will to the Great Will of good, not the extinction of an imaginary will before the throb of the Universe."

I think we may reasonably set beside the above the following now familiar passage from Mr. Bertrand Russell's *Free Man's Worship*. Here of course the attitude adopted is one not of patience but of defiance.[1]

"Brief and powerless is man's life; on him and all his race the slow sure doom falls pitiless and dark. Blind to good and evil, reckless of destruction, omnipotent matter rolls on its relentless way; for Man, condemned to-day to lose his dearest, to-morrow himself to pass through the gate of darkness, it remains only (1) to cherish, ere yet the blow falls, the lofty thoughts that ennoble his little day; (2) disdaining the coward terrors of the slave of Fate, to worship at the shrine that his own hands have built; (3) undismayed by the empire of chance, to preserve a mind free from the wanton tyranny that rules his outward life; (4) proudly defiant of the irresistible forces that tolerate, for a moment, his knowledge and his condemnation, to sustain alone, a weary but unyielding Atlas, the world that his own ideals have fashioned despite the trampling march of unconscious power."

The first part of such a passage might well have been written by an Indian philosopher, but his remedy for the situation would not have been defiance, so much as the abandonment of the life in which suffering of such a poignant kind was inevitable, in favour of the life of mystical absorption. "Of course," he would say, "birth and marriage and death and all ordinary human

---

[1] This is a marvellously fine attitude, but it is an exacting one to maintain, and one wonders whether Mr. Russell has not since abandoned it first for a more ordinary and less admirable one, and then for "the resignation which is based not on pessimism but on unconquerable hope," the latter of course being approximate to that professed by Christians, even though he may not realise it.

occupations are fraught with misery, but that is because we cling unwisely to that which is really illusion. If we seek blessedness we should abandon all these things and in simplicity and solitude seek to be absorbed into the life of infinite being which is beyond consciousness." Most Western sociologists at present regard with amazement, if not abhorrence, such a solution of human problems. They will be wise to consider the probability that a day is not far distant when an increasing number of them will view it with favour.

The choice so made gets rid of the dualism in finite existence by abandoning what most people call "life," and this has even been done by some Christians, who, unlike their Master, said that the whole of human society was so deeply infected with evil and so utterly corrupt, that Deity had doomed it to destruction, and it was man's business to save himself out of it as quickly as he could. The alternative choice preferred by Jesus Himself involves the admission that perhaps we may not be able completely to unify our conception of the whole of reality at present, and that in some way suffering and evil are necessary concomitants of the world-process. The elements of this choice will be expounded elsewhere,[1] but it is necessary to refer to them here. Obviously it is one which regards ethical value as not subordinated to a temporary and non-moral world-process, but as an essential part of the eternal order of things, and therefore that its emergence in the world-process is not accidental or meaningless, but a true expression of the quality of reality. How this expression is compatible with the existence of

[1] In Volume 6 of the series.

suffering and pain, except in so far as these appear to be the result of what is called "sin," is of course not clear. It seems as though the Ultimate Reality, or Deity, in working towards the perfect realisation of ethical value, chooses to risk the temporary appearance of evil. This may be due to the voluntary self-limitation involved in the creation of finite universe. Anyhow it seems clear that on this reading of the facts, suffering is not confined to living finite beings but is experienced by Deity Himself.

Returning to the main subject of this chapter we may affirm then that the general metaphysical pessimism which we have described is the fundamental basis of Hindu religion. It is sometimes said that the ideas of cosmic retribution, or Karma, and of rebirth and transmigration, or Samsara, are equally characteristic of it, but although this might seem to be the case, actually even these themselves are conditioned by the preceding belief that the whole world of phenomena is simply more or less purposeless energy thrown off by the Supreme Being. The Indian, it has been said, thinks of this world as a circular and unending journey, an ocean without a shore, a shadow play without even a plot. It is but the manifestation of some exuberant force giving expression to itself in joyous movement. Whether human individuals can feel this joy unless they adopt the contemplative life is regarded as questionable. Ordinary life seems to be regarded as inevitably involving suffering, and release is to be sought not as in the case of Christians in the re-making and re-orientation of life, and in the re-direction of activity, but in the withdrawal from any kind of activity and the attainment of an exalted state of absorption which is really not so much a state of consciousness as of unconsciousness or even hypnotic trance.

Hinduism is so hospitable a system that Hindus themselves would reject the above as a fair description of the whole of it, and would quite correctly assert that it makes room for almost every variety of belief and cultus. Thus it chooses to allow its adherents, provided that they observe the customs of the caste system, to hold non-theistic views which regard the Ultimate Reality as simply an association of fixed natural laws of which no explanation is offered: but it also makes room for a measure of theism and for every conceivable variety of polytheism and idolatry. Nevertheless, we must, I think, insist that it is precisely the fundamental conception of the purposelessness of the world-process which makes this hospitality possible; for if there is no *telos* in the universe, then all features in the process have an equal right to be there, and are all equally unimportant. There is a place for the criminal caste as well as for the warrior caste, for the temple prostitute and for the world-renouncing ascetic.

To continue beyond this, and to give as lively as possible a picture of the countless varieties of temple cultus practised by Hindus would be only necessary, if our purpose were to compose a detailed treatise upon the religious life of the peoples of India: but it is not necessary in an outline such as this, since what specially differentiates Hinduism from other religious systems is not its rich and varied types of cultus.

These it shares in common with the polytheistic and polydaemonistic systems all the world over. The distinctive feature of Hinduism is its vagueness. It is impossible to tie it down and to fix it anywhere. Hindus in argument are for ever shifting their ground, and seem incapable of agreeing to any positive doctrine which involves the negation of any other doctrine. This is no injustice to them, for it is simply the logical result of their outlook on life.

To say then that Christ is the crown of Hinduism is not really correct. Hinduism can have no crown, but, as has been truly said,[1] leads towards the abyss. It may be right that we should all go in the direction of the abyss of the unknowable and indefinable, but at least we ought to know that we are going there. I do not think, therefore, that I am disparaging Hinduism in thus describing its ultimate tendency.

(It is true that the comparatively modern development of *bhakti* offers a different kind of goal, or at any rate appears to do so, but to this we will attend presently.)

Sir Charles Eliot declares that as a form of life and thought Hinduism is definite and unmistakable. This does not contradict the assertion of vagueness and lack of consistency to which we have referred, but is due to his recognition of certain broad principles which pervade the whole of Indian religion. The first of these is the conviction that salvation or blessedness is attainable by knowledge of a certain sort. He who in this manner knows Deity attains to Deity, and is even identical with Deity. Ceremonies and

[1] Dr. Otto at the Jerusalem Congress.

ascetic practices may be needful steps in the direction of such knowledge: but he who possesses it stands above them. In the second place, all Hindus lay stress on asceticism, and assume that no one who is in earnest about religion or philosophy will fail to observe chastity and only eat to maintain life. (Most Europeans find it difficult to appreciate the almost habitual vegetarianism of Indians.) No one in India setting himself up to be a teacher stands the slightest chance of gaining a hearing unless he is ready to adopt both these practices.[1] In addition there are two main ideas in which practically all Hindus believe: the first of these is a polytheistic pantheism, the second the idea of a continuous chain of existence, involving an infinitude of re-births conditioned by cause and effect.

This concept of the chain of existence and its idea of retributive justice, or Karma, demands a rather more detailed consideration, since not a few Western thinkers other than the members of the Theosophical Society seem inclined to favour it as an explanation of life and its phases. Let us begin by stating it in as clear terms as we can.

The Indian view is that while the body at death breaks up, there passes on into another equally transitory tenement something which is continuous in being, and which eternally shows itself in perishable forms, but does not perish with them any more than wine

[1] The traditional scheme of life for the Hindu is that of child, student, householder, and finally ascetic. It is the ideal for man to end his days untrammelled by wordly cares, in the contemplation of the Atman, while the ideal leader is always the Mahatma, who has forsaken the married state, or passed beyond it.

when the glass containing it is broken, or fire when it passes from fuel which it has consumed, to envelop a fresh supply. This might suggest that to Indian thought there was no such thing as personal immortality; but fundamental to that thought is the principle of Karma, that is to say that whatever deeds are performed in any particular temporary state of existence determine the conditions of the subsequent state of existence, so that the permanent element, whatever it is, is reborn in that condition which it has earned by reason of the viciousness or virtue of its previous behaviour. Doctrines of transmigration are not confined to India, but the doctrine of Karma is purely Indian. The precise form in which it is held is different in Buddhism from what it is in Hinduism, since Buddhist thought is conditioned by the distinction (to which we shall refer in its proper place) between pure being or *sub*sistence, and being in process or *ex*istence. That which passes on from state to state is not positively recognised as a soul or atman but all that can pass on is the desire for continued existence in process. The object of attaining saintliness in Buddhism is to extinguish this particular desire, and when such extinction is achieved, the chain of births is broken and the elements which combine around that desire as a nucleus are dispersed, so that the individual expression no longer exists, but sinks back into the universe of pure subsistent being. In the Vedanta philosophy, however, the soul is accompanied in its migrations by a subtle body, which, though material, is transparent and invisible, and is a counterpart of the mortal body.

It is evident from the foregoing account that the belief in Karma is bound up not only with the belief in transmigration of souls but also with the belief in the unity of life, so that one can be reborn in a bird or reptile or avatar according to one's deserts. Plainly, as it stands, this must either mean that the individual soul can be imprisoned in the physical integument of a lower animal or promoted to occupy the position of an angel—(in which case the soul is regarded as a separate entity), or else that there are no *souls*, but only *one* soul, the Atman, so that the apparent separateness of the individual is an illusion. Yet if this latter be the case, it is hard to see how the one Atman can acquire merit from itself. Karma seems in spite of itself to pre-suppose a gap between the soul and its Creator, who rewards or punishes it and permits it to acquire character in transit through this world. A further difficulty about accepting the doctrine is that it ignores the factor of heredity. The pre-existence of an individual in some other sphere seems contradicted by the obvious connection between the child and the family tree, not only in physical feature but also in character.

Within the limits, then, indicated above (*i.e.* a polytheistic pantheism coupled with the idea of a continous chain of existence), may be found nearly every variety of belief and practice, including an almost indescribably base cultus of sexuality, and a chaste monotheistic devotion to a personal God, as well as a monistic philosophy.

The stability of this enormous system is considerable, and it seems as though many of the elements in Indian nationalism are actually favourable to its continuance. It must be plain, however, that this continuance is closely connected with the strange inconclusive temperament so characteristic of natives of India. This temperament may be due partly to climate, partly to tradition. It has been accompanied by a great aptitude for abstract thought, displaying itself in a talent for pure mathematics and metaphysical speculation, but also by great indifference to the sufferings of the proletariat, and by a neglect in applying intelligence to the improvement of sanitary, agricultural, and other social conditions. It has not bred a race of rulers, and it has placed India again and again at the mercy of conquerors inspired by more bracing creeds. Indians as a whole are perhaps the most naturally spiritual people in the world, and it cannot be that they should fail in the long run to make a great and influential contribution to the sum total of world religion. Yet at the same time the value of that contribution seems likely to be limited by the peculiar and distinctive conditions under which Indian life is lived. These conditions render it probable for example that the development of Christianity in India will involve an emphasis upon aspects of it which make a less effective appeal to northern Europeans or North Americans, and that ideas that are especially agreeable to the Indian temperament will not easily find acceptance away from the heat-belt and among active and practical Nordic peoples.

The primitive period of Indian religion, though far distant, is of more than mere antiquarian interest. Its deities are for the most part personifications of natural forces and so far resemble those of other early races of mankind, worship being distributed among them impartially. There is, however, a literature connected with this worship which is both considerable and interesting, and which is generally known as that of the Vedas. The first of these is a collection of over one thousand ancient hymns, which have been compared in parts to the Hebrew or Babylonian psalms. This is divided into ten books and the whole collection is known as the Rig-Veda. Another section, called Yajur-Veda, consists of instructions about sacrifice and ritual, and a third, called the Sama-Veda, is a compilation of verses from the hymns, intended to be used by the priests in ceremonies connected with the sacred plant from which the liquid Soma was brewed. The fourth collection, known as the Atharva-Veda, is again a collection of hymns divided into twenty books and some 730 in number. These mostly reflect the popular and magical side of religion and are of the character of charms and incantations.

The poetic value of this literature is considerable, and the deities celebrated in it bear names which show their Aryan origin. Thus Agni the god of fire is obviously the same as the Latin Ignis, and Varuna the god of the sky is obviously the same as the Greek Ouranos, while Dyaus, who also personifies heaven, is the same as Zeus, and Mitra, a solar deity, was worshipped under the name of Mithras in the Roman empire in the early part of the Christian era. Of these deities the most important for the purpose of our survey is Vishnu, who afterwards became one of the most popular objects of cultus in the whole of India. It is probable that the majority of the believers in this early period were polytheists, yet temples and idols do not seem to have been employed, while in some of the hymns there are actual traces of a tendency towards monotheism, and suggestions that the manifold forms in which the One Supreme Being manifested Himself to the sons of men in order that they might understand the richness and full complexity of his being, were only forms and not separate beings possessed of any permanence. Interest in this early Vedic religion has been much stimulated in India during the past fifty years and has led to the development of a special reforming movement known as the Arya-Samaj, the object of which is to stimulate pride among Indians on behalf of their ancient traditions. One specimen of a hymn addressed to Agni may here be given.

O worthy of oblation, Lord of Prospering powers, assume thy robes, and offer this our sacrifice.

Sit, ever to be chosen, as our Priest, most youthful, through our hymns, O Agni, through our heavenly word.

For here a Father for his Son, Kinsman for Kinsman worshippeth, and friend, choice worthy, for his friend.

Here let the foe destroyers sit, Varuna, Mitra, Aryaman like men, upon our sacred grass.

O ancient Herald, be thou glad in this our rite and fellowship; hearken thou well to these our songs.

Whate'er in this perpetual course we sacrifice to God and god, that gift is offered up in thee.

May we be our dear household Lord, Priest, pleasant and choice worthy; may we, with bright fires, be dear to him.

The gods, adored with brilliant fires, have granted precious wealth to us; so, with bright fires, we pray to thee.

And, O Immortal One, so may the eulogies of mortal men
    belong to us and thee alike.
With all thy fires, O Agni, find pleasure in this our sacrifice,
    and this our speech, O Son of strength.

It appears that the more strictly Vedic period,
so-called, shades gradually into the second or Brahmanical period, and that its chief characteristic is the
development of a literature which inculcates punctilious
and elaborate ritual, involving the necessity for a
carefully trained class of person who shall be able
correctly and minutely to carry it out. Such a class,
once it has come into existence, will be likely to acquire
exclusive rights and privileges, and this is the main
though perhaps not the sole explanation of the development of the caste of the Brahmans, which, beginning
originally as an hereditary priesthood, ended by
securing for itself temporal dignity and power of
singular permanence.

The final section of Vedic literature is that which
is known as the Upanishads. These are prose theological writings dealing with the nature of Deity, and
of the cosmic process, and with the proper mode of
living the spiritual life, *i.e.* by means of (1) Tapas or
asceticism (literally the burning up or consuming of the
desires of the body), and (2) Yoga or self-control,
which consists in various practices for inducing higher
states of consciousness through the control of breathing,
the concentration of the eyes, and the posture of the
limbs.

Some of them are late, while others appear to be
very ancient. The meaning of the name appears to
be "that which destroys" *i.e.* that which destroys

ignorance and passion in the soul by the revelation of the Supreme Being.

The following selections may be taken as typical:

(i)

*Liberation into the real Brahma by relinquishment of all desires, mental activity, and self-consciousness.*

*Om*! One should be in a pure place, himself pure (*suci*), abiding in pureness (*sattva*), studying the Real (*sat*), speaking of the Real, meditating upon the Real, sacrificing to the Real. Henceforth, in the real Brahma which longs for the Real, he becomes completely other. So he has the reward (*phala*) of having his fetters cut; becomes void of expectation, freed from fear in regard to others (as fully) as in regard to himself, void of desire. He attains to imperishable, immeasurable happiness, and continues (therein).

Verily, freedom from desire (*niskamatva*) is like the choicest extract from the choicest treasure. For a person who is made up of all desires, who has the marks of determination, conception, and self-conceit, is bound. Hence, in being the opposite of that, he is liberated.

On this point some say: "It is quality (*guna*) which by force of the developing differentiation of Nature (*prakrti*) comes to bind the self with determination (and the like), and that liberation results from the destruction of the fault of determination (and the like)."

(But) it is with the mind, truly, that one sees. It is with the mind that one hears. Desire, conception, doubt, faith, lack of faith, steadfastness, lack of steadfastness, shame, meditation, fear—all this is truly mind.

Borne along and defiled by the stream of Qualities, unsteady, wavering, bewildered, full of desire, distracted, one goes on into the state of self-conceit. In thinking

"This is I" and "That is mine" one binds himself with himself, as does a bird with a snare! Hence a person who has the marks of determination, conception, and self-conceit is bound. Hence, in being the opposite of that, he is liberated. Therefore one should stand free from determination, free from conception, free from self-conceit. This is the mark of liberation (*moksa*). This is the pathway to Brahma here in this world. This is the opening of the door here in this world. By it one will go to the farther shore of this darkness, for therein all desires are contained. On this point they quote:—

> When cease the five
> (Sense-) knowledges, together with the mind,
> And the intellect stirs not—
> That, they say, is the highest course.

## (ii)

### *The unitary world-soul, immanent yet transcendent*

As the one fire has entered the world
And becomes corresponding in form to every form.
So the Inner Soul (*antaratman*) of all things
Is corresponding in form to every form, and yet is outside.

As the one wind has entered the world
And becomes corresponding in form to every form,
So the one Inner Soul of all things
Is corresponding in form to every form, and yet is outside.

As the sun, the eye of the whole world,
Is not sullied by the external faults of the eyes,
So the one Inner Soul of all things
Is not sullied by the evil in the world, being external to it.

*The indescribable bliss of recognising the world-soul in one's own soul*

The Inner Soul (*antaratman*) of all things, the One Controller,
Who makes his one form manifold—
The wise who perceive Him as standing in oneself,
They, and no others, have eternal happiness!

Him who is the Constant among the inconstant, the Intelligent among intelligences,
The One among many, who grants desires—
The wise who perceive Him as standing in oneself,
They, and no others, have eternal peace!

"This is it!"—this they recognise
The highest, indescribable happiness.
How, now, shall I understand "this"?
Does it shine (of itself) or does it shine in reflection?

*The self-luminous light of the world*

The sun shines not there, nor the moon and stars,
These lightnings shine not, much less this (earthly) fire!
After Him, as He shines, doth everything shine,
This whole world is illumined with His light.

### (iii)

Thou art Brahma, and verily thou art Vishnu.
Thou art Rudra.   Thou art Prajapati.
Thou art Agni, Varuna, and Vayu.
Thou art Indra.   Thou art the Moon.
Thou art food.   Thou art Yama.   Thou art the Earth.
Thou art All.   Yea, thou art the unshaken one!

For Nature's sake and for its own
Is existence manifold in thee.
O Lord of all, hail unto thee!
The Soul of all, causing all acts,
Enjoying all, all life art thou!
Lord (*prabhu*) of all pleasure and delight!

Hail unto thee, O Tranquil Soul (*santatman*)!
Yea, hail to thee, most hidden one,
Unthinkable, unlimited,
Beginningless and endless, too!

### (iv)

*The saving knowledge of the one, kindly, immanent*
*supreme God of the universe*

The One who rules over every single source,
In whom this whole world comes together and dissolves,
The Lord (*isana*), the blessing-giver, God (*deva*) adorable—
By revering Him one goes for ever to this peace (*santi*).

He who is the source and origin of the gods,
The ruler of all, Rudra (the Terrible), the great seer,
Who beheld the Golden Germ (Hiranyagarbha) when he
    was born—
May He endow us with clear intellect!

Who is the overlord of the gods,
On whom the worlds do rest,
Who is lord of biped and quadruped here—
To what god will we give reverence with oblations?

More minute than the minute, in the midst of confusion
The Creator of all, of manifold forms,
The One embracer of the universe—
By knowing Him as kindly (*siva*) one attains peace for ever.

He indeed is the protector of the world in time,
The overlord of all, hidden in all things,
With whom the seers of Brahma and the divinities are
    joined in union.
By knowing Him thus, one cuts the cords of death.

By knowing as kindly (*siva*) Him who is hidden in all
    things,
Exceedingly fine, like the cream that is finer than butter,
The One embracer of the universe—
By knowing God (*deva*) one is released from all fetters.

That God, the All-worker, the Great Soul (*mahatman*)
Ever seated in the heart of creatures,
Is framed by the heart, by the thought, by the mind—
They who know That become immortal.

When there is no darkness, then there is no day or night,
Nor being, nor non-being, only the Kindly One (*siva*) alone.
That is the Imperishable.  That (is the) choicest (splendor)
    of Savitri (the Sun).
And from that was primeval Intelligence (*prajna*) created

Not above, not across,
Nor in the middle has one grasped Him.
There is no likeness of Him
Whose name is Great Glory (*mahad yasas*).

His form is not to be beheld.
No one soever sees Him with the eye.
They who thus know Him with heart and mind
As abiding in the heart, become immortal.

(v)

### The imperishable source of all things

That which is invisible, ungraspable, without family,
    without caste (*a-varna*)—
Without sight or hearing is It, without hand or foot,
Eternal, all-pervading, omnipresent, exceedingly subtile;
That is the Imperishable, which the wise perceive as the
    source of beings.

As a spider emits and draws in (its thread),
As herbs arise on the earth,
As the hairs of the head and body from a living person,
So from the Imperishable arises everything here.

By austerity (*tapas*) Brahma becomes built up.
From that food is produced;
From food—life-breath, mind, truth,
The worlds, immortality too in works.

He who is all-knowing, all-wise,
Whose austerity consists of knowledge—
From Him are produced the Brahma here,
(Namely) name and form, and food.

(vi)

### The eternal indestructible soul

The wise one (*i.e.*, the soul, the *atman*, the self) is not born,
    nor dies.
This one has not come from anywhere, has not become
    anyone.
Unborn, constant, eternal, primeval, this one
Is not slain when the body is slain.

If the slayer think to slay,
If the slain think himself slain,
Both these understand not.
This one slays not, nor is slain.

### (vii)

Verily, he is the great, unborn Soul, who is this (person) consisting of knowledge among the senses. In the space within the heart lies the ruler of all, the lord of all, the king of all. He does not become greater by good action nor inferior by bad action. He is the lord of all, the overlord of beings, the protector of beings. He is the separating dam for keeping these worlds apart.

Such a one the Brahmans desire to know by repetition of the Vedas, by sacrifices, by offerings, by penance, by fasting. On knowing him, in truth, one becomes an ascetic (*muni*). Desiring him only as their home, mendicants wander forth.

Verily, because they know this, the ancients desired not offspring, saying: "What shall we do with offspring, we whose is this Soul, this world?" They, verily, rising above the desire for sons and the desire for wealth and the desire for worlds, lived the life of a mendicant. For the desire for sons is the desire for wealth, and the desire for wealth is the desire for worlds; for both these are desires.

That Soul (*Atman*) is not this, it is not that (*neti, neti*). It is unseizable, for it cannot be seized. It is indestructible for it cannot be destroyed. It is unattached, for it does not attach itself. It is unbound. It does not tremble. It is not injured.

Him (who knows this) these two do not overcome— neither the thought "Hence I did wrong," nor the thought "Hence I did right." Verily, he overcomes them both. What he has done and what he has not done do not affect him.

This very (doctrine) has been declared in the verse:—

> This eternal greatness of a Brahman
> Is not increased by deeds (*karman*), nor diminished.
> One should be familiar with it. By knowing it,
> One is not stained by evil action.

Therefore, having this knowledge, having become calm, subdued, quiet, patiently enduring, and collected, one sees the Soul just in the soul. One sees everything as the Soul. Evil does not overcome him; he overcomes all evil. Evil does not burn him; he burns all evil. Free from evil, free from impurity, free from doubt, he becomes a Brahman.

"This is the Brahma-world, O king," said Yajnavalkya. (Janaka said): "I will give you, noble sir, the Videhas and myself also to be your slave."

(Yajnavalkya continued): "This is that great, unborn Soul, who eats the food (which people eat), the giver of good. He finds good who knows this.

"Verily, that great, unborn Soul, undecaying, undying, immortal, fearless, is Brahma. Verily, Brahma is fearless. He who knows this becomes the fearless Brahma."[1]

The documents are a curious medley of quotations, prose discussions, dialogues, hymns and ritual directions. There is little consistency or unity about them, but perhaps some development is traceable in the reference of the World-Ground to Water, then to Space, then to Non-being, Being or the Imperishable. The entire collection has until recently been treated by Indians as having for them as much value and importance as the New Testament has for the Christian, and it has

---

[1] The extracts are from R. E. Hume, *The Thirteen Principal Upanishads.*

been maintained that it contains the germ of many ideas which are familiar to religious philosophers in the west, especially the concept of the Absolute. It is estimated that there are about 250 Upanishads, not all of equal importance; and they have been the subject of many commentaries, of which we will mention as the most important that of Sankara, a Brahman who lived in the south of India about the year 800 A.D. and his school, and that of Ramanuja, about the year 1017 A.D. Sankara's chief work was an elaborate interpretation of teaching concerning the Supreme Being or Brahman which had been previously put together from the Upanishads by a scholar whose date is uncertain, Badarayana. The actual views of Sankara are representative of the purest abstract Hinduism.[1] To him Deity was ineffable, indescribable, and incapable of localisation. He is credited with the famous saying :

"Lord pardon my three sins. I have clothed thee in form who art formless; I have described thee in praise who art ineffable; and in visiting shrines I have ignored thine omnipresence."

Ramanuja tended on the whole to interpret Badarayana's sutras in a theistic sense, and he therefore represents on the theoretical side the strain of theistic devotion which is never wholly absent from sections of Hinduism, while his work is really a protest against the views represented by Sankara. It is probable, however, that the latter represents more truly the main stream of

[1] Yet it must be noted that Prof. Otto has lately concluded that even Sankara is not as antitheistic as has been alleged. This is difficult to follow, for if he was not, why did Ramanuja oppose him in the interests of theism?

tradition, according to which Brahman is the soul of the
universe, the one and only Atman, which pervades all,
in and through whom all things have their being.   What
Brahman is to the universe, the atman, with a small 'a,'
is to the individual human being.   Yet the fundamental
abstract idea which lives and moves in the minds of
multitudes of ordinary Indians is that represented by
the word Advaita or non-duality, expressed in the
curious little phrase, "tat tvam asi," "Thou art that,"
or again "soham," "I am that," or once again the
maxim "The doer and he who causes to do are one," or
fourthly "Atmanam Atmana pasya," "discern the self
by the Self." Atman and atman are one.  It would be
impossible in a work of this kind to expound fully the
whole of the doctrine of the Upanishads, but those who
know India well insist that the intuition of reality here
expressed is fundamental as a controlling influence in
Indian life.  At the same time while it is plain that
there can be no treaty of peace between such a monistic
pantheism and even the most mystical form of Christian
theism, there are signs that the ultimate implications of
this pantheism are being realised by Indian thinkers,
and that they are being led to a modification which may
yet lead to a panentheistic reconciliation between the
two.

Even within the Upanishads there are signs that the
monistic or Vedanta philosophy is not everywhere in
possession, but that the alternative dualistic philosophy
of India called the Samkhya has here and there asserted
itself; though not to the same extent as in the great
classic of the Gita, to which reference shall presently be
made.

Samkhya is in a sense the scientific world-theory of its day. According to its classical teaching there are two ultimates.

(a) Souls which are for ever many and separate (like the primary selves in Dr. McTaggart's well-known system).

(b) Nature or prakriti.

Nature is composed of three ultimate constituents or gunas (*i.e.* strands of a rope). These are lightness, movement, and heaviness, and their corresponding mental qualities, goodness, passion and dulness. In what is indeed the Yoga philosophy there is a kind of controlling God who is a sort of super-soul—not a creator, but a being who aids other souls to their goal; but in classical Samkhya this being is not introduced, and the purpose of the life of each soul is to free itself from prakriti. In the Gita, as we shall see, the idea of the super-soul of Yoga is enlarged to the size of a real controlling Deity—the Lord of the Song.

Other subsequent aspects of Indian religion need equally to be emphasised. Buddhism and Jainism, which will be dealt with rather more fully in succeeding sections, may be regarded as definite developments of the third philosophical period of Hinduism. Jainism has never made many converts, while Buddhism in spite of its wide appeal did not permanently take root in India but swept on, and by and by declined in the face of new popular cults, which are of great importance.

These it is which must next be described.

Their development is obscure and cannot be dated; it is, however, very different from that of earlier Vedic polytheism, in which, as we have seen, worship is more or less impartially distributed among the various gods. The new tendency is sometimes called sectarian, for it tends to select one great God, usually either Vishnu or Siva, upon whom all devotion, lyrical enthusiasm and thought, are centred. "He is" says Sir Charles Eliot, almost God in the European sense; but still Indian deities, though they may have a monopoly of adoration in their own sects, are never entirely similar to Jehovah or Allah. They are at once more mythical, more human, more philosophical, since they are conceived not as creators and rulers external to the world, but as forces manifesting themselves in nature. An exuberant mythology bestows on them monstrous forms, celestial residences, wives and offspring: they make occasional appearances in this world as men and animals; they act under the influence of passions which, if titanic, are but human feelings magnified." The philosopher accommodates them to his system by saying that Vishnu or Siva is the form which Brahman the Supreme Spirit assumes as Lord of the visible universe, a form which is real only in the same sense in which the visible world itself is real.

It is not our purpose to give a detailed account of these great quasi-theistic cults. They constitute, of course, a large part (not the whole) of that popular religion of India which the Moslem invasion and occupation has not been able to suppress. Islam and Hinduism thus exist side by side acting and re-acting upon one another. It is said that in discussions with the representatives of modern theistic religion Hinduism presents itself as being monotheistic, but that for the common people it still appears as polytheism. Some think that southern or Dravidian race-influence is to be seen at work in these later movements and that the result is a fusion of southern polytheism and northern Yoga; and this is certainly a plausible reading of the data.

The educated Hindu declares that the gods worshipped by the common people are merely forms in which the supreme God has at one time or another appeared. Therefore the worshippers of those Gods actually adore in them the supreme and only God. In the same way they say that the idols, whether pillars, statues, or sacred trees which are reverenced by the common people, are only symbols or localisations of the supreme God, who is not really more present in one spot than another, but for convenience sake is thought of as though he were for the time being associated with some particular piece of wood or stone.

Popular Hinduism is a reaction against the frigidity of philosophic pantheism. Many Indians have felt starved by the latter, and have said, like Tulsi Das, "the worship of the impersonal laid no hold upon my heart." They consider that Deity is not only the ground of existence but also one who loves the world, and who, if not exactly philanthropic, is at any rate philo-cosmic. This involves a personal relationship between God and man, and although it may lead ultimately to absorption in Deity, it tries at the same time to regard this merging into Deity as a loving act of surrender. The classical expression of this relationship is to be found in the famous Bhagavadgita or Song of the Highest, a lengthy philosophical poem forming part of the great Indian epic called the Mahabharata.

In it the God Vishnu appears to an Indian king who is about to go into battle, and grants him a revelation of himself in the person of Krishna, the greatest of his incarnations. The poem demands much study, and contains many difficult passages; and it has obviously been revised and enlarged. The following passage may be quoted as typical of its mystical teaching.[1]

## Gita. Eleventh reading. Verses 15 to 46.

15. I see, Lord, in thy body all the Lords of Heaven and diverse hosts of beings, Lord Brahma seated on his lotus-throne, and all the seers and snakes divine.

16. With many arms and bellies and mouths and eyes do I behold thee, on all sides infinite of form; no end in thee, no middle, nor yet beginning do I see, O Universal Lord, O Universal Form.

17. With crown and mace and disc—a mass of glory gleaming on all sides—do I behold thee; hardly may I gaze on thee; as burning fire or sun resplendent round about incomprehensible.

18. Thou art the Imperishable, learning's highest theme; thou art the supreme treasure-house of this universe; thou art the changeless guardian of eternal law; thou art the Person from everlasting—so I deem.

19. With no beginning, middle, or end I see thee; thy might is infinite, thine arms are infinite; the sun and moon thine eyes; thy mouth of kindled fire; with thine own radiance dost thou heat this universe.

20. For by thee alone are these interspaces of heaven and earth pervaded, and all the quarters of the sky; when it beholds this form of thine, marvellous, terrible, shudders the threefold world, O Mighty One.

21. Verily unto thee do those hosts of deities draw near; some in affright laud thee with folded hands; crying 'All Hail.' Great Seers and Perfect Ones in hosts praise thee with hymns of praise abounding.

22. The Spirits of Destruction; and of the Sun, the Radiant Lords, the Spirits of the Sky, all lesser Lords, the Horsemen Twain, the Storm-Lords, and those who quaff the steam, the hosts of the Celestial Choir, of Goblins, of Devils, and of Perfect Ones—all gaze on thee astonished.

---

[1] Translation by J. D. P. Hill of Benares. There is also one by E. J. Thomas (Wisdom of the East Series). The primitive and local character of the poem will be evident from the passage quoted.

23.  Beholding thy great form with many mouths and eyes, with many arms and thighs and feet, with many bellies, a form of terror with many teeth, the worlds do quake, O thou of mighty arm, and I quake too.

24.  For when I see thee touch the sky, with varying hues agleam, with open mouths and wide resplendent eyes, my inner being quakes; nor constancy I find nor quietude, O Vishnu!

25.  And when I see thy mouths inspiring terror with their teeth, like to the fire of Doom, I know not the quarters of the sky nor find I happiness; be gracious, Lord of Heavenly Lords, Home of the universe.

26.  And all those sons of Dhritarastra, together with the hosts of kings, Bhisma and Drona and yon son of the charioteer, and our chief warriors also,

27.  Hasten to enter thy fearful mouths inspiring terror with their teeth; some, caught between the teeth, are seen with heads crushed;

28.  As many river torrents flow to meet the sea, so do these heroes of the world of men enter thy flaming mouths;

29.  As moths in rapid course enter a lighted fire to their destruction, so do the worlds to their destruction enter in rapid course thy mouths.

30.  Thou lickest up all the worlds around, devouring them with flaming mouths; thou fillest the whole universe with thy glory; thy dreadful rays blaze forth, O Vishnu!

31.  Tell me, who art thou of dread form? Reverence to thee, O chief of Heavenly Lords! Be gracious! Thee I desire to know as primal; for thy forthcoming to action I do not understand.

The Blessed Lord said:—

32.  Doom am I, that causes worlds to perish, matured and here come forth to destroy the worlds; even apart from thee not one of the warriors drawn up in ranks opposing shall survive.

33.  Therefore arise, win glory, defeat thy foes, enjoy wide sovereignty! I have already slain these men; be thou no more than a mere left-handed bowman!

34.  Drona and Bhisma and Jayadratha and Karna and other mighty warriors too, when I have slain, slay thou! Tremble not! Fight! Thy rivals shalt thou conquer in the fray.

Samjaya said:—

35.  When he heard this word of Kesava, the wearer of the crown folded his hands and trembled, and did once more obeisance; bowing, he spoke to Krisna, with faltering voice and all afraid.

Arjuna said:—

36.  Meet is it, Hrisikesa, that thy praise should move the universe to joy and love, the Monsters fear and run to every quarter; and all the hosts of Perfect Ones do reverence.

37. And wherefore should they not do reverence to thee, O Mighty One, the First Creator, greater even than Brahma? Infinite Lord of Heavenly Lords, Home of the universe! Thou art the Imperishable, Being, Not-being, That Supreme!

38. Thou art the Primal Lord of Heaven, the Ancient Person; thou of the universe the Treasure-house Supreme; thou art the knower and that which must be known, and the Supreme Abode; by thee O infinite of form, is the universe pervaded.

39. Thou art Vayu, Yama, Agni, Varuna, Sasanka, Prajapati, and the Great-grandsire; reverence, reverence to thee a thousand times, and yet again and again reverence, reverence to thee!

40. Reverence to thee from before and from behind! Reverence to thee from all sides, O All! Of boundless strength art thou and measureless might! Thou fillest all; therefore art thou all!

41. Whatever rude word I have spoken, thinking of thee as comrade, saying O Krisna! or Yadava! or Comrade! not knowing this thy majesty, in negligence or love,

42. And whatever disrespect has been shown to thee by way of jest, whether we played or rested, sat or ate, alone or in sight of men—for all this O Never-falling, I crave pardon of thee who art incomprehensible.

43. Thou art the Father of this world, of all that moves and does not move, thou art to be adored, its Master reverend, there is none equal unto thee; how could there be a greater in the threefold world, O thou whose power knows no rival?

44. Therefore I bow myself and prostrate my body and crave grace of thee, the Lord adorable; as father with his son, as comrade with his comrade, as lover with his beloved, so shouldst thou bear with me O Heavenly Lord!

45. Now have I seen what none has seen before; therefore am I delighted though my heart quakes for fear; show me that other form, O Lord of Heaven; be gracious, Lord of Heavenly Lords, Home of the universe!

46. I wish to see thee even as thou wast, with crown, with mace, with disc in hand; take on once more that four-armed shape, O thousand-armed, O Universal Form![1]

Other instances of this aspect of Indian religion are to be found in the writings of the so-called Bhakti

[1] Principal Cave has shown that until about forty or fifty years ago the Gita was almost forgotten and unknown in India, and that the revival of its influence is largely due to the reaction against Christian propaganda. This of course diminishes our estimate of the worth of Hinduism when left to itself, and leads us to speculate as to the interpretation put upon the Gita at the time it was written. But in any case the poem was a great achievement upon the part of the person or persons who originally composed it.

poets, such for example as Tukaram.   Bhakti means
devotion, and is essentially a fervid emotional attitude
towards Deity.   It is a general term for the devotional
products of that theistic period in Hindu history which
began roughly at a date corresponding to the early
mediaeval period in Europe, and is still going on,
influenced by the impact of Christian thought and
propaganda.   To those who profess it, the doctrine of
Advaita or non-duality does not give room to breathe.
Two or three typical Bhakti poems may here be quoted.

The first is the utterance of Yamunacarya (an immediate
predecessor of Ramanuja), in relation to Vishnu:—

> The vessel of a thousand sins, and plunged
> Deep in the heart of life's outrageous sea
> I seek in thee the refuge of despair;
> In mercy only, Hari, make me thine . . .
> But for Thee I am masterless;  save me
> There's none to earn Thy mercy.   Since our fate
> Weaveth this bond between us, Master mine,
> O guard it well and cast it not away . . .
> Lord Madhara, whatever mine may be,
> Whatever I, is all and wholly Thine.
> What offering can I bring, whose wakened soul
> Seeks all Being bound to Thee for aye?
>
> Trans. L. D. Barnett, *The Heart of India*, p. 42.

The second is a typical poem by Tukaram (seventeenth
century A.D.), born near Poona in 1608:—

> Thee, Lord of pity, I beseech,
> Come speedily and set me free.
> (Yea, when he hears my piteous speech,
> All eager should Narayan be.)
> Lo, in the empty world apart,
> I hearken, waiting thy footfall.
> Vitthae, thou father, mother art!
> Thou must not loiter at my call.
> Thou, thou alone art left to me,
> All else, when weighed, is vanity
> Now Tuka pleads, thy gift of grace complete;
> Now let thine eyes behold thine equal feet.
>
> Trans. N. MacNicol.

The third is a Saivite bhakti hymn, written by an unknown poet:—

> When thou didst make me thou didst know me all:
> But I knew not of thee. 'Twas not till light
> From thee brought understanding of thy ways
> That I could know. But now where'er I sit,
> Or walk, or stand, thou art for ever near.
> Can I forget thee? Thou art mine, and I
> Am only thine. E'en with these eyes I see,
> And with my heart perceive, that thou art come
> To me as lightning from the towering sky.
> If my poor heart but choose the better part,
> And in this path doth worship only God,
> His heart will stoop to thine, will take it up
> And make it his, the heart shall serve for both.

Trans. L. D. Barnett, p. 92.

The fourth is a brief account of the religious experience of Tukaram:—

"Step by step he supports me: my life is led on to perfection. I have found an assured place in him, and the world I have left void. My spirit goes forward on the path. I am filled in the flesh with growing joy. Tuka says, In this mortal world I have joined the pervading spirit."

Other specimens of this type of devotion will be found under the heading of Sikh sacred literature, and in the materials provided at the beginning of Volume 2 in this series (*Religious Experience*).

The difficulty which Westerns must inevitably feel about all this fervour is the uncertainty as to the character of the deity to which devotion is directed, and sometimes the apparent unattractiveness of that character even when defined. Christians feel that they have 'a sure word' on this point, and know what they mean when they speak of God, but that Hindus do not. Thus, for example, some of the Bhakti hymns are directed towards a being who is represented in the form of a most repulsive image to be described as arousing feelings of awe and horror.   Again, some of the devotion which in Europe is expended upon the Madonna is directed, in India, to a divinity of the female sex, it is true, but not a kindly mother, for the terrible goddess Kali is the personification of ruthless and destructive nature.   Or, again, much popular worship, involving little gifts of flowers, rice and so forth, and the crooning of hymns, is bestowed upon Siva, the personification of the principle of life in its richness and zest, and this, as practised in most ages, has involved a certain element of grossness in the cultus.

Some have felt that the deification of sexuality has created a morbid mentality which exercises a baleful influence over millions of Indian citizens, enervating their manhood and rendering them craven and lacking in that courage which is indispensable for self-government.

The cult of Vishnu more easily excites affectionate devotion, because the latter is usually regarded under his name of "the Preserver."   It is modified monotheism and represents the benevolent God as incarnate under a number of different forms, which include fish, tortoise, boar, man-lion, dwarf, all of which are mythical and possibly relics of totemism.   Later incarnations may, however, contain historical elements. Thus Rama and (in certain aspects) Krishna were probably warrior heroes, although their stories have been very much elaborated by the addition of legendary details, so that it is possible that Krishna may have even received into his story elements from tales about Pan or Dionysus.

THE DANCE OF SIVA, OR THE ZEST OF LIFE.

(*See* p. xii.)

Yet in the Gita even Krishna is, as we have seen,
conceived as a monstrous being "with many arms and
bellies and mouths and eyes."

Siva means propitious, and therefore, like the word
Eumenides, is a complimentary title timidly bestowed
upon a dangerous god. He was originally known as
Rudra (? dark-red) and, like his female counterpart
Kali, personifies the destructive force of nature. He is
the man-slayer and the sender of disease, but if he
restrains these activities he can give life and health. It
is thought that the development of these cults may
have been affected by invasions from the north-west
corner of India. However this may be, there is certainly
no little resemblance between Krishna and Siva on the
one hand and Apollo and Dionysus on the other. The
Vedic deities are inclined to be abstractions, but these
later ones are much more of personalities. In no case,
however, (even in that of Vishnu) is the deity of Hindus
a deity of righteousness like the Yahweh of the Hebrew
prophets or the Wise Parent of Christians. Moral
distinctions do not seem to count with It, and there is
no background to life corresponding to that implied for
example in the utterances of Amos. Such a view of
the Supreme Being might of course become prevalent
in the West; and the prospect is enough to make
most of us shudder, in spite of the reassurances of
Mr. Aldous Huxley.

The real development of Bhakti proper belongs to a
period later than the time of Christ, and roughly
corresponding to our middle ages. Thus the specially
known Marathi Bhakti poets, of whom there are said to
have been over a hundred and fifty, seem to have

flourished towards the end of the thirteenth century, specially in connection with Vishnuism.

The protective and benevolent character of Vishnu renders him extremely popular, and it is difficult to be sure how far such popularity is due to Christian influence. Closely connected with the character of Vishnu is the doctrine of Ahimsa or non-injury,[1] which, although primarily connected with the sanctity of animal life, is now expanded into a universal pacifist benevolence. Sir Charles Eliot says of it:

"This beautiful doctrine, the glory of India, if not invented by the Buddha, at least arose in schools which were not Brahmanic, and were related to the Jain and Buddhist movements. It formed no part of the Vedic religion, in which sacrifice often meant butchery."

In Hinduism to-day it meets with extensive even if not universal acceptance.

The Moslem invasion of India belongs properly to another chapter, but it cannot wholly be ignored here, since about 76,000,000 of the population acknowledge Islam as their faith. As early as the year 664 an Arab force made its way into Afghanistan and took Kabul, making many proselytes. Towards 717 the conquest of Sind was carried out, and thence the Arabs advanced and took Multan. By 1030 the western districts of the Punjab were subdued, and in 1206 Kutt-al-Din proclaimed himself sovereign at

[1] No feature of Hinduism has been more widely displayed by Mr. M. K. Gandhi than this doctrine of Ahimsa. It lies at the root of passive non-co-operation which disdains to fight. It links him with the Quakers. It renders him at a distance attractive to many who love the Christianity of St. Francis. But how far is its intensification in him due to his admiration for the life of Christ? And how far is he sincere, how far subtle?

Delhi over the whole of Northern India. During the next hundred and twenty years Moslem power was extended to Southern India. In the fifteenth century Moslem power in India broke up into a number of independent states, but these were re-united into a great Indian Empire by the Moghul Akbar (1556–1605) and his successors. Akbar was tolerant of Hinduism and tried to establish an eclectic religion, including elements drawn from all the faiths which were recognised in his empire. In the main, however, Islam in India has remained pure and rigid, somewhat like Ulster Protestantism in relation to Southern Irish Catholicism. The Moslem buildings of North India are familiar for their austere and beautiful architecture, so expressive of the pure but hard monotheism of their founders. To many they present a pleasing contrast to the gross and often dirty shrines of Hinduism.

Islam has naturally affected Hinduism, and certain results have followed in the form of hybridisation. One of the most important religious teachers in India during the fifteenth century of our era was a Mohammedan weaver called Kabir (exact date uncertain), who attached himself to a Hindu teacher of later Vishnuism called Ramanand, and his disciples. These latter were themselves typical exponents of that Bhakti to which we have already referred. Kabir stands midway between Islam and Hinduism, leaning on the whole in the direction of the latter. He is, as he says, a child of Ram and Allah. "O God, whether Allah or Ram, I live by Thy name." The teaching of Kabir is known as the Kabirpanth, and there are about a million persons who hold themselves to be his direct followers. The writings of Kabir and his friends are full of beauty, and were preserved by a Hindu of Lahore called Nanak (1469–1538), who came under Moslem influence and was greatly attracted by the doctrines of the Kabirpanth. After many years of wandering up and down throughout India Nanak ended by founding a new religion and also a political group, that of the Sikhs, whose customs are so distinctive that the members tend to think of themselves as a separate race. The Sikh faith is a blend of Hinduism and Islam and its adherents number approximately 2,200,000. The founder gave the community a stable organisation under a succession of teachers or gurus, of whom the fourth, Ram Das (1575–1581) erected the celebrated golden temple at Amritsar, and the fifth, Arjun, his son, was the first hereditary guru of the sect, and the compiler of the Sikh scriptures. This literature, which is known as the Granth, comprises hymns, prayers and aphorisms not only by Nanak and his successors, but also by Kabir and his associates, the Vaishnavite Bhakti poets. It is rich and full of mystical beauty, and the whole collection is treated by the Sikhs with the same respect as the Koran in Moslem circles. A few extracts from it are here given.

The first is by Namdev, a disciple of Ramanand:

There is one God of various *manifestations* contained in and filling everything; whithersoever I look there is He.

Maya's variegated picture hath so bewitched *the world*, that few know *God*.

Everything is God, everything is God, there is nothing but God.

One string holdeth hundreds and thousands of beads; God is the warp and woof.

Waves and foam and bubbles cannot be distinct from water.

This illusion, *the world*, is the play of the Supreme God; on reflection *thou shalt* not *find it* different from Him.

Fleeting phantoms, illusions of dreams man deemeth real advantages.

My guru instilled into me right ideas, and when I awoke *to reason* my mind accepted them.

Saith Namdev, behold the creation of God, and reflect on it in thy mind;

In every heart and in all things uninterruptedly there is only the one God.

The next two are by Kabir:

The name of God is my wealth;
I cannot tie it in a knot, or sell it for my livelihood.
The Name is my field, the Name is my garden.
I Thy slave, O *God*, perform Thy service and *seek* Thy protection.

Thy Name is my wealth, Thy Name my capital;
I know none but Thee.
Thy Name is my kindred, Thy Name my brethren,
Thy Name my associates, who will assist me at the last moment.

Saith Kabir, I am a slave to him
Whom *God* keepeth in the world, but *who is* indifferent to it.

\* \* \* \*

If God dwell only in the mosque, to whom belongeth the rest of the country?

They who are called Hindus *say* that God dwelleth in an idol: I see not the truth in either sect.

O *God*, whether Allah or Ram, I live by Thy name,
O Lord, show kindness unto me.

Hari dwelleth in the south, Allah hath His place in the west.

Search in thy heart, search in thy heart of hearts; there is His place and abode.

The Brahmans *yearly* perform twenty-four *fastings* on the eleventh *day of the dark and light halves of the lunar month ;* the Musalmans fast in the month of Ramzan.

The latter put aside eleven months of the year, *and* say that the Treasure is in one alone.

What availeth the Hindus to bathe *at Jagannath* in Urisa (Orissa), what *the Musalmans* to bow their heads in a mosque?

With deception in their hearts they repeat prayers; what availeth them to go on a pilgrimage to Makka?

The men and women Thou hast created, *O God*, are all in Thy form.

Kabir is a child of Ram and Allah, and accepteth all gurus and pirs.

Saith Kabir, hear, O men and women, seek the sanctuary of the one God;

O mortals, only repeat God's name, and then shall you be assuredly saved.

In Kabir's presence a Brahman and a Muhammadan priest were reviling each other's sacred books. The Muhammadan expatiated on the merits of sacrifice.

The remaining three are by Rav Das, another disciple of Ramanand:

God, God, God, God, God, God, God;

By remembering God, saints and sinners are saved.

Through the name of God, Kabir became renowned, and the accounts of his sins of many births were torn up.

Namdev, as in duty bound, gave milk to God to drink;

Wherefore he had not the pain of being born again in the world.

The slave Rav Das is dyed with God's love,
And so, through the favour of the guru, he shall not go
to hell.
They who think not of God shall be condemned.

\*　　\*　　\*　　\*

When there was egoism in me, Thou wert not with me;
now that Thou art with me, there is no egoism.
Huge waves are raised by the wind in the ocean, but
they are only water in water.
O God, what shall I say?　Through illusion things are
not as they are supposed to be.
A king sleepeth on his throne; in a dream he becometh
a beggar;
He suffereth pain at losing his empire, *though* it is intact:
such hath been my condition.
Like the story of the rope and the serpent, I have now
had the secret explained to me.
On *seeing* several bracelets I erroneously supposed *that
they were distinct from the gold ;* but what I then said I
now say no longer.
In all things the one Lord assumeth various shapes;
God sporteth in all hearts.
Saith Rav Das, God is nearer to us than our hands and
feet; it is what taketh place by His will that taketh place.
Rav Das so loves God that he feels he has a claim on
His mercy.

\*　　\*　　\*　　\*

I remember Thee, O God, in my heart; I behold Thee
with mine eyes; I fill mine ears with Thy hymns and
praises;
I make my mind the honey-bee, I put Thy lotus feet
into my heart, and with my tongue I utter Thine ambrosial
name.

May my love for God not decrease!

I have bought it dear in exchange for my soul.

Without the companionship of the saints no love is produced, and without love no service is performed for Thee.

Rav Das offereth one prayer to God—preserve mine honour, O my sovereign Lord.

God's name is for Rav Das equal to all the Hindu oblations.

Jainism is another development from Hinduism. According to the last census the number of Jainas in India amounted to nearly a million and a quarter, and probably a good many escaped being counted. This might seem to indicate that they were not important enough to be mentioned in our outline. They are, however, a people whose influence is out of proportion to their numbers. Their standard of literacy is higher than that of any other community in India except the Parsis (495 males and 50 females per thousand), and their level of morality is also exceedingly high. It is said that one hardly ever hears of a criminal Jain. There seems no doubt that their founder Mahavira was an historical character, and that he was born between 570 and 569 B.C. Legend has been busy in framing marvellous stories of his birth, childhood and initiation. He was a typical Hindu ascetic, who practised mendicancy and self-torture and developed complete indifference to worldly possessions and to pain, while he exhibited the most intense absorption in meditation. For twelve years he wandered about, never staying more than one night in a village, or five nights in a town except during the rainy season, meditating upon the meaning of things and, as the records inform us, free from sin.[1]

In the thirteenth year of his wanderings Mahavira attained to enlightenment, that is to say he saw what he believed to be his great contribution to man's knowledge of the meaning and purpose of life. Brahmanism had declared that birth into a particular caste was all-important. Mahavira, however, said that it was revealed to him that compared with the law of consequences, of cause and effect, called by Indians Karma, birth and caste were of little importance; what mattered most was the destruction of the consequences of Karma. So far it would seem that Gautama and Mahavira were in agreement. It is strange that the two great leaders never met, since their periods of activity overlapped by about thirty-five years. The difference between them lay in the choice of a method whereby to break the chain of cause and effect. Mahavira taught that the proper method was ascetic discipline of the body, and he carried this to so complete a degree that he discarded and taught his followers to discard all clothes. The Buddha quite as definitely rejected the extreme forms of asceticism and declared that he had found a better way, the way of mental discipline, coupled with simplicity and moderation in food and drink. Obviously there is a much greater sanity about the Buddhist scheme than about that of the Jainas, and it is not surprising that the latter have remained a relatively small community. On the other hand, while Buddhism has almost completely died out in India and has made its greatest conquests outside their country,

[1] Margaret Stevenson, *Notes on Modern Jainism*, p. 37.

the Jainas remain apart from the Hindus as a small but quite distinct community, which would seem to shew that there is something about them which has a greater power of persistence. As far as one can judge, the reason is to be found in the greater affinity between Jainism and organised Hinduism than between Hinduism and Buddhism. One expert indeed has said that Jainism represents the theological mean between the two others. Actually it is one of a number of reforming sects which developed in India round about the sixth century A.D. and it seems to be the only one of these sects which has survived quietly and unobtrusively till to-day. It is said that it is more speculative and less enterprising than Buddhism, but that it is also less clerical in its organisation. It protested against the exclusiveness of priests who wished to limit membership of an ascetic community to persons who were born of the Brahman caste. Also, curiously enough, it has come to be the chief exponent of Ahimsa. It would perhaps be fanciful to compare the position of Jainism in India with that of Quakerism in Christendom, yet there are certain features in both which seem to suggest that they belong to the same type of development.

Most striking of all, however, is the curious theory of the relation of the human spirit to the whole of reality which is held by the Jainas. Whether they derive this teaching from Mahavira himself or from the collective thought of his followers cannot, perhaps, be determined, but at any rate the doctrine, whatever its origin, is clear and unmistakable. Jainism regards it as fundamental that there is no power higher than man. This might seem to suggest that the Jainas are atheists, but they are only atheists in the sense that Auguste Comte and his followers were atheists, that is to say, that both direct their reverence and worship towards Humanity, or rather towards a limited number of specially heroic and enlightened individuals who are held to exemplify what Humanity stands for.  In principle this is a form of insistence upon the Divine Immanence, though its special expression may seem to some of us exaggerated. The Jainas call the individuals who are supposed to exemplify humanity Tirthankaras, and say that there are twenty-four of them, the last two being Mahavira and his immediate disciple. These Tirthankaras are defined as persons who have made the passage across the ocean of worldly illusion, and who have reached the further shore where they will be for ever free from action and desire.  Such persons will have entered into a state of passionless and ineffable peace.  It seems that the ultimate reality is thus plurality of souls, no one of which is supreme, though all are perfect.  This pure unfettered spirituality is called by the Jainas "Jiva" and it is probable that except for a certain amount of influence coming in from outside the Jainas do not regard Jiva as involving the complete identity of all souls in one super-soul.  Jiva then may be regarded as the deity of the Jainas, and as a conception of reality it bears a striking resemblance to that put forward by one of the most eminent British philosophers of modern times, Dr. J. E. McTaggart.  That there is much truth in the idea of a commonwealth of souls can scarcely be denied, and it is hardly surprising that thinkers of widely different races and ages have been attracted by

Q

it and have emphasised it. We should, however, beware of regarding it as the whole or final truth.

The history of religion in India since the advent of the British raj has been naturally influenced by the West. At first there was very little Christian propaganda, but as the hold of the British tightened, opportunity for the latter increased. So far as the missionaries themselves were concerned, it was entirely sincere and disinterested, and due to their horror at the obscene monstrosities of Indian polytheistic practice. The officials of the raj, however, avowedly tolerated the missionaries because they thought that their influence would tend to make the natives more submissive to British rule.

During the nineteenth century the growth of Christian work of all kinds was steady, and soon began to produce reactions. Hindus themselves came under its influence in the mission schools, and some of the more enterprising saw the necessity of reforming their native faith. They set about this in two directions. Some of them frankly adopted as much Christianity as they could, while at the same time remaining Hindus. Others took the line that the religion of the Vedas, the pure Aryan faith and practice, had been corrupted in later times, and sought to revive and regenerate Hinduism itself. The great majority of the upper-caste Indians, however, remained conservative.

More recently there has been a tendency to break away from religion altogether. This is due to three causes:—

(1) to the large number of Indians who have been educated under the auspices of the raj in the modern

schools of science and philosophy, and who have thereby been rendered agnostic or secularist.

(2) to the disgust of the younger generation of Indian nationalists at the ceaseless clash between Hindus and Moslems. Better, it says, cut out religion entirely, if it is so potent a source of weakness and disunion. Let us unite India for Swaraj upon a non-religious basis.

(3) to the proletarian propaganda of Russian Communists, who are able to say to the masses: "Look, what good has your national religion ever done for you? It has left you in the mud, and has only fostered the interests of the rich high-caste people."

Indians are so naturally religious that they cannot be happy in the face of such propaganda.

It is becoming increasingly evident that a simple form of Christianity, detached from foreign influence, and from indefensible dogmas about creation and atonement,[1] is what the bulk of Indians in their hearts are seeking. The historical Jesus reigns in the hearts of nearly all Indians who know of him, even when their national pride debars them from openly confessing it. Hinduism is in consequence growing more and more theistic and is repudiating some of its characteristic tenets. The future would seem to lie between a thoroughly Indian form of Christianity and an orientalised secularism: but it will never be easy for the Indian mind to accept the significance of the historical course of events.

[1] I do not mean by this an undogmatic Christianity, but one the dogmas of which are properly defensible, and not those of western fundamentalism; and one which is not burdened with over-definition.

## OF BUDDHISM.

Buddhism is a gigantic development emerging from the religion of India in the third or philosophical period, and essentially adopting an international missionary and propagandist outlook which Hinduism has never equally possessed. It originated in the sixth century B.C., and the extent of its operations, so far as territorial expansion goes, is greater than that of any other world-view except the Christian. It is estimated that in 1920 there were approximately 138,000,000 Buddhists in existence, as compared with 564,000,000 Christians.

The founder, Gautama, whose first name was Siddhartha, was born probably about 483 B.C.,[1] the son of a Hindu of high rank belonging to the Kshatriya or warrior caste. His mother died soon after his birth and his sister took her place and reared him. Like most Hindus he married early and he had one son. At the age of twenty-nine a sense of the futility of ordinary life with its conventional round overtook him. Actually it is said that this was due to his meeting successively on one day an old man, a sick man, a corpse being carried to burial, and an ascetic. He thereupon determined to abandon the married state and to become an ascetic himself. This procedure in a Hindu of some twenty or thirty years his senior would not have been regarded as anything but natural and normal: the unusual feature about Gautama was that he abandoned so early the life of the married householder. He began his new career by practising the extremest forms of austerity, and at

---

[1] The traditional date is 554 B.C.

an age when Christ was entering upon the crucial phase of His ministry, Gautama was still seeking for a solution of his uneasiness, and continued for some time, (according to tradition six years), travelling along what he at length realised was the wrong road.

Finally he and five other ascetics were on their way to the sacred city of Benares, and his companions having left him for a time, Gautama sat under a great pipal or sacred fig tree to meditate.

Suddenly he perceived with perfect clarity the significance of life, and the true and right path for human beings to follow. He rejoined his companions and proceeded to convert them one by one; and so successful was he in his task that he gradually became the revered leader of an enormous Sangha or body of monks, and died a natural death when he was somewhere over eighty years of age.

It is believed that at any rate in 1912 there were actually fewer Buddhists in existence than Hindus, but this is due to the enormous population of India. Buddhism in some form prevails extensively in the extreme north of India, in Tibet, Burma, Ceylon, Siam, Indo-China, China and Japan. It has in recent times attracted interest in Central Europe, and appears to be not unsuccessful in coming to terms with modern culture. In spite of its many varieties, it preserves to nearly as great a degree as Christianity the influence of the personality of its founder. A fair estimate of it by a western Christian is not easy, since the form and expression of its founder's teaching were more markedly determined by contemporary modes of Indian thought than the teachings of the historical Jesus were by

contemporary modes of Jewish thought. In consequence
it is commonly asserted that, in so far as Buddhism is a
religion, it is a religion without a personal god; but this
is only true in the same sense in which it may be said of
some forms of the higher Hinduism that they represent
the ultimate reality as beyond description in those terms
of personality which they reserve for the numerous deities
of the Hindu pantheon. Brahm, though not exactly like
the Greek ἀνάγκη, or necessity, is nevertheless regarded
as indefinable, because personality to these thinkers
involves not only the association with a number of
qualities of doubtful repute such as anger, desire,
jealousy and so on, but also the sense of limitation
involved by the distinction between "myself" and "other
persons." Hence a kind of reverent reluctance to think
of the ultimate reality in terms of personality. It will
be seen that here at the outset is something with which
a large element in modern thought has much sympathy.
Buddhism, however, as it appears in the authentic
teaching of its founder, does not affirm or deny anything
about the personality of Deity. It simply leaves it on
one side as something to be regarded with impartiality,
and only concerns itself with the manifest effects of the
rule of Deity as seen or thought to be seen in the
unerring justice of natural law.

The Buddha has sometimes been compared with
Luther, and Buddhism has been described as a sort
of Protestant reformation of Hinduism. This is a
generalisation which must not be unduly pressed, but
there is a good deal of truth in it. Buddhism like
Protestantism was a great simplification of devotional
practice. It cut away the necessity for an elaborate

temple system, since Gautama insisted that each of his disciples must be "a lamp unto himself"; and theoretically a Buddhist after proper instruction should be able to pursue his course of spiritual progress unaided. It is true that subsequent developments have diverted the system from its primal simplicity, but even so it depends chiefly for its vitality upon a number of individuals banding themselves together to practise exercises which produce a special state of consciousness. There is no Buddhist church in our sense of the word, only the Sangha or monastic community, with lay adherents.

The fundamental basis of the Buddha's teaching is said to consist in the realisation of what are called the Four Noble Truths. These are

(1) The truth concerning suffering.

(2) The truth concerning the cause of suffering.

(3) The truth concerning the removal of suffering.

(4) The truth concerning the way to the removal of suffering.

The sum of these is that existence involves suffering, since existence involves the urge or craving for further existence, conceived as rebirth in the chain of finite being. Suffering is removed by the cessation of existence, and this is achieved by the pursuance of what Buddha described as the eightfold path, consisting of right belief, right decision, right speaking, right action, right living, right striving, right reflection, right meditation.

The question naturally arises as to what is meant by "right." The scheme is as follows: The disciple should believe in the four noble truths and in the impermanence of individual existence and of the elements of which it is composed. This leads to the decision to renounce the world, and to occupy oneself with the highest good, and the next four steps are concerned with the practice of the moral code as enjoined by the Buddha, consisting briefly of the prohibitions of murder, theft, lying, drunkenness and sexual irregularity, with the positive side, involving compassion and mercy to all living creatures (conceived as a passive sentiment rather than in the form of positive acts of goodwill), of liberality, not, however, to the poor but to the ascetic, and of purity, which, as celibacy, is enjoined only upon the monk, the layman being merely forbidden to commit adultery. Lying is taken to include slander and evil-speaking. Right thought consists in self-control and submission, and right meditation in the practice of the spiritual exercises enjoined by the Buddha, which are in effect a common-sense reformation of Hindu yoga.

The final goal in this scheme is the attainment of Nirvana, which is described by a Singalese Buddhist as bliss unspeakable, and by a Siamese as "not consciousness, but ineffable happiness."

It is beyond dispute that the person of Gautama, in spite of the fact that he himself repudiated the idea that his followers should lean upon him or his merits, much less offer him worship, has been elevated almost universally in the Buddhist world to a position in which he is identified with Deity. It is true that a Singalese monk in reply to a question from Professor Pratt as to the existence of Gautama in a spiritual sphere, naïvely

replied: "Buddha finish." Nevertheless the general
attitude of the devout is certainly that prayers and acts
of reverence may be directed towards the symbolical
image of Gautama, not because as a finite individual he
can hear them or be aware of them, but because he
represents in symbolic form our correct attitude
towards the power behind the Universe, so that by
offering him "puja" we are really doing obeisance to
this power, since we are *ipso facto* identifying ourselves
in will and spirit with the correct attitude towards it
which he, the Buddha or fully enlightened one, has
prescribed. It is not to be supposed that the simple-
minded peasant necessarily thinks in this way, but it
seems certain that it is the attitude of the more
sophisticated Buddhists. In either case the conclusion
may be drawn that with the great mass of mankind,
rightly or wrongly, the *direct* worship of the impersonal
or even the superpersonal is an impossibility, and that
for the true and best possible principle of belief and
action to be acceptable to the bulk of human beings it
must be connected with its symbolic embodiment in
an historical personage.

Buddhism has undeniably performed for Eastern
peoples something of the intellectual, moral and
spiritual service which Christianity has done for Europe
and America, though it is a question whether its
essential teaching is really detachable from the
specifically Indian framework of Karma, re-incarnation
and the meaninglessness of history, which the Western
mind finds it so difficult to accept. Its chief tenet
seems to be that life is suffering, and that Gautama
discovered a way to be free from suffering. But what

is this way? Detach it from the peculiar jargon in which Gautama expressed it, and it is very little different from the specifically Christian point of view that happiness is to be found in unselfishness and detachment from bondage to temporal things and temporal interests. The way to acquire this habit of mind is made to consist in the patient practice of what is called "the middle way" or "the eightfold path," which includes the eight correct practices, previously enumerated, and especially the avoidance of extremes.

This latter counsel so strangely resembles the teaching of Aristotle that one group of anthropologists[1] to-day hazards the conjecture that the intellectual influence of Greece extended eastward at a far earlier date than the time of the more obvious Hellenic influences upon northern Buddhism. It is, however, necessary to reflect that Aristotle was a contemporary of Alexander and lived considerably later than the Buddha. If the doctrine of the golden mean was to be found much earlier than Aristotle, then of course it would not be impossible for it to have been derived from the West; but if, on the other hand, its statement in Aristotle is a new feature of Greek ethics, then it is quite possible for it to have travelled in the reverse direction, and it is at least conceivable that it may have come westward through the conquests of Alexander. In any case the doctrine is also found among Chinese thinkers, and may have concurrently developed in a number of different spots.

So far it is not difficult to feel that Gautama was a sort of prophet who inculcated virtues and principles

[1] Messrs. Elliott Smith and Perry, etc.

which are compatible with Christianity. It is when we come to examine the teaching more closely and in greater detail, that we find certain fundamental differences.

The spirit of detachment in Buddhism seems incompatible with the Christian virtue of benevolence, since it belittles human love between persons, even at its best, and has no notion of making the world in which we live a pleasanter and more beautiful place by the application of religious principles to the betterment of social conditions.

Yet if this is true (and it is difficult to deny its truth), the same criticism may be levelled at organised expressions of Christianity existing in past centuries and not by any means extinct to-day. Certain types of unreformed Christianity have frankly refrained from interesting themselves in social reform, and have taught and practised a dual standard of morality, one for the laity and another for the monk, which is of course almost exactly what the Buddhists have done, and for which they have been rather unjustly criticised.

It has also been said that the Buddhist system, in theory at any rate, gives no place to women. But here again it has to be admitted that the Buddha did at any rate before his death come to allow that there might be a place in his scheme for nuns; while it has taken some nineteen hundred years for organised Christianity (and then not the whole of it) to give the full spiritual equality to women which Christ Himself always seems to have approved, and which St. Paul accepted in principle, but was hampered by his inherited Jewish prejudices from embodying in practice.

The most serious criticisms which Buddhism has to face are that it is

(*a*) Pessimistic.

(*b*) Atheistic.

It has been said that the view that it is pessimistic is largely due to the fact that the first popular diffusion of knowledge in Europe about it was due to Schopenhauer! This is partly true, but I think we must allow that Schopenhauer did not merely misrepresent Buddhism, but that he was attracted to it because of certain world-renouncing elements in it which appealed to him and which he therefore emphasised.[1] Christianity is not merely world-renouncing but world-transforming, and the Buddha, in common with other Indians and indeed in company with some Christians, doubts the value of any such transformation. It must be admitted that in the form of an earthly paradise a transformed world seems a somewhat inadequate goal. It is the *metanoia* or transformation of finite minds into the harmonious social existence of the kingdom of God which is really worth achieving; and yet it must also be remembered that so long as God chooses us to be inhabitants of this planet and to occupy it in a state of probation, so long are we bound to express ourselves by the way in which we organise the details of our earthly life. It is difficult to imagine such an institution as a Buddhist Social Union or an Industrial Buddhist Fellowship, except in so far as a certain amount of Japanese Buddhism is copying from Christianity. Buddhism of

[1] He also read it in Deussen's edition of the sacred Books of the East, and extracted congenial portions. The naïve, primitive and uncongenial elements are ignored.

the purer sort cannot on principle be interested in the
details of a world-process which it believes to be
inherently futile and therefore evil.

Reference has already been made to the detached
attitude maintained by Gautama towards Deity. He
certainly believed that the gods and goddesses of the
Hindu pantheon were probably real beings, but only
finite on a larger scale. Above them and round them
was the infinite and inexorable Whole to which all
were subject, both great and small, but like a true
Indian he refused to bind himself as to the nature of
this ultimate Entity. He evaded questioning upon it,
and would not commit himself even as to its existence
or non-existence. But we Westerns use the word
existence in a different way from the Easterns. For
us a thing must either exist or not exist; while the
subtle Indian mind conceives of a third condition of
being which is not non-existence or sheer negativity,
nor existence which is phenomenal, but *subsistence*. It
has been suggested that Buddhism is thus in its pure
form a kind of Asiatic Platonism. Both Deity and the
Buddha, and indeed all souls who have freed themselves
by following the middle path, *subsist* though they do
not exist. They are eternally real and belong to the
world in which there is neither space nor time. The
real Deity is thus manifest to us through the eternal
law which prescribes suffering to those who desire
existence, and Nirvana to those who desire eternal life;
and this Absolute Reality unfailingly rewards those
who seek the latter.

There is much ground, therefore, for regarding the
Buddha not as an atheist, but as equally with Socrates

and Plato a "Christian before Christ," in the sense in which the phrase is used by an early Greek apologist. Yet when this has been granted there is plainly a deep chasm between Gautama and Jesus. The Buddha's teaching of benevolence is far below that of the Christian inculcation of $\dot{\alpha}\gamma\dot{\alpha}\pi\eta$ or active good-will. 1 Cor. xiii has no equivalent in Buddhist literature. The saying attributed to Jesus about hating one's relatives is obviously a poetical exaggeration intended to indicate the utter detachment of the Christian on active service, to be balanced by the fact that Jesus loved passionately all around Him and not least His own mother, and that His self-offering in the fulness of His manhood is the supreme instance of $\dot{\alpha}\gamma\dot{\alpha}\pi\eta$ in His life. For the sake of the multitudes whom He loved He desired to bring in the Kingdom, and He found that He could only do this by giving Himself. Contrast with this the story of Gautama's comment on the behaviour of one of his disciples.

A man, it is said, who had left wife and child in order to become a disciple of Buddha, came in his wanderings to the town where they lived. The woman learned the presence of her husband, betook herself with her child to where he was, and said to him, "See, here is your little son; give me support." The man would not vouchsafe her one look, but kept silence, and remained silent while she put forward her request a second and third time. Finally she laid her child down before the man, saying, "that is your son, nourish him," and went forth. When, however, she looked back after a short time and saw that the man was not even looking at the child, she returned and took the child again with her, saying to herself, "not even his little son matters to him."

The story ends with the remark that the Buddha with his supernatural eye observed the incident and remarked:

"Over your coming he rejoices not, over your departure he grieves not, him whom I see freed from love and desire, him I call a true disciple of the Buddha."

This leaves us with matter for reflection.

In the expansion of Buddhism there are two great divisions. The first of these is called the Hinayana or little vehicle, and its typical home is Ceylon, where, however, it is surrounded with a rich growth of animistic cults. It aims at the preservation of the traditional teaching of the Buddha himself, and its classic literary products are the Sutras or discourses, a few typical extracts from which may here be given.

The position of the sacred literature of Buddhism is not quite the same as that of Christianity, for whereas practically all Christians acknowledge the scriptures of the Old and the New Testament, and a great many also accept the Old Testament Apocrypha, there are four or five authoritative lists of Buddhist writings which do not agree together. In general, however, we may say that the Pali canon which is accepted by the Buddhists of Ceylon, Burma and Siam most closely resembles the Bible of Protestant Christianity, in that it excludes the possibility of further revelation, and only contains the writings which were recognised by the Council of Asoka. This canon, therefore, is definitely Hinayana, and is closed. The Mahayana collections of Buddhist texts, however, are open to unlimited additions, since the very principles of Mahayana involve the possibility that fresh

revelations by new Bodhisatvas may occur from time to
time. Broadly speaking we may say that the Pali
canon is mostly primitive, and the Sanskrit texts are on
the whole later. Very little can be gleaned from the
earlier writings, however, as to the biographies of
Gautama and his companions, for Hindus are not
interested in biography and therefore seldom write
about it. The Pali texts mostly consist of (1) Sutras,
short discourses or sermons or strings of aphorisms, and
(2) the Vinaya or codes of monastic rules. The following extracts will serve to illustrate the nature of this
literature, and the concluding passages will be seen to be
of classic interest as showing the position which
Gautama himself believed that he was meant to occupy
in the movement of his creation.

(A)

Reverence to the Blessed One, the Holy One, the Fully-Enlightened
One.

1. Thus have I heard. The Blessed One was once staying at
Benares, at the hermitage called Migadaya. And there the Blessed
One addressed the company of the five Bhikkhus, and said:

2. "There are two extremes, O Bhikkhus, which the man who
has given up the world ought not to follow—the habitual practice,
on the one hand, of those things whose attraction depends upon
the passions, and especially of sensuality—a low and pagan way
(of seeking satisfaction) unworthy, unprofitable, and fit only for
the worldly-minded—and the habitual practice, on the other hand,
of asceticism (or self-mortification), which is painful, unworthy, and
unprofitable.

3. "There is a middle path, O Bhikkhus, avoiding these two
extremes, discovered by the Tathagata—a path which opens the
eyes, and bestows understanding, which leads to peace of mind,
to the higher wisdom, to enlightenment, to Nirvana!

4. "What is that middle path, O Bhikkhus, avoiding these two
extremes, discovered by the Tathagata—that path which opens the
eyes, and bestows understanding, which leads to peace of mind, to

the higher wisdom, to full enlightenment, to Nirvana? Verily! it is this noble eightfold path; that is to say:

| "Right views; | Right livelihood; |
|---|---|
| Right aspirations; | Right effort; |
| Right speech; | Right mindfulness; and |
| Right conduct; | Right contemplation. |

"This, O Bhikkhus, is that middle path, avoiding these two extremes, discovered by the Tathagata—that path which opens the eyes, and bestows understanding, which leads to peace of mind, to the higher wisdom, to full enlightenment, to Nirvana!

5.  "Now this, O Bhikkhus, is the noble truth concerning suffering.

"Birth is attended with pain, decay is painful, disease is painful, death is painful. Union with the unpleasant is painful, painful is separation from the pleasant; and any craving that is unsatisfied, that too is painful. In brief, the five aggregates which spring from attachment (the conditions of individuality and their cause) are painful.

"This then, O Bhikkhus, is the noble truth concerning suffering.

6.  "Now this, O Bhikkhus, is the noble truth concerning the origin of suffering.

"Verily, it is that thirst (or craving), causing the renewal of existence, accompanied by sensual delight, seeking satisfaction now here, now there—that is to say, the craving for the gratification of the passions, or the craving for (a future) life, or the craving for success (in this present life).

"This then, O Bhikkhus, is the noble truth concerning the origin of suffering.

7.  "Now this, O Bhikkhus, is the noble truth concerning the destruction of suffering.

"Verily, it is the destruction, in which no passion remains, of this very thirst; the laying aside of, the getting rid of, the being free from, the harbouring no longer of this thirst.

"This then, O Bhikkhus, is the noble truth concerning the destruction of suffering.

8.  "Now this, O Bhikkhus, is the noble truth concerning the way which leads to the destruction of sorrow. Verily! it is this noble eightfold path; that is to say:

| "Right views; | Right livelihood; |
|---|---|
| Right aspirations; | Right effort; |
| Right speech; | Right mindfulness; and |
| Right conduct; | Right contemplation. |

"This then, O Bhikkhus, is the noble truth concerning the destruction of sorrow.

9.  "That this was the noble truth concerning sorrow, was not, O Bhikkhus, among the doctrines handed down, but there arose

R

within me the eye (to perceive it), there arose the knowledge (of its nature), there arose the understanding (of its cause), there arose the wisdom (to guide in the path of tranquillity), there arose the light (to dispel darkness from it).

10. "And again, O Bhikkhus, that I should comprehend that this was the noble truth concerning sorrow, though it was not among the doctrines handed down, there arose within me the eye, there arose the knowledge, there arose the understanding, there arose the wisdom, there arose the light.

11. "And again, O Bhikkhus, that I had comprehended that this was the noble truth concerning sorrow, though it was not among the doctrines handed down, there arose within me the eye, there arose the knowledge, there arose the understanding, there arose the wisdom, there arose the light.

12. "That this was the noble truth concerning the origin of sorrow, though it was not among the doctrines handed down, there arose within me the eye; but there arose within me the knowledge, there arose the understanding, there arose the wisdom, there arose the light.

13. "And again, O Bhikkhus, that I should put away the origin of sorrow, though the noble truth concerning it was not among the doctrines handed down, there arose within me the eye, there arose the knowledge, there arose the understanding, there arose the wisdom, there arose the light.

14. "And again, O Bhikkhus, that I had fully put away the origin of sorrow, though the noble truth concerning it was not among the doctrines handed down, there arose within me the eye, there arose the knowledge, there arose the understanding, there arose the wisdom, there arose the light.

15. "That this, O Bhikkhus, was the noble truth concerning the destruction of sorrow, though it was not among the doctrines handed down; but there arose within me the eye, there arose the knowledge, there arose the understanding, there arose the wisdom, there arose the light.

16. "And again, O Bhikkhus, that I should fully realise the destruction of sorrow though the noble truth concerning it was not among the doctrines handed down, there arose within me the eye, there arose the knowledge, there arose the understanding, there arose the wisdom, there arose the light.

17. "And again, O Bhikkhus, that I had fully realised the destruction of sorrow, though the noble truth concerning it was not among the doctrines handed down, there arose within me the eye, there arose the knowledge, there arose the understanding, there arose the wisdom, there arose the light.

18. "That this was the noble truth concerning the way which leads to the destruction of sorrow, was not, O Bhikkhus, among the

doctrines handed down; but there arose within me the eye, there arose the knowledge, there arose the understanding, there arose the wisdom, there arose the light.

19. "And again, O Bhikkhus, that I should become versed in the way which leads to the destruction of sorrow, though the noble truth concerning it was not among the doctrines handed down, there arose within me the eye, there arose the knowledge, there arose the understanding, there arose the wisdom, there arose the light.

20. "And again, O Bhikkhus, that I had become versed in the way which leads to the destruction of sorrow, though the noble truth concerning it was not among the doctrines handed down, there arose within me the eye, there arose the knowledge, there arose the understanding, there arose the wisdom, there arose the light.

21. "So long, O Bhikkhus, as my knowledge and insight were not quite clear, regarding each of these four noble truths in this triple order, in this twelvefold manner—so long was I uncertain whether I had attained to the full insight of that wisdom which is unsurpassed in the heavens or on earth, among the whole race of Samanas and Brahmans, or of gods or men.

22. "But as soon, O Bhikkhus, as my knowledge and insight were quite clear regarding each of these four noble truths, in this triple order, in this twelvefold manner—then did I become certain that I had attained to the full insight of that wisdom which is unsurpassed in the heavens or on earth, among the whole race of Samanas and Brahmans, or of gods or men.

23. "And now this knowledge and this insight has arisen within me. Immovable is the emancipation of my heart. This is my last existence. There will now be no rebirth for me!"

24. Thus spake the Blessed One. The company of the five Bhikkhus, glad at heart, exalted the words of the Blessed One. And when the discourse had been uttered, there arose within the venerable Kondanna the eye of truth, spotless, and without a stain, (and he saw that) whatsoever has an origin, in that is also inherent the necessity of coming to an end.

## (B)

### THE END OF GAUTAMA

Now when the Blessed One had thus entered upon the rainy season, there fell upon him a dire sickness, and sharp pains came upon him, even unto death. But the Blessed One, mindful and self-possessed, bore them without complaint.

Then this thought occurred to the Blessed One, "It would not be right for me to pass away from existence without addressing the disciples, without taking leave of the order. Let me now, by a strong effort of the will, bend this sickness down again, and keep my hold on life till the allotted time be come."

And the Blessed One, by a strong effort of the will, bent that sickness down again, and kept his hold on life till the time fixed upon should come. And the sickness abated upon him.

Now very soon after the Blessed One began to recover; when he had quite got rid of the sickness, he went out from the monastery, and sat down behind the monastery on a seat spread out there. And the venerable Ananda went to the place where the Blessed One was, and saluted him, and took a seat respectfully on one side, and addressed the Blessed One, and said: "I have beheld, Lord, how the Blessed One was in health, and I have beheld how the Blessed One had to suffer. And though at the sight of the sickness of the Blessed One my body became weak as a creeper, and the horizon became dim to me, and my faculties were no longer clear, yet notwithstanding I took some little comfort from the thought that the Blessed One would not pass away from existence until at least he had left instructions as touching the order."

"What, then, Ananda? Does the order expect that of me? I have preached the truth without making any distinction between exoteric and esoteric doctrine; for in respect of the truths, Ananda, the Tathagata has no such things as the closed fist of a teacher, who keeps some things back. Surely, Ananda, should there be any one who harbours the thought, 'It is I who will lead the brotherhood,' or, 'The order is dependent upon me,' it is he who should lay down instructions in any matter concerning the order. Now the Tathagata, Ananda, thinks not that it is he who should lead the brotherhood, or that the order is dependent upon him. Why then should he leave instructions in any matter concerning the order? I too, O Ananda, am now grown old, and full of years, my journey is drawing to its close, I have reached my sum of days, I am turning eighty years of age; and just as a worn-out cart, Ananda, can only with much additional care be made to move along, so, methinks, the body of the Tathagata can only be kept going with much additional care. It is only, Ananda, when the Tathagata, ceasing to attend to any outward thing, or to experience any sensation, becomes plunged in that devout meditation of heart which is concerned with no material object—it is only then that the body of the Tathagata is at ease.

"Therefore, O Ananda, be ye lamps unto yourselves. Be ye a refuge to yourselves. Betake yourselves to no external refuge. Hold fast to the truth as a lamp. Hold fast as a refuge to the truth. Look not for refuge to any one besides yourselves. And how, Ananda, is a brother to be a lamp unto himself, a refuge to himself, betaking himself to no external refuge, holding fast to the truth as a lamp, holding fast as a refuge to the truth, looking not for refuge to any one besides himself?

A BODHISATTVA (CHINESE).

(*See* p. xii.)

"Herein, O Ananda, let a brother, as he dwells in the body, so regard the body that he, being strenuous, thoughtful, and mindful, may, whilst in the world, overcome the grief which arises from bodily craving—while subject to sensations let him continue so to regard the sensations that he, being strenuous, thoughtful, and mindful, may, whilst in the world, overcome the grief which arises from the sensations—and so, also, as he thinks, or reasons, or feels, let him overcome the grief which arises from the craving due to ideas, or to reasoning, or to feeling.

"And whosoever, Ananda, either now or after I am dead, shall be a lamp unto themselves, and a refuge unto themselves, shall betake themselves to no external refuge, but holding fast to the truth as their lamp, and holding fast as their refuge to the truth, shall look not for refuge to any one besides themselves—it is they, Ananda, among my bhikkhus, who shall reach the very topmost Height!—but they must be anxious to learn."

The type of Buddhism which is called the Mahayana or great vehicle is less dependent upon the historical Gautama, and indeed it has been said that it could get on very well without him, since it assumes that the teaching of the middle way is associated with the appearance of a long chain of holy and inspired persons known as Bodhisattvas, of whom Gautama is only one. The development of this great system, which is to be found prevailing over areas as widely apart as Tibet and Japan, is the work of a number of teachers, but also of a vast syncretistic process in which (as for example in Japan), a number of sacred personages wholly unconnected with Buddhism are incorporated within it by being declared to be Bodhisattvas. It represents, in fact, the Buddhist philosophy of life accommodating itself to the polytheisms prevailing in the various countries of its adoption.

The classic literary product of the Mahayana is known as the "Lotus." Its date is unknown, though it is recorded in a catalogue of Chinese sacred Buddhist books between A.D. 265 and 316. It is not an historical but an idealised account of the life of the Buddha, and exhibits much richness of detail and imagery. A short extract giving its concluding passage follows here:

Thereupon the Lord Sakyamuni, the Tathagata, etc., rose from his pulpit, collected the Bodhisattvas, took their right hands with his own right hand, which had become strong by the exercise of magic, and spoke on that occasion as follows: "Into your hands, young men of good family, I transfer and transmit, entrust and deposit this supreme and perfect enlightenment arrived at by me after hundred thousands of myriads of kotis of incalculable Aeons. Ye, young men of good family, do your best that it may grow and spread."

A second time, a third time, the Lord spoke to the host of Bodhisattvas after taking them by the right hands: "Into your hands, young men of good family, I transfer and transmit, entrust and deposit this supreme and perfect enlightenment arrived at by me after hundred thousands of myriads of kotis of incalculable Aeons. Receive it, young men of good family, keep, read, fathom, teach, promulgate, and preach it to all beings. I am not avaricious, young men of good family, nor narrow-minded; I am confident and willing to impart Buddha-knowledge, to impart the knowledge of the Tathagata, the knowledge of the Self-born. I am a bountiful giver, young men of good family, and ye, young men of good family, follow my example; imitate me in liberally showing this knowledge of the Tathagata, and in skilfulness, and preach this Dharmaparyaya to the young men and young ladies of good family who successively shall gather round you. And as to unbelieving persons, rouse them to accept this law. By so doing, young men of good family, you will acquit your debt to the Tathagatas."

So addressed by the Lord Sakyamuni, the Tathagatas, etc., spoke the following words: "We shall do, O Lord, what the Tathagata commands; we shall fulfil the command of all Tathagatas. Let the Lord be at ease as to this, and perfectly quiet." A second time, a third time the entire host of Bodhisattvas spoke in one voice the same words: "Let the Lord be at ease as to this, and perfectly quiet. We shall do, O Lord, what the Tathagata commands us; we shall fulfil the command of all Tathagatas."

Thereupon the Lord Sakyamuni, the Tathagata, etc., dismissed all those Tathagatas, etc., who had come to the gathering from other worlds, and wished them a happy existence, with the words: "May the Tathagatas, etc., live happy." Then he restored the Stupa of precious substances of the Lord Prabhutaratna, the Tathagata, etc., to its place, and wished him also a happy existence.

# LOTUS

Thus spoke the Lord. The incalculable, innumerable Tathagatas, etc., who had come from other worlds and were sitting on their thrones at the foot of jewel trees, as well as Prabhutaratna, the Tathagata, etc., and the whole host of Bodhisattvas headed by Visishtakaritra, the innumerable, incalculable Bodhisattvas, Mahasattvas who had issued from the gaps of the earth, the great disciples, the four classes, the world, including gods, men, demons, and Gandharvas, in ecstasy applauded the words of the Lord.

The striking feature of the "Lotus" is that it identifies the historical Gautama with a special manifestation of the great Purusha. Now Purusha, a term of the current philosophy, denotes a mental concept which is almost identical with that of the Greek Logos. So close is the parallel, that some have found in it a further piece of evidence for the genetic relation between Greek and Eastern thought. "In the metaphysical discussions reported in the Upanishads and in the Vedic hymns behind them, it had acquired a peculiar meaning. In common use it denoted simply man, a human being. But the early thinkers in their search for the Ultimate Reality used it to designate what we call Spirit. Here was the ground of all existence, the fundamental fact of all our consciousness. Thought, feeling, all that passes within us moment by moment, all that makes up what we call our personality, was only possible through its presence within us. That presence was constant, and gave us the power to know ourselves distinct from others, but at the same time it united us with them in a common life which pervaded all things. Purusha dwelt in the heart, unseen, smaller than the small, and yet he transcended the world and was greater than the great. Language failed to define it, for it might be conceived as a point, without parts or dimensions, and yet it was boundless like space. Source of all our mental activity,

it was itself "made of mind." As such it was an
Infinite Person, who needed neither hands nor feet
wherewith to grasp or run, who could see without eyes,
hear without ears, the universal Knower, who yet veiled
himself from recognition save by those who trod the
highest way."[1]

True there are actual differences between Indian and
Greek ideas as to the Incarnation of the Purusha. The
Indian is on the whole more naïve, more picturesque,
more precise in richness of detail than the Greek. The
Purusha when appearing would be identifiable by thirty-
two signs upon his person, among them being wheel-like
disks upon the soles of his feet, giving forth a thousand
rays. Manifestations of the Purusha in the past were
believed to have been twenty-four in number, and the
earlier Buddhism predicted that there would only be one
in the future; but later Buddhist theology as reflected
in the Lotus makes provision for a limitless number of
manifestations of the Purusha, Buddha-to-be, or
Bodhisattvas, sometimes of the male, sometimes of the
female sex. All these constitute a commonwealth of
holy souls which has been not unfitly compared to the
mediaeval conception of the communion of saints, and
has certainly points of resemblance with the Jiva of
Jainism.

The foregoing description of Buddhist principles may
leave a false impression with the reader, if it leads him
to suppose that the four noble truths (with especial
reference to all that the fourth truth implies) are well-
known and acceptable to all Buddhists. It has been
pointed out by observers that they are not nearly so

[1] J. Estlin Carpenter, *Christianity and Buddhism*.

prominent as we might have expected them to be. Whether this is due to the influence of Christian ideas, leading Buddhists to stress the sympathetic and co-operative side of their master's teachings, or whether it is the reaction of human nature against the doctrine of the cultivation of indifference, it is difficult to say. A prominent Singalese monk once declared to Prof. Pratt:[1]

"I have mother and father and sisters but leave them all to themselves and think of myself only and my salvation. I have to think of my own salvation only and not somebody else's. You have mother and father and sisters? Leave them all to themselves and think only of yourself, pay no attention to them. If you get rid of lust, anger, and ignorance you will have happy life. To love your husband or your father very dangerous. If you live pure life without attachments you will be young and good-looking when you will attain eighty or hundred years. If I live good life I will be young and well with no infirmities when I get old."

This seems quite correct as a popular reproduction of the orthodox attitude, and I am informed that there is plenty of it to be found in *e.g.* such a thoroughly Buddhist country as Siam. At the same time there are certain features about Buddhism in practice which render it rather different from what it is in theory.

First, there is often a tendency to distinguish between good desires and bad desires, and to hint that not all desires are bad, and therefore that not all desires need be quenched. Thus a Siamese Buddhist once sought to distinguish between sexual love and love in the sense of

[1] *The Pilgrimage of Buddhism.*

desire for people's true welfare. The former he depreciated, the second he allowed. Christians, however, would demur that on the one hand not *all* sexual love need be bad, while on the other even desire for the welfare of others may lead to suffering and so to the invasion of one's inner citadel by discomfort. In any case the Siamese referred to was contradicted by a friend standing by, who said that love and hate alike must be extinguished.[1]

Second, Buddhism in practice allows a much larger place than theorists commonly suppose to the conceptions of heaven and hell. This again may be due to non-Buddhist influence; but the important rôle it plays in popular belief can scarcely be overestimated.

Third, a fair judgment upon Buddhist thought is much hindered by the wrong translation or definition of terms. Neither "consciousness" nor "extinction" mean what they mean in the terminology of Christians. Consciousness is not to be identified with the being of the noumenal, but with that of the phenomenal self. Existence is not the same as being, but merely "having a position in Samsara, the river of becoming." Extinction in the sense of not being born again does not imply "ceasing to be." This may seem to be so, if reference be made to the simile of the fire which goes out. But as Schrader reminds us,[2] "The common Indian view, since the oldest time, is that an expiring flame does not really go out, but returns into the *primitive pure invisible state* of fire which it had before its appearance as visible fire." (The italics are mine.)

Without necessarily subscribing to this Indian view,

[1] Pratt, *op. cit.*, p. 86.    [2] In his Introduction to the Pâncarâtra.

we may well say that obviously the teaching of the Buddha here assumes the correctness of it, and implies that beside rebirth and non-rebirth there is a term which may be properly used, *i.e.* Pari-Nirvana, which is beyond definition, because we have no categories in which we may adequately express it, but which is certainly not a negative one.

The average effects of Buddhist teaching must be compared, not with the highest results of the teaching of Christ, but with the average effects of the latter as seen in the diffused and diluted sentiments prevalent in so-called Christian countries. Even a comparison on these terms shows a favourable balance on the Christian side, because even nominal adherents have in each case a different background, so that the nominal Christian is *inclined* to be rather more truthful and more altruistic than the nominal Buddhist.

In any case there can be no reasonable doubt that the theory of the good life is in the long run really different in the two systems. The Christian parent or pastor giving himself utterly in vicarious suffering for the welfare and uplifting of children or parishioners is an impossible character in pure Buddhist theory. It may be argued that the correct mode of life for a human being is that which glorifies indifference to others and treats love of one's fellow creatures as dangerous—as we shall see, the Stoics held this view also. But correct or not, it is not the same mode of life as that which says "who is weak and I am not weak? who is caused to stumble and I burn not?" The question we have to ask ourselves is: "which is the better?" Our answer will carry with it a greater measure of theology than we expect.

It would be a serious omission in such a survey as

this not to refer to the important criticisms of the
accepted view of the Buddha and his teaching which
have been set forth lately by Mrs. Rhys-Davids.
Briefly she maintains that the accepted version of
the Way is a perversion of the original, due to a
morbid overgrowth of monastic pessimism.    Primitive
Buddhism according to her was a development of
Indian thought coming approximately in date between
the composition of the sixth and eighth Upanishads,
and distinct from the philosophy of the latter in that
it sought to stress *becoming* rather than *being*.    The
Upanishads said "tat tvam asi," thou *art* that; the
Buddha implied " tat tvam bhavavi," thou *becomest*
that.    Man in fact rightly regarded was not identical
with the Highest, but potentially capable of becoming it.
Mrs. Rhys-Davids maintains that the textual evidence
renders it probable that the concrete Eight-fold way
was not part of the original "New Word" of Gautama,
but an organisation of his teaching due to "revising
Sangha editors."    What then was the "New Word"?
The authoress is convinced, after forty years study,
that it is most clearly contained in a Sutta coming
near the end of the third collection, said to have been
delivered to the five friends, and called " the Discourse
of Turning the Dharma-Wheel."    The gist of this
sermon as she gives it, is that men are mostly inclined
to walk either in the way of self-indulgence or as mere
slaves of external rules and regulations, whereas
Gautama's suggestion is that they should adopt the
middle way between these two, *i.e.* walking according
to the will to be better, and by repeated choices of
the better way, gradually "wayfaring in the way to

the utterly well." Each man is to be captain of his own ship, and steer it for himself. He is not to be priest-ridden, but "a lamp unto himself," working out the best road to the Highest which he by his very nature is becoming, or bound-to-become.

If this reading of the primitive teaching of Gautama be correct, it makes him out to be what Christians would call a Pelagian, *i.e.* one who stresses human capacity to achieve rather than the absolute necessity of Divine grace and man's powerlessness without it. It also makes him to be a teacher of ethics pure and simple, rather than a proclaimer of religion, since it reduces his distinctive authentic teaching to a proclamation of practical method, and leaves his background of doctrine regarding Deity (whatever it was) untouched, and even ignored. So far as Deity is acknowledged it is only in so far as the genius of the Buddha is identified with an expression of the Self-Existent Being. This seems at least to be the way of the Mahayana. Of course, if the will which steers a man to choose to become better be re-described as the Inner Light, then Quakerism can link hands with Gautama, and the latter becomes once again "a Christian before Christ." But the guidance of the Inner Light involves a more passive, or at least submissive attitude than seems implied in Gautama's alleged doctrine of "the will to become." The sense of human dependence upon a Greater-than-self, a "Wider Self" is fundamental to any Christian position, and Christianity claims here to be more radically correct than Buddhism, however primitive. In any case, much must depend upon the verdict which subsequent critical study passes upon Mrs. Rhys-Davids' handling of the Pali texts.

The first phase in the history of Buddhism extends from the death of Gautama to the reign of an important Indian king known as Asoka. The latter ascended the throne in 273 B.C., while the death of the Buddha probably occurred somewhere about the year 400—we cannot fix the chronology nearer than that. Up to the accession of the king the Buddhist movement seems to have been spreading more or less as a school of thought, not greatly to be distinguished from others with which it was contemporary. With the advent of Asoka, however, a profound change ensued. The king himself was a convinced Buddhist, who had himself for a time lived the life of a monk. He inherited large dominions, and extended them during the first ten years of his reign by a series of military operations until finally his empire came to stretch from Afghanistan to the Ganges delta and southwards also to Madras. We cannot discover exactly when Asoka became converted to the tenets of Buddhism, since his own assertion is that for more than two and a half years after his conversion he was simply a lay believer of a rather easy-going type, but that he then joined the Sangha and devoted his energies seriously to the propagation of his beliefs throughout his dominions. The chief evidence which we possess for the beliefs and policy of Asoka is derived from a series of thirty or forty remarkable inscriptions scattered over nearly the whole of India and carved upon rocks or pillars. These inscriptions were inscribed by order of the king, and are either in the form of edicts ordering or prohibiting certain actions as being harmonious with or inimical to the principles of Buddha, or in the form of sermons setting forth those principles for the benefit of his subjects.

Some have seen in these inscriptions an attempt at the popularising of the teaching of Buddha for the multitude, but it seems much more likely that Asoka was making his appeal to the educated, for his edicts and sermons would not have been of any use to the vast multitude of illiterate persons who even to this day abound in India. Actually the inscriptions were probably on the level of the best general culture of Asoka's day and reflect the authentic teaching of Gautama himself. That there is development in the gospel proclaimed by the king may be conceded, but that he knew and sincerely accepted the real teaching of the Master seems quite certain. There is a genuinely primitive emphasis in the edicts.

Asoka declared his sorrow for the bloodshed which stained the earlier part of his reign, and declares his intention of henceforth devoting himself to missionary enterprise on behalf of his new faith. He seems to have been as good as his word, and to have travelled about his dominions not merely in order to visit as a pilgrim the various spots connected with the career of Gautama, but also to introduce the Way into as many different localities as possible, erecting pillars, setting up rock inscriptions, and building monuments. According to tradition he died after reigning about forty years (that is to say about 232 B.C.). His policy had a decisive influence on the movement, because he seems to have been the first person in high position who was not only governed by the thought of the world-wide spread of the teaching, but who also conceived of the spread of the teaching in a practical way.    There is no real parallel between him and Constantine, nor between him and St. Paul, although their influence upon the spread of Christianity led to much the same results as did that of Asoka in the case of Buddhism.[1]

Buddhism to-day occupies an interesting position. In its southern Hinayana form it seems to be in a fairly healthy condition, due, as Pratt thinks, to its "tough-minded" philosophy.    It loses less from naturalism than from Christian propaganda, and it is less vulnerable to the attacks of science than some forms of Christian belief.    It sometimes takes hold where faith in Christianity has ceased, and offers at any rate a way of escape from sorrow and suffering.    Moreover it is practical, and does not depend upon authority.

[1] *Note on the Second Pillar Edict.*    It has been pointed out by Mrs. Rhys-Davids that the edicts of Asoka support her theory that ancient Buddhism was different from the monastic corruption of it, and that Asoka's own version of it is essentially primitive.    She says that the advice given in the Edicts stresses three points: (1), the positive satisfying human worth of the good life in the world; (2), the interesting nearness of the next step, the Beyond in that good life, the bright world awaiting such lives; (3), the all-importance in the good life of the human fact of growing or of becoming.    In the Edicts, which taken all together do not occupy many pages of print, there are some eighty references to Asoka's subjects becoming so and so, to their making to grow, to their making to become this or that in their welfare; and the compound word "Bhava sudhi" she thinks is best translated as salvation by growth or becoming. The good life is never static, it is always a walking in a way.    Thus the Second Pillar Edict runs as follows:

"Dear-to-Devas Piyadasi King thus has said: 'Dhamme is excellent, now how much is dhamme?    Few evil tendencies, many virtuous (deeds), kindness giving truth purity."

He then goes on to speak of his own efforts to reign worthily, and then concludes: "This dhamme-writing was caused to be written that they might walk in accordance and that it might long persist.    And he who will thus ever walk will do good deeds."

Mahayana Buddhism, however, appears to be mori-
bund in many localities, except perhaps in Japan, where
it has copied Christian methods. Thus, although in
Cambodia the Hinayana is strong, across the border in
Annam the Mahayana is nearly extinct—due in part to
French secularist influence, although it is said that it
was nearly defunct when the French arrived.

In China the influence of Buddhism is steadily
declining. In a few places it retains its strength, but in
many localities, *e.g.* round Canton, the temples have
been taken over by the state and turned into schools.
In the lower Yangtse valley it is actually reviving. In
Manchuria it is decrepit. In Shansi it is quietly dying
out. This shrinkage has been going on for a long time,
and Western influence has only accelerated it. In
Corea Buddhism is nearly dead, and is kept alive mainly
by Japanese colonists. In Japan organised Buddhism
seems to have some future. It is developing a new
philosophy, is giving a thorough education to its priests,
and is imitating Christian methods of social service.
All these developments may prolong its life—but for
how long?

## OF THE RELIGION OF CHINA

The Chinese present to the Western thinker a problem
which he has not always been willing to face. Not only
do they constitute an enormous proportion of the
world's population,[1] but their culture is so ancient and
thorough-going that it is probable that when it comes to
be understood it will be found not far inferior to that of
Greece. Of course it is very different, and it has
suffered both petrifaction and deterioration, but the

[1] In 1931, about one-fifth, *i.e.* 438 millions.

Chinese have produced a small number of profound thinkers whose wisdom and character have had an incredibly strong influence upon their nation, so that it has developed certain special features traceable in origin to the men who first taught their importance. To take one or two instances, no nation blessed with vital or even volcanic energy has cultivated such complete control of itself as the Chinese. It is true that this practice of control has its dangers in the form of occasional outbursts of furious temper, but in the main the Chinese nature is extraordinarily tranquil and serene. As human beings they probably rank highest in physical vitality, and it may be that they have not even yet given to the world the full benefit of this endowment; but more important than their vitality is their national practice of poise which has gone on for thousands of years under the encouragement of the wisdom of their philosophers. It has thus become second nature, and it is probable that this natural poise is to a great extent the source of the energy of the nation. Yet to understand why self-control has been taught we have to go back to the theories of the meaning of life set forth by Lao-tzǔ, Kung-fu-tzǔ (Confucius), and other teachers, and these we must approach historically.

The Chinese, although long centuries have unified them into a fairly homogeneous nation, contain a number of different types. Until recently only Neolithic remains had been found, but since the beginning of the twentieth century rich Palaeolithic deposits have come to light, especially in the loess area, and it now seems clear that early man was at least as active in

China as in France[1]. It is not yet possible for us to estimate the real significance of the discovery of alleged sub-human remains at Peking. A considerable Neolithic culture datable at about 2000–1500 B.C. has been found in the north-east and north-west, and in the north-west has been found pottery resembling early specimens unearthed in Babylonia, and dating from before 3500 B.C. This culture is regarded as the eastern expansion of a great prehistoric one which spread from Central Asia to Iran, Syria, and Egypt, long before 4000 B.C. Physically, these early Chinese may have had a more European appearance, but Central Asiatic tribes, Turki, Tungus, Mongols, and Manchu invaded the country at various times and modified the early type, while there are also connections with Siam and Burma.

The influence of Mongolian man has not yet been worked out, and it is not impossible that this species of human being may prove to have had a uniformly disturbing influence upon theistic religion: certainly in his nomad condition he does not seem to have taken very well to Christianity or to have had a very strong sense of a transcendent personal deity, his own natural religion being that of ancestor and spirit-worship conducted through sacred men known as Shamans. It is, however, a mistake sweepingly to assume (as perhaps von Hügel does in one of his essays) that there is a general Mongolian temperament which is hostile to theism, although, as we have seen in the section dealing with Buddhism, some Indian thinkers maintain that the

[1] See Vol. IV, Archives de l'Institute de Pal. Hum, *Le Paléolithique de la Chine*, 1928; Boule. Breuil, Licent, etc.

essential features of pure Buddhism are not at all Indo-Aryan but rather Mongolian, and that this is the reason for the failure of Buddhism to maintain itself in India, and for its success in Tibet and other Mongolian areas. We may doubt, however, whether the Mongolian temperament is in general more hostile than any other to a theistic outlook, while the attacks of the Huns and Turks upon the Christian church were really no worse than those of the early Danes, and are merely a sign of crude and savage barbarism, unless we are to assume, what is by no means certain, that the Danish invasions were looting expeditions led by Nordics, but composed mainly of north Mongolian savages.

Mongolian man divides into three groups, the northern, southern, and oceanic. Of these, the northern comprises the various types of Turk, and a number of peoples such as the Finns, Lapps, Bulgars and Magyars: of all of whom it must be said that they have been greatly modified by intermarriage with northern and western Europeans, of Nordic and Alpine stock.  To this same northern group also belong the various peoples of East Siberia and the Manchus of China.  There is a strong element of northern Mongol in the Japanese and the Korean.  The southern Mongols include the Chinese proper, the Burmese and Siamese, the peoples of French Indo-China, and the various tribes of Tibet and the Himalayas.  The oceanic Mongols include most of the peoples of the East Indies, the Malays and proto-Malays, and, strange to say, the inhabitants of Madagascar.

We know very little about the origin of the civilisation of China but it appears (though not the most ancient) to be the oldest continuous culture in the world. Some think that it came from south-west Asia and point to the resemblances between Akkadian and Chinese words and astronomical systems. These, however, need not imply actual colonisation, but only trading intercourse, either by caravan routes (which are certainly of great antiquity), or by traffic sea-borne from a port called Eridu at the head of the Persian gulf, which was a centre of commerce some four or five thousand years ago.

If we were to make an exhaustive survey of religion in China, we should have to take account of very much which resembles what is to be found in other countries. Thus, for example, we should find the cultus of domestic deities very much resembling that of the Lares and Penates of the Romans[1], and a large survival of more or less primitive nature-worship, which in China is officially known as Taoism, and which does not rise above the level of bargaining with daemons in order to obtain favours from them, and to avert disasters due to their possible malevolence. It is unfortunate that the Taoist system should have adopted Lao-tzŭ and the Taoist philosophers as its patrons, since Taoism as religion has nothing whatever to do with it, and its name is an unlucky choice, for it gives the erroneous impression that the philosophy of Lao-tzŭ is the background of religious belief and practice, and this can hardly be said to be the case. Probably Taoism as religion is a degeneration from an earlier polytheism of a more dignified type, and it is not an insignificant fact that the more orthodox philosophers hardly disputed

[1] This point is made by Warde Fowler, in one of his later essays.

the primitive religious background of earth and sky worship or of the existence of dragons and daemons, though they did not profess to teach about them. It is the so-called heretical philosophers, Wang Ch'ung and Chuang-tzŭ, who ridicule certain aspects of religious belief and practice—and as we shall see, Chu Hsi at a later date attacks image-worship.

Again, the Buddhism of China is not very different from a good deal of Buddhism in other places. Ideas of sacrifice and reverence for departed spirits occur in China just as in other countries. It is rather in the proportion which the various practices observe that the distinctive character of Chinese religion is to be found. Thus by far the largest part of Chinese piety is domestic, and consists in prayers said at home, and in the cultus of revered ancestors.

In the recently discovered records of oracles dating from about 1700 B.C. there appears to be no mention of Deity—only of ancestors. It is also probable that everyone did not have an ancestor, in the sense of a surviving spiritual forbear. Only certain aristocratic (to use our own phraseology "significant") personalities were believed to survive[1]; and in such a world there was perhaps no President, but only a community of ancestors, —a sort of Chinese counterpart to the Jiva of Jainism. But ancestor-worship was then and is now in the main a purely selfish process—all ultimately for the benefit of the living.

It is said that many men and women who would call themselves Buddhists in China never go near a temple.

[1] Cf. the early Egyptian restriction of the Ka to persons of high rank.

Communal, in the sense of congregational, worship is something of which the Chinese have very little conception. Yet primitive Chinese religion had its communal festivals just as Greece had. Individualism in religion seems therefore to be a later growth. So far as there is any real private piety of a personal nature, it is a mixture of Taoism, Confucianism, and Buddhism, with Buddhism as perhaps the strongest spiritual element of the three. An English scholar,[1] who has spent over thirty years in the study of the Chinese people, is of opinion that among the educated classes, while actual atheism is or was exceedingly rare, there is a good deal of scepticism, combined with a sense of awe in the face of the invisible powers of the universe, and that many possess the reverent mind of Confucius, and comfort themselves with the philosophic satisfaction that in doing their duty they are fulfilling their destiny in this life, and making themselves ready thereby for their destiny in a future life, whatever form the latter may take. But this will be felt to be a description which would apply quite as well to many persons in the West, and it is merely an indication of the way in which, beneath a veneer of local and national differences, the processes of the human mind are similar all over the planet. The same observer says that the official religion of China is almost, if not entirely, a material worship for material benefit, a mass of childish superstitions of meagre moral value, degrading to intelligent men and almost devoid of spiritual inspiration. (The above, of course, is a pre-war view).

After this it is not surprising to hear from an educated Christian the statement that the people of China are

[1] W. E. Soothill.

steadily ceasing to regard seriously their old systems of religion and morals. For them there is now little left but the choice between some form of Christian belief and total irreligion. Educated Chinese are quick to criticise the weak points in the presentation of Christianity, and to detect inconsistencies in the lives of those who profess it, but even so they recognise that it is something stronger and greater than anything which they have inherited from even the wisest of their ancestors, and that the best that the latter have been able to give is to be found in Christianity in greater fulness. Western studies are rapidly transforming the outlook of the Chinese student class, and it less and less cares to read the ancient classics of the nation, especially since they are written in a script which it is endeavouring to discard for a new phonetic type; while the books which really interest it are published in England, France and America, and the modern Chinese student can of course read Western print. Nevertheless, the complete abandonment of interest in ancient Chinese wisdom would be regrettable, since its depth and clear-sightedness render it worthy of respect, and it is easy to understand that from a Christian point of view its values and teachings have not unjustly been held to furnish a propaedeutic for the gospel.

The origins of Chinese civilisation are as hard to disinter from the depths of the past as those of any other people. It is true that we have traces of documents believed by some to carry us back to about 2000 B.C., which are embedded in the two famous Chinese classics known respectively as the Shu-King and the Shih-King, the book of history and the book of poetry, and from which attempts have been made to reconstruct some picture of the ancient Chinese. As, however, the epoch in question is roughly some fifteen hundred years, it may be dangerous to conclude that we have really anything more than extremely fragmentary and partial records of so long a period. In general these ancient Chinese appear to have been not unlike the Greeks as depicted in Homer. They had wives and also concubines, they preferred sons before daughters, they hunted and fished, they tilled the soil, they fought, and were organised under a sort of feudal system, if we may borrow a term from the West. Their religious world was pluralistic. There were spirits of heaven and of earth, spirits of departed ancestors, and daemons of storm and drought. Ancestor worship was already practised, and there were spirits of hills and rivers. Supreme honour seems to have been given to a mysterious entity called Shang-ti, and there is also reference to T'ien. It is very difficult to know what is meant by this Being. Some would suggest that T'ien simply means the bright sky, the azure heaven. Others think that it means supreme ruler. The sovereign alone worships Shang-ti. Other men venerate the inferior spirits.

There has been no small controversy about the Christian adoption of the term Shang-ti to translate the Christian God. It has been said that the term indicates a particular deity, and that it is rather as though St. Paul, in preaching the one true God, had called him "Zeus." Hence in the seventeenth century the Dominicans and Franciscans persuaded the Pope to decree (in spite of Jesuit opposition) that Roman Catholic missions should

use an entirely different term, T'ien-Chu, as an appella-
tion for God. This term was supposed to be free from
heathen taint, although as a matter of fact it was really
the name of an inferior Chinese deity. To-day there is
a return in certain quarters to the use of the word
Shang-ti, and there seems considerable justification for
its employment. Shang-ti is certainly described in the
book of history as though he were the supreme personal
god, although in the book of poetry Shang-ti is frequently
identified with the visible heaven, or at least referred to
in terms which are applicable only to the sky.

Can we discover during the long period covered by
the documents any development of ideas? Strange to
say the only one of any importance is the gradual
depersonalisation of Shang-ti, which is exactly the
opposite of what we should expect. Chinese thought
develops in the direction of philosophy and ethics, but
Chinese religious practice remains most of the time on
a typical polydaemonistic level.

The origin and development of this philosophical
movement requires us to make a further brief historical
survey. Whereas between the actual Chinese and their
neighbours to the south there was from the earliest
times racial intercommunication, between them and
their neighbours to the north and west, the nomads of
Central Asia, there was generally hostility, and whenever we find an admixture of racial elements from this
direction it has invariably taken place as the result of
warlike invasion. To this very day there is a substantial difference between the north and south, and it does
not seem easy for the two halves of China to work
together, even though they were long united, prior to

the revolution, under a single government. Differences
of climate and of physical geography combine to
accentuate this difference. The common tie which
unites the Chinese, therefore, is their national culture or
rather its spiritual aspect. China has often been
conquered, but this special and distinctive ordering of
life has remained constant, and amidst eras of political
weakness and disintegration it has gone on maintaining
itself steadily. It is therefore important to understand
how this culture of theirs came to take shape.

It appears that the stable development of Chinese
civilisation derives from the early population (whatever
its composition) settled in the valleys of the Huang-ho
and the Wei-ho. From these river valleys the population spread north, south and east, reaching the sea, the
important Yang-tse valley and even further south, but
not the mountainous west. The sea at first does not
seem to have attracted them, and for long they remained
ignorant of the Japanese islands. Later legends
ascribe the developments of early culture to mythical
emperors, of whom five are named, somewhat resembling
the seven kings of early Rome. The classical literature
of a later date speaks of a golden age, that of the
Emperors Yao, Shun, and Yü, but of the real historical
personages we know next to nothing, except perhaps
that under Yü China became divided into nine
provinces. The main point about these early rulers is
that they were not hereditary, but were religious
functionaries selected for the worthiness of their
characters, and their duties were in consequence
religious rather than administrative. The importance
of this is seen in the remarkable ceremonies connected

with the white marble Altar of Heaven at Peking, which were exclusively performed once a year by the emperor himself, and which, although discontinued for a time after the revolution, and in any case not quite compatible with Protestantism (though they might have been somehow preserved by a Catholic emperor) are a standing and mysterious testimony, as some will hold, to the prevalence in early China of the worship of a "high god." Whether this high god who was worshipped under the open heaven was regarded as the sole deity, or merely as a sky-god presiding over a populous pantheon of lesser spiritual beings is uncertain. At any rate the religious character of the imperial office in these early times overshadowed the political. The ruler was no despot, but controlled by certain sacred duties and by the moral law, responsible alike to Heaven and to his subjects. Heaven, emperor and people thus stood in an ordered relationship. In process of time, however, the imperial office became hereditary. The first three dynasties of Hsia, Shang and Chou are to a great extent legendary, but during the Chou dynasty history begins to be somewhat clearer, though its political details do not here concern us. With the beginning of the eighth century China appears less as a centralised empire and more as an aggregate of great fiefs. The emperor was less the absolute ruler than the head of a league of princes, whose members maintained themselves to a greater or lesser degree in positions of independence. Theoretically there was no private property in land, since all the land was the absolute possession of the emperor, by whom it was parcelled out to individual families for cultivation. In practice the usufruct passed from father to son, so that a sort of rule of inheritance sprang up. The family appears to have been the smallest unit in this agricultural system. The individual had no special rights, and his life was subservient to the needs of the community. In the division of the land among the subjects of the emperor a certain area was always reserved as state property, and thus arose the nine-field system, in which eight families, each having its own small-holding, were grouped together, and cultivated the ninth plot in common, the latter containing the well which gave them their common water supply, and the produce of which was paid to the state as revenue. As each family was the unit, the male head of the family was of paramount importance, since through him the unit derived its continuance. To him, therefore, the highest respect was due, and filial piety has in consequence ever been the outstanding feature in Chinese ethics, and the main source of the stability of Chinese culture.

Such in outline was the political and social condition of China at the time when Lao-tzŭ and Confucius were born, in the years 605 and 551 B.C. Their homes were in the feudal provinces of Chu and Lu respectively. Lu comprises a small corner of what is to-day the province of Shantung, which at that time was not by any means one of the more important feudal states, so that its princes were in no great degree immersed in the political rivalries of the period. Indeed the teaching of these masters was so contrary to the spirit of the time, which was concerned with the struggles of the individual feudal war-lords to obtain in turn the mastery, that, although it was intended to bring about a regeneration of the life of the state, it had at the time almost no results. Nevertheless, for the future development of the Chinese character it was of the very greatest importance, and indeed it may truly be said that in an age in which the central government of China was almost as ineffective as it is to-day, and in which the peace of China was almost as much disturbed as it is now by the selfish rivalries of local military leaders, the real foundations of the subsequent spiritual life of the country were being remade by the two great teachers Lao-tzŭ and Kung-fu-tzŭ (Confucius). Neither of these two men lived to see peace and unity established in his afflicted country, but after a series of bitter civil wars a new dynasty, associated with the prince of Ch'in, came to the fore as the holder of paramount military power among feudal lords. One of these Ch'in rulers, Chao-hsiang, in the year 255 B.C. overthrew the ineffective emperor and so brought to an end the Chou dynasty, which had been in occupation since the year 1122 B.C. A nephew of this prince, Shih-huang-ti, in the year 246 assumed the rule of the province of Ch'in, and after a vigorous campaign finally in the year 221 seized the empty imperial throne and proclaimed himself the first emperor of the new Ch'in dynasty. The importance of this change can hardly be exaggerated. The new emperor was a genuine and very able Asiatic autocrat. He abolished the feudal system, converted China from a federal to a centralised state and with an iron fist saved China from disintegration and gave her a well organised provincial government. The great wall of China was completed to protect the north against invasion, and the imperial power was extended over the whole of the actual area of what is China to-day.

One curious feature of the policy of this indefatigable ruler was his determination to sweep away all previous traditions. The extermination of everything that had gone before appeared to him as a necessary step in the promotion of his reforms, and he therefore gave order for the destruction of all literature which might possibly contain the expression of principles contrary to the new system. His hatred directed itself especially against the teaching of Confucius, which, in its respect for tradition and its adherence to the historical standpoint, stood in the sharpest opposition to the intentions of the emperor. Accordingly in the year 213 he ordered an essential part of the old literature of the Chinese people to be burned. The enmity of the emperor did not, however, extend to the followers of Lao-tzŭ, since the doctrines of the latter appeared to lay less stress upon tradition. Confucius, it seems, had given utterance not merely to his own opinions but to the characteristic principles long cherished in the family life of the Chinese people. "From Yao went the tradition to Shun, from Shun to Yü, from Yü to T'ang, from T'ang to Wên, Wu and Chou-kung, from Wên, Wu, and Chou-kung to Kung-fu-tzŭ, from Kung-fu-tzŭ to Mêng-tzŭ; but when Mêng-tzŭ died, the tradition went no further." So wrote a Chinese chronicler. Indeed the teachings of Confucius had found so ready a reception among the Chinese people that it needed more than the edict of a tyrant to eradicate them.

The prohibition remained in force only a short time. The great autocrat died suddenly in the year 209 and his entire system of government quickly broke up. His successor was a weak ruler, and once again the country was rent by civil war. After three years an adventurer called Liu Pang, the son of a peasant, who had raised himself to be ruler of the province of Han, seized the capital, and the emperor and his councillors perished in the flames of the burning palace. Liu Pang overcame all his competitors and took possession of the central government. He rebuilt the imperial palace, took the title of emperor, and founded the famous Han dynasty, which continued in power from 206 B.C. to 220 A.D. Its rule embraces the most brilliant period of Chinese history. In spite of the overthrow of Shih-huang-ti's successor, the general principles of his policy remained secure, and upon a theocratic basis was founded an absolute imperial monarchy with an hereditary succession. The appointment of state officials was thrown open to public competition, and decided by an examination in the standard literature of China. In fact the Han period opened with a spiritual reaction in favour of Confucianism. Shih-huang-ti came to be looked upon as guilty of a blasphemous outrage upon the most sacred treasures of China, and the nation reverted with relief to the teaching delivered some three hundred and fifty years earlier, which it no doubt somewhat idealised. Confucius himself became a sort of national saint and his system a compendium of state dogma and correct conduct.

It is now time to examine the system itself and to see what it actually contains.

What we call Confucianism is a philosophy of life and conduct, mildly tinged with religious sentiment, towards which the most substantial contribution was made by Confucius himself, but which inherited its basic ideas from his predecessor Lao-tzŭ and was further developed by his successors Mêng-tzŭ and Mo-tzŭ. The general idea which it contains is that the course of nature is good. It is not necessarily easy to understand, but on the whole it is just and moral, and therefore men should submit to its decrees. Nothing can happen to them but what is in the course of nature, and therein are prescribed principles and rules for the right conduct of human beings. This natural course of the universe is called Tâo, and is a universal law common to all ages, the hidden principle of all life. It will be seen that this teaching greatly resembles that of the Stoic philosophers, and sentiments akin to it may be found in the confessions of Marcus Aurelius.[1] Like that of some Indians this general conception of a single principle in the universe is an attempt to form what we should now call a monistic philosophy. It differs from their attempt, however, in its optimism. Whereas the Indians regard the cosmic process as either evil, futile, or meaningless, the Chinese believe it to be wholly good; whereas by the Indians Deity is described in terms of negation, to the Chinese He is the sum-total of the forces operating in the universe. Chinese thought is in consequence faced with a dilemma which it can never satisfactorily overcome. Its ideals are very nearly as pure and lofty as those inculcated by Jesus,

---

[1] The possible connection between the speculative thought of Greece and China cannot be easily dismissed. We know that the influence of Greek decorative art is traceable in Chinese monuments found in Corea. May there not also have been an interchange of ideas?

and its assertion is that these ideals may be discovered
in the working of the forces of Nature, so that
meditation upon nature will lead to the discovery
of the highest ethical principles. But it happens
(as T. H. Huxley saw), that these principles cannot
really be discovered by merely contemplating natural
processes, for some of these processes connected with
the struggle for existence appear to conflict with
the highest ethical principles. The Chinese, therefore,
(as Schweitzer has pointed out) have either to idealise
these processes in a strained and unnatural way, in order
to bring them into line with the requirements of their
noblest sages, or else to explain away the teaching of
these sages until it is reduced to a level which accords
with what we know of the harsher aspects of the world
processes.

"In so far as the Chinese philosophers are ethical, they
idealise the natural forces at work in the world and ascribe
to them ethical character. In so far as they dare to face
reality, they must turn the wick of the lamp of ethics down,
till in the end it is reduced to a dimly-burning light.
Slaves of their monism, they run after an illusion—as if
religion could justify itself on the mere basis of knowledge
of the world. If they cannot comprehend the meaning
of the world as the activity of the forces of love, they land
in a cold religion if not in scepticism: thus there are indeed
some Chinese thinkers who say the meaning of the world
is that in the expectation of inevitable death we enjoy
life."[1]

The main difference between Lao-tzŭ and Confucius
would seem to have been that the former inculcated a

[1] Schweitzer, Lectures at Selly Oak, 1923, p. 59.

kind of quietist mysticism, in which action and true thought are eschewed, since nature is so beneficent that it is better not to interfere with her machinery; while the latter favoured a practical conservatism, in which the duties of one's day and station were carefully prescribed and were to be carried out with balance and moderation, avoiding all extremes.

In a sense Confucianism taken by itself is not a religion, for it prescribes no ordered ceremonies or sacrifices. This, however, is due to our common practice of regarding religion only in its institutional aspect. Confucianism is certainly a way of life based upon a belief in a responsive Deity, the proper relation to whom is to be maintained not by some departmental ceremony or ceremonies but by the ordering of the whole life. The interest, however, is less in Deity than in the ordering of life. Yet Confucius himself, though pre-eminently practical and this-worldly, was not indifferent towards Deity. He spoke of Heaven, and said that the ideal man stood in awe of the ordinances of Heaven; and again, "Heaven has entrusted me with a mission"; but his attitude towards this mysterious entity was cold and reserved.

There are certain other general ideas in Chinese thought which we will now proceed to describe.

The first of these is man's natural tendency to be good. This is taught by Mêng-tzŭ, who declares that every man possesses within himself four principles of benevolence, justice, propriety, and wisdom, and that a man has but to obey the law in himself in order to be perfect. In the eleventh century A.D. a little book was compiled for the use of Chinese youth, the opening sentence of which embodies this early teaching of Mêng-tzŭ, and runs:

"Men at their birth are by nature radically good."

It must be noted however that Mêng-tzŭ himself, in order to accommodate his theory to the facts of life went on to say that the goodness of mankind is potential rather than actual.

"Men possess a moral nature; but if they are well-fed, clad, and housed, without being taught at the same time, they become almost like the beasts."

The great end of learning therefore, he says, is to recover and develop this goodness, since the common condition of men is that they have either never realised their potentiality, or have drifted away from it.

The next idea is that of what is called Li, or propriety. According to Confucius there is a correct relation to almost any person or situation which you may encounter in the course of your life, and in this everyone must be trained from childhood, so that it becomes instinctive. The result is that a quiet courtesy and savoir-faire are characteristic of even the most uneducated Chinese.

A third idea is that of Ch'êng, which means the quality of harmony with Tâo or nature. It is sometimes translated as sincerity. It is more than Li, which means appropriate procedure in any particular circumstance. Ch'êng means rather character, the right attitude in all circumstances; and in "the Doctrine of the Mean," a treatise of Confucius, the general principle of avoidance of extremes or of defect and excess is as clearly enunciated as in the teaching of the Buddha about the Middle Way, or of Aristotle in his

Nicomachean Ethics; so that, as we have elsewhere observed, there is the bare possibility that the three thinkers were not wholly independent of one another.

The next idea is that of Chung, which denotes loyalty or conscientiousness. The term is variously translated, but seems to mean strict and honourable consistency.

The fifth and sixth ideas are those of Shu and Jên, which are respectively the negative and positive aspect of thoughtfulness for others.

Shu is usually expanded into what we know as the silver rule, which is found stated in the Analects as follows: "Tzŭ Kung asked: 'Is there some single word which I may take as the rule of conduct throughout life?' The master said, 'Is not Shu the word? What you would not wish done to yourself, never do to others.'" Jên may be translated as active benevolence and he who habitually practises Jên is called the Chün-tzŭ or "princely man," very much the same as the English "gentleman."[1]

Confucius said "the princely man does not act contrary to Jên even during the course of a single meal, or when he is hurried or when he fails." Jên in the Analects is defined as loving one's fellow-man and being a true man. To know what Jên is we must know what man's true nature is.

The later Chinese thinkers as distinct from Lao-tzŭ are much more insistent than he is upon active goodwill, and some of their sayings show a very close approximation to those of Jesus Christ.

[1] The Chinese statue figured opposite p. 234, though Buddhist, seems influenced by this idea, and might very well represent a Chün-tzŭ.

Thus one of them, Mo-tzŭ says:

"We must do what Heaven desires us to do, and refrain from doing what Heaven does not desire us to do. What is it that Heaven desires and what is that which Heaven hates? Heaven desires that men should love and be of use to one another, and does not wish them to rob one another. How do we know that? From the fact that Heaven loves all without exception, and ministers to the needs of all. And this is known from the fact that Heaven possesses and nourishes them all without exception."

It has been pointed out that in the fifth century B.C. China produced a number of teachers of the type of Mo-tzŭ who preached universal peace and disarmament. Of these a contemporary writer said:

"They sought to unite men through an ardent love in universal brotherhood. To fight against lusts and evil desires was their chief endeavour. When they were reviled, they did not consider it a shame: they were intent on nothing but the redemption of men from quarrelling. They forbade aggression, and preached disarmament in order to redeem mankind from war. This teaching they carried throughout the world. They admonished princes and instructed subjects. The world was not ready to accept their teaching, but they held to it all the more firmly. It was said that high and low tried to avoid meeting them, but that they forced themselves upon people."

It is difficult to realise that this incredibly high teaching precedes Christianity by several centuries. Its effects, however, were limited. That it did influence the spirit of the Chinese people profoundly may be judged from the very low esteem in which the military profession has been held in China, at any rate until recent times. Nevertheless, a mere philosophy of conduct must always fail in its effects, because it lacks the driving power which is furnished by the warm and affectionate relationship with a personal god. "Heaven" is too vague a conception to stir the imagination.

Chinese philosophy crystallised into an extremely conservative movement and steadily lost influence, until finally in the first century of our era the northern type of Buddhism invaded China and showed itself as a philosophical system more ready than Confucianism to come to terms with Chinese ritual practices and mythology. It was this accommodating character which enabled it to take root, and not its theory, which was hardly a formidable rival to that of the native philosophers. It is now said to be in rapid decay. In the tenth century there was an attempt at an introduction of Shintoism from Japan, but this did not attain to great importance. Confucianism then revived and finally produced in the eleventh century a really great teacher called Chu Hsi, who is wrongly reported to have taught a kind of materialistic monism comparable with the modern system of Haeckel. Thus it is said that he denied a personal God and the immortality of the soul. Everything to him was li, eternal unconscious changeless law, and ch'i, all matter. Existence he is represented as saying is like a sea composed of waves, which, however, are only temporary discontinuous appearances of the one substance, water. Ancestor-worship is merely the expression of gratitude towards those who have passed on life to us; recognition as it were of past waves, long since vanished.

In view of the importance of Chu Hsi and of the injustice with which his system is sometimes described, it seems worth while to dwell a little more fully upon his theory of the universe. In the first place, what exactly does he mean by his term ch'i? A French writer translates it as *matière*, but since there is nothing in the whole cosmos into which ch'i does not enter, so that it is "the primordial substance . . . . . . invisible and intangible, the source from which spring all phenomena, the basis, not only of all that we call matter, but of every form of existence, material or spiritual, physical or psychical," ch'i must, according to that interpretation, include spirit as well as matter, so that these may be regarded as the twofold manifestation of one substance (very much like what a modern physicist has called "mind-stuff"). Li, on the other hand, is translated by the same French writer as *forme* or *formel principe*, which may mean in English principle or law, but, says Chu Hsi, "heaven (the self-existent) is law." In other words li is the Supreme Ultimate. It is a guiding and directing principle which determines the form of everything that exists and causes it to be. It is thus capable of description in the same terms as the Logos of the fourth gospel. "Without it hath not anything been made, and that which was made in it was life"; li in fact is that which vivifies and constructs or composes and informs the whole. It is, however, very difficult to agree that li is impersonal, since we are told that love, righteousness, reverence, and wisdom are component principles of it, and these to us are attributes of mind. Chu Hsi himself seems to recognise this, for although he says that li is a property of mind rather than mind

itself, he goes on to add that li apart from mind would
have nothing in which to inhere, while li is not conscious
apart from its vehicle of manifestation.    Moreover li is
ethical.    Plainly it is much more than law; it is that
which gives law, and it is that all-pervading abiding
unity which remains constant amid the changes and
chances of this fleeting world.

What then is the relation between li and ch'i?    It is
very easy to arrive at contradictory conclusions.    One
commentator finds in it an uncompromising materialism, another a species of monotheism combined with
pantheism.    It is safer to avoid labels and to look at the
statements of Chu Hsi himself.    He says that in the
whole universe there is no ch'i apart from li nor li apart
from ch'i.    But this is not dualism, since there is
nothing antagonistic in the relations of li and ch'i.    We
are told, however, that from eternity li is antecedent and
ch'i subsequent.    It seems, therefore, that what Chu
Hsi has really thought out for himself is much the same
as that Western system which says that deity is eternal,
but that his generation of matter is also eternal.    Li is
eternal but eternally generates ch'i.    How anyone can
call this materialism it is difficult to see; on the contrary
many of us would feel that it was remarkably good
natural theology.    Its importance lies in the fact that
Confucianism has come to us reshaped by Chu Hsi and
has remained until the present age of disintegration
substantially the same for the last seven hundred
years.

It is perhaps worth noting that Chu Hsi, in spite of his
distance from us, had a remarkably clear perception of
the process by which cosmos was evolved.    He takes

the old twofold activity of the ether, known to the Chinese as Yin and Yang, or, as we should say, inertia and energy, for granted. Yin and Yang are produced by the rotation of the ether, and follow each other in endless succession, and by their interaction in differing degree produce what are called the five agents, from which the whole cosmos is evolved on a vast scale in a cycle of four periods corresponding to the four seasons of the solar year, each of which is said to typify love, beauty, service, and reserve.[1]

Chu Hsi had a clear doctrine of human nature. This nature, he says, is like a decree imparted by Heaven, flowing from the latter as a stream of water; each of us is as if one took a bowl and filled it from the stream. Our nature then is nothing less than the individuation of the immaterial principle previously defined as li.

What then is the place of free-will, and how are we to account for evil?

Chu Hsi's answer is that by *individuation* li ceases to be that absolutely pure nature of which it can only be said that it is good. It is like a stream, which, issuing pure from its source, has somewhere on its way become turbid and muddy. Individuation is not itself evil but is the cause of the possibility of evil. How then, finally, can this evil be purged? The answer is by conversion. If we ask what is the method of this conversion we are told by self-culture. The process must be wholly from within. When men, he says, have sought the conversion of the physical element in their constitution, their success and their return to their original nature are not imparted from without. Man holds within himself all that is needed for his own redemption.

[1] Some may see in this a faint resemblance to the Hegelian dialectic.

It is said that Chu Hsi's teaching upon the nature of mind is not easy to follow, but that it may be summed up in the following paragraph: "Mind is a form of the primordial Ch'i. In contrast to the body it is the pure and refined portion of Ch'i, the positive mode, active, expanding, independent of gravitation or resistance. But mind itself has its negative and positive modes and thus has a double manifestation in soul and spirit, or as sentient mind and intellectual mind.

Chu Hsi's views led him into controversy with the Buddhists, since the latter, although they agreed with him in declaring that the individual mind is one with and a part of the universal mind, taught, nevertheless, that it was man's business to sink his individuality and to lose it in the universal. Chu Hsi, on the other hand, taught that man's business was to develop his mind to the utmost and to bring it into harmony with its source; and that by this means his individuality would not be obliterated but intensified, and the cardinal virtues perfected.

In conclusion we may well ask whether Chu Hsi has any claim to be regarded as a theist. It is quite clear that the word T'ien is used in the classics in at least three different senses, as the sky, the ruling power, and law. Chu Hsi declares that these are synonyms for the same being, regarded from different points of view. But it is quite clear that he thought of the supreme ruler as personal. He was, however, strongly opposed to image-worship and anthropomorphism, and on these grounds was charged with atheism. It has been pointed out that (1) he draws a distinction between saying that the Supreme Ruler is a man in the heavens and saying that he is a man *as it were*, and (2) he denies that the universe has become what it is by a process of self-evolution. He represents the mind of the universe as its Pilot, the organ of conscious personality in the Divine Being, whose attributes are love, righteousness, reverence and wisdom; and of these, in point of view of priority, love is the first, and in point of view of greatness, love is the greatest.

It may be asked, "How was it that this lofty scheme of natural theology should have come to be regarded as materialistic and atheistic?" The answer must be that even if the implications of his system were theistic, these implications did not receive so much attention as some of his other doctrines. He was a philosopher, not an evangelist, a thinker rather than a prophet; and in his desire to stress the spiritual nature of deity, he laid less emphasis upon the personality of deity. Moreover the general tendency of the temperament of the average Chinese is materialistic.

The monism of Chu Hsi gradually gained prestige and was taught from the fifteenth century onwards in all the schools, and has remained the official philosophy until recent times, even though in 1906 the curious national system of examination in the Chinese classics was abolished, owing to emphasis on those features in it which we have indicated and perhaps also owing to a temper of agnosticism. It has been thus comparatively easy for the non-Christian educated Chinese to adopt Western materialistic systems of thought such as those of Spencer and other exponents of nineteenth-century naturalism, and it is perhaps hardly surprising that men whose mental outlook is inherited from the later Confucianism should find an affinity between themselves and the non-Christian teachers of modern Europe, especially the Russian dialectic materialists. Indeed the individual terminology of the Chinese thinkers should not be allowed to obscure the resemblance between their thought and that of much Western philosophy. It seems that for the brain of the *hominidæ* there are only a certain limited number of types of solution to the riddle of the universe which are capable of being propounded, and that those which come last are not necessarily the best, but may be just those which are consequent upon the arrival of a decadent state of society, or the decay of national energy. Or perhaps they come round again and again as thought moves in spirals.

The history of Buddhism in China is rich and varied, though, as has been said, it is in many areas rapidly on the decline. There are also a certain number of Moslems in China, amounting perhaps to 4,000,000. It is sometimes said that China has three religions, Taoism, Confucianism, and Buddhism, but it is now coming to be recognised that this is not the best way of describing the situation. The real religion of China is the belief in spirits, whether of departed human beings or of natural forces, expressing itself in ceremonial. Confucianism and Buddhism, as well as the teachings of thinkers not strictly connected with either system, are really not religions at all in this ceremonial sense, but attempts at the construction of a philosophy of life. These systems of thought survive with the multitude by coming to terms with Taoistic religion. Hence at bottom there is only one religion of China, though the great systems of philosophy, two of them native and one imported, have divided it into three groups.

By far the most important feature for us to-day, however, is the impact made upon China by extraneous modes of thought, acting on her from different directions. Thus from Britain and America has come reformed Christianity, partly in a liberal, partly in a fundamentalist guise, together with a certain amount of scientific, materialist, and humanist philosophy. France and Russia are, on the other hand, influencing China in the direction of positivism and atheistic communism. The effect of the considerable Roman Catholic community cannot be ignored, especially because of its tendency, at any rate until recently, to aim at political influence.

About so vast a country in such a period of rapid change and transformation no general statement can safely be made. But it seems probable that when the temporary nationalist antagonism to Christian propaganda has subsided the wise Chinese leaders[1] will be seen to be leading their people in the direction of an indigenous and enlightened Christian faith, although the embarrassment of the latter by secularism on the one hand and obscurantism on the other must for some time be severe. A modern correspondent writing in the Spring of 1931 said:

"Idol-worship is hardly a subject worth discussing in modern China—it is dead, save among the most ignorant country peasants, or among the weakly superstitious. The

[1] It is not an insignificant fact that the President of the Chinese Republic during the year 1930 received baptism at the hands of Methodists.

cry is 'Christ or Lenin'—'God or no God.' That is the challenge we have to answer. Always materialist by nature, many young Chinese have fallen an easy prey to the shallow scientific materialism of Moscow."

On the other hand it is said by some who have visited China since the friction with Japan, that the key positions in her public life appear to be held by Christians, and that it is the policy of such men which is destined to determine the future of the country and its inhabitants.

## APPENDIX

The following extracts from Chinese classics (Legge's translation) may serve to illustrate their characteristics.

I. Two typical passages (*a*) from the Shu-King or book of historical documents, which embodies passages dating from as early as the twenty-fourth century B.C., but collected and amplified at much later dates.

In the spring of the thirteenth year there was a great assembly at Mâng-king. The king said, "Ah! ye hereditary rulers of my friendly states, and all ye my officers, managers of my affairs, hearken clearly to my declaration.

"Heaven and earth is the parent of all creatures; and of all creatures man is the most highly endowed. The sincerely intelligent (among men) becomes the great sovereign; and the great soverign is the parent of the people. But now, Shâu, the king of Shang, does not reverence Heaven above, and inflicts calamities on the people below. Abandoned to drunkenness and reckless in lust, he has dared to exercise cruel oppression. He has extended the punishment of offenders to all their relatives. He has put men into offices on the hereditary principle. He has made it his pursuit to have palaces, towers, pavilions, embankments, ponds, and all other extravagances, to the most painful injury of you, the myriads of the people. He has burned and roasted the loyal and good. He has ripped up pregnant women. Great Heaven was moved with indignation, and charged my deceased father Wan to display its terrors; but (he died) before the work was completed.

"On this account, I, Fâ, the little child, have by means of you, the hereditary rulers of my friendly states, contemplated the government of Shang; but Shâu has no repentant heart. He sits squatting on his heels, not serving God nor the spirits of heaven and earth, neglecting also the temple of his ancestors, and not sacrificing in it. The victims and the vessels of millet all become the prey of wicked robbers, and still he says, 'The people are mine; the (heavenly) appointment is mine,' never trying to correct his contemptuous mind.

"Heaven, for the help of the inferior people, made for them rulers, and made for them instructors, that they might be able to be aiding to God, and secure the tranquillity of the four quarters (of the kingdom). In regard to who are criminals and who are not, how dare I give any allowance to my own wishes?

"'Where the strength is the same, measure the virtue of the parties; where the virtue is the same, measure their righteousness.' Shâu has hundreds of thousands and myriads of officers, but they have hundreds of thousands and myriads of minds; I have (but) three thousand officers, but they have one mind. The iniquity of Shang is full. Heaven gives command to destroy it. If I did not obey Heaven, my iniquity would be as great.

"I, the little child, early and late am filled with apprehensions. I have received the command of my deceased father Wan; I have offered special sacrifice to God; I have performed the due services to the great earth; and I lead the multitude of you to execute the punishment appointed by Heaven. Heaven compassionates the people. What the people desire, Heaven will be found to give effect to. Do you aid me, the One man, to cleanse for ever (all within) the four seas. Now is the time!—It should not be lost."

### (b) from the Shih-King or book of Poetry—a typical ode.

How vast is God, The ruler of men below! How arrayed in terrors is God, With many things irregular in his ordinations. Heaven gave birth to the multitudes of the people, But the nature it confers is not to be depended on. All are (good) at first, But few prove themselves to be so at the last.

II. From the Appendices to the Yi King, a curious text based on a number of ideograms made up of straight lines, which are said to symbolise moral, spiritual and political ideas. The Yi was in existence before Confucius (at least twelfth century B.C.), and the Appendices are attributed to him.

### (a) Appendix III, Section II, Chapter 5.

40. The Master said:—"Virtue small and office high; wisdom small and plans great; strength small and burden heavy—where

such conditions exist, it is seldom that they do not end (in evil). As is said in the Yi, 'The tripod's feet are overthrown, and the ruler's food is overturned. The body of him (who is thus indicated) is wet (with shame):—there will be evil.'"

41. The Master said:—"Does not he who knows the springs of things possess spirit-like wisdom? The superior man, in his intercourse with the high, uses no flattery, and in his intercourse with the low, no coarse freedom:—does not this show that he knows the springs of things? Those springs are the slight beginnings of movement, and the earliest indications of good fortune (or ill). The superior man sees them, and acts accordingly without waiting for (the delay of) a single day. As is said in the Yî, 'He is firm as a rock (and acts) without the delay of a single day. With firm goodness there will be good fortune.' Firm as a rock, how should he have to wait a single day to ensure his knowing (those springs and his course)? The superior man knows the minute and the manifested; he knows what is weak, and what is strong:—he is a model to ten thousand."

## (b) Appendix IV, Chapter 6. (Confucius on the marks of the princely man.)

The great man is he who is in harmony, in his attributes, with heaven and earth; in his brightness, with the sun and moon; in his orderly procedure, with the four seasons; and in his relation to what is fortunate and what is calamitous, in harmony with the spirit-like operations (of Providence). He may precede Heaven, and Heaven will not act in opposition to him; he may follow Heaven, but will act (only) as Heaven at the time would do. If Heaven will not act in opposition to him, how much less will men! how much less will the spirit-like operation (of Providence)!

## (c) Appendix V. (Showing a passage in which Confucius refers to deity.)

God comes forth in Kan (to His producing work); He brings (His processes) into full and equal action in Sun; they are manifested to one another in Lî; the greatest service is done for Him in Khwan; He rejoices in Tui; He struggles in Khien; He is comforted and enters into rest in Khân; and He completes (the work of the year) in Kan.

All things are made to issue forth in Kan, which is placed at the east. (The processes of production) are brought into full and equal action in Sun, which is placed at the south-east. The being brought into full and equal action refers to the purity and equal arrangement of all things. Lî gives the idea of brightness. All things are now made manifest to one another. It is the trigram of the south. The sages turn their faces to the south when they give audience to all under the sky, administering government towards the region of brightness:—the idea in this procedure was taken from this. Khwan denotes the earth (and is placed at the south-west). All things receive from it their fullest nourishment, and hence it is said, "The greatest service is done for Him in Khwan." Tui corresponds (to the west) and to the autumn—the season in which all things rejoice. Hence it is said, "He rejoices in Tui." He struggles in Khien, which is the trigram of the north-west. The idea is that there the inactive and active conditions beat against each other. Khan denotes water. It is the trigram of the exact north—the trigram of comfort and rest, what all things are tending to. Hence it is said, "He is comforted and enters into rest in Khan." Kan is the trigram of the north-east. In it all things bring to a full end the issues of the past (year), and prepare the commencement of the next. Hence it is said, "He completes (the work of the year) in Kan."

N.B.—"God" in the above = Shang-ti, and Legge has a note in his preface defending this translation.

III. From the Hsiao King, a treatise on filial piety, dating from before the Han dynasty. Chapter VII. *Of filial piety in relation to the three powers.*

The disciple Zang said, "Immense indeed is the greatness of filial piety!" The Master replied, "Yes, filial piety is the constant (method) of Heaven, the righteousness of Earth, and the practical duty of Man. Heaven and earth invariably pursue the course (that may be thus described), and the people take it as their pattern. (The ancient kings) imitated the brilliant luminaries of heaven, and acted in accordance with the (varying) advantages afforded by earth, so that they were in accord with all under heaven; and in consequence their teachings, without being severe, were successful, and their government, without being rigorous, secured perfect order.

"The ancient kings, seeing how their teachings could transform the people, set before them therefore an example of the most extended love, and none of the people neglected their parents; they set forth to them (the nature of) virtue and righteousness, and the people roused themselves to the practice of them; they went before them with reverence and yielding courtesy, and the people had no contentions; they led them on by the rules of propriety and by music, and the people were harmonious and benignant; they showed them what they loved and what they disliked, and the people understood their prohibitions.

"It is said in the Book of Poetry,

'Awe-inspiring are you, O Grand-Master Yin,
And the people all look up to you.'"

IV. From the Lî Kî or Collection of treatises on propriety or ceremonial, with comments by Confucius. Its text has probably been correctly preserved for eighteen hundred years, but it is composed of strata of various dates. The extracts are from Book VIII, in which sacrifices to the dead are dealt with.

19. A superior man has said, "What is sweet may be tempered; what is white may be coloured. So the man who is right in heart and sincere can learn the (meaning of the) rites." The rites should not be perfunctorily performed by the man who is not right in heart and sincere. Hence it is all important (in the performance of them) to get the proper men.

20. Confucius said, "One may repeat the three hundred odes, and not be fit to offer the sacrifice where there is (but) one offering of the cup. He may offer that sacrifice, and not be fit to join in a great sacrifice. He may join in such a sacrifice, and not be fit to offer a great sacrifice to the hills. He may perform that fully, and yet not be able to join in the sacrifice to God. Let no one lightly discuss the subject of rites."

V. From the Lî Kî. Book X. (The Pattern of the Family.) Section I. (A curious description of filial piety.)

(1) The sovereign and king orders the chief minister to send down his (lessons of) virtue to the millions of the people.

(2) Sons, in serving their parents, on the first crowing of the cock, should all wash their hands and rinse their mouths, comb their hair, draw over it the covering of silk, fix this with the hair-pin, bind the hair at the roots with the fillet, brush the dust from that which is left free, and then put on their caps, leaving the ends of the strings hanging down. They should then put on their squarely made black jackets, knee-covers, and girdles, fixing in the last their tablets. From the left and right of the girdle they should hang their articles for use:—on the left side, the duster and handkerchief, the knife and whetstone, the small spike, and the metal speculum for getting fire from the sun; on the right, the archer's thimble for the thumb and the armlet, the tube for writing instruments, the knife-case, the larger spike, and the borer for getting fire from wood. They should put on their leggings, and adjust their shoe-strings.

(3) (Sons') wives should serve their parents-in-law as they served their own. At the first crowing of the cock, they should wash their hands, and rinse their mouths; comb their hair, draw over it the covering of silk, fix this with the hair-pin, and tie the hair at the roots with the fillet. They should then put on the

jacket, and over it the sash. On the left side they should hang the duster and handkerchief, the knife and whetstone, the small spike, and the metal speculum to get fire with; all bestowed in the satchel, the great spike, and the borer to get fire with from wood. They will also fasten on their necklaces, and adjust their shoe-strings.

(4) Thus dressed, they should go to their parents and parents-in-law. On getting to where they are, with bated breath and gentle voice, they should ask if their clothes are (too) warm or (too) cold, whether they are ill or pained, or uncomfortable in any part; and if they be so, they should proceed reverently to stroke and scratch the place. They should in the same way, going before or following after, help and support their parents in quitting or entering (the apartment). In bringing in the basin for them to wash, the younger will carry the stand and the elder the water; they will beg to be allowed to pour out the water, and when the washing is concluded, they will hand the towel. They will ask whether they want anything, and then respectfully bring it. All this they will do with an appearance of pleasure to make their parents feel at ease. (They should bring) gruel, thick or thin, spirits or must, soup with vegetables, beans, wheat, spinach, rice, millet, maize, and glutinous millet—whatever they wish, in fact; with dates, chestnuts, sugar and honey, to sweeten their dishes; with the ordinary or the large-leaved violets, leaves of elm-trees, fresh or dry, and the most soothing rice-water to lubricate them; and with fat and oil to enrich them. The parents will be sure to taste them, and when they have done so, the young people should withdraw.

## VI. The following passages are from the Tâo Teh King, or description of the Tâo. (Li as defined in the writings of Chu Hsi seems much to resemble Tâo.)

The Tâo that can be trodden is not the enduring and unchanging Tâo. The name that can be named is not the enduring and unchanging name.

(Conceived of as) having no name, it is the Originator of heaven and earth; (conceived of as) having a name, it is the Mother of all things.

> Always without desire we must be found,
> If its deep mystery we would sound;
> But if desire always within us be,
> Its outer fringe is all that we shall see.

Under these two aspects, it is really the same; but as development takes place, it receives the different names. Together we call them the Mystery. Where the Mystery is the deepest is the gate of all that is subtle and wonderful.

The Tâo is (like) the emptiness of a vessel, and in our employment of it we must be on our guard against all fulness. How deep and unfathomable it is, as if it were the Honoured Ancestor of all things!

We should blunt our sharp points, and unravel the complications of things; we should attemper our brightness, and bring ourselves into agreement with the obscurity of others. How pure and still the Tâo is, as if it would ever so continue!

I do not know whose son it is. It might appear to have been before God.

We look at it, and we do not see it, and we name it "the Equable." We listen to it, and we do not hear it, and we name it "the Inaudible." We try to grasp it, and do not get hold of it, and we name it "the Subtle." With these three qualities, it cannot be made the subject of description; and hence we blend them together and obtain The One.

Its upper part is not bright, and its lower part is not obscure. Ceaseless in its action, it yet cannot be named, and then it again returns and becomes nothing. This is called the Form of the Formless, and the Semblance of the Invisible; this is called the Fleeting and Indeterminable.

We meet it and do not see its Front; we follow it, and do not see its Back. When we can lay hold of the Tâo of old to direct the things of the present day, and are able to know it as it was of old in the beginning, this is called (unwinding) the clue of Tâo.

All-pervading is the Great Tâo! It may be found on the left hand and on the right.

All things depend on it for their production, which it gives to them, not one refusing obedience to it. When its work is accomplished, it does not claim the name of having done it. It clothes all things as with a garment, and makes no assumption of being their lord:—it may be named in the smallest things. All things return (to their root and disappear), and do not know that it is it which presides over their doing so;—it may be named in the greatest things.

The Tâo, considered as unchanging, has no name.

Though in its primordial simplicity it may be small, the whole world dares not deal with (one embodying) it as a minister. If a feudal prince or the king could guard and hold it, all would spontaneously submit themselves to him.

Heaven and Earth (under its guidance) unite together and send down the sweet dew, which, without the directions of men, reaches equally everywhere as of its own accord.

As soon as it proceeds to action, it has a name. When it once has that name (men) can know to rest in it. When they know to rest in it, they can be free from all risk of failure and error.

The relation of the Tâo to all the world is like that of the great rivers and seas to the streams from the valleys.

## Of Mediterranean Religion in Crete, Greece and Rome.

Greek religion is of special interest for three main reasons. First, it presents a development occurring among one of the most gifted peoples that the world has ever produced. Secondly, it stands out as almost the only example of the evolution of an aesthetically attractive religion suitable to a great and progressive nation out of an original primitive faith without any serious break. Thirdly, its decline teaches plain lessons which later ages much need to learn.

In the development of Persian and Hebrew religion there is evidence of an actual breach with the traditions of the past; but in the case of the Greeks there is unbroken continuity in the development which their religion exhibits from the lowest to the highest stage of their cultural development. The archaeological discoveries of the last ten years have demonstrated that the Greek people emerged from a fusion of two different races in prehistoric times, and that the Greek religion was also a fusion of two separate faiths. The racial blend is that of tall fair Nordics with short dark wiry Iberians, a blend which seems to produce great ability coupled with physical beauty and vigour. (It is sometimes said that the British people may flatter themselves that their best stocks are instances of a similar blend!) The actual development of Greek polytheism is perhaps to-day only of archaeological interest, and seems to those who study the vicissitudes of religion in India to be paralleled by phenomena occurring in that country, but the remarkable feature about religion as it came to express itself in the city-states, and especially in Athens, is that the actual practices of primitive times were retained under more splendid circumstances as the outlet for the devotion of a people no longer primitive.

The precise relation of the civilisation and religion of the Mesopotamian peoples, of those of Egypt, and of those of Crete and pre-historic Greece, is still a matter of much dispute. There are those who say that the civilisations of Crete and of Mycenae in Hellas were derived directly from the Nile Valley. Others, however, prefer the view that their development is more directly connected with Babylonia and Lydia; and it seems indeed from the specimens of decorative art which have been found that they have much more in common with the art of these countries than with that of Egypt.

Much attention has of late been devoted to the wonderful and mysterious civilisation which flourished in Crete and which is centred upon the royal palace at Knossos. Its extraordinary antiquity is beyond dispute. The most ancient strata in the island carry us back to the early neolithic, and there is the same kind of contrast between the cultures of these primitive strata and the glorious artistic achievements of the golden age of Knossos, that there is between the predynastic cultures of Egypt and those of the old kingdom. The chronology is roughly as follows:—

(1) Neolithic or so-called "pre-Minoan," perhaps going back five thousand years to (let us say) 8000 B.C.

(2) Early Minoan in three stages, beginning about 3400 B.C., and extending to about 2100 B.C.

(3) Middle Minoan in two stages. The age of the great palaces in Crete beginning about 2000 B.C., and ending in a great earthquake about 1700 B.C.

(4) Transitional }
(5) Late Minoan } both these subsequent to 1700 B.C.

This civilisation of course gets its label from the name of the half-legendary priest-king, Minos,[1] who reigned at Knossos; and it appears to have been accompanied by a somewhat advanced religion; the most striking feature of which was probably the worship of the female principle or the Great Mother.[2] The origin and distribution of this worship has in itself been the subject of much study. It is a perfectly spontaneous development such as we might expect to discover among any race of human deings, and it is natural also to find that it is not unconnected with a tendency which sometimes occurs in the primitive community to trace descent through the mother and to exalt the influence of the mother of the family. However all this may be, it is certainly remarkable that the worship of the Great Mother under various guises is equally characteristic of the small dark Mediterranean whites, and of the Dravidian peoples of Southern India. These, as it were, take kindly to conceiving their supreme divinity in female form, and to this, rather than to any real justification to be derived from the narrative of the New Testament,

[1] But Minos was also probably the name of a god, who had to make way for Zeus, and so was reduced by the invaders to the level of a king—the son of a god.

[2] "Married to her son," as she seems to have been conceived in some cases. The predominant symbol of this cultus was the double axe, which may be a conventionalised form of the thunderbolt, since the lightning seems to have been regarded as the act whereby the heaven fertilised or touched the earth.

must be attributed the readiness of the Mediterranean races to venerate the Madonna.

The earliest element in Greek religion is plainly of the same type as the religion of other savage peoples. It is associated with three great festivals, in each case connected with the original cultus of what was possibly a totem-animal—a snake, a sow and a bull; the first representing perhaps the powers of the under-world or of the earth, the second the power of fertility, and the third force and vitality. It appears that early Mediterranean religion, of which we discover traces at Knossos and Mycenae, concerned itself with mysterious ceremonies connected with these three creatures, and especially with the bull. Thus the first element in this religion is reverence for a dangerous and mysterious force. The development of this into the cultus of a deity in human form involves a peculiar transition. Almost the earliest, if not quite the earliest, representations of the human form in prehistoric art show the man or woman wearing the head or skin of a sacred animal. This is true in the case of the ancient carved bones found at Teyjat in the South of France within recent years, and it is also true of the picture of the so-called medicine-man painted on the wall of the cave of Trois Frères in the Pyrenees; we have also seen that it is probably the case with the curious men-animals of Babylonia, and it certainly appears to be so in Egypt. We learn from the best authorities that men covered their heads with the mask of a beast, and it has been suggested that the Minotaur was a man wearing the skin and horns of a bull in connection with a magical dance. (I myself have seen an obviously magical dance performed by three Tibetans wearing the heads of antelopes). The significance of this is that the mysterious and dangerous force of the animal is thought to be connected with its characteristic features, and the man who wants to get close in touch with the force puts on the skin of the animal. He then comes to feel as though he is the animal; and it has been suggested that the medicine-man or sacred-man is the original θεός, the human being in contact with the mysterious power who in this way was able to control the course of nature. It has further been suggested that sooner or later this identification breaks down, because the medicine-man is incapable of living up to his pretensions. He makes mistakes. His spells fail to work. He inaccurately forecasts the future. It is not far from this to the assumption that the medicine-man is only the fallible deputy of the infallible but inaccessible divine power, which is (though but imperfectly) mediated through him to humanity. This theory, it will be seen, may almost be described as an early form of what in relation to the divinity of Christ is called the kenotic theory.

The second element in the development of Greek religion is due to the invasion of a quite different race of people from the north. They were more like some of our own Anglo-Saxon ancestors, in that they were probably big fair people with fine clear-cut features, and their religion probably resembled that of the early Norsemen. It has been pointed out that Mount Olympus was not one particular mountain, but that there were several heights bearing that name. In other words the gods of Olympus were mountain gods, the anthropomorphic deities of a race of hill-men; and as such they came to be imposed upon the people dwelling by the Mediterranean.   There was one further difference between the two sets of people.   Whereas the Mediterranean folk, as we have seen, traced their descent through their maternal ancestors, the people from the north traced descent through their fathers.   The two types of family organisation are quite well known and are found in other parts of the world; but the point here is that they naturally influenced the respective religions of the two peoples.   In the Mediterranean, although they believed in a god of the sky whom they called Kronos, they also believed, as we have seen, in the great Earth-Mother, and her cultus seems to have been the more important of the two.   She was represented as fertilised by the descent of Kronos, which might either mean the rays of the sun or the descent of the lightning (which sometimes tears up the earth) but in either case it was *she* who was important, and it is significant that, when what appear to be ancient sacred images have been found belonging to this early culture, they always represent a woman, holding in her hand snakes which are dangerous and mysterious creatures dwelling in the earth.   The people from the north, on the other hand, though they believed in a sky-god and an earth-goddess, gave the ultimate sovereignty to the god Zeus.[1]   When, therefore, Zeus displaces his Mediterranean counterpart he does not become subordinate to the Great Mother. It needs very little intelligence to see that the sub-conscious effect of these two types of belief has had an

---

[1] This imposition of a supreme sky-god, as dominating the community of divine beings, seems to come from the northern plains in all cases, and to be introduced all along the line, from east to west.

influence far beyond the disappearance of the old pagan
religion.   The tendency of the Mediterranean peoples
to prefer what is called the Catholic form of Christianity
with its exaggerated emphasis upon the Virgin-Mother,
and the northern European preference for Protestantism with its male Saviour, who teaches people to say the
Lord's Prayer rather than the Angelus, is obviously so
extraordinary a phenomenon that it cannot be accounted
for by saying that two sets of theologians argued out the
matter differently.   The secret of the difference is
obviously racial, and connected with a non-rational
emotional prejudice.   In other words, it is in the blood.

Prof. Gilbert Murray has divided the history of Greek
Religion into five stages, with only four of which we are
here concerned.

(1)   The primitive period.

(2)   The Olympian or classical stage.   Sixth and fifth
centuries B.C.

(3)   The bankruptcy of the Olympian religion and
the collapse of the city state in the fourth
century B.C.

(4)   The failure of nerve, from the end of the fourth
century B.C. to the third century A.D.

(5)   The pagan revival of the fourth century A.D.

The second stage is the one which naturally interests
us most.   In this a new type of cultus, less barbarous,
more human, and less totemistic and gross,[1] was super-
imposed upon the Aegean religion.   Its deities were

[1] Sir Arthur Evans holds that in morality and decency the religion
of the Mediterranean was superior to that of the invaders from the
north, but Murray seems to disagree with him.

men and women of a larger growth rather than forces of nature, and this had its dangers from the point of view of theology, since if you got in the way of the lightning your injury might be a lamentable accident, but if to be struck meant that a personal god had deliberately thrown a thunderbolt at you, then some reason had to be found for his action. "A being who claims to be the moral equal of man must not behave like a charge of dynamite, and strike well-intentioned people dead in his rage at their harmless and unintentional errors." But the attempt at fusing two types of religion together had other unhappy results. The forces of nature and fertility were still worshipped as deities, mostly of the female sex: but they became associated with a smaller number of male deities, and hence instead of purer morals we get the association of religion with the very reverse of monogamy, and even with promiscuity. Further, in the fifth century, the real religious emotion in Greece was devotion to the city-state personified. The local female divinities of these poleis were much more important to their citizens than the greater gods and goddesses who did not belong to any particular city, and therefore were only half-heartedly believed in. An urbanised population, detached from direct contact with the soil, demanded then, as in other ages, a different kind of outlet for its religious instincts.

The Olympic deities in the heyday of their worship were regarded as twelve in number, including Apollo as a late-comer, but excluding Dionysus. They formed six pairs; Zeus and Hera, Ares and Aphrodite, Apollo and Artemis, Hermes and Hestia, Hephaistos and Athene; but of these Zeus, Athene and Apollo occupied the positions of importance.   Hera and Artemis appear to be genuine Greek names, but Aphrodite has never been explained from Greek language, and may possibly be an old Aegean name of the goddess of nature recast in Greek mouths.   At any rate it seems likely that the worship of Aphrodite was an Aegean growth, which was afterwards promoted and influenced by the Phoenician cult of Astarte.

The development of the cults of Apollo and Dionysus demands some notice.   Both deities seem to have been introduced into Hellas from outside, but, for the matter of that, perhaps most of the Hellenic deities are importations.   (Aphrodite is certainly a goddess of passion introduced from the regions of the sun).   Apollo is also thought to be a solar deity who has some connection with the north of Europe, although perhaps his cultus came southwards by way of Asia Minor.   Obviously, whatever he afterwards became, he was in the beginning a personification of the sun in his splendour.   His great sanctuary (as is well known) was at Delphi, whence his oracle exercised for some centuries an almost unique influence.   It is curious how all special ideas of expiation for blood and of purification for criminal offences, especially murder or manslaughter, become centred round the cult of Apollo.   It is true that such purificatory rites were in the main pieces of external ceremonial; but, nevertheless, the idea that a particular god valued human life and was displeased at its destruction was of great importance, and undoubtedly opened the way to glimpses (though only glimpses) of higher morality.   Another peculiar feature about the cults of Apollo and Dionysus is that they are early

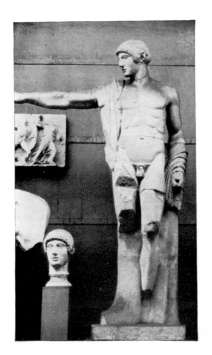

APOLLO.

(*See* p. xii.)

instances of missionary religions. Whereas most Greek cults, like local nature-worship everywhere else, were tied to particular spots, the worship of Apollo seems to have spread from place to place, until it was found nearly everywhere in Greece.

Of Dionysus we shall have much to say later on. At this period it is sufficient to record that he is another instance of a migratory cult, and that his worship appears to have spread from Thrace southwards. His mother, according to the myth, was Semele, a proper name which appears to mean (in the original Thracian) the earth, and perhaps Dionysus is a vegetation deity in some way connected with the barley-crop, from which even in early times an intoxicating drink was brewed. If this is so, it would account for the curious connection which has always existed between Dionysus and alcoholic ecstasy.

The religion of the "lively Grecians" in its outward expression appears a joyous and beautiful thing. There are signs, however, that it was built upon an earlier foundation of fear of the bad sacred. Nevertheless, in its flourishing stage, as the expression of the abounding life of its votaries and the projection of noble ideas it demands our admiration. Let us take the descriptions of two of the chief ceremonies of which we have record. The one is the Daphnephoria, a festival connected with Apollo, as it was observed at Thebes and recorded by a traveller.[1] He writes:—

"They wreathe a pole of olive wood with laurel and various flowers. On the top is fitted a bronze globe from which they suspend smaller ones. Midway round the pole

[1] See Jane Harrison, *Themis*, p. 438.

they place a lesser globe, binding it with purple fillets, but the end of the pole is decked with saffron. By the topmost globe they mean the sun, to which they actually compare Apollo. The globe beneath this is the moon; the smaller globes hung on are the stars and constellations, and the fillets are the course of the year, for they make them 365 in number. The Daphnephoria is headed by a boy, both of whose parents are alive, and his nearest male relation carries the filleted pole. The Laurel-bearer himself, who follows next, holds on to the laurel; he has his hair hanging loose, he wears a golden wreath, and he is dressed out in a splendid robe to his feet and wears light shoes. There follows him a band of maidens holding out boughs before them, to enforce the supplication of the hymns."

The other festival is the Panathenaia, as observed in Athens (in the middle of the fifth century) during the month of July, and living for us in white marble in the famous frieze of the Parthenon, which was brought to England by Lord Elgin early in the reign of Queen Victoria and is preserved in the British Museum. (The account is an abbreviation of that compiled by Miss Jane Harrison).

The Parthenon was the temple (*i.e.*, the palace) of the maiden goddess Athena, the personification of the spirit of the city of Athens,[1] and in the shrine within it was the great image of Athena in gold and ivory, symbolising her presence in precisely the same way that an image of Siva in a South Indian temple symbolises the presence of the deity who is the embodiment of life's superabundant energy. Outside the shrine, and running round the top of the building was the sculptured representation of the worship

[1] We have seen this idea to have obtained at an earlier date in Sumeria.

of the goddess, who was accompanied in theory by eleven other deities. The procession so depicted brought the whole of Athens together, just as the Lord Mayor's show in some sense brings each year the whole of the city of London together, except that the Panathenaia was only held every fifth year. In the frieze we see the procession beginning to form, and the youth of Athens mounting on its horses. After the cavalry we come to the chariots; then follow the sacrificial beasts, sheep and cows, then the instruments of sacrifice; flutes and lyres and baskets and trays for offerings; men carrying olive boughs in blossom; and maidens with water vessels and drinking cups. The procession is met by a band of magistrates who face it at the east end of the temple just as it enters. The central ceremony appears to have been the offering to the goddess of a sacred robe or peplos woven and em- broidered by the young women of Athens, and received, as we see represented in the central slab of the frieze, by the priest of Athena from the hands of a boy, after which solemn reception it was placed like a doll's dress upon an ancient image, one far older and more primitive than the gold and ivory statue. The day of the festival was believed to be the birthday of the goddess and was the opening of the first month of the Athenian year. Its object no doubt was to bring about the renewal of the life of the ground, parched by the summer heat, for without rain the life of the year dies out and has to be renewed. This renewal is brought about not by making a new image each year, but by redressing the image and offering it each fifth year a new robe. (This of course does not explain why the ceremony became quinquennial. Perhaps the interval may have been due to motives of economy.)

Most important for us to-day, however, is not the origin of Hellenic beliefs and worship so much as a third

feature, *i.e.* the disintegration of this splendid and
artistic polytheism before the criticism of free thought.
The actual heyday of Hellenic worship was short (less
than a century perhaps) and as in the case of other
religions[1] the observance of the pageantry outlasted the
vitality of the creed.   Here it seems that perhaps there
really is a break in development, and that philosophy
performed somewhat the same service for the Greeks
that prophecy did for the Hebrews.   At the same time
the utterances of the prophets, so far as they have come
down to us, are almost always accompanied by a
positive element, whereas much Greek speculation is
merely negative and destructive.   It is said that this
negative criticism was in the beginning rendered possible
by the frank anthropomorphism of the Homeric epics.
Whatever the origin of these great poems, in their
finished form they embody the work of a school of
thought which depicted the deities of the Greek pantheon as being neither more nor less than akin to human
beings animated by passion and cruelty.   These epics
originated in Ionia, that western tip of what we call
Asia Minor, which until the recent sack of Smyrna was
for long centuries the home of a Greek population:
and it was this epic poetry with its anthropomorphism
which uprooted the belief in the supernatural and paved
the way for the explanation of the world on naturalistic
lines.   Natural philosophy accordingly developed freely
in Ionia, but was at first confined to a narrow circle,
since that province was politically insignificant.   It went
on, however, to be transplanted towards the beginning of
the fifth century B.C. into Italy, and towards the end of

[1] See note on page 346.

the same century into Athens, the spiritual metropolis of Hellas, where it encountered a certain amount of hostility. Athens, having during the previous century attained a high degree of wealth and prosperity, became involved in 431 in a war of rivalry with her neighbour Sparta. Now as long as the city was prosperous and successful, her authorities were ready to smile indulgently upon modernists and freethinkers; but the type of statesman thrown up by this war was not altogether friendly to them, for the city-state regarded religion of the traditional polytheistic type as an expression of the idea of the State, and its maintenance as a patriotic duty; and seeing that Athens was fighting for her very existence, the Government regarded with intense hostility anything that was likely to endanger its relations with the gods. Moreover, it seems to be a resultant feature of most wars that they lead temporarily at any rate to a revival of conservatism in religion, if not of actual superstition, accompanied by a profound scepticism. This is the explanation of the notorious attack on Socrates in 399 B.C., which ultimately led to his condemnation. We must not, however, suppose that the politicians were always able or even willing to suppress free thought or the expression of so-called anti-religious symptoms. (Actually, of course, there was more of what we should call real religion about Socrates and his pupil Plato than about some of the Greek philosophers and playwrights whose utterances apparently passed uncondemned).

The Milesian philosophers of Ionia, whose methods of free investigation when transplanted led to this trouble, were what are now called monists, and the chief of them,

Thales, who flourished about 600 B.C., derived all that exists from a single watery element. Aristotle, however, says that Thales taught that all things are "full of gods," by which one supposes that he meant "possessed of a spiritual or mental element."

Pythagoras, important as he seems, is a half-legendary figure. We hear of his leaving Samos in the Aegean about 532 B.C. and going to the south of Italy, where he established what in India to-day would be called an Ashram, or school for his pupils, in philosophy and mysticism. These pupils in fact became a species of religious order, with an elaborate ceremonial derived perhaps from the Orphic mysteries. Pythagoras himself professed a monism in which the basic element was air. The multiplicity of forms in the world around us arises in his view out of this one unlimited and simple world-substance, through the action upon it of another principle, that of determination. These two from all eternity have been linked together and yet are opposed to each other, and from their perpetual attraction and repulsion all things have sprung, their forms being determined by ratios of numbers.

Heracleitus, who flourished in Ephesus about 490 B.C., was what we should call a pluralist, and found the meaning of the Universe in its perpetual flux. The only unity to him is the feature of activity, which is the common property of the ever-changing multiplicity of things. Parmenides, who taught at Elea[1] in South Italy about 480, was another definite monist, and carried the doctrine to its extreme conclusion. The real world—

[1] Hence the phrase, the Eleatics, describing both those who followed him and also his predecessor Xenophanes.

the whole of that which is—was according to him, one, indivisible, and unchangeable, without beginning or end, growth or decay, unmoving and immovable. The defect of this view was that it had to explain away the differences which manifest themselves to us between the many entities which the world seems to contain, but did not account for them satisfactorily, and soon led therefore to a reaction in the direction of pluralism, exemplified in the teachings of Democritus (*c.* 460) with his doctrine of atoms, and of Empedocles (*c.* 490), who made out the four basic elements from which the Universe in its endless multiplicity is derived to be earth, air, water and fire.

It can hardly be a matter for wonder that such a series of independent thinkers should have found the naïve mythology and crude polytheism of the populace, and even the cultured and conventionalised religious pageantry of the city-states inadequate and unsatisfying.

We will now give a few instances showing the kind of criticism which crops up at intervals from the period of the Homeric epics onwards. Earliest of all is probably that of Xenophanes, the founder of the Eleatic School, who left Colophon in Ionia in 532 to settle in Sicily and afterwards in South Italy, and who declared that if the animals could speak they would certainly say that Deity was like one of themselves. He taught that there was but one only God, akin to mortals neither in mind nor form, and he attacked the cult of images in the form of statues, and the mythology recounted in the pages of Homer and Hesiod. Not enough remains of his writings however to enable us to decide whether his god was a real god or merely a philosophical principle, and whether he was only a philosopher or also a religious reformer.

There are also utterances of Heracleitus which are directed with the greatest possible acuteness against the outward forms of worship. It is not clear whether these men were aiming at overthrowing the religion which they had inherited, or whether they were seeking to purify it, through radical reform. In any case their criticism was without the consequences which resulted from similar criticisms at a later date. In his *Apology*, Plato represents Socrates as referring to a certain Anaxagoras who is being accused of atheism. Socrates says that the teachings of this man have been confused with his, and that although he on the whole agrees with the astronomical speculations of Anaxagoras, he himself believes in a spiritual deity, though he does not identify him with the sun.

Anaxagoras (to do him justice) taught that the ultimate element in the universe was Nous, usually translated mind, which is unlimited, and has power over all things that have life, both great and small. We cannot be sure, however, whether he regarded Nous as personal. Probably he was as much open to misunderstanding as the Chinese Chu Hsi, with his doctrine of li. He was one of the two tutors of Pericles, the great Athenian statesman of the fifth century.

Socrates was preceded by, and is indeed himself one of, the popular philosophical teachers known as sophists, who figured as public instructors of youth, and engaged in open discussion. It is difficult to believe that apart from political animosities it would have been considered worth while to prefer the charge of unorthodox religious opinions against him, since other sophists had also treated the nature of the gods as an open question. Thus one of the earliest of them, Protagoras (*c.* 415), says: "In the matter of the gods I have not been able to attain the knowledge of their existence or non-existence or of what form they are; for many things hinder the attainment of this knowledge, both the obscurity of the subject and the shortness of human life." The main point here, of course, is that Protagoras treats the existence of the gods as something to be demonstrated by argument, and this involves an appeal to reason, which undermines the authority of a supernatural religion.

Diagoras, a contemporary of Protagoras, was the typical atheist. His own sufferings had rendered him sceptical, and he declared that the injustice of the world proved that there was no deity who punished evil and guarded the virtuous. When someone pointed out to him in a temple the votive pictures of persons who had had a safe voyage by sea, as evidence that the god in question had protected them, he replied: "those who are shipwrecked do not get painted."

Bur it was not only the philosophers who were the distinctive critics of religion; it was also the dramatists, who in their youth had received their education at the hands of the sophists. Many will be familiar with the way in which Aristophanes gently pokes fun at the Greek gods. He represents the builders of cloud-cuckoodom as interposing their newly-constructed state between earth and heaven, and so cutting off the smoke of the sacrifices from the gods, who are starved into making a treaty with them. In the *Clouds* the

theories of natural philosophy are displayed, when
Zeus is represented as being deposed by a whirlwind
(Δῖνος), and a revolt against the ethic of conventional
religion is hinted at when it is pointed out that Zeus
with his thunderbolt does not limit his use of it (as he
ought), to the punishment of perjurers and profane
persons, but also occasionally strikes harmless mountain
tops, beautiful trees, and even his own temples. There
is a fragment of a drama entitled Sisyphos, written by
Kritias, one of the best known pupils of the sophists, in
which the thesis is maintained that men at first lived
like wild beasts without law and order; might was right;
and this was only remedied by the invention of laws and
punishments whereby right might take the place of
might. But since men now began to practise injustice
in secret, a certain wise and cunning fellow invented the
gods who hear and see all, so that mankind should not
be able to enjoy unrighteousness in secret. Religion
thus becomes a mere tool for the maintenance of order
in the state, a moral robot policeman for upholding
legal conventions, but so cleverly constructed as to be
beyond criticism.

In the hands of Euripides the religion of the day is
fiercely attacked. Of course Euripides was limited by the
conventions of the Athenian playwright, both as regards
his subject-matter and its treatment. He was only
allowed to draw from the ancient stories of the gods; he
had to observe the dramatic unities and conventions;
and his plays were intended to be acted at religious
festivals. The less intelligent of his audiences probably
thought that he was giving them the usual correct
picture of piety rewarded and vice and irreverence

punished. It is quite evident, however, that Euripides is often writing with his tongue in his cheek, that he hates and despises the Greek gods, and that to those who have eyes to see and ears to hear, he represents them as despicable. His attitude is well summed up in the famous outburst of Hecuba:

"If the gods do something shameful, then are they not gods."

In another place in the same play, the *Bellerophon*, he represents one of his characters as saying bitterly that there can be no gods who protect small states against the aggression of greater ones, otherwise there could be no tyranny. Belief in the oracles now began to decline, and we can see the beginning of this in the writings of Herodotus and Sophocles.

At first this scepticism was associated with the upper and educated classes, and was suspected by the popular democracy, whose interests were bound up with the maintenance of the stability of the state, which was believed to depend in no small measure on the maintenance of the state religion. Hence the prosecutions of Socrates and others. By the third century, however, these prosecutions ceased, for the religious indifference which was the result of the work of the critics had seized upon the whole people. We hear in Xenophon of a typical young man who does not sacrifice, does not consult the oracle and mocks those who do so. Plato in the work which he wrote in his old age (the *Nomoi*) recommends, as we shall see, that atheists shall be shut up and admonished, and if they persist be punished with death. But Demosthenes only uses the names of the gods conventionally, regards Tuchê or chance as controlling life, and says that the oracle of Apollo at Delphi is a cheat. The Athenians at the end of the century blasphemously defied a popular hero, and a song was publicly sung in which the contempt for the old gods was expressed in the words:

"Either they are far away or have no ears, or else do not exist or care not a whit about us."

After this, blasphemy in some cases became a fashionable pursuit, while in art the gods are no longer represented with reverence, but merely as convenient excuses for making statues in which the technique is the real interest.

Meanwhile the explaining away of the myths in a naturalistic fashion went on steadily. At first it was mainly allegorical and physical, but in the case of Euhemerus (340) a new explanation was offered. The gods, he said, were really human beings who by might and cunning had persuaded men to worship them. His book was one of the first to be translated into Latin and his popularity is evident from the way in which he is singled out for abuse.

The effect of what is called Euhemerism was to encourage the depersonalising of the idea of Deity. Side by side with the conception of Tuchê or chance, and Anankê, necessity or fate, both of which are blind and capricious, we find the conception of τὸ θεῖον, a vague sublime quality not wholly unlike the "sacred" or the "numinous" in our modern jargon. This was thought to manifest itself especially in the lives of eminent men, and so justified the euhemeristic explanation of the origin of worship. It was actually justifiable as well as natural to treat heroes, generals, and kings with divine honours. The first man to receive divine worship in this way was Lysander, the conqueror of Athens (*d.* 395 B.C.). Altars were raised to him as to a god, sacrifices were offered and hymns sung in his honour. A hundred years later at Athens Demetrius and Antigonus were similarly given divine honours. The "Dionysia" were rechristened the "Demetria" and the last day of every month was called "Demetria." It is not a far cry from such practices to the deification of emperors, although the Roman practice comes some centuries later. The point is that men argued the possibility that the divine principle might manifest itself in the lives of human beings of exceptional power and ability.

The unbelief of the declining period of Greek fortunes was accompanied by much uneasiness. Side by side with scepticism flourished a large amount of superstition, such as is ridiculed by Theophrastus (*d.* 287 B.C.). In addition to this there began the immigration of foreign deities, possibly with the idea that as less was known about them they might be more credible than the ones which had been explained away. There was also a considerable resort to astrology.

It would be a mistake, however, to suppose that there was no constructive thought during the later period of Greek history. Although Socrates (470–399) is usually thought of as a destructive critic, he was in reality a remarkable mixture of prophet and rationalist, claiming that from childhood he had an inner voice which seemed to him divine, and which afforded him constant guidance. Indeed at his trial the indictment does not charge

him with atheism but with introducing strange supernatural beings who are not the gods recognised by the
authorities of the city of Athens. Whether his views of
religion are given correctly by his pupil and biographer
Plato (427–347) it is hard to say, but one thing at any
rate is certain, namely that the latter develops and
displays positive beliefs of his own which are of a
strongly normative character and deserve careful
attention.

Plato is sure that there are certain truths about God
which are capable of demonstration, and that their
denial leads straight to the formation of bad character.
Hence the denial of these truths is an offence against
society and should be punished as such. In Plato's
view there is therefore a natural or philosophical
theology which is not necessarily opposed to or com-
plemented by revelation, but is "natural" in the sense
of being concerned with a proper account of things as
they are in φύσις, nature, or reality.

Plato regards three types of misbelief as harmful,
(1) pure atheism, (2) Epicureanism or the doctrine of
the indifference of the gods, (3) that the gods can be
bribed, by gifts and offerings, to acquit the offender.

" It is morally less harmful to believe in no god than
to believe in a careless god, and better to believe in a
careless god than a venal one."

Plato says that he can prove the existence of God or
gods as against these three so-called heresies. His
arguments against atheism are of some interest, and
they clearly establish his position as the creator of
philosophical theism. He proceeds thus: All bodily

movements are ultimately dependent on mental voli-
tions.    Therefore the world is caused by the activity of
one perfectly good soul, the ἀρίστη ψύχη.  He points out
that atheism arises from two sources, first the materialistic theory of the Ionian scientists who professed to
explain the order of nature upon what we should call
purely mechanical principles, with no reference to plan
or design; secondly to the theory of the sophists that
moral distinctions are of a purely conventional and
relative character.   Plato aims at refuting both these
theories, and shews that all motions of bodies which we
are able to investigate closely are preceded by movements of soul, so that, as he says, τέχνη (or purpose)
precedes τύχη (what happens), and not τύχη τέχνη.
Plato's notion is that evil is traceable to the disorderly
motion of the soul.   If these ideas were not actually to
be read in Plato's *Nomoi*, one would be tempted to
suppose that they were modern ideas put into his mouth.
Their actual presence shews what a very little way we
have got in pure thought since the days of the great
Greeks.   We are still, in spite of our accumulated
information, compelled to choose between Plato's
theism and its opposite.

Once he has demonstrated the theistic position, it
becomes easy for him to refute the other two forms of
misbelief, *i.e.* that which maintains the indifference of
deity towards human affairs, and that which holds it
capable of being flattered or bribed into the betrayal
of Justice.   (It is rather curious that throughout the
argument Plato seems careless about the use of the
singular or plural, and sometimes speaks of God, sometimes of the gods).

Of the first allegation—that the gods (*sic*) are indifferent, Plato says that since we ourselves are conscious of disliking idleness, carelessness and injustice, and further that since Deity, whether singular or plural, is the Self-Existent Origin of ourselves, therefore Deity cannot be possessed of qualities which are fundamentally opposed to our own. But further, says Plato, our opponents do not deny the existence of Deity, nor even the perfection and omnipotence of such a self-existent Being. But perfection as an attribute excludes the possibility of indolence and ignorance alike. It is indeed a much better explanation of life than complete predestinarianism to assume that God assigns to human souls their places in such a manner as to ensure the defeat of evil, while He leaves the fashioning of men's characters to themselves; and it is more correct to say that man was created to fit into his own place in the universe than in order that the universe might minister to his convenience. With regard to the allegation that the gods are venal and can be bribed or bargained with, Plato insists that it is impossible to suppose Deity to be worse than even moderately good men. On the contrary it is a better explanation to suppose the world, as he says "to be full of many goods and also of evils and of more evils than goods, and that there is an immortal conflict going on among us, which requires marvellous watchfulness; in which conflict the gods are our allies and we are their property."

Finally Plato prescribes a certain scheme of punishment for dealing with persons who teach heresy.

If, he says, a man is guilty of any impiety in word or deed, anyone who happens to be present shall give information to the magistrates, who shall be bound to prosecute under penalty, and who, if they refuse to act, shall themselves be tried for impiety. Persons convicted under these conditions shall be liable to three forms of imprisonment, the first of these being confinement in the ordinary common prison, the second, committal to a house of reformation. the third, banishment to a penal settlement in some wild and desolate region. Plato points out that from each of the three causes of unbelief arise two sorts of impiety, so that there are actually under this count six different types of offence which are worth distinguishing and which should not all have the same punishment. In other words, each of the three types of impious person may be either honest or dishonest. If they are honest they are to be placed in solitary confinement for five years, and if they repent at the end of that time they shall be restored to society, but if they again offend they shall be punished with death. Those who are dishonest are to be imprisoned for life, and when dead their bodies are not to be buried but thrown over the frontier, while anyone venturing to give them burial is himself to be liable to prosecution for impiety.

These proposals have been given in detail for the obvious reason that they have provided the model for all subsequent religious persecution, and indeed not only for all subsequent attempts by states to coerce men into adopting or eschewing private beliefs, but also for most penal systems. Thus it will be obvious that the prison system of Great Britain provides ordinary gaols for short-term sentences, others as reformatories or Borstal institutions, and others again of the type of

Dartmoor for long or life sentences. Again, the same threefold division was observed by the Tsarist government in Russia in dealing with seditious persons, the extreme penalty being banishment to Siberia, and it appears that the Bolshevik and Nazi authorities treat offences against communistic and fascist theory in much the same way. Finally we have of course the supreme instance of the working of a penal code directed against impiety in the provisions of the Roman church for the conduct of the Holy Office of the Inquisition, though none of Plato's punishments can compare in cruelty with the handing over of an incorrigible offender to the secular arm with prayers that there might be no shedding of blood, *i.e.* that the person in question might be burned alive. (It is obvious that execution by burning was a barbarous practice taken over from the pagan southern Europeans, like bullfighting: it has, however, spread to other parts of the globe, and has been indulged in by Protestant Christians as well. There are of course records of the burning of witches in Great Britain, and of the lynching of negroes by whites in the United States).

Whether Plato is to be burdened with the guilt of having taught the world to persecute may be disputed. The case of Socrates shows clearly that the practice of penalising the unorthodox, whether in religious or political opinions, was already well-established before Plato wrote, so that all that can be said about the coercive proposals contained in the *Laws* is that they show that he thought that if you could arrive at a true and absolute doctrine about God, it would become *ipso facto* a necessary part of the erudition of a good citizen, and that to dispute it ought to be punished as not only dangerous, but as an insult and an act of disloyalty towards the very foundations of the universe. The nineteenth century thought differently, though it is not easy to say how much of its liberalism was due to an uneasy suspicion that, certainty being impossible, all opinions must therefore be tolerated, and how much to the basic principle that force is not an attribute of deity and that truth is so majestic that she can always win her way by persuasion. But the twentieth century seems inclined to abandon freedom and to go back to Plato in his last phase, since within the last thirty years we have had penal enactments against theists, pacifists, communists, and anti-fascists.

The whole point about it, of course, is that Plato assumes that no reasonable person will regard his propositions as doubtful, and therefore to reject them will imply moral turpitude. It is certainly much more difficult to condemn the repression of freedom of opinion if one believes that certain propositions about the nature of reality are capable of complete demonstration, especially if belief or disbelief in such propositions has a direct bearing upon conduct. The horror with which most of us regard the story of the proceedings of the Holy Office is not entirely bred of our objection to its ferocious torturings and burnings. It is in a measure excited by the conviction that a part of Catholic belief is simply not true. Bolshevik Russia, Fascist Italy, and Nazi Germany, have been guilty of persecuting their internal enemies within the last ten years, and the defence in all three cases has been the

x

assertion that the tenets of communism and fascism comprise truths which it is pernicious to deny. It is quite possible to imagine a state of society where scientific eugenists were rulers, in which it would be a penal offence to beget a child without a licence or to make a public speech against sterilisation of the unfit. Toleration begins when men grow doubtful as to the infallible truth of their judgments, and is in any case impossible on all points. There are some opinions which no community can allow to be publicly expressed, even though they may be held in secret. In general a universal tolerance springs from two causes:

(a) The belief that no knowledge is final and complete, but that human opinion moves on towards a future goal and is in need of continual revisions.

(b) The conviction that coercion is not the way in which to get the best service out of any individual.

It is a relief to turn to another aspect of Plato's work.

We have seen that Deity to Plato is the self-moving mover. The origin of the cosmos is in the purposive contemplation of this mover, who contemplates the "forms" (which are an essential part of Plato's theory of the universe) and reproduces them in the order of the sensible world. Although to students of the dialogues "form" is a familiar technical phrase, it may be serviceable to explain its meaning to the general reader.

It is well to remember that Plato's conception of the world is not cut and dried. He did not himself write out his scheme nor did he encourage his followers to do it. What he wished was that they should love truth and pursue it as a quest. The only set principle by which he holds that this quest should be guided is that the temporal can only be understood in relation to the eternal. Everything which we apprehend is a particular instance of some general or universal idea or form, very much indeed what the mediaeval philosophers called "universals." There is in fact a whole eternal world of "forms" which are the proto-types of all the things with which we are familiar. Thus we are acquainted with particular examples of circles. These, however, are but copies or instances of what we may call the heavenly idea of the circular. Similarly in many things around us we recognise an element which we call the beautiful, of which we see particular instances, such as beautiful children, flowers, or statues. These, however, are but fleeting instances of beauty subject to change and decay. They are particulars of a universal or heavenly form which is eternal. The supreme form is that of good, which is the fundamental motive of the whole cosmos. The difficulty involved in this theory plainly appears when we ask, is there a form corresponding to everything within the scope of our experience? Is there for instance a form corresponding to the particular phenomenon of mud, dirt, or hair?

At this point Plato's consistency seems to break down, and he says that although the theory would seem to demand forms for everything, at the same time he is inclined to reject this conclusion.

Obviously, so far as detailed expression is concerned, the theory belongs to the age in which it was conceived, and we cannot claim for it any entire finality, but as a general principle it demands respect, *i.e.* as the principle that the groundwork of all events in space-time consists of a succession of ideas (here called forms) which subsist in the eternal mind of God and find expression in the patterns woven in our material cosmos. Whatever we may think of this conception, it is quite impossible to understand much of the early literature of the Christian movement, and indeed much of the literature of late antiquity, without taking it into account. Thus, for example, we find Plutarch explaining the myths of Greek religion and the personalities of the Alexandrian divinities by saying that they are merely particular likenesses or symbols of the eternal reality, and that their meaning is allegorical rather than literal. Similarly the Alexandrian Jew, Philo, treats the stories of the Old Testament as allegories; and echoes of the same method may be found in certain passages of St. Paul, in the Epistle to the Hebrews, and in the writings of the Alexandrian theologians, Clement and Origen, at the beginning of the third century A.D. The influence of Platonism upon early sacramental theory was profound, and it is still a vital element in Christian thought. But it contains what must seem to many one grave weakness, namely a dualism between the world of forms and the world of things.

Plato, though he inclines towards monotheism, is not prepared to give us any definite teaching as to the nature of God, and, as we have already seen, he now and then speaks of gods in the plural. Sometimes he says that the good life consists in imitating God, and that nothing on earth so much resembles God as the just human being, and he also says that God brought the world into being because He was not only free from all jealousy but wished to have created souls to share His perfection. It is a commonplace that when words fail him in giving an exact description of anything, he falls back on a myth, and tells a tale which is to give the likeness or copy of the truth.

Aristotle (384–322) is in almost every respect different from Plato, although he manifestly takes over, as a pupil from his master, a large amount of his actual terminology, if not of his thought. Whereas Plato aims at discovering the meaning of the universe from one's own mind, feeling that our acquaintance with what lies outside us is simply opinion, the former regards the study of the external world as of the first importance, and is actually in many ways the founder of scientific method, with its observation, classification, experiment and deduction. With all this Plato seems to have little or no concern. We may even suppose that he has an entire contempt for them. Possibly he felt that the men of his day were too imperfectly equipped for their scientific observations to be of any value; but if he does so he at the same time shows no desire to improve that equipment. To him God is the measure of all things and the universe is less important. To Aristotle the universe and its inhabitants are important, and religion as concerned with Deity matters less. Curiously enough, there is also less interest in the problem of the future life. He is pre-occupied with human society as it exists, with the world of Nature which surrounds it, and not with the unseen world. We may assume that he was less a precursor of a type which will ultimately replace the Platonic, than himself an instance of a type which will always coexist with the Platonic. Such men owe their strength to the faculty they possess for abstracting a certain entire group of elements from the sum total of possible human experiences and of concentration upon it. They have the merit that their feet are ever firmly planted upon the earth. The trouble about the Platonist is that he tends to be sadly unpractical, and loses his head in the clouds.

It has been said that Aristotle's is the most comprehensive intellect in the history of thought. Certainly one of the ablest and most widely influential groups of writing in the world, next to that of the Bible, is the trilogy formed by the *Ethics*, *Politics*, and *Poetics*. Although the interests of Aristotle are scientific rather than religious, it seems fitting to give a brief account of his system, if only because of the effect which it has had indirectly upon the philosophical theology of the Roman Catholic church. To Aristotle what we call the real substance of any individual being is something which is distinct in thought from its external expression. The first he calls εἶδος or form, the second ὕλη or matter. Form organises, defines, and makes concrete the matter of each individual unit. Matter, therefore, is not distinct from spirit but is relative to it; it never exists by itself but only, so to speak, in form. We may almost say that matter is simply a pattern in which spirit arranges itself and not something separate from spirit. It is obvious that this kind of monism may lead to a materialistic conclusion in which spirit becomes only an etherealised sort of matter. Aristotle does not, however, draw this conclusion, but rather (though quite inconsistently), that form in the shape of reason can and does exist prior to and apart from its union with and expression in matter, and he even suggests that the soul may inhabit the body just as a sailor lives on a ship. Clearly there is here no final position. Deity to Aristotle exists as pure form.

To Aristotle there are four kinds of cause in Nature: the material cause, let us say the stone out of which a statue is made; the formal cause, that is to say the pattern which it is made to assume (*e.g.* Nurse Cavell); the efficient cause, *i.e.* the sculptor, in this case Frampton; and the final cause, the purpose for which the statue was made, *i.e.* to commemorate the sacrifice of a good woman. Aristotle declares that this final cause or purpose is the real cause which has to be discovered about anything before the human mind can be satisfied about it and so come to rest. Obviously this theory is the basis of his ethics. Before we can understand the meaning of the development (or as we should say the evolution) of any species of animal, or pre-eminently of man, we must consider not merely its origin but its final aim. He firmly believes in what we call teleology, though not necessarily that the *telos* of any particular development is an ultimate or distant one; sometimes it may be a near and immediate *telos*, or, as we should say, a limited objective. Here we come to his theology, such as it is. He believes that time and change are necessarily eternal. The only continuous change is motion.

But we can only be satisfied by an explanation of motion which relates it to a cause of motion which is itself unmoved. Now, since such an unmoved mover must by reason of his own nature be precluded from being a cause falling into any one of the first three classes, he must be a final cause or better still the final cause, keeping things moving by drawing them with the longing to fulfil a purpose. Deity Himself, since He is perfect, can desire nothing, can love nothing but what is perfect, and can know nothing but what is perfect, that is Himself. But the desire for Deity moves the intelligences of the universe which inform its matter, and draws them by making them long for communion with Deity. It is a curious theory, and it is strange that it should have indirectly exerted so much influence upon Catholic theology, for it seems to have little or nothing in common with the conception of Deity held by Jesus of Nazareth. It seems, indeed, as though the effort to fit Christianity on to this philosophy, however ingenious and well-meant, has been an effort to fit one alternative solution of the problem of existence on to another which is incompatible with it, and that this has led astray many generations of religious thinkers. Some may not feel able to accept the Christian theory of God, and may even prefer Aristotle's remote and impersonal Deity: but when it comes to a question of consistency, it seems that one or the other must be given up.

The actual immediate influence in the Hellenic world was less that of Aristotle than that of Plato, and out of the latter's system there developed a number of more or less distinct philosophical schools, of which we will mention two, associated respectively with Epicurus and Zeno. Epicurus (341–270 B.C.), rejected any notion of a purpose in Nature, and consequently denied that there was any moral government to be discerned in the universe. We should describe him to-day as a thorough-going materialist. He and his followers taught that pleasure was the sole good and pain the sole evil. Such a philosophy may lead to a life of sensual indulgence, but in practice, since indulgence frequently leads to pain, it actually involves the withdrawal from the world as the means of attaining true pleasure. Absence of pain is the highest good, and all virtues are compacts of expediency to prevent discomfort. The followers of Epicurus adhered very loyally to his teaching, and it appears reproduced for us with but little variation in the poetry of the great Roman Lucretius, whose sombre verse breathes a resolute resistance bred of inevitable despair. It is not surprising to learn that at a comparatively early age Lucretius went mad and committed suicide.

Zeno (336–264 B.C.) is said to have been a Phoenician whose home was in Cyprus, and who abandoned trade for philosophy, establishing himself at length in Athens about the year 310, where he set up a school for instruction in a colonnade known as the Painted Porch or Stoa. (Hence the name of Stoic as applied to his disciples.) He was succeeded by Chrysippus (280–207) who organised the teaching of Zeno into a system which has had a remarkably long life. According to this system Deity *is* the *universe*, which is thought of and described sometimes as fire, sometimes as spirit or breath, sometimes as Nature, reason, providence or destiny. Whereas, according to Plato, it is only the ideas of phenomena which really exist, the Stoics held that it was this refined material substance alone which existed, and everything, from the popular gods to the soul of man and the world of his experience, is of the nature of a series of emanations from Deity, into whom they will eventually be reabsorbed. The object of life for man, therefore, according to the Stoic, must be to live in accordance with Nature, that is to say, in harmony with the purpose and principle of the universe. Each individual contains a fragment of the divine reason, whereby man can, if he will, live in accordance with Nature, and whatever disharmony there may be is due to the failure of the individual to recognise this and submit to it. There appears then in this system to be a distinct place for human free-will. Zeno himself insisted that the speculation in which the Greek mind delighted could not be an end in itself, that end being to live in conformity with Nature. Speculation, therefore, is only necessary in order that we may know what Nature is, and hence the Stoic division of study into physics, logic and ethics. The end of such study, however, is not the study itself but the discovery of what Nature is, in order that the knowledge thus gained may be applied. Nothing is good to the Stoic but virtue, and nothing bad but vice. Those things which are commonly called good or bad are merely conditions under which virtue may be practised, and to the ideal wise man these conditions are indifferent, since nothing can happen to him which is not part of the system of the universe, and he will therefore be able to be calm and self-sufficient even in extreme adversity. Zeno, however, was not a complete individualist, for he strongly insisted upon the unity of the universe and on man's duty as part of the whole.

Since all men partake of the divine nature, all are citizens of one great Commonwealth, and have the obligation of mutual service: but it must be noted that such service is not to be animated by feelings of goodwill, pity or compassion, but only by the sense of duty. For the Stoic it can never be right in the cause of compassion to surrender one's inner citadel and to sacrifice one's internal calm. Here, of course, we see a very sharp distinction between the Stoic and the Christian theory of life.

According to the Stoic teaching, the soul, as a fragment of the indestructible universe, survived death, but not as an individual. Being by nature an emanation from the divine Fire or Spirit (a fragment of it, so to speak), it will eventually be reabsorbed into its Source. Zeno taught that there was evidence of purpose and providence in the natural course of events, but he regarded that course as of infinite duration, and as consisting of a series or cycle of universes, each of which is emitted and brought into being and sustained through stages of deterioration till it has finally run down and completed its course, when another will take its place and again another, and so on for ever. There is no future consummation or ultimate purpose towards which this series can be said to be working, although we are told that we need experience neither fear nor discomfort at the dissolution of that which is natural. At the same time we must not expect to find our true beatitude in the future.   If we are to have any satisfaction, any happiness, any sense of eternal life, we must look for it here and now; and since we plainly cannot always have what we like, we must school ourselves to like what we can have.

By far the most famous Stoic religious poem is what is called the hymn of Cleanthes (331–232), the successor of Zeno, which is here given in translation.   In it, as we shall see, the supreme principle is personified as Zeus.

### THE HYMN OF CLEANTHES

O God most glorious, called by many a name,
Nature's great King, through endless years the same;
Omnipotence, who by thy just decree
Controllest all, hail Zeus! for unto thee
Behoves all creatures in all lands to call,
We are thy children, we alone, of all,
On earth's broad ways that wander to and fro,
Bearing thine image wheresoe'er we go.
Wherefore with songs of praise thy power I will forth show.
Lo! yonder heaven, that round the earth is wheeled,
Follows thy guidance, still to thee doth yield
Glad homage; thine unconquerable hand
Such flaming minister, the levin-brand
Wieldeth a sword two-edged, whose deathless might
Pulsates through all that nature brings to light;
Vehicle of the universal Word, that flows
Through all, and in the light celestial glows
Of stars both great and small.   O King of Kings
Through countless ages, God! whose purpose brings
To birth whate'er on land or in the sea
Is wrought, or in high heaven's immensity;
Save what the sinner works infatuate.

Nay, but thou knowest to make crooked straight;
Chaos to thee is order; in thine eyes
The unloved is lovely, who didst harmonize
Things evil with things good, that there should be
One Word through all things everlastingly.
One Word—whose voice, alas! the wicked spurn.
Insatiate for the good their spirits yearn,
Yet seeing see not, neither hearing hear
God's universal law, which those revere
By reason guided, happiness who win.
The rest unreasoning diverse shapes of sin
Self-prompted follow; for an idle name
Vainly they wrestle in the lists of fame.
Others inordinately riches woo,
Or, dissolute, the joys of flesh pursue
Now here, now there, they wander, fruitless still
For ever seeking good and finding ill.
Zeus the all-bountiful, whom darkness shrouds,
Whose lightning lightens in the thunder-clouds,
Thy children save from error's deadly sway;
Turn thou the darkness from their souls alway;
Vouchsafe them unto knowledge to attain;
For thou by knowledge art made strong to reign
O'er all, and all things rulest righteously;
So, by thee honoured, we will honour thee,
Praising thy works continually with songs,
As mortals should; nor higher meed belongs
E'en to the gods, than justly to adore
The universal law for evermore.

This remarkable system of teaching presents obvious
affinities with much that goes by the name of
Christianity,[1] and it is an accepted fact that the early

[1] A useful survey and comparison of Stoic and Christian doctrines
is to be found in the Haskell Memorial Lectures delivered by the
late Dean Rashdall, and entitled "Conscience and Christ."

Christian church baptised a good deal of the Stoic philosophy and admitted it as not incompatible with Christ's teaching.

Two of the best known later exponents of Stoicism, Seneca and Epictetus, are actually contemporary with Christ, while the famous Stoic Emperor, Marcus Aurelius Antoninus (A.D. 177), although he bitterly persecuted the early Christian movement, has had the satisfaction of seeing himself almost canonised and his famous book of meditations treated as a devotional classic, set by some nearly on a level with Thomas à Kempis' *Imitation of Christ*. This, of course, may be partly due to the presence of a movement around the Emperor which he could not wholly ignore, even though he might react against it. His Stoicism, like that of his contemporaries, may be compared with the Hinduism of a reforming movement, owing an unacknowledged debt to Christianity. In any case there is a wide gap chronologically between Zeno and the Antonines, and all are agreed that Stoicism developed and altered very much during that interval. Thus *e.g.*, by the time of Epictetus (A.D. 90), the primeval stuff of the universe had become identified with reason.

Perhaps for us the most important feature about Stoicism is its clear-sighted anticipation of the picture of the universe given to us by the modern biologists. No one can fail to be impressed with the resemblance between the simple Stoic account of the universe and some of those which have been written by scientists during the past twenty years. The enormous area of research which lies between the two seems to make but little difference.

The fundamental difference between the Stoic and the Christian standpoint is easy to detect, and it is remarkable to see that there is a similar difference between the essentially Christian standpoint of to-day and some contemporary scientific philosophy. The difference is this: Stoicism viewed the cosmic process as an eternal repetition of cycles leading nowhere, each cycle ending in a dead level of inertia. Some cosmogonists to-day believe, as we have seen, that the super-universe is settling down to a somewhat similar dead level of inertia, and others that there is a winding-up as well as a running-down process going on all the time, and therefore that history endlessly repeats itself. But the Christian belief, inherited from the Hebrews, is, as we shall see later on, that in the successive phases of evanescence there is a purpose or series of purposes which is being worked out, and that the course of the whole, even though possibly spiral, is not cyclic, but makes for permanent achievement and infinite progress.

The most interesting religious feature in later antiquity is the development of religious confraternities which transcended the boundaries of class and race. The earlier conception of even a great god or goddess is that he or she represents a divine power connected with some locality, either a city-state or a piece of territory. Gradually, however, there grows the idea that strangers and foreigners may become fellow-citizens with those who are under the immediate patronage of the god, and so his cultus takes on an international form, and candidates for admission to the fraternity of his worshippers may be drawn from a number of different places. He may almost be said to take on missionary activities. Side by side with this there comes a second idea, that by a process of training, culminating in a solemn dramatic ceremony, the individual may experience rebirth into the fraternity of the worshippers of the god, and by this solemn experience become purged from base and perishable elements and acquire the immortal nature of the divine being himself. Hence the growth of what are rather roughly grouped together as mystery-religions. The various systems differ so much from one another that, beyond the two principles above stated, they have hardly anything else in common. Chronologically they extend over a long period, and must not be supposed to be limited to the time when the Christian church began its mission. There are obvious similarities between the entry into Europe of the worship of Dionysus which preceded Christianity by several centuries, and the entry of the worship of Mithras, which was very nearly contemporary with the apostolic age but perhaps a little later. There has been much vague and loose writing about the mystery religions, and their influence upon first-century Christianity has probably been exaggerated, since at that time the corrective influence of Hebrew religion was strong enough to check any unwarrantable intrusion of pagan ideas. In the second and following centuries, however, there are definite signs that the practices of contemporary mystery-cults are shaping the religious practices of Christians.

What we have to remember is that, as soon as Christianity moved out of its exclusively Jewish surroundings, it inevitably came to include in its membership Gentiles, many of whom, as people of religious habits prior to their conversion, were familiar with the customs of the fraternities connected with such gods as Sarapis, Isis, Apollo, or Bacchus (Dionysus-Zagreus). It would be almost impossible for them not to carry these ideas into their new environment, and to read the significance of the new religious practices which they were adopting in the light of the old. Moreover, however true it may be that in Judaism the moral and spiritual teaching of the prophets was never entirely obliterated, it was nevertheless associated with the survival, which apparently was tolerated by all Jews up to the destruction of the temple, of animal sacrifices, sacred meals, ceremonial mutilation and lustrations. Even after the destruction of the temple all the practices which could be carried on without it continued. There is, therefore, by no means the great gap between Judaism and Paganism which some have imagined. Gentiles becoming Christians would no doubt in the first century be struck by the peculiarity of certain specially Jewish practices, but they would regard them as belonging to the same world of mysterious ceremonial as their own. It would be the spiritual and moral teaching of the prophets, of Jesus and of the apostles, especially St. Paul, which would constitute the real *differentia* and which would condition their ideas about such things as the reception of the sacraments.

The main characteristics of these so-called mystery-religions may be summed up as follows:

The centre of worship is a divine personage in human

form, not perhaps the highest god, but a divine person of considerable eminence, representative no doubt of some great natural force. Each of these sacred beings was believed to have gone through some strange and often grotesque experience, and it was believed that if human beings were prepared to submit to a process of discipline, secret instruction and mystic ceremonial, they might actually share, as it were by proxy, in this great experience, or at least participate in the benefits which that particular episode was believed to yield for mankind.

Chief of these benefits was supposed to be that of rebirth into immortality, by which the initiate escaped the pangs of death and passed through the gates of everlasting life. It does not appear that any very exalted moral standard was required of candidates by initiation, but it is difficult to judge fairly, because in any case the best pagan morals are not identical with those of the Christian movement. At the same time the candidates were undoubtedly expected during the period of preparation to abstain from certain foods and from sexual intercourse. What teaching they were given we cannot exactly say. It may be that it was merely a series of mythical stories and their supposed meaning, or it may have been, if we are to trust the Hermetic literature, a series of lectures on the cosmogony of the day. In any case the whole scheme is obviously a more or less refined and artistic development of the initiation-customs of primitive man, the chief extension being in the direction of admitting not simply boys and girls at the age of puberty, but any individuals who applied for the privilege. It appears that to visit Eleusis for initiation was rather like visiting Ober-Ammergau for the Passion Play, or making a pilgrimage to mediaeval Canterbury, in the sense that it was possible to combine a pleasant holiday with the acquisition of merit or the performance of a pious practice.

The greater mysteries of Eleusis were connected with the story of Demeter and Korê, the Earth mother and her daughter; but the lesser mysteries of Eleusis were connected with the cultus of Dionysus. This god was not worshipped by the Greeks until the fourth century B.C., when his ceremonies were introduced from Thrace. It is a curious story. According to the myth he was the offspring of Zeus and a woman, and was torn in pieces by a race of giants and eaten by them. His father Zeus then restored him to life and gave him authority over the human race, who being descended from the giants inherited both their guilt (a sort of original sin) and also (strange though the idea seems to us) the actual nature of Zeus, through their ancestors having devoured his son. It was held, therefore, to be the duty of the human race to purge itself of the baser titanic element, and to be born again like Dionysus, through a process of mimetic communion with him. It seems to have been held that this communion was established in the sacred ritual, so that the devotee of Dionysus after initiation was born again and inherited bliss. The name "Orphic" as applied to these mysteries derives from their supposed invention by a Thracian prophet called Orpheus. The existence of such a person has been doubted. Perhaps the most that can be said is that there was probably at some time or other a prominent leader in Thrace who, whatever his name, organised the cultus and gave it driving force. Its whole circumstances, however, are strikingly un-Greek, and resemble in their violence and extravagance an Asiatic cult, which is not improbable, seeing that the Thracians are racially connected with some of the peoples of Asia Minor. Thracian influence began to make itself felt at Athens in the days of Socrates, and the Orphic mysteries established at Eleusis must have been a centre of influence right on to the time of Christ, since in the early years of the second century A.D. we find Justin Martyr, a Christian apologist, referring to the strange resemblance between Christ and Dionysus.[1]

It has often seemed strange that the worship of Christ should have spread so rapidly in the Gentile world; and the view has been expressed that persons familiar with the Orphic mysteries would readily accept a tale so similar to the one taught in their initiation, when it was seen that the hero was a historical character and not a mythical one like Dionysus-Zagreus. However this may be, it is certainly striking evidence that in the whole of the earliest Christian art Christ is conventionally represented either as Orpheus, Dionysus, or Apollo, and there is no attempt at portraiture.

Our knowledge of the actual ceremonies accompanying these greater initiations is fragmentary. There are a number of casual references to them in the classical writers. Thus, for example, Demosthenes sneers at Aeschines for having become a convert to the worship

---

[1] Some have maintained that St. Paul must have been acquainted with the Dionysiac mysteries because there was a cult of the god at Tarsus, his native place. This however cannot be proved.

of Dionysus, and says that he goes about performing ridiculous antics and shouting "Bad have I escaped and better have I found." We have a rather long account of an initiation into the mysteries of Isis in the pages of the *Golden Ass* of Apuleius, but this of course is fiction and of a comparatively late date. We have also a few representations in sculpture of the ceremonies connected with the initiation of persons into the mysteries at Eleusis, and the ceremonies connected with the fraternity which worshipped Mithras.

Putting together these various pieces of information, we arrive at a general idea of what went on. It seems that the candidate was probably veiled at the beginning of the ceremony, and also clad in special vestments. Certain prescribed sentences were recited, and votive offerings made. A number of curious pieces of dramatic ritual also accompanied the ceremony, which, we are bound to admit, bore a strong resemblance to the initiation rites connected with freemasonry, or to the practices of some of the older friendly societies. At the final moment the candidate appears to have been unveiled and confronted with a solemn spectacle, possibly either a colossal image of the god himself or a slow procession of priests wearing head-dresses to represent the principal inhabitants of Olympus. Our information is vague, for the officials of mysteries love to surround their proceedings with secrecy. Of one thing we may be sure; the initiation was carefully staged, and calculated to produce a powerful effect upon the mind of the candidate.

How long such an effect lasted is of course uncertain. Apuleius makes his hero say that he was "for some

time after" a "cultor frequens" of Isis, thereby imply-
ing that such a state of affairs did not last for ever.
Later he was initiated into the mysteries of Osiris.
It was possible for an extremely zealous person to
be a member of a number of fellowships, for we have
record of a nobleman in the reign of the Emperor
Valens who was connected with four, and of the wife
of a prefect who was consecrated to five.

Mithraism is a form of sun-worship, which had a
remarkable vogue about the second century A.D. The
legend about Mithras represents him as a young and
handsome man who pursued and killed a bull by
driving a sword into its back and causing its blood to
flow and to fertilise the soil. The name Mithras is
obviously a form of the name Mitra, which is the name
of a Vedic solar deity. There can be little doubt that
Mithras is really the triumphant sun, whose rays in the
springtime pierce like a sword the surface of the earth
and cause germination to take place. It may be, however, that combined with this nature myth there is the
reminiscence of some virile hero of the matador type.
The cult of Mithras travelled westward from Persia and
seems to have been extremely popular in the Roman
army. This carried it to the confines of the empire,
traces of it having been found in the neighbourhood of
the Roman wall in Northumberland. Membership of
the confraternity of Mithras was restricted to the male
sex, and this limited the appeal of what might otherwise
have proved a formidable rival to the early Christian
society. As it happened, however, the Mithraic fellowship gave way before the spread of a wider and more
hospitable community, the Catholic Church, in which

many of the customs of the mystery-fellowships were combined with acceptance of the Christian God-story. Mithraism in fact also bears no small resemblance to modern freemasonry, and it may well prove to be the case, if the history of the latter should ever come to be scientifically investigated, that it may be found to have partly derived at least some of its institutions from those of Mithraism. The meetings of the Mithraic fellowship were held in a building somewhat resembling in size and style a masonic temple; and the remains of one such mithraeum have been found in Rome.

Early Christian writers were struck by the resemblance between the Mithraic and the Christian communion, in the former of which bread and a cup of water were administered to the members. As in masonry there were a number of grades or degrees through which the candidate had to pass in order to reach full membership. These were seven in number, and known respectively as Crow, Griffin, Warrior, Lion, Persian and Courier of the sun.

Under Diocletian, in 307, Mithras was for the time dignified with the title of "Protector of the Empire." Hence, when Christianity became a *religio licita*, it did so in a *milieu* in which Mithraic worship was its fashionable competitor.

It may seem curious that in an age succeeding one in which philosophy had reached to a refinement of outlook similar to that of our own day, these more or less magical and decidedly non-intellectual secret fellowships should have had such a vogue. Doubtless it was partly a matter of reaction, and in any case among the educated there was still plenty of philosophy, some of it of a sceptical nature. We are given to understand, however, that the real explanation of the attraction exercised by the fellowships of the various mysteries was the failure of nerve on the part of the world of late antiquity. It seems to have lost confidence in itself, and it certainly believed that the world was running down rapidly and approaching death. Whether after the conflagration which the Stoics predicted there would be a fresh start, or what that fresh start would be, and whether anyone would survive to share it,—these things were doubtful. In any case one's own death was approaching, and it seemed worth while to seize any opportunity of σωτηρία or salvation, of being born again, "not of corruptible seed but of incorruptible," which existing religious systems had to offer.

No one can doubt that it was in the form of a mystery-religion that Christianity conquered the Mediterranean world. This casts no slur upon its reputation. It conquered because its Hero was an historical person who was believed to be the precise moral image of the invisible god, because of its intense pure morality, its firm and exclusive claims, and its confident optimism. No one can doubt equally that it deserved to conquer. Whether conquest in this form has best served the interests of preserving and transmitting the essential message of Jesus may, however, be disputed.

## THE ROMANS.

It is easier to say that the Romans and their religion were of decisive importance for the history of European religion, and indeed of European society in general, than to explain why they were and how they came to be so. Superficially there would seem to be very little reason why a small area of central Italy should have reared a race of people strong and talented enough to found and rule a great empire, with a high enough birth-rate to produce (for a number of centuries at any rate) a sufficiency of man-power to administer and defend it, and withal to bestow a legacy of law upon the world of the future, the importance of which is not denied even by those who dispute the soundness of some of its principles.

As far as we can judge, the causes of Roman greatness lie in the conjunction of a number of favourable conditions. Chief of these were the blending of race and the physical geography of the land that bred the Roman stock. As far as we are able to tell,[1] the Umbrians, Samnites and Latins developed as the result of a blending of the predominant Mediterranean stock with a number of Alpine peoples led by Nordics, under the influence of a rival race, the Etruscans, whose origin is not certainly known, but whose main element is said to be traceable to Lydia in Asia Minor, and whose skin colour apparently was a venetian red. Etruscans and Latins were settled near one another in the centre of Italy, and for a time Etruscan kings seem to have ruled in Rome, where their influence may perhaps have been similar to that of Norman-French kings in England. At any rate, in the sixth century B.C. the Romans threw off the Etruscan yoke and established an aristocratic republic, peculiar because its head

[1] In the *Cambridge Modern History* Prof. Giles himself shows that this is a doubtful hypothesis.

consisted of *two* annually elected magistrates or consuls
with an advisory body called a Senate, a system of veto
checking the action of both. The other important
element contributing to the greatness of the Roman
people was the fact that they grew and consolidated
themselves in a mountainous country. They were
sturdy hill-folk, hardy, virile and masterful, and of
a most enduring vitality. Those who think of Italy
in terms of the Campagna forget that the genuine
Roman owed his virtues largely to the same causes
as the peoples of the north of England, living in the
neighbourhood of the Pennines or the Scotch moors.

This, then, was the race which conquered and held for
many generations the whole of the Mediterranean world,
and ruled from Persia to Hadrian's wall. Of its earliest
religion there are abundant traces to show that it was
typically pluralistic. It acknowledged numerous local
spirits connected with trees, springs and rocks, and,
most familiar of all, the lares[1] and penates or little gods
of the household and farm. Later it sought the favour
of the greater gods, Jupiter or Dyauspater, the god of
the bright sky, a typically Aryan deity, closely akin to
the ancient Vedic gods; and others such as Juno, Mars
and Venus, obviously corresponding to the more
important deities of the Greek pantheon. But there
were also a large number of not very important but
extremely popular divinities who presided over the
different scenes of human life. These were hardly in
some cases personifications—they were powers or

---

[1] The lar was probably the boundary-spirit of the farm-lands,
and his worship was brought into the house by the slaves of the
family. (Warde Fowler.)

"numina." Thus there was Tutela or "protection,"
sometimes worshipped in masculine form as Janus, the
spirit who protected the door of the house; there were
the Semones, spirits of the corn sowing; there was
Pomona, the goddess of the apple harvest, and Pales
who presided over the herds of kine; there was Divus
Robigus, a spirit invoked for protection against the
robigo or corn disease, and even Cloacina, the spirit
presiding over the drains. All these divinities had
their proper ritual, with which they were approached in
the course of an elaborate calendar, and their days
were marked in the form of neuter plural words such as
the Robigalia and the Ambarvalia. In process of time
the simpler animistic religion received modifications
and additions from Etruscan, Greek and Oriental
sources. From the Etruscans it probably derived, at
any rate, the characteristic form of its three great
divinities, Jupiter, Juno and Minerva. From the
Greeks it received (c. 217 B.C.) (through the identification of its principal divinities with corresponding
Greek ones), a considerable mingling of mythology, art,
and ceremonial. Towards the end of the days of the
Republic the old Roman religion with its personification
of abstract virtues and forces had been transformed
into something richer and more grandiose, though there
still remained Vesta, the goddess of the hearth fire
(with her sacred virgins) and, perhaps most important
of all, the deity whose ministrations were in the hands
of the Pontifex Maximus with his college of sacred
ministers. The pontifex is the bridge-builder, important
in this case as the medicine-man who maintained
friendly relations with the god of the river Tiber, over

whose waters the bridge had to be built connecting its two banks.

With the establishment of the Principate (34 B.C.) the Roman Emperor came to concentrate in his hands not only all secular and military power but religious as well. Nominally both consuls and senate still continued to exist, but it was Augustus and his successors who really ruled, and with their secular offices also combined that of Pontifex Maximus; while after his victory at Actium in 31 B.C. when he became, from a military point of view, master of the Mediterranean world, Augustus proceeded to Rome and made a great show of reviving the ancient glories of the old Roman religion, including many of the distinctively early Roman customs, and instituting especially the festival of the secular games, which, in the form in which he caused it to be observed, was really a festival introduced from the East.

It seems strange that with the elaborate religious revival which Augustus sought to procure we find at the same time a marked decline in the vitality of faith. It is rather as though we had stumbled upon an ancient parallel to the modern situation in which the splendours of neo-Catholic cultus are accompanied or immediately followed by a disintegration of concrete belief on the part of the populace.[1] Augustus preferred the worship

[1] A friendly critic says: "You seem to hint in this sentence that we may at present be actually witnessing a real 'Untergang des Christentums.'" I do not mean this conclusion to be drawn, but I do think that the story of Greek and Roman religious pageantry is a serious warning to all ritualists. What has happened before may happen again (as apparently it has in Russia) if the intellectual foundations and moral witness of the religion in question are in any way deficient. Beauty must not be divorced from truth.

of Apollo, to whom he said that he owed his victory at Actium; but Apollo was a Greek divinity, not a Roman one, and with the importation of Greek anthropomorphic ideas about the gods real damage was done to Roman religion.

It has been well remarked that the old Roman numina were not anthropomorphic, and that when, through Greek influence, it came to be suggested that they were, and indeed not only no better than men, but in most cases actually worse, the idea of divinity rapidly deteriorated, and the way was opened for ridicule, and finally for utter scepticism.

It seems clear from a study of Roman literature after the time of Virgil (40 B.C.), and even to some extent from Virgil's own writings, that in literature the gods were less and less represented as objects for genuine belief. Apollo, for instance, simply becomes a picturesque title for the spirit of poetry, and Mars a synonym for war. Virgil, however, still believes in a principle of Divinity in the universe, manifesting itself in many ways. It is by no means certain that his successors were as full of faith as he was. Of course it is precarious to draw conclusions as to the beliefs of a nation, or even of all the members of its educated class, from the

The saving of the situation for us is that the Christian religion has a strong intellectual basis and also a vigorous moral influence. At the same time one fears that those who are interested in ceremonial are not always the same set of persons who profess an intellectually water-tight Christian credo, or bear a robust moral witness, but lean upon the thought and practice of others, without acknowledging their indebtedness to them. But I have no wish to attack those who have done so much to make worship beautiful, and I give thanks for those (happily not a few) who have succeeded in combining moral witness, a forward-looking faith, and the consecration of art to worship.

fragments of literature which happen to have survived, but at the present time it must be admitted that what we have got is not very encouraging material. Horace is sometimes sceptical and mocking, sometimes poses as sharing in rural piety, sometimes seems to show sympathy with the beliefs of the educated Stoic, and in any case is ready to give more or less divine honours to the emperor. On the other hand, Propertius and Ovid seem to be totally destitute of any religious beliefs or signs of reverence.

Readers will remember the famous sentence of Gibbon, in which he says that to the philosopher the popular cults were all equally false, to the mob all equally true, and to the statesman all equally useful. This generalisation we can hardly accept. All philosophers were not sceptics, but in many cases held that behind the naïve stories about the gods lay deep and mysterious truths, which the stories themselves only served to represent in picturesque form. Such a defence was perhaps not entirely useless in arresting the decline of popular religion, but it was a feeble rampart against the onslaught of Christian enthusiasm, inspired by a group of definite and well-attested historical events.

What, then, was the legacy of Rome, judged from a religious point of view? Less theological we may say than ecclesiastical. She bequeathed, to those that came after, her spirit of discipline and sagacious government. In so far as the Christian church of the West stepped into the shoes of the Empire, it inherited the organic structure of the imperial court with its Ministers of State, and of the imperial religion with its divine vicegerent who is Pontifex Maximus, while the gods many and lords many of the Roman pantheon and of the towns, villages and local sanctuaries of the Empire as often as not become Christian saints.   There is, however, little or no legacy in thought, and all that we can say is that through the provincial system of the Roman Empire there was mediated and conveyed to the west the heritage of Greek philosophy which Roman culture preserved even where perhaps it hardly appreciated it.[1]

## OF MIDDLE AND NORTHERN EUROPE.

The religion of the middle and northern Europeans deserves some notice.   Formerly it was usual to divide it into that of the Celtic and that of the Teutonic peoples.   Such a division, however, to-day needs to be qualified by consideration of the racial composition of the peoples in question.   We now know that the Celts proper were of the same racial group as the central Europeans, of whom they simply represent a particular group or earlier wave which gave its name to other and later ones.   We think of them as peopling Gaul, Britain and Ireland, and we assume that the languages called Celtic were the languages of these people.   But it needs to be remembered that the Celts were Alpines crossed with Nordics who swept over areas in western Europe which had previously been peopled by short

[1] Some present-day writers say that the Roman spirit of practical common sense, respect for tradition, social solidarity and individual personality is being re-born in the various fascist movements of modern Europe, and that this is a necessary reaction against the excessive development of the Greek spirit of speculation and un-bridled self-expression which has dethroned God and made man in his stead the Lord of the Universe, and which when unchecked seems to lead to a dissolution of the body and to moral chaos,

dark inhabitants, and that the latter were descendants and offshoots of the old dark belt of long-headed peoples, sometimes called rather vaguely the Mediterranean race. It needs also to be remembered that these in their turn had already received modification from their contact with still earlier inhabitants, and from admixtures of other earlier races whose origin is obscure, such as the tall handsome people known to us as the "prospectors," and round-headed migrants such as the so-called "beaker folk." These infusions began in times before the introduction of metals and went on into the bronze age.

We have therefore to consider the religious beliefs:

(a) of the dark whites and their predecessors.

(b) of the round-headed Alpine stock.

(c) of the genuine Nordics.

(d) of the Slavs and northern Mongols.

It is true that one school of anthropologists regards the round skull as not being a sign of a separate race, and treats the Alpines as though they were a localised variety of Nordic. This view seems now, however to have given way before the classification set forth above.[1] It is improbable that there was much difference in beliefs between the dark whites of north-west Europe and those of the Mediterranean. Any who wish to study the subject will find that they will gain a good idea of it from a treatise upon early Mediterranean religion in Crete or on the folk-lore of the small dark inhabitants of Corsica. We cannot pretend to any

[1] The red hair and greenish-blue eye of some Celts are only variants of Nordic features, possibly due either to soil and diet, or to crossing with Alpo-Carpathian stock, and are akin to albinism.

direct knowledge of the religious beliefs of the "prospectors" or of the "beaker folk," and can only judge
that it must have been similar to that of other primitive
peoples of a similar level of culture with which we have
still direct contact. It is not easy to say whether there
was much difference between the religious beliefs and
practices prevailing among Alpine and Nordic peoples,
and in any case the religion of the Celtic-speaking
people preserved in their remains is that of a composite
Alpo-Nordic population, in which the leadership is
generally Nordic, for it has been noticed that the tall
fair-haired long-headed Nordic man from the Northern
plains appears to have over-lorded the aboriginal
populations wherever he went, while the Alpines,
though sturdy, extremely industrious, and peaceful,
are on the whole of a docile temperament, and do not
run to leadership, though physically their round skull
is a dominant, so that they are able to transmit it in
marriage to their superiors. It is thus not easy to
determine how far there can be said to be a distinctly
"Alpine" attitude to religion. In general the Alpine
race, as its name indicates, has developed in the
mountainous belt running east and west in Europe and
western Asia. Its outlook is therefore that of a series
of groups living in sharply divided valleys and gorges,
and is in consequence lacking in the breadth of outlook
characteristic of plain-dwellers. The Celts, however,
can hardly be regarded as pure Alpines, but when
they come before us as an expanding people dwelling
beyond the Rhine in north and west Germany, have
migrated thither from the mountainous regions of south
Germany, Switzerland, Bohemia, Moravia and Hungary,

and are already strongly blended with and dominated by Nordic or proto-Nordic stock, so that they must already have been influenced by Nordic religious ideas. If we take the ordinary division of so-called Celtic languages into Q-group and P-group, we notice that the former includes Erse, Manx, and Gaelic, and the latter Breton, Welsh and Cornish. Yet the peoples associated with these dialects are very largely the descendants of the short dark population. The latter must therefore have adopted the languages of their conquerors, contributing at the most a number of pre-Celtic words and intermarrying as well.

It seems, therefore, that in considering Celtic religion we are confronted with the religion of central Europeans, modified by blending with Nordic and Mediterranean elements, and that perhaps we never get it quite pure except in parts of Ireland. It has been said that its characteristic features are the prominence of nature-deities, the practice of human sacrifice, the simplicity of the worship (which, like that of Japanese Shinto, took place more often in natural surroundings than in temples) the power of the priesthood, the general practice of magic, and the strong belief in immortality. This account does not indicate any very striking peculiarities. So far as it is correct, it fails to indicate a type of religion greatly differing from that of some tribe in the Pacific, except in the names of its divinities and perhaps to some extent in its mythology. The calendar was determined by the phases of the moon, and the year began in November, which opened with a feast known as Samhain, when ceremonial fires were kindled. There was also an important festival about May-day, at which again ceremonial fires were lit, called Beltane fires (the meaning of these words is uncertain—perhaps Samhain was the Celtic name for the deity of the underworld). There were also festivals at the beginning of February and August and at the end of June. All these festivals were presumably recognised and as far as possible transformed by the Christian church, so that we have All Saints' Day at the beginning of November, Candlemas Day, or the Feast of the Purification, on February 2nd, St. Philip and St. James' Day on May 1st, and Lammas Day on the 1st of August, which was associated with a festival of St. Peter. Midsummer Day was appropriated to the memory of St. John the Baptist, while the festival of Christmas occupied the place of some mid-winter celebration. The assignment of these days probably strikes us now as a little meaningless, but we have to try to put ourselves in the place of the early Christian missionaries who found the pagan festivals in existence and felt that they had to do something with them. If people insisted on dancing and lighting fires, it was better that they should do so in connection with some historical Christian character. Our missionaries, as we know, often adopt a similar policy in India and Africa to-day.[1]

[1] The above remarks seem to need a little qualification on account of the subsequent superimposition of Anglo-Saxon, Jutish and Danish invaders upon the British population. We need to observe, however, that it is no longer asserted that entire areas had their British inhabitants exterminated by the invaders. In many places, especially on the north side of the Chilterns and in the hill country in the north of England the earlier inhabitants survived, and whether Christian or non-Christian their customs must have been carried

The strong probability has been demonstrated that a great many Christian burial grounds with a sacred building in the centre occupy the precise spots where pre-Christian religious rites were performed. The details of the evidence are too numerous to be given here, but it seems to have been demonstrated that with the pre-Christian inhabitants of these islands there was no sacred place where there was no burial. "Every place where there was burial was holy ground, and there could be no holy place where no burial was." These ancient burials were further associated with the construction of circles, and it is more than likely that although the circle was associated with tribal meetings and tribal games, it was also the mark of a sacred area within which religious ceremonies took place. From this it has been suggested that the true derivation of the word church is not as given in the middle of the ninth century by Walafrid Strabo—from the Greek κυριακόν—but on the contrary that the word kirk or church has no connection with the Greek, but means a circular place of pagan burial—ciric.[1] Here

over into the new régime. There was, therefore, probably inter-marriage and fusion of cultural practices; but further, it is by no means certain that the religious practices of the invaders were so very different from those of the people whom they conquered. Both were polytheists and both were influenced in their religious calendar by the course of nature. At the same time they were divided very likely in marriage customs and in emphasis upon the rights of the male parent. The conversion to Christianity came in every case by way of people who had developed their Christian customs amid non-Teutonic surroundings, and therefore the festivals provided for the Teutonic converts, though modified (as Gregory the Great advised that they ought to be), by the existing practices of those converts, were the festivals of the Churches (whether Gaelic, Italian, or Celtic from Ireland) which converted them.

[1] So Hadrian Allcroft, *The Circle and the Cross*, and his evidence seems good.

again the evidence is too detailed to be given in a small compass, but it seems quite convincing. In Scotland the name of kirk constantly attaches to circles which are commonly accounted pre-historic, and this seems to be equally the case south of the Tweed, and to be connected in some cases with the locality in which a circular earthwork exists.

What is called Druidism needs a few words of explanation.

The actual word "Druid" is evidently a symbol for a religious expert or authority, since in an ancient writing Christ Himself is spoken of as God's Druid. What we call Druids, however, were plainly the priesthood of the Celtic peoples of Gaul, Britain, and Ireland, at the time of the Roman invasion and occupation. The reason why so much attention has been focussed upon them is because early authorities describe them as possessing great power and importance. The best explanation of this is that the Celtic-speaking peoples, after having peacefully settled in north-west Gaul, evolved out of a condition in which the king performed priestly functions, into an order of society in which priests were differentiated from kings. It is admitted that in the Marne area of France there was a great and special development of the typically Alpo-Celtic la Tène civilisation. Now it so happens that we have remarkable evidence of the preservation in this area of pre-Celtic artistic tradition, and art and religion being so closely akin, there is an equal probability of the persistence of native religious tradition. It would not, therefore, be surprising if in this area Celtic religion came to be built upon pre-Celtic Iberian religion.

The invasion of England followed. But it has been pointed out that these invaders were the descendants of the people who had settled in the Marne area and probably intermarried with its population. On swarming across the Channel they would therefore not feel as much as their forefathers the strangeness of the religious and social system of Iberian Britain, and would easily incorporate this native religion with their own, recognising it as an undiluted form of what had already been fused with the faith of their fathers in the Marne area, and most likely for this very reason treating it with respect. This would account for the report made to Caesar that the origin of Gallic Druidism was in Britain. It is argued, therefore, that the highly elaborate Druidic system developed both in name and form in Gaul, and was then carried westward even as far as Ireland, but that it owes its differentiated priesthood to Celtic contact with non-Celtic peoples.[1] The remains of Neolithic pre-Celtic religious rites cannot therefore strictly speaking be called Druidical, though it is extremely probable that they were taken over in many instances and used by Druids.

We are accustomed to derive our knowledge of the religion of these pre-Teutonic peoples from classical records, especially the writings of Caesar, Pliny and Diodorus; but we are also able to glean considerable information from archaeological remains, and in the Paris museums are to be found statuettes of many Gallo-Roman deities. In the main we may say that while the Celts of Gaul were affected by the

[1] This, at any rate, is the latest theory, given by Mr. T. D. Kendrick.

neighbourhood of the Romans, the peoples of Britain and Ireland were less influenced in this way. It would be impossible without unduly enlarging this book to give any detailed description of the many obscure divinities with strange names which abounded among the Celts, and it would also prove an exceedingly complicated task to dissect Celtic religion and to isolate the properly Celtic elements in it from those which it inherited from the aboriginals.

The Teutonic peoples are commonly divided into the western group comprising the Anglo-Saxons, the southern group comprising the Saxons, Frisians, and Alamanni and the northern group comprising the Swedes, Danes, Norwegians and Icelanders. The eastern group comprising Goths, Vandals and Burgundians became merged in the populations whom they subjugated.

The earliest period in the history of these peoples of which we have certain knowledge shows them as possessing the features of a relatively high culture. Their work in bronze and gold is of a high order. Among their religious symbols occur the double axe and the solar disk, which seem to betoken a penetration of ideas from the Mediterranean as far as Scandinavia during the bronze age. The two most important nature deities were Wodan or Odin and Donar or Thor. The former appears as the god of war, the protector of warriors, who gathers those who fall in battle to the dwelling-place of the elect, Valhalla, whither they are conducted by attendant maidens or Valkyries. Wodan himself from his high place rules what are called the nine worlds. He appears on earth sometimes as the

wild hunter with his eight-footed horse Sleipnir,
accompanied by a noisy rout, sometimes as a one-eyed
man with a broad-brimmed hat and accompanied by
ravens, in which guise he is god of wisdom and of spells.
The conception of Wodan as the all-father and king of
the gods may be a later development, and even perhaps
intensified by Christian influence. Some of his attributes seem to have been transferred to St. Michael, St.
Martin, and St. Nicholas, at any rate in German
legends. The worship of Wodan necessarily demanded
bloody sacrifices. With him also is connected the
drinking of mead, which like the *soma* of the Eastern
Aryans is thought to bestow divine wisdom. Donar
or Thor is the good and encouraging deity who is
represented as riding through the air in a chariot drawn
by two rams. The oak is sacred to him. His weapon
is the famous double hammer Miollnir, with which he
conquers the powers opposed to him. Wodan appears
to have replaced an older conception of the god of war
who was known as Tiu or Tyr. In the description of
the Scandinavian Temple of Upsala (afterwards
replaced by a Christian cathedral) it is reported by a
chronicler that beside the images of Wodan and Donar
also stood that of Frey, who was a god of fertility and
peace. We also hear of the female divinity Frija.
Caesar and Tacitus make the attempt to equate these
Teutonic deities with Graeco-Roman ones; but it is by
no means clear that their identifications are more than
guesses.

Meanwhile the records of German polytheism have
for us a little more than an archaeological interest, since
it was the faith of our Anglo-Saxon forefathers, and

was therefore at one time by people of our own race felt to be a plausible explanation of the world. I propose, therefore, to record at this point some reflections which have been made upon polytheism in general, since we have now had (in this and preceding sections) a number of different types of it presented to our notice. It is said that the ability to conceive gods in man's own image was a late and difficult achievement, and we have already pointed out that the early Roman numina were qualities rather than persons. Polytheism is therefore a sign of a pluralistic tendency, and not necessarily of anthropomorphism. Even to-day it is urged that there are many people who, in spite of professing a higher religion, retain, nevertheless, polytheistic minds, in that the several centres of their own private interests are each still apt to be regarded as the centre of the universe. The development of anthropomorphic deities in Greece was plainly a humanising of the natural, rather than a degradation of the supernatural. It is not by any means fair to charge polytheism with evil results. No doubt it had its limitations, and only gave a temporary advantage, but there can be no reasonable doubt that there was something about it which helped on the advance of civilisation, making Deity to be no longer shapeless, or brutish, but at least approximating to the standard of some human beings. It gave a greater freedom of mind and encouraged men to adventure, and by the fusion of deities of different types, made possible the formation of composite states. There also appears to have been a connection between polytheism and the development of private property. It was never capable, however, of being made into a theological system, and as soon as the attempt was made it was seen to be irrational. As we have already observed, the Greeks criticised it to death, while Catholic Christianity has only managed to retain it by strongly subordinating the cult of saints to that of God Himself, and by tolerating such legends as are unbearable to educated people. It is an unfailing mark of polytheism that it has no ideas beyond civilisation and no quarrel with it. It creates the state, but is then shut up within it as state religion.[1] Hence in Babylon, Egypt, India and Greece it deteriorated with the decline of the state. Moreover polytheism, having no quarrel with civilisation, is unable to lift it or preserve it from corruption by setting up an independent standard beyond that of the natural. Most of us are familiar with the boast made by Ethelbert of Kent that the gods of his people were virile warriors. The gods of polytheism with all their splendour are indeed just what the Psalms call them, idols, mere imaginative figments having no more and no less reality than the primitive emotions from which they spring. They are not historical facts like the career and character of Jesus Whom the Self-Existent universe has produced, nor are they to be compared with the Deity Whom Jesus claims to reveal, and Who is everlasting, without body, parts or passions.

To resume then, Teutonic religion, although the names of its chief deities are well-known to us, and although its mythology and general outlook are discernible in the Icelandic Eddas and in the early

[1] Cf. Oman, *The Natural and the Supernatural*, p. 395 ff.

English poem of Beowulf, must be regarded to a
large extent as religion that has become teutonised,
since it is difficult to avoid the conclusion that much of
it shows signs of affinities with what we get in Babylonia
and in the Mediterranean. Perhaps the two more
distinctly Nordic features are: (1) the belief in a supreme
sky-god. (In this respect there is resemblance to the
high-god beliefs of other peoples, though the influence
of the Nordic sky-god is, as we have already seen, of
exceptional importance). (2) the well-attested picture
of the familiarity which prevailed between the Teutons
and their gods. The phrase "the beloved friend Thor"
is typical, and differs widely in spirit from the numinous
awe of the Mediterranean folk.

Much has been made of the Teutonic divinities, chiefly,
one supposes, because of their appearance in the Operas
of Wagner, and from the fact that they have given their
names to some of the days in our week. Evidence as to
the earlier customs and beliefs of their worshippers is
thought to be accessible in the famous treatise, the
*Germania* of Tacitus. We may doubt the accuracy
of Tacitus' information, but at the same time we cannot
help recognising that some of the practices to which he
refers correspond to similar ones which are known to
have existed among our Anglo-Saxon forefathers. It is
indeed by no means impossible to obtain a very fair
notion of what the latter believed by reading a version
of the Teutonic legend of the ring of the Nibelungs, but
with the details of this we need hardly concern ourselves,
since its influence now belongs entirely to the past. (At
the same time it must be remembered that the story, as
it appears in the Operas of Wagner and in the various

popular narratives based upon the latter, has been treated very freely, and has had imported into it ideas and elements which are not primitive, and which belong to a later date. In spite of this, however, the quasi-Homeric polytheistic atmosphere is well preserved).

One single point demands special mention. The difference between the practice of the Mediterranean, Alpine and Nordic peoples with regard to the existence and duties of sacred men is strongly marked. Generalisations are always fraught with hazard, yet it seems impossible to avoid in this matter indulging in an inference which is of the nature of a generalisation. It has been noted that, whereas in Egypt and in the Minoan civilisation a class of sacred men developed who were not necessarily kings or chieftains, and whereas among Alpine peoples there is also a tendency in the same direction, among the Greeks of the post-archaic age (possibly as the result of Achaean or proto-Nordic influence) there was no class of priests, but priestly functions were exercised by ordinary laymen, who at the most were sometimes temporarily nominated for the office, much as we should nominate the mayor of a town. In western Europe among the Teutonic peoples it is also recorded that priests do not seem to have been a class, but to have combined sacerdotal functions with civil ones. In Celtic Britain it has been pointed out that certain areas show the same combination, whereas in others, possibly those in which Alpine and Iberian influence was stronger, the sacred men were a distinct set of people from the chieftains. It must be obvious to anyone who studies later European history that the

Teutonic peoples on the whole have a marked aversion to the existence of a separate class of sacred men. In Ireland, on the other hand, and in those parts of England and the Continent where the Alpine and Mediterranean strain in the population is still strong, the priest as an institution is still of importance. The implications of this can obviously lead to controversy.

At the same time a distinction must be drawn between those who desire a sacred official to act as their representative before Deity, whether he be of a separate caste or not, and those who feel no need of such an ambassador at all, even a temporary one, chosen from among themselves. And further, while the depreciation in the emphasis laid upon sacred men as a separate class is specially characteristic of the central and northern European, it would seem to be a mental feature which may occur anywhere, and which is possibly due to a special type or level of brain development which has not yet been fully investigated by psychologists. It is not impossible that the separation of chieftainship and priesthood is in some cases due to an evolutionary process in which functions hitherto held together become differentiated. But this does not account for the repugnance felt by some groups for a sacerdotal order. One wonders sometimes whether it is due to racial rather than religious antagonism. The whole problem is most difficult and offers no easy solution.

## THE SLAVS AND ESPECIALLY THE RUSSIANS.

The Slavs are generally regarded as a branch of the Alpine race. In the west the latter are, as we know, blended with Nordics to form what we call the Celtic peoples, but the true Alpine has usually dark brown hair and is broad or thick-set. Typical specimens of these people were seen in England during the Great War in the persons of the Serbian refugees. In the area bordering on the Baltic the Slav, again through blending with Nordics, appears with fair hair and blue or grey eyes. The population of Russia consists mainly of a mixture of Slavs from this so-called Alpo-Carpathian group of Alpine peoples, combined with various types of northern Mongol; but before them there seems to have been quite a different kind of population of early Nordic peoples, who have disappeared, and in this part of the world only survive in numbers in Latvia and Lithuania, and in a few special areas in New Russia. As we know, there has been since 1914 an earnest desire on the part of non-Russian Slavs to unite under one government, so that they are grouped to-day in the two states of Czecho-Slovakia and Jugo-Slavia.

The religion of the early Slavonic peoples seems to have been a pluralistic nature-religion. The names of the deities are known. Svarog was the god of fire and Dazbog was the sun-god. Perun was the sky-god. Obviously in the latter we have a variation (explainable by Grimm's law) of the name of the Aryan sky-god Varuna. A mediaeval chronicler says of the Prussian Slavs: "They vainly worshipped all creatures as god, to wit, sun, moon and stars, thunder and lightning, birds and four-footed beasts. They had also sacred woods, fields, and streams." Another writer says that beside greater and lesser spirits they worshipped a highest god as creator of heaven and earth. It is evident, therefore, that there was nothing distinctively noteworthy about the pre-Christian stage of Slavonic religion.

What of course is a singular problem is the effect of Mongolian influence upon the temperament of the Russian and other peoples. It has sometimes been asserted that the influence of the northern Mongols has been adverse to religion. This is perhaps a prejudiced view, due partly to the treatment of the Christian church by Attila and his Huns, and to the supposed Mongolian element in many Russians of the type of Lenin. At the same time there appears to be a vein of hardness and cruelty in the Mongolian character, which is liable, unless tamed, to break out in sinister fits of ferocity; though one doubts whether the typically Bolshevik attitude towards all religions is not quite as much the fruit of French positivism and Semitic atheism working upon an unstable situation fraught with proletarian bitterness, as of any supposed influences from north-east Asia.

## Chapter VI

## OF THE ARABS, MOHAMMED, AND THE RELIGION OF ISLAM

It will be best to begin this section with some account of the life of the founder and his people, the Arabs.

The latter are a Semitic people who originated in the large and partially arid peninsular which bears their name. Isolated there from other Semitic stocks, they developed strong individuality both in language and culture, and preserved great purity of breed. They fluctuated between nomadism and settled life, but their real determining influence has been the desert rather than the city. At the period of which we are shortly to speak they were probably ripe for expansion, and since the days of Mohammed they have spread in all directions, carrying with them their language, their distinctive dress, and the new creed which, though proclaimed as universal by its founder, has ever for them possessed the quality of a national faith. They have blended their stock with that of many other peoples and have provided sovereigns and aristocracies to a number of less virile and enterprising races.

Mohammed himself was born about 570 A.D., the posthumous child of Abdulla, a member of a local Arab family of the Quraish tribe, to whom was entrusted the guardianship of the national sanctuary, at Mecca, known as the Ka'aba. Of his early youth and manhood little is known that can be called history. There is,

however, a great difference between the attitude of the
New Testament towards the boyhood of Jesus and that
of tradition towards the boyhood of the Prophet. It is
only in Christian apocryphal writings that we get a
great deal of legend, and no serious Christian to-day
pays any attention to it, while he is able to accept
critical analysis even of the canonical gospels without
alarm. On the other hand the most puerile stories
about Mohammed are implicitly believed by vast
multitudes of devout Moslems. (Of course it may be
retorted that in Continental Catholic circles there is
much credulity, but even so, the balance of restraint
is considerably on the Christian side).

The only certain facts about the early life of the
Prophet are his connection with the Ka'aba, and his
journeys to Syria with Abu Talib from the age of twelve
and upwards, during which he appears to have heard
and seen much of both Jews and Christians, and to have
formed his opinions about them. We can safely say
that he never knew Christianity in anything but a
corrupt and idolatrous guise, and we can hardly think
what he would have made of the beliefs and practices
of some of the modern reformed churches, though it
seems possible that he would have passed a favourable
opinion upon them.

At the age of twenty he was engaged in a war
commonly called the sacrilegious war, because it was
fought in a sacred country and during the sacred
months. He seems to have shown himself during this
time a very steady and dependable person, and to
have earned fully the title of "the Faithful" which his
countrymen bestowed upon him. It was owing to this,

no doubt, that a certain wealthy widow, Khadija, chose him to conduct her commercial affairs. He afterwards became her husband, and from that date until the beginning of his mission he seems to have behaved as an extremely quiet, sincere, and on the whole honest man.

Until he was forty he lived in Mecca, a comparatively obscure individual, about whose inner life we can only hazard speculations. We may assume that he pondered upon the beliefs of the Jews, with which his writings show him to have had very close acquaintance; and also that the polytheistic paganism of his own country-men failed to satisfy him. After he had turned his fortieth year he began to talk to his wife and a few other friends about certain ideas which had come to possess him, chiefly with regard to the unity and absoluteness of God, the fear of hell, the iniquity of idolatry and the reward of the faithful with paradise. At first he and his associates remained an insignificant sect, but after a few years Mohammed began to preach more boldly and to aim at forming a powerful party. The leaders of the local religion naturally opposed him; his followers were scattered; and he himself appeared in the courtyard of the national sanctuary and made a sort of recantation, in which he said that perhaps the many divinities of Mecca might after all be real beings. No sooner had he done this than he repented of it, and made no secret of his regret that he had allowed himself to play the coward. His position was now more unsatisfactory than ever. He had been at work for ten years; he was a man of fifty; his wife Khadija and some of his friends were dead; and when he fled from Mecca to a neighbouring town he was stoned and driven out of it and had to return to Mecca. Then at last he got his chance. The city of Medina, possibly as the result of Jewish influence, opened its gates to him, and in the autumn of 622 occurred the famous Hijra or flight of the Prophet from Mecca to Medina, which he reached by making a roundabout journey in order to avoid his enemies, since the latter knew very well what was on foot, and were determined to assassinate him if possible, before he could find time to establish himself in his new stronghold. Moslem chronology dates its beginning from this event.

For several years the Prophet kept up a series of typical Bedouin raids upon his neighbours, who at length raised an army of ten thousand men with the idea of sacking Medina. Mohammed, however, by the advice of a Persian, fortified the town with a trench and a wall, and refused to give battle. By indulging in Fabian tactics he prolonged the campaign until the rains began to fall, when the besieging army became uncomfortable and finally melted away. Eventually the leading men in Mecca came over to his side and a treaty was arranged by which the Meccans agreed to accept his religious beliefs so long as their city was allowed to continue to be the centre of pilgrimage.

In 629 Mohammed entered Mecca and destroyed its last idol; and soon after by the same sort of methods as he had hitherto employed, he made himself master of all Arabia. As long as Khadija lived he seems to have been monogamous, but after her death he married two other wives, one of them the famous Ayesha, who always remained his favourite; and he subsequently

added a large number of other women to his establishment, "developing a disagreeably strong interest in
them, as many men do in their declining years." It is
said on good authority that one Jewess, Sufiyya,
was married to him on the evening of the day on
which her husband had been captured in battle and
executed.

The picture we get of the founder of Islam is thus, as
it appears, a curious one. "A being of commoner clay
than Jesus, Gautama, or even Mani; vain, egotistical,
tyrannous, and a self-deceiver."[1]

Then in 632, when he was in his sixty-second year,
he died.

Probably most readers will be familiar with the
account of Mohammed given by Carlyle in his *Heroes*,
where the Koran is described as "the confused ferment
of a great, rude, human soul." There seems no doubt
that he was an extraordinary mixture of good and evil,
subject probably at times to epileptic fits and even
melancholia. He was a thorough-going Arab of
aristocratic lineage, full of deep religious feelings and at
first intensely sincere, so that much of the earlier part
of his book is fervent and earnest. He thought of
himself as a sinner, and never claimed perfection; at
the same time we are bound to admit that on the most
humanistic estimate his character compares but feebly
with that of the historical Jesus. Mohammed lived
partly by plundering caravans, and it is recorded by
Al Kindy that he engaged in twenty-nine campaigns

[1] H. G. Wells, *The Outline of History*. I have followed Mr. Wells
here pretty closely, because he is favourably disposed to Mohammed,
and his admissions are therefore all the more important.

and nine pitched battles. If a caravan was weak he
attacked it. It is also undeniable that he cruelly
massacred some Jewish tribes. (Moslem massacres have,
as we know, occurred even since the Great War in parts
of Asia Minor). It is difficult to understand how such a
warlike character can compare with that of the Prince
of Peace, who exhorted men to love their enemies.
Again it seems quite certain that Mohammed's extraordinary initial success had the effect of turning his
head and spoiling his whole character. He came to
believe that he could safely indulge where he had
placed a restraint upon others, and then proceed to
invent a supposed private revelation to justify his
action. It appears that his adopted son Zaid had a
wife of whom the Prophet became enamoured. He
allowed Zaid to know this and encouraged him to
divorce her in order that he might marry her. This
was contrary to all custom and somewhat strained the
loyalty of his followers; whereupon the Prophet
composed the thirty-third Sura in which he makes
Almighty God legalise the marriage in express terms
of approval. This is not the only time that we find
Mohammed consciously or unconsciously confusing the
voice of God with his own unregenerate desires. Thus in
the same Sura Mohammed is given permission to marry
as many wives as he pleases " as a special privilege above
all other believers"; and again, a theory is invented
that one passage in his book can be abrogated by
another and later passage. This is quite a different
thing from the progressive revelation alleged to exist
in the Christian scriptures, and is plainly an attempt to
use revelation for private ends. By the time he reaches

this point Mohammed is no longer overwhelmed by the splendour of God. The earlier chapters of the Koran are short and for the most part vividly poetical. The later ones are long-winded, dull and prosaic. His whole career has been very well summed up in the following passage:

"A strong faithful man of a religious temperament becomes a convert to the monotheistic creed of his supposed ancestors, Abraham and Ishmael. For a time he is absorbed by the new idea, but not for some years does it occur to him that he is commissioned to preach it. He has four classes of people to deal with, (1) idolators, (2) a few sincere seekers after truth, the Hanifs, (3) Jews, and (4) Christians. He begins to preach at Mecca sincerely, and after much persecution and suffering flees with a few disciples to Medina.

"Here he begins to succeed. He looks round him and finds Jews and Christians professing a religion something like his own. He endeavours, and hopefully endeavours, to bring them back to the original and, as he thinks, the pure and only true faith of Abraham. (The Qur'an speaks in two different voices at two different times about Jews and Christians). He is disappointed, for they fail to respond. He then begins to talk of religious warfare, and to accuse them of tampering with their Scriptures, which had prophesied his coming as the Seal of the Prophets. He bitterly persecutes the Jews. He conquers the Meccans. He receives deputations from various Arab tribes, and at last just at the close of his life there dawns on him the idea of a universal empire and universal faith. One Prophet, One Faith, for all the world."[1]

When he was within a year of his death, Mohammed

---

[1] Canon Dale, of Zanzibar.

made a last journey from Medina to Mecca, and for this occasion the following speech is recorded of him.[1]

"Ye people: Hearken to my words; for I know not whether, after this year, I shall ever be amongst you here again. Your lives and property are sacred and inviolable amongst one another until the end of time.

"The Lord hath ordained to every man the share of his inheritance; a testament is not lawful to the prejudice of heirs.

"The child belongeth to the parent; and the violator of wedlock shall be stoned.

"Whoever claimeth falsely another for his father, or another for his master, the curse of God and the angels and of all mankind shall rest upon him.

"Ye people! Ye have rights demandable of your wives, and they have rights demandable of you. Upon them it is incumbent not to violate their conjugal faith nor commit any act of open impropriety; which things if they do, ye have authority to shut them up in separate apartments and to beat them with stripes, yet not severely. But if they refrain therefrom, clothe them and feed them suitably. And treat your women well, for they are with you as captives and prisoners; they have not power over anything as regards themselves. And ye have verily taken them on the security of God, and have made their persons lawful unto you by the words of God.

"And your slaves, see that ye feed them with such food as ye eat yourselves, and clothe them with the stuff ye wear. And if they commit a fault which ye are not inclined to forgive, then sell them, for they are the servants of the Lord, and are not to be tormented.

[1] The speech may not, as it stands, be authentic, but the 300 millions of Moslems accept it as such and observe its maxims as their rule of life.

"Ye people! hearken to my speech and comprehend the same. Know that every Moslem is the brother of every other Moslem. All of you are of the same equality."

It is said that the bulk of the people, who at the present day accept this utterance as that of a divine message, do not trouble very much whether the founder of their religion was a good man or not. They hold that his teaching was better than his conduct, and indeed it can scarcely be denied that Mohammed had a curious knack of attracting and holding friends. His closest confidant was Abu Bakr, and Abu Bakr never faltered in his allegiance. He was strong and clear-sighted, actually a stronger character than his master, though less imaginative. If Mohammed had the ideas, Abu Bakr carried them into effect. It is no small testimony to the personality of Mohammed, that with all his faults he was able to win and to hold such a man in this way.

Something should now be said about the volume in which the founder's teaching afterwards became embodied, and to which reference has already been made. It is composed of a number of Suras or chapters, 114 in all, of enormously varying lengths. Thus, the longest Sura, known as "The Cow," contains 286 verses, the next in length, "Al Araf," 205, and a third, "The Family of Imran," 200; while of others Sura cx, with three verses, and "The Daybreak," with five verses, are little more than ejaculations or aphorisms. The Koran is not in any sense a continuous treatise; and the manner in which it was put together sheds interesting light on the way in which the books of the Hebrew prophets came to take shape.[1] Each Sura is supposed to represent the verbal expression of an inrush of revelation upon the prophet's consciousness. In the lifetime of Mohammed, these scattered fragments were not collected, but they were afterwards put together by Abu Bakr as his immediate successor at the suggestion of another friend Omar, who afterwards became the third Caliph. Both these men preserved a large part of the Suras in their memories, and they appointed Zaid, Mohammed's secretary and adopted son, to carry out the task of recording them in writing, while Zaid for his part declared that he gathered them together "from date-leaves and tablets of stone and from the breasts of men." Their arrangement was thus not necessarily chronological, but in order of length, beginning with the shortest. For reasons already stated, however, it seems that the shorter Suras are the earlier ones. Upon the result of all this process of collection was bestowed the name "Koran" (that which hath been recited). To a casual reader it may appear dull and wearisome beyond measure, but scarcely any other work suffers so much in translation, for the Suras are written in a kind of rhythmical (almost rhyming) prose, which lends itself to emotional recitation, and the original in style greatly resembles the Hebrew book of Psalms.

The following passages illustrate the teaching of the Koran. They are from Rodwell's translation, which is a most successful attempt at a reproduction, not only of the rhythmic flow of the Arabic, but also of its poetic idiom.

[1] And even the Christian Gospels.

### (i)

Praise be to God, Lord of the worlds!
The compassionate, the merciful!
King on the day of reckoning!
Thee *only* do we worship, and to Thee do we cry for help.
Guide Thou us on the straight path,
The path of those to whom Thou has been gracious;. with
    whom thou art not angry, and who go not astray.

### (ii)

O thou ENWRAPPED in thy mantle!
Arise and warn!
Thy Lord—magnify Him!
Thy raiment—purify it!
The abomination—flee it!
And bestow not favours that thou mayest receive again
with increase;
And for thy Lord wait thou patiently.
For when there shall be a trump on the trumpet,
That shall be a distressful day,
A day, to the Infidels, devoid of ease.
Leave me alone to deal with him whom I have created,
And on whom I have bestowed vast riches,
And sons dwelling before him,
And for whom I have smoothed all things smoothly
down;—
Yet desireth he that I should add more!
But no! because to our signs he is a foe
I will lay grievous woes upon him.
For he plotted and he planned!
May he be cursed!  How he planned!
Again, may he be cursed!  How he planned!
Then looked he around him,
Then frowned and scowled,

Then turned his back and swelled with disdain,
And said, "This is merely magic that will be wrought;
It is merely the word of a mortal."
We will surely cast him into Hell-fire.
And who shall teach thee what Hell-fire is?
It leaveth nought, it spareth nought,
Blackening the skin.
Over it are nineteen *angels*.

None but angels have we made guardians of the fire:
nor have we made this to be their number but to perplex
the unbelievers, and that they who possess the Scriptures
may be certain of the truth *of the Koran*, and that they
who believe may increase their faith;

And that they to whom the Scriptures have been given,
and the believers, may not doubt;

And that the infirm of heart and the unbelievers may
say, What meaneth God by this parable?

Thus God misleadeth whom He will, and whom He will
doth He guide aright: and none knoweth the armies of
thy Lord but Himself: and this is no other than a warning
to mankind.

Nay, by the Moon!
By the Night when it retreateth
By the Morn when it brighteneth!
Hell is one of the most grievous woes,
Fraught with warning to man,
To him among you who desireth to press forward, or to
remain behind.

For its own works lieth every soul in pledge.    But they
of *God's* right hand
In their gardens shall ask of the wicked;—
"What hath cast you into Hell-fire?"
They will say, "We were not of those who prayed,
And we were not of those who fed the poor,
And we plunged into vain disputes with vain disputers,

And we rejected as a lie the day of reckoning,
Till the certainty came upon us"—
And intercession of the interceders shall not avail them.

### (iii)

Praise be to God and peace be on His servants whom He hath chosen! Is God the more worthy or the gods they join with Him?

Is not He who hath made the Heavens and the Earth, and hath sent down rain to you from Heaven, by which we cause the luxuriant groves to spring up? It is not in your power to cause trees to spring up! What! A god with God? Yet they find equals for Him!

Is not He, who hath set the earth so firm, and hath made rivers in its midst, and hath placed mountains upon it, and put a barrier between the two seas? What! A god with God? Yet the greater part of them have no knowledge!

Is not He *the more worthy* who answered the oppressed when they cry to him, and taketh off their ills, and maketh you to succeed your sires on the earth? What! A god with God? How few bear these things in mind!

Is not He, who guideth you in the darkness of the land and of the sea, and who sendeth forth the winds as the forerunners of His mercy? What! A god with God? Far from God what ye join with Him!

Is not He, who created a Being, then reneweth it, and who supplieth you out of the Heaven and the Earth? What! A god with God? SAY: Bring forth your proofs if you speak the truth.

None either in the Heavens or in the Earth knoweth the unseen but God. And they know not

When they shall be raised.

—Yet they have attained to a knowledge of the life to come:—yet are they in doubt about it:—yet are they blind about it!

And the unbelievers say: "When we and our fathers have been dead shall we be taken forth?"

### (iv)

And when I taught thee the Scripture, and Wisdom, and the Law, and the Evangel: and thou didst create of clay, as it were, the figure of a bird, by my leave, and didst breathe into it, and by my leave it became a bird; and thou didst heal the blind and the leper, by my leave; and when, by my leave, thou didst bring forth the dead; and when I withheld the children of Israel from thee, when thou hadst come to them with clear tokens: and such of them as believed not said, "This is nought but plain sorcery";

And when I revealed unto the Apostles, "Believe on me and on my Sent One," they said, "We believe; and bear thou witness that we are Muslims."

Remember when the Apostles said:—"O Jesus, Son of Mary! is thy Lord able to send down a furnished Table to us out of Heaven?" He said:—"Fear God if ye be believers."

They said:—"We desire to eat therefrom, and to have our hearts assured; and to know that thou hast indeed spoken truth to us, and to be witnesses thereof."

Jesus, Son of Mary, said:—"O God, our Lord! send down a table to us out of heaven, that it may become a recurring festival to us, to the first of us and to the last of us, and a sign from thee; and do thou nourish us, for thou art the best of nourishers."

And God said:—"Verily, I will cause it to descend unto you; but whoever among you after that shall disbelieve,

I will surely chastise him with a chastisement, wherewith I will not chastise any other creature."

And when God shall say:—"O Jesus, Son of Mary: hast thou said unto mankind—'Take me and my mother as two Gods, beside God?'" He shall say:—"Glory be unto Thee! it is not for me to say that which I know to be not truth; had I said that, verily thou wouldest have known it: Thou knowest what is in me, but I know not what is in Thee; for Thou well knowest things unseen!

"I spake not to them aught but that which thou didst bid me—'Worship God, my Lord and your Lord'; and I was a witness of their actions while I stayed among them; but since thou hast taken me to Thyself, Thou hast Thyself watched them, and Thou art witness of all things:

"If Thou punish them, they are Thy servants, and if Thou forgive them . . . . Thou, verily, art the Mighty, the Wise!"

God will say:—"This day shall their truth advantage the truthful. Gardens shall they have 'neath which the rivers flow, and remain therein for ever": God is well pleased with them and they with Him. This shall be the great bliss.

Unto God belongeth the sovereignty of the Heavens and of the Earth, and of all that they contain; and He hath power over all things.

It is now time to consider the actual teaching embodied in this curious complex of written and oral tradition. The process of extracting a theology out of the pages of the Koran presents itself as tedious, for the reader finds little that is consecutive in the teaching, and is chiefly impressed by the wearisome repetition of the command not to join gods with God, while the frequent references to the torments of hell (often accompanied by lurid details), are emphatically repulsive. Still, despite evident weakness, there is a peculiar dignity and power about this wild string of half-incoherent utterances, and the intense perception of monotheistic sovereignty which they display is overshadowing. Allah is not a proper name, but is a contraction of Al Ilah, literally the Deity or the strong or mighty one. The other primitive Moslem name is Rabbi or Lord. From these it appears that the earliest conception of God proclaimed by Mohammed was that of absolute power. God guides and misleads whom he will, and is the Unconditioned Disposer; but his power is tempered with mercy. This overpowering sense of divine majesty, as experienced by the prophet, displays itself in a fertile variety of names, purporting to set forth the different aspects of the being and action of Deity. "Most excellent names hath Allah; by these call ye upon him and stand aloof from those who pervert his names." These names are reckoned in tradition as ninety-nine, and Moslems use rosaries of ninety-nine beads to aid in their recital. They divide themselves under five heads: (1) self-subsistent unity (2) omnipotence, (3) omniscience, (4) justice and (5) mercy. Some of the names are not found in the Koran explicitly, but are derived from passages which imply them.

Creation is described as an absolute act of Allah, and the details of it are those of Genesis i, as amplified by the Talmud. In spite of the intense unitarianism, there are curious traces of emanations, which seem to imply distinctions within the godhead. Such an emanation is called amr, and through it the divine spirit is said to proceed. Thus it is declared by Mohammed:

"Thus did we inspire thee with the spirit proceeding from our amr." Although Mohammed strongly opposed giving the title of Son of God to Christ, he evidently did so, not because he ignored this special gift, for he represents Allah as saying: "Some of the apostles we have endowed more highly than others . . . . we have given Jesus, the son of Mary, manifest signs and we strengthened him with the Holy Spirit," but because his belief in divine transcendence makes him most unwilling to call any human being a son of God: while his knowledge of the Christian Trinity was a completely erroneous one, *i.e.* that it consists of three separate deities strung together, God the Father, Jesus Christ and the Virgin Mary.[1] To us it must seem, therefore, that the Moslem reiteration against coupling gods with God rests upon a ludicrously frail foundation. We can, however, only conclude that the vulgar manifestations of Oriental Christianity left grave suspicions in the mind of the prophet about their tritheism; and whatever the doctrines of Christian theologians may be, it is by the popular devotions which it permits, or fails to condemn, that a theology must be judged.

Islam would appear to be a genuinely Semitic faith. It is much more than a mere republication of prophetic Judaism, though it certainly seems to have been influenced by the Old Testament. It is, as we have seen, a tremendous affirmation of the transcendence of Deity, and in this lies its strength. The word Islam

[1] Sura v, 116. "When Allah shall say: O Jesus Son of Mary, hast thou said unto mankind: Take me and my mother as gods beside Allah? Jesus will deny with indignation."

THE PEARL MOSQUE AT AGRA.

(*See* p. xii.)

itself means "to deliver the face," an idiom signifying "to submit one's self wholly."

Allah, as represented in the Koran and in the utterances of Moslem teachers, closely resembles the Veiled Being spoken of by Mr. Wells in his war-book: "God the Invisible King," or the Ananke of the Greeks, and the Necessitas of the Odes of Horace. The Deity of Islam is really Power, unlimited, arbitrary and inscrutable, and the appeal of Islam has been due even more to the fact that this corresponds very closely to a considerable section of human experience, than to the tendency of certain temperaments to react strongly against the approach to Deity, through the medium of localised symbols. Thus, when the scientist says that he recognises the probability that the Universe is controlled by a great spiritual being, but that he doubts the benevolence of that Being, or when a woman who has suffered a great sorrow says that she resigns herself into the hands of her creator with the words "I am sure that they are wise hands, but I somehow wish that they were kinder," in both cases the affirmation as to the nature of Deity is almost exactly on a par with that of Islam. Leaving on one side for the moment the problem of localisation, we may say that if this teaching about arbitrary transcendence represented the whole of the genuine experience of Deity, Islam would have much to commend it as the universal religion of mankind.

We might almost say that the influence of what has been called "astronomical intimidation," *i.e.* the discovery of the vastness and seeming incomprehensibility of the universe, actually strengthens the case for something resembling the Moslem creed. It is, however, impossible to agree to this without reserve, since to do so is to ignore another large section of human experience, *i.e.* that of the Divine loving-kindness. The Christian experience derives, not simply from the prophetic teaching of Jesus, but also from the verification of that teaching in human experience, and that verification involves the affirmation that if we take a large enough view of the purpose of Deity, it is reasonable to conclude that the latter is not only purposive rather than arbitrary and capricious, but that the purpose is benevolent in the sense in which the word is used of a human being of the wisest and best sort. The importance of this can hardly be exaggerated. Among the Moslem names for Allah, we find that the two commonest are "the compassionate" and "the merciful." It would appear, however, that the compassion and mercy are those of an inscrutable and entirely arbitrary tyrant, and that St. Paul, in his strange outpourings in the ninth chapter of Romans, is strongly Semitic and Jewish, though hardly Christian, when he says: "Therefore hath He mercy on whom He will have mercy and whom He will He hardeneth." The higher conception is that of the twenty-third Psalm, "though I walk through the valley of the shadow of death I will fear no evil . . . surely loving-kindness and mercy shall follow me all the days of my life."

The critical point is what is meant in Hebrew by the Semitic word for "loving-kindness." The word is חֶסֶד, and if we wish to understand its meaning we must recognise that חֶסֶד = kindness and benignity. Thus the "benevolent man" is חָסִיד, and perhaps the most striking explanation of what it means to be חָסִיד is to be found in the fact that the feminine form חֲסִידָה can also be a noun and not merely an adjective, and (as a noun) is the Hebrew for "stork"; the implication of which is that the stork is a bird showing intense and self-sacrificing affection for its young. חֶסֶד, therefore, does not mean the capricious kindness of a despotic ruler, about whom it may be said that you never know what he will do next, and that, if he is kind as a human being is kind, it may be an accident that he happens to behave as though he were a human being, or that in the particular instance he has chosen to be merciful, and to spare when he might have crushed. חֶסֶד means that quality, which ensures to you that the possessor of it, whatever he may be doing to you at the moment (possibly hurting you), is really inspired with an unfailing spirit of goodwill towards you, and may be trusted to maintain that spirit. It is probable that many human beings suppose that loving-kindness involves avoiding on all occasions doing or permitting anything to be done to another, which might cause the sensation of pain or suffering. It does not appear that the prophetic genius of Judaism at its maximum, conceived this to be the meaning of חֶסֶד. On the contrary, it firmly believed that the love of God might mean an attitude of love, not precluding the possibility of the suffering of the loved one.

This notion of divine benevolence may be difficult to those who live in certain parts of the world, and it has been significantly observed, that although Islam has penetrated into temperate and even cold climates, it is essentially a religion of the heat belt, and that it seems to be associated with the hot desert areas of the planet, and to be specially acceptable in tropical Africa. Colonel Buchan thinks that these physical conditions have largely produced it: "It is the empty desert and the empty sky that cast their spell over the Moslem, these, and the hot strong antiseptic sunlight, which burns up all rot and decay. It isn't inhuman, it's the humanity of one part of the human race." The movement which appeared about thirteen hundred years ago as a new and novel phase of religious life, is still a living and potent force, and in Africa is still spreading, though it is probable that its finest and most conservative expression is to be found among the Wahabi Moslems of Arabia. Up to the period of the Great War it preserved an almost solid front against Christianity and indeed against any other form of religious faith, and it seemed to be holding its own people. Since the War it has lost ground heavily, not least owing to the revolution in Turkey and the abolition of the Caliphate by Kemal Pasha. It is said that it is not holding the younger generation either in East Africa or in Egypt, and that the Mullahs or Moslem clergy, whether in Persia or Afghanistan, are almost everywhere opposed to the introduction of modern education and western civilisation, because they hold them to be dangerous to the purity of the faith of Islam. The situation in Moslem countries is therefore so unstable, that it is difficult to say anything really satisfactory about it. One thing is certain, and that is that it is suffering adversely from the influence of materialism and from the break-up of old pre-scientific views of the world, quite as much as any other traditional faith; and this is making it look in some countries wistfully towards the Christian movement, which it has hitherto been taught to misunderstand and to caricature, and which it now sees to be a more effective bulwark than its own inherited tradition against a materialism which it is learning to dread.

The immediate development of Islam was the work of Abu Bakr, to whose strength its success was almost entirely due. If there had been more men like Abu in the early days of the movement it might have swept the world. The Arabs, with a series of small armies of fine physique and unflinching confidence, carried all before them. This was the swarming period of a great race. The Arabs were well led, and the peoples with whom they fought, Byzantines, Persians and Central Asiatics, were spiritless and decadent. They prevailed, as has been said, because they possessed the best social and political order the times could offer. They found everywhere peoples who were being badly governed by systems both selfish and unsound. "Theirs was the broadest, freshest, and cleanest political idea that had yet come into actual activity, and it offered better terms than any other to the mass of mankind. They were obviously during their best years cleaner, more just and more merciful, than their neighbours."[1] Unfortunately those best years were short-lived. The first two Caliphs, Abu Bakr and Omar, were completely in earnest; but with Othman, the third caliph, there

[1] Wells, *Outline of History.*

comes a deterioration. Simplicity begins to give way
to luxury, and the national succeeds the religious as the
motive for conquest. Finally there is a miserable
quarrel over the succession. In 656 Othman was
murdered, and Ali, the nephew of the prophet and also
his son-in-law, seized the caliphate in spite of the fact
that his right to the succession was disputed. He, in
his turn, was murdered in 661, and the headship of the
new religion became a prize to be squabbled for by the
followers of two women, Ayesha, the favourite widow
of Mohammed, who supported Othman, and Fatima,
the wife of Ali, who supported her husband's claim.
"The world of Islam was rent in twain by the spites,
greeds, and partisan silliness of a handful of men and
women in Medina."[1] This division still endures, and
Moslems to this day are divided into the Sunnis, who do
not limit the caliphate to the direct heirs of Mohammed,
and the Shiahs who maintain that Ali and his family
had the hereditary right to the caliphate.

It is perhaps hardly worth while to trace in detail the
further expansion of Islam. In Spain, Sicily, Malta
and Greece, it made no permanent settlement. On the
other hand it firmly established itself in North Africa,
in India, in Persia, and, of course, wherever the Arab
element was dominant in the population. In more
recent times it has spread among the Malays, and has
swept downwards to central Africa, and eastward into
China. (In 1920, Moslems were said to number in all
two hundred and twenty-one millions). While for a
time its chief means of expansion was military, in later
centuries it has been the Arab trader who has acted as

[1] Wells, *op. cit.*

its apostle, and its attractiveness lies in the main in four things.

(1) The stark simplicity of its doctrine of deity.

(2) Its immediate admission of all converts to terms of equality, in obedience to the concluding words of Mohammed's last sermon.

(3) The ease and precision with which its devotional exercises are performed.

(4) The attainableness of its moral standard. It is no great hardship to forswear pork and alcohol in the tropics, whereas in a hot climate sexual laxity is difficult to avoid. But it is easier to be a good Moslem than to be a good Christian, because the standard demanded is not so high.

The five compulsory practices or pillars of Islam are:

(1) Kalimah, or the recital of the creed.

(2) Salat, or the recital of the five daily prayers, accompanied by ablutions.

(3) Fasting.

(4) Zakat, or Almsgiving.

(5) Haj, or pilgrimage.

To these some would add as a sixth, "jehad," or the Holy War, but this is not now regarded by all as essential to the same extent as the other five.

There is denunciation of usury and games of chance, but polygamy is granted to all.

As Islam expanded from Arabia, it had, like Christianity, to adapt itself to wider horizons, and in process of time to decide what might be regarded as proper development from teaching originally given to the prophet, and what might be rejected.

Three lines of development are recognised:

(1) Sunna, or custom, which is certified by a succession of teachers, and is based on the hadith or tradition regarding the words and deeds of the prophet.

(2) Ijma, or unanimity of opinion among teachers at all times and in all places. (This somewhat resembling the Vincentian canon in Christianity).

(3) Qiyas, or inferences and deductions which inevitably followed from the original teaching.

It is not surprising to find that in the process of expansion Islam has divided into a large number of sects, of a ritual, political and theological character. In Christianity the test of belonging to a denomination is in the main one of communion, or at least of acceptance of a credal formula. In Islam the test is the ability to pray behind a particular leader or Imam.

The Arab civilisation of the Middle Ages was of a high order. Its characteristic architecture is to be seen alike in the Moorish palaces of Spain and in famous Taj Mahal at Agra in India. It revived the study of Aristotelian philosophy and science, and made great contributions in the realms of mathematics.

The eulogy of Islam given in the *Outline of History* will doubtless be familiar to many.

"What appealed to them was that this God, Allah, he preached, was by the test of the conscience in their hearts a god of righteousness, and that the honest acceptance of his doctrine and method opened the door wide in a world of uncertainty, treachery, and intolerable divisions, to a great and increasing brotherhood of trustworthy men on earth, and to a paradise, not of perpetual exercises in praise and worship, in which saints, priests, and anointed kings were still to have the upper places, but of equal fellowship and simple and understandable delights, such as their souls craved for. Without any ambiguous symbolism, without any darkening of altars or chanting of priests, Mohammed had brought home these attractive doctrines to the hearts of mankind."

That is probably the best that can be said, and it is a good deal. Unfortunately, however, the Deity of intense power and majesty preached by Mohammed, although he is sometimes called by "beautiful names," does not seem in reality to have the same moral qualities as the Deity whose character is unfolded to us in the character of Christ. Mohammed's declaration concerning equality seems to have been an impulsive remark, subconsciously derived from Christianity or Judaism, probably the latter, since it does not say "every human being is the brother of every other human being." Indeed, the general structure of society implied in the teaching of Mohammed, involves polygamy, slavery, divorce, war, revenge and duplicity. In addition to this, the will of Allah is throughout represented as the will of an arbitrary numen. The beautiful names mean very little. They are almost like the flattery of a slave cringing before a despot and trying to wheedle him into a good temper. There is a great gulf between this attitude and that of the free Christian man who can

stand up fearlessly and without flattery address Deity
as "Father."

One who has lived for many years in first-hand
contact with Moslems,[1] writes:

"The Eternal Being is regarded by Muhammadans as
separated from man by an impassable chasm. Those
profound words, the germs of Christian theology, that
God made man in His own image and after His own
likeness, would be indignantly repudiated by the Muhammadan. Man's justice is no measure of the divine justice.
There is no affinity. The idea of communion and fellowship
with God (impossible without such affinity), is blasphemous
to the Muhammadan. It follows that His commands do
not aim at creating a likeness between God and man, do
not aim at making him a son of God, do not aim at revealing
the nature of God, but are the arbitrary commands of an
oriental despot. It is precisely at this point that our
Christian prepossessions lead us astray. We read into
passages in the Qur'an which describe the name and
attributes of God Christian conceptions of those attributes.
If we remember that the Qur'an is supposed to be the
perfect revelation of the Eternal Will of God, and that
He has commanded everything in it because He willed
to command it, and that if He wills to alter it He can
alter it, you must face one of two conclusions, either (1)
that there is a fixed moral standard and the passages in
the Qur'an which enjoin slavery, polygamy, divorce, and
religious warfare are immutable, or (2) that there is no
fixed moral standard anywhere, no 'Rock of Ages.' The
commands are not the revelation of a moral and righteous
governor of the Universe, they are the arbitrary commands
of an oriental despot. There is no fixed moral standard
at all. If you tell a Muhammadan that Muhammad sinned

[1] Canon Dale, of Zanzibar.

in the matter of Zainab, he will reply, 'He did not sin, because God commanded it.' What is a moral impossibility to us, that God should command a breach of the moral law, is by no means inconceivable to them. Sin with them is disobedience to an arbitrary will, rather than an offence against the holiness of God or a falling short of the glory of God. The will is arbitrary, it can be changed at pleasure, they say that it actually has been changed!

"Now this conception of arbitrariness is the evil genius of Islam. It is necessary to read the Qur'an through, and let the repetition of the words 'if God will,' 'what God will,' 'when God pleases,' produce the required impression on the mind. Then you will begin to see how the arbitrariness of the will of God, as they conceived it, led them on to their rigid theory of predestination and *kismet*."

" To quote from the Qur'an:

'Had thy Lord pleased He would have made men of one nation, but they will not cease to differ save those on whom the Lord has had mercy. For this has He created them and the Word of Thy Lord is fulfilled, I will surely fill hell with jinns and mankind altogether.'

'We have created for hell many of the jinns and mankind.'

'Thus God leads astray whom He pleases and guides whom He pleases, and no one knows the hosts of the Lord save Himself. And every man's destiny have we fastened on his neck.'

"Now to see how the traditions support this view.

"The traditions are taken from two of the authorised collections—these of Al Bokhari and Abu Muslim. 'God touched Adam and brought forth another family, and said, "I have created these for hell, and their actions will be like unto those of the people of hell." Then a man said to the

Prophet, "Of what use will deeds of any kind be then?"
He said, "When God createth His servant for Paradise
his actions will be deserving of Paradise until he die."
'The first thing which God created was the Pen (of
power). And he said unto it "Write" and it said "What
shall I write?" And God said "Write down the quantity
of every individual thing to be created"; and it wrote down
all that was and that will be to eternity.'

But the most astounding passage of all is one quoted
by the well-known Oriental traveller, Mr. Palgrave, who
says that when in the Nejd he heard it again and again
from admiring and approving Wahhabis. 'When God
resolved to create the human race He took into His
hands a mass of earth, the same whence all mankind
were to be formed, and in which they after a manner pre-
existed, and having divided the clod into equal parts, He
threw one half into hell saying, "These to eternal fire and
I care not," and the other half into Paradise and said,
"These to Paradise and I care not."'

The importance of the above quotation from Palgrave
can hardly be exaggerated, since he got his facts
first-hand from intimate knowledge of Arabia from
inside. It will be seen from this, how vast is the
difference between the spirit of resignation in Islam and
in Christianity. The latter may be summed up as
intelligent, loyal and affectionate trust, the former as
dumb submission. What is the effect on character?
This doctrine of the arbitrary will of God was introduced
into Christianity by Augustine, and developed by
Calvin. It does not belong to the teaching of Christ.
Alike in Islam and in Calvinism, it produces a strong,
virile, and unbending type of character, not without
dignity, but tending inevitably to harshness and

cruelty. In the West it on the whole favoured a republican oligarchy and antisacerdotalism. In the East it might have developed in this way, but although in the political theory of primitive Islam, as we see it in the person of the great Caliph Omar, there is a distinctly republican spirit, the oriental peoples were on the whole not ready for this sort of government, and the Moslem world gradually drifted into Sultanism.

"The Arabs never grappled with the problems . . . of the stable progressive state; everywhere their form of government was absolutist and subject to the convulsions, changes, intrigues and murders that have always characterised the extremer forms of monarchy."[1]

The influence of Islam is in the direction of ethical mediocrity. Among the primitive peoples of Africa and the East it has effected a certain cleansing and simplification of life. It gets rid of idols and fetishes, encourages bodily cleanliness, and trains people in habits of spiritual prayer. But as it tolerates slavery, polygamy and war, it disturbs the moral standard of the African village very little, and this renders it easier of acceptance than the Christian creed, which makes infinitely higher demands on the character, and sets forth a standard difficult of attainment. The standard of Islam is easily attainable. It is a half-way house between primitive and Christian morality, and once a convert has reached it, he is content to stop there, and it is found in practice extremely difficult to get him to shift and to struggle after the Christian ideal.

It appears, then, that the aim and end of life according to Islam is a disciplined life of submission, abstemious

[1] Wells, *op. cit.*

in food and drink though not in sex matters, motivated by a very definite paradise of sensual delights. Such a scheme cannot satisfy to the full the claims of human nature, and we therefore find the development known as Sufism, which provides an outlet for those who find ordinary Moslem practices inadequate for the satisfaction of the mystical temperament.

The name Sufi is first met with about the end of the second century after the Hijra. It is supposed to be derived from Suf, the name of the garment of coarse, undyed wool, worn by Christian ascetics, and it is of course difficult to know how far the Sufi is an independent development, and how far he owes anything to his Christian neighbours. It is, however, quite unreasonable to say that there is anything actually inconsistent with the teaching of Mohammed in Sufism, since the prophet was himself a man of strong intuitive genius, and it is his followers for the most part who have reduced his teachings to a system. It is not difficult for the pendulum to swing from extreme emphasis upon transcendence to extreme emphasis upon immanence, provided that we are concerned with the life of feeling and devotion, rather than of thought. The real change, however, which cannot be denied, and which may be due to Christian influence, is the change from submission to a transcendent potentate who cannot be expected to exhibit affection towards his slaves to mystical union with a celestial lover. Indeed, the records of Sufism are so full of passages about the Beloved, that it is difficult often to distinguish them from passages in Eckhart. The golden age of this Moslem mysticism occurs in Persia after the devastation of western Asia by the hordes of Mongolian nomads, and there is a rich literature of Persian poetry which illustrates the sentiments of these spiritual dreamers. One of them may here be quoted:

> With my Beloved I alone have been
> When secrets tenderer than evening airs
> Passed, and the Vision blest
> Was granted to my prayers,
> That crowned me, else obscure, with endless fame,
> The while amazed between
> His beauty and His majesty
> I stood in silent ecstasy,
> Revealing that which o'er my spirit went and came.
> Lo, in His face commingled
> Is every charm and grace,
> The whole of Beauty singled
> Into a perfect face
> Beholding Him would cry,
> "There is no god but He, and He is the Most High!"

Súfism still exists, but its palmy days are over, and with the waning of the vitality of Islam it is natural that it should decline, since loss of faith naturally produces a cooling of fervour, and so creates a temperature unfavourable to the growth of mystical piety.

There are at least four orders of Súfis, one of them known as the dancing dervishes. The Súfi is an ascetic who has much more in common with Hinduism than with Islam as usually represented. He uses extremely symbolical language, and he is badly misunderstood by the westerner, who takes, for example, the Rubaiyat of Omar Khayyam as the musings of a drunken philosopher, whereas they are in reality pure mysticism, "wine" meaning "ecstasy," "the tavern" "the secret chamber of the soul," "beauty" "the perfection of God," "the keeper of the tavern" "one's own spiritual director."

It seems on the whole most probable that the mysticism of the Sufis and that of mediaeval Christianity both derived from the common influence of Neo-Platonic thought, mediated especially through the writings of the Pseudo-Dionysius. Just as Neo-Platonism developed probably through Plotinus from India, so what we have here in Sufism is a modification of Islam not unlike that to be found in the writings of Kabir and among the Sikhs.

The fundamental issue between Islam and Christianity is found just where too often they are supposed to resemble each other, namely, in their idea of God. Each is monotheistic. As against idolatry, polytheism and pantheism, Christians feel a strong sense of agreement with Islam, and they seem to themselves to breathe a purer air when they pass out of a Hindu temple, with its idols, and often its obscenity, into the austerity and simplicity of a Mohammedan mosque. Also there can be no doubt that Mohammed thought he was setting forth the true conception of God, which in some measure the Jews and Christians whom he knew had corrupted, although his methods of proclamation were different from theirs. Even so, however, he believed at first that it was the same God. "Our God and your God is one," says the Koran. But they are not the same God at all. In the prevalent Moslem view there are, as we have seen, seven attributes of God, and ninety-nine names. The early Moslems, the companions of Mohammed and their followers, held, however, that inquiries into the nature of God and His attributes were not lawful.

It was sufficient, as Mohammed had taught, to

"Say: He is God alone:
God the eternal!
He begetteth not, and He is not begotten;
And there is none like unto Him."

Moslem apologists for Islam have sought to Christianise the God of Islam. Ayed Ameer Ali first describes the Christian doctrine, and especially the historic view of Jesus and His revelation of God as Father, and then transfers the whole Christian conception to the Allah of Mohammed. But the facts of history cannot be so easily dissipated. The Moslem view of God has been seen both in itself and in its effects to be defective in its unmoral autocracy, its irresponsible fatalism, its implication in human sin, the mere verbalism of its compassion, its inadequacy in holiness and love, the capriciousness of its justice, its repudiation of the conception of fatherhood, and its denial of the possibility of the immanence and indwelling of God.

Two testimonies from outside the missionary ranks will suffice:

Johannes Hauri, in his study of Islam, says:

"What Mohammed tells of God's omnipotence, omniscience, justice, goodness, and mercy sounds, for the most part, very well indeed, and might easily awaken the idea that there is no real difference between his God and the God of Christianity. But Mohammed's monotheism was just as much a departure from true monotheism as the polytheistic ideas prevalent in the corrupt Oriental Churches. Mohammed's idea of God is out-and-out deistic. God and the world are in exclusive, external, and eternal opposition."

And James Freeman Clarke calls it the "worst form of monotheism," and says:

"Islam saw God, but not man; saw the claims of Deity, but not the rights of humanity; saw authority, failed to see freedom—therefore hardened into despotism, stiffened into formalism, and sank into death . . . . Mohammed teaches a God above us; Moses teaches a God above us, and yet with us; Jesus teaches—God above us, God with us, and God in us."

In order to be perfectly just we must point out that Islam came into existence just over thirteen hundred years ago, and that, therefore, it might be proper to compare its present condition with that of Christendom at the beginning of the fourteenth century A.D., rather than with that of Christendom as it is to-day. Against this, however, may be set the probability that even were we to give it another six hundred years it is unlikely that Islam would ever develop into the position at present occupied by Christianity. No doubt six hundred years might see a great modernising of Moslem teaching, an abandonment of much credulous superstition and the assimilation of the residuum to something very like a deistic unitarianism. Indeed we see such a process actually at work in the activities of the comparatively modern Ahmadiyah sect. But there are two reasons why it is most unlikely that even six hundred years will bring Islam to a higher

level in which it would compare favourably with
Christianity in 1930.

(1) Islam as a system is much more vulnerable than
Christianity to critical study.    Scientific investigators
can ruthlessly handle the documents of the Bible and
the records of the Early Church, sifting the grain from
the chaff, and at the end the essential and vital soundness of the judgments of Jesus and the significance of
His brief career remain unscathed.    It is otherwise with
the utterances of Mohammed.    An intensive study
of the Koran convinces of the injustice, ignorance
and unsoundness of some of its most important
statements.

(2) Even when we have stripped away these, the bare
transcendent monotheism of Mohammed remains
inferior to the much more fully balanced Christian
doctrine of Deity, and is an entirely different thing
from the qualified transcendence taught in Christianity.
The two creeds are alternatives and not identical.    Only
a superficial survey of Moslem theology can leave the
impression that the differences are negligible.    In
essence they are as wide apart as the heaven.    If
liberal Moslems seriously endeavour to christianise
their inherited dogmas about Allah, they will not long
remain genuinely Moslem except in name.    It may be
that many of them feel that there is a good case to be
made out for a quasi-Mohammedan form of deism; but
if this is so, they should adhere to the pure stream of
their traditional faith and not contaminate it with the
oil of Christian theism.

There is a marked difference, of course, between the
prophetic monotheism of the Koran and the scholastic

Mohammedanism of the Middle Ages with its attempts to state Islamic dogma in Aristotelian terms.

Space forbids a detailed account of these later developments of Moslem theology, and of the large number of sects and schools of thought, but some mention must be made of the important division which arose as the result of hot debate upon the relation of divine omnipotence to human freewill. This began as early as the first century after the prophet's death, and those who took the view that Allah could not predestinate the actions of men, because he was a moral being who was bound to do that which was righteous, received the name of Mu'tazila, which means "the Seceders" or secessionists. These liberal Moslems insisted not only that Allah was not beyond good and evil, but that theology should be subject to investigation by the reason. They refused to accept as final such phrases as "God the Most High has said," and demanded enquiry. This attitude, of course, had its dangers, and led some of them into a state of scepticism, but nevertheless it encouraged others to establish Moslem theology on a firm logical foundation, by insisting that nothing repugnant to philosophy should be taught as of faith. It is these philosophical Arab teachers with whom the Catholic schoolmen of the Middle Ages were in close contact, and it is strange to reflect that in the thirteenth century there was almost a possibility of a real understanding between the two groups. We may sum up the situation in the words of a historical expert: "East and West were then intellectually much more closely allied than they have ever been since. Save for the central dogmas of the

Trinity and the Incarnation, the schoolmen could as often as not find as many allies in the opposing camp as in the ranks of their own army." This fortunate condition came suddenly to an end, not only owing to the different attitude of the Turks, but also to the banishment of the Moors from Spain and to the end of the Arabian Moslem Empire upon the shores of the Mediterranean.

The dominance of Islam in its ancient strongholds is to-day severely shaken. The following three comments from observers are sufficient evidence of this.

The first is from an American educational worker in Egypt. The second and third are from a ten years' survey of missions in Turkey and Persia.

(1) "The day was when in any café or railroad train in Egypt the dominant topic of conversation was religion. The questions of supreme interest were those of theology and philosophy: 'Do the decrees of Allah allow man to be free? Is it not blasphemy for Christians to claim that Jesus is the Son of God? Can a Moslem accept interest on his loan? Is not the Koran the very word of God?' And the sheikh, the exponent of such learning, was held in high honour. To-day all that is changed. As some one has said of Moslem Egypt: The old creed, 'There is no God but Allah and Mohammed is the Prophet of Allah,' has been displaced by the creed, 'There is no God but Cotton and the Egyptian Pound is the Prophet of Cotton.' Not the minaret of the mosque, but the chimney of the cotton mill dominates village life to-day. Theology is barely tolerated. As for the sheikh, he is the butt of joke and satire in every Egyptian popular

theatre. The questions that matter to-day are: Is any religion credible? Has not science discredited all belief in God? What is the true pathway of nationalism? What of the economic order? What of sex and the social order? What principles determine right and wrong? Can any faith be placed in international agreements? How banish disease? What form of government best suits the country?"

(2) "An effort has been made to impress on the Turkish mind that Islam was a system imposed on the Turks by the Arabs. The Turks, it is said, had an honourable history in the world before they became Moslem. This feeling is shown in a newly published text-book of history now in use in all the higher schools, which explains that Islam was forced on the Turks by Turkish political leaders after centuries of fighting with the Arabs, and while polite about the influence of Christianity in the world, adopts in its earlier chapters an almost atheistic view. Another movement which throws light on the same point is what may be called the cult of the White Wolf. During the Great War Enver Pasha, then Minister of War, sent out to the army a prayer for use by the soldiers invoking the aid of the White Wolf, a pre-Islamic war god of the Turks. Now-a-days, on the stamps and on the paper currency the White Wolf has reappeared, and the story has been introduced into school reading books. This has not led to any worship of the legendary wolf, but it has increased the tendency to regard all religion as myth or legend. With the prohibition of the study of Arabic in all schools, a generation is growing up that cannot study the Koran in the original, and with the abolition of

the *medressehs*, no new religious teachers are being produced. Islam, therefore, grows weaker every year, while there is a greater tendency towards the study of other religions."

(3) "The Government's attitude towards religion is not very active. It curbed the influence of the *mullahs*, and by so doing has indirectly encouraged the people in their rebellion against the former autocracy of the religious leaders, who had steadily opposed all movements for reform. The educated classes have long ceased to have any respect for their clergy."

## NOTE TO CHAPTER VI

IN order to show how the prophetic belief of Mohammed was capable of being treated by a philosophical theologian of his own community it may be of some interest to give here in an appendix the following short dogmatic treatise which was composed by Abu 'Abdallah Mohammed ibn Mohammed abu Jusuf as-Senusi in North Africa in the year 1490, that is to say 895 years after the hijra. It happens to be somewhat popular as a means of instruction:

In the name of God the merciful and compassionate! Praise be to God, and peace and blessing upon the prophet of God!

Know, that the judgment of reason hath three categories: necessity, impossibility, and possibility. The necessary is that of which non-existence is inconceivable, the impossible is that of which the existence is inconceivable, the possible is that of which the existence is as conceivable as the non-existence.

It is before all things necessary for every man who is under obligation to perform the duties of a Moslem according to the law, that he know what in respect of our Lord the Mighty and Exalted is necessary, what is impossible, and what is possible. Even so is it also his duty to know the relation of the self-same categories to the Prophet—upon whom be blessing and peace.

To the category of that which for our Lord, the Exalted and Mighty is *necessary*, there belong twenty attributes:

(1)  Being:
(2)  Existence from eternity:
(3)  Existence to eternity:
(4)  That He the Exalted One is distinct from temporal things:
(5)  That He the Exalted One existeth of Himself, that is that He needeth no embodiment and no determining principle.
(6)  Unity, that is that He hath no equal beside Himself neither in His essence nor in His attributes nor in His activity.

Thus far be there six attributes of which the first is essential (grounded in the divine essence) namely Being, and the following five are negative. Furthermore there are necessary for him, the Exalted One, seven other attributes, which are called the conceptual attributes, namely:

(1)  Omnipotence,
(2)  Will,

both of which have for their object all which is possible.

(3)  Knowledge, which hath for its object all that is necessary, possible, and impossible.
(4)  Life, which hath no object.
(5)  Hearing,
(6)  Sight,

both of which have for their object all that existeth.

(7)  Speech, which is without word or sound, and which hath the same object as knowledge.

Further there be seven attributes which are called the ideal attributes, and which are logically bound up with the first seven, namely that He the Exalted One:

(1)  Is Almighty;
(2)  Willeth;
(3)  Knoweth;
(4)  Liveth;
(5)  Heareth;
(6)  Seeth;
(7)  Speaketh.

To the category of that which is impossible in respect of God the Exalted One, there belong attributes, which are the opposites of the first twenty, namely:

(1)  Non-existence;
(2)  Temporal emergence;
(3)  Entry into non-existence;

(4) Resemblance to temporal things, as though He were a corporeal being, that is to say that His exalted essence should occupy a specific amount of empty space, or as though He were a quality inherent in a body, or as though He occupied a position in regard to material things or they to Him, or as though He were limited by space or time, or as though temporal predicates could be appended to His Exalted Being, or as though the predicates small or great could be appended to Him or as though purposes concerning activities or judgments could be ascribed to Him.

(5) Even so is it impossible with Him the Exalted One that He should not be self-existent in the sense of being an attribute dependent upon something else even as the soul is upon the body, or had need of a determining principle.

(6) Even so is it impossible with Him the Exalted One that He should not be unique in His self-sufficiency, as though He were subject to conditions, or as though there existed other beings like Him in essence or attributes, or as though there were some force working alongside of Him in the performance of activity. (For God Himself is the only active One, and all that happens in the activities of men, happens through an ever reiterated process of creation, and man is only able to do anything through appropriating to himself that which God hath done.

(7) In like manner is it impossible with Him the Exalted One to be incapable of anything which is possible and that anything should be set in existence in the world if its existence is opposed to Him, that is if He the Exalted One doth not will it, or that it should come to pass through an oversight, or without His knowledge, or that it should come to pass through the mere chain of cause and effect, or through the nature of things.

(8) Even so little is it possible that God should be ignorant, or that He should have a like imperfection in relation to anything accessible to knowledge.

(9) Impossible to Him is death, deafness, blindness and dumbness. The opposites of the ideal attributes proceed clearly from the foregoing.

That which denotes the *possible* in relation to God, that is the performance or the non-performance of all that which is possible.

The proof for the existence of God the Exalted One is the temporal origin of the world; for if it had no one who could have caused it to originate so that it existed through itself, then of logical necessity the case would arise that one of two similar possibilities (existence and non-existence) although equal to its opposite yet overcame it without adequate reason; and that is impossible.

The proof of the temporal origin of the world is its association with temporal accidents, motion, rest, and the like; and that which is associated with the temporal is itself temporal.

The proof of the temporal origin of these accidents is the perception that they pass from non-existence to existence and from existence to non-existence.

The proof for the necessity of the primordial existence of God the Exalted One is that if He were not in being from eternity, He must have arisen in time and then would need someone on whom to depend for His existence. And this would involve either a vicious circle or an endless chain of contingent beings, themselves in need of a creator.

The proof of the existence of God the Exalted One to eternity is that if it were possible for non-existence to be predicated of Him, it would then be impossible to credit Him with primordial existence; for His existence would then belong to the category of the possible, not to that of the necessary; and the existence of the possible belongs only to the category of the temporal. But we have already established the necessity of His primordial existence.

The proof that He the Exalted One is distinct from temporal things is that if He were to resemble any of them He would then like them have arisen in time; but that is impossible since thou knowest already that it has been established that He the Exalted One hath existence from eternity to eternity.

The proof that He the Exalted One is self-existent is that if He were to need support He would be an attribute; but an attribute can possess neither conceivable nor ideal attributes, and our Lord Mighty and Exalted possesseth of necessity both kinds of attributes; He is therefore Himself no attribute. And further, were He to be in need of a determining principle, He would then be of temporal origin. But we have already established the proof of His eternal being.

The proof that He the Exalted One hath of necessity *unity* is that if He were not unique, the logical consequence would be that nothing would exist in the world, because He would, in that case, of logical necessity, be without power to create.

The proof that He the Exalted One of necessity hath the attributes of omnipotence in will, knowledge, and life, is that if a being possessing these did not exist, none of the things which are temporal could exist either (as they do).

The proof that He the Exalted One hath hearing, sight and speech is to be found in the Koran, the tradition, and the agreement of the pundits. Further, if He had not these attributes, it would then be logically necessary that He should have the attributes which are opposed to them; but these are imperfections, and any imperfection is for Him the Exalted One impossible.

The proof that activity or non-activity in matters which are possible belongs for Him (the Exalted One) to the category of the possible, is that if it were conceivable that the one or the other were to Him the Exalted One either compulsory or impossible, then that which is possible would become changed into the compulsory or impossible; but that is inconceivable.

With regard to the apostles of God, upon whom be blessing and peace, the following are necessary; veracity, fidelity, and communication to His creatures of that which they are commanded to transmit to them.

The opposites of these attributes, namely lying and infidelity, or the concealment of that message which is entrusted to them, these are impossible to the apostles, upon whom be peace, and further it is impossible that they should do anything that is excluded either by counsel or command. That is possible in regard to them which belongeth to human infirmities, as for example sickness and the like, so long as it detracteth not from their high dignity.

The proof of the necessity of their veracity is that without it God the Exalted One must have lied when He authenticated their teaching through wonders, which convey the divine message: "My servant is in all things which he communicates from me endowed with veracity."

The proof of the necessity of their fidelity is that if they showed themselves to be unfaithful in that they transgressed any precept which forbade or dissuaded, then that which they were commanded or advised not to do would become a pious act; for God the Exalted One hath commanded us to imitate them in word and deed, and God the Exalted One doth not command men to transgress a prohibition or exhortation. The same proof holds good for the third attribute of the apostles.

The proof of the possibility of human infirmity in regard to these latter persons is the perception of its existence in them. That existence is permitted either in order to make their reward greater, or to provide a rule of conduct for mankind, or to wean them from worldly things, or to demonstrate to them that that which is of this world is in the eyes of God the Exalted One contemptible, and that He hath no pleasure in the world save as the place in which His prophets and holy ones win their reward, having always under consideration the circumstances under which they live in the world.

The content of all this confession of faith is contained in the words: "There is no god save Allah and Mohammed is the apostle of God." For the significance of the divine is that God is independent of all other things and that everything else is dependent on Him. The meaning of the words: "There is no god but Allah," is that there is no one else save God the Exalted One who is independent of all other things and on whom all other things depend. From the fact that the Mighty and Exalted One is independent of all other beings there followeth of necessity His being, His existence from eternity to eternity, His separateness from temporal things, His self-existence, and His freedom from imperfections. Thereby it is established that He the Exalted One hath of necessity hearing, sight, and speech; for if He did not of necessity possess these attributes, then would He need someone to have called Him into existence, to sustain Him, or to guard Him from imperfections. Further it follows that He the Exalted One is free from designs in His actions and judgments, for otherwise He would be dependent upon that which satisfies His purpose. But He the Mighty and Exalted is independent of all other things. Further it follows herefrom that it is not necessary for Him the Exalted One either to do or to leave undone any of the things which it is possible for Him to do. For in that case it would be conceivable that one of these possibilities, as for example the granting of rewards in the future life, might become a necessity, and in this case He the Mighty and Exalted One would become dependent on this circumstance for His perfection, since only that which pertaineth to the perfection of Him the Exalted One is to Him necessary. But He the Mighty and Exalted One is independent of all other things. From the circumstance that all other things are dependent upon Him the Exalted and Mighty, it follows of necessity that He the Exalted One hath the attributes of life, omnipotence, will, and knowledge; for if one of them were to be lacking then it would not be possible for any one of the things temporal to exist, and there would be nothing to be dependent upon Him.

But He is the one upon whom all other things depend. Further to Him the Exalted One there pertaineth unity; for if there were a second god beside Him, then would nothing be absolutely dependent upon Him, because neither god would be omnipotent; but He is the one upon whom all other things depend.

Further follows from the above the temporal emergence of the whole world; for if any part of it were eternal it would be independent of Him the Exalted One; but now is He the one upon Whom all other things of necessity are dependent.

Further it follows from the above that none of the things which exist can produce any effect by itself. Else would it be the case that this effect was not dependent upon our Lord the Exalted and Mighty One.

But now is He the very one upon whom all other things without exception and under all circumstances are dependent; and this applies in the case of anyone's claim that any one of the things which exist is able independently by its own natural constitution to produce an effect.

Were one, however, to suppose that this effect had been produced by some power delegated by God, as many unwise persons hold, that would also be impossible.

For in that case our Lord the Mighty and Exalted, in carrying out one of His designs would Himself be dependent upon one of His means of action. But that is a contemptible argument, since thou knowest that He the Exalted and Mighty is independent of all other things.

It is now clear to thee that the phrase: "There is no god but Allah," includeth the three categories which it is the duty of everyone embracing the life of a Moslem to know, in their relation to our Lord the Exalted and Mighty. It embraceth in relation to Him the Exalted One that which is necessary, that which is impossible, and that which is possible.

With our confession: "Mohammed is the Apostle of God"—God grant him blessing and reward him with salvation!—is implied the belief in the other prophets and the angels and the revealed books and the last day, because he, peace be upon him, has provided the corroboration of all these. From this follows the necessity of the veracity of the apostles, upon whom be peace, and the impossibility that they can lie. For else were they not true apostles of our Lord the Exalted and Mighty One who knoweth the deep and hidden things. Further followeth therefrom the impossibility that they should ever commit any forbidden deed; for they are sent that they may instruct mankind by their words, their deeds and their silent approval. And it is inconceivable that in all these there should be any contradiction of the commands of our Lord the Exalted and Mighty, who hath chosen them out from among all His creatures, and hath entrusted to them the secret of His revelation.

There followeth also from the preceding word the possibility of the presence in them of every human infirmity; for that prejudiceth neither their apostleship nor their exalted rank with God the Exalted One; but on the contrary maketh these all the greater.

It is now clear to thee, that the two divisions of the confession of faith, for all that they contain so few words, nevertheless embrace all the articles of faith which that person must know upon whom are incumbent the duties of the Moslem in relation to His apostle, upon whom be peace. Perchance it lieth in the circumstance that they be so short and yet embrace all that we have expounded, that the divine Lord has ordained them to be the expression of the faith present within the heart, and acknowledgeth that faith in no man except He know them. He that understandeth them therefore must oft repeat them, the while he recalleth to himself the articles of faith which they embrace, so that with their content they fully penetrate his flesh and blood; for he will thereby come to behold countless mysteries and wonders, if it be the will of God the Exalted One.

With God is refuge; other than Him there is no Lord, and to Him only may we pray.

We beseech Him who is exalted and praised that He may so ordain it, that we and those whom we love may in the hour of death recite the confession with full consciousness.

God bless our lord Mohammed, that he may be mindful of such as do this and unmindful of such as leave it undone!

May God the Exalted One be gracious to all the companions of the prophet and likewise to all who follow them with faith even to the day of judgment! Salvation to the apostle of God, and praise be to God the Lord of the worlds!

OF THE RELIGION OF THE MAYAS, AND
OTHER EARLY PEOPLES OF THE
AMERICAN CONTINENT

THE so-called Maya peoples of Central America present a singular problem both to the anthropologist and the student of religion. Their great centre of civilisation was formerly supposed to be Mexico, but the ruins of important cities have also been discovered in the mahogany forests of Yucatan and British Honduras, and elsewhere, and these show the existence of a highly developed art and architecture. Who these peoples were still remains an enigma. It has been suggested that they are part of a vast wave of colonisation extending eastward and westward from either Egypt or Mesopotamia, and leaving its traces in the megalithic monuments of such far-separated places as Easter Island and Stonehenge. Whatever the value of this theory, it is certainly remarkable that the practice of building in a particular way with huge blocks of stone should be as widely distributed as it is, if there were no genetic relation between the various peoples who practised it. There is also a certain similarity between the Maya teocallis, the Mesopotamian ziggurats, and the Egyptian pyramids. Another curious phenomenon is the use in Mexico of what appears to be the conventionalised representation of an elephant in the decorations carved on the buildings. It is said that it is difficult to believe, therefore, that the Mayas are entirely unconnected with some of the other early peoples whose cultures resemble theirs, and whose traces are distributed round the equatorial belt to such a uniform extent that they have not unsuitably been described as the children of the sun.

Leaving such speculations on one side, however, we have to reckon with the probability that the primitive inhabitants of these Central American provinces came from the direction of British Columbia. The languages of the native Indian tribes of the north-west greatly resemble the language of the Nahuas of Mexico, and the art-forms of the two peoples are strikingly similar. Still more remarkable is the tradition prevailing among the Nahuas that their ancestors reached the Mexican plateau from the north. Probably the migration was gradual, and occupied a number of stages, spread over a long period of time. This does not explain where the tribes of the north-west originated, nor does it account for the great cultural developments of the Aztecs and Peruvians; and it tells us nothing about the possible external influences which may have touched them during their settlement in Central America. Much still remains a mystery. It has been shown, however, that the connection of the Mayas with Egypt or with any other external culture is most unlikely. The old Mayas had no knowledge of metals; the Maya chronological cycle is unlike any other known; while almost nothing about these people suggests any Eurasiatic influence.

We may distinguish several periods in the early history of Central America. First a primitive culture; second, what is called the Old Maya Empire; third, a period of disintegration and barbarian invasion; fourth, a New Maya Empire, ending with the Spanish invasion. The dates of these periods are not at all clear, although the Mayas had an elaborate, and, so far as we can discover, unique system of chronology by cycles. This latter gives us as the earliest possible date the year 3485 B.C. which has been regarded as an impossible one. It is thought more likely that the Old Empire prevailed from about the first to the third or fifth centuries of our era, and that it collapsed partly through pestilence, partly at the hands of invaders. Its population is believed to have been racially different in the bulk from its ruling caste, and this raises the insoluble question as to the origin of that caste. After the collapse of the Old Empire its great cities of Copu, Uaxactum and Palenque seem to have remained deserted until their discovery in the nineteenth century. On the other hand the New Empire which followed created a further series of cities, Chichén-Itzá and others, and remained in existence till the arrival of the Portuguese off the coast in 1493.

As a result of careful field work it now seems fully established that through a series of unpremeditated, accidental, and long continued migrations a portion of the human race, consisting of the yellow-brown peoples from Asia and Polynesia, reached America from Siberia by way of Alaska and a land-bridge which is now partially under the sea. The beginnings of this migration may be dated approximately as from 25,000 to 10,000 years ago, and were due to increase in population and to shortage of food. They were wholly fortuitous and continued in waves throughout some thousands of years, the last wave being that of the Eskimos. No American civilisations therefore can be very old, and most of the highest are indeed not old at all. Thus the Old Maya Empire may be dated between 50 and 700 A.D., and the New Maya Empire falls between 900 and 1200 A.D., with an intervening period of decline. The Toltec period lasted from 1201 to 1458 and then declined, and was in a state of decadence at the time of the Spanish invasion.

In the Andean area there was an advanced archaic period between 100 B.C. and 600 A.D. in the highlands with an extension to the coast during the next two hundred years, and then after a period of decline a revival which led to the establishment of the Inca Empire in the fifteenth century; though it is thought that the latter was on the verge of disruption at the time of the European invasion.

It was the enterprise of the Spaniards under Cortes which led ultimately to the discovery for Europeans of these hitherto unknown peoples. Cortes landed in Mexico in 1519 and further south another band of adventurers led by Pizarro established the beginnings of Latin civilisation in Peru in the year 1530.

The conquest was accompanied by great cruelty, not perhaps greater than that with which the Mexicans and Peruvians were accustomed to handle their own defeated enemies, and the invaders, who were accompanied by

2 D

Catholic clergy, were much impressed with all that they saw, and recorded it in a series of chronicles, some of them written by Jesuit missionaries, and furnishing lively accounts of the Maya religious customs.

The American historian, Prescott, constructed a connected story from these, and in the nineteenth century his work was widely read and esteemed. Then followed a reaction, during which it was alleged that he had over-estimated the importance of the Spanish evidence, and that so far from the Mayas and Incas being highly civilised folk, they were really only just emerging from barbarism. Since then much archaeological research has taken place ; and it seems likely that these American cultures will be permanently judged as somewhat on a par with that of the ancient Sumerians, though of course of a much later date, contemporary with the middle ages in Europe. They are distinctive and interesting, but repulsive on account of their extraordinarily low valuation of the individual human life.

The Maya and Andean civilisations are late in development but verge upon those of Sumeria and Egypt in elaborateness of architectual and pictorial art. They are inferior in that they show no great literary productions, and are perhaps what the earlier stages of Sumerian and Egyptian cultures might have been like, when emerging from savagery. It is very difficult to know to what extent the so-called Inca hymns, of which two are here appended, have been influenced in their transmission by the Biblical ideas and language familiar to their transmitters, the Catholic missionaries, and in any case they were not put in writing, but were transmitted orally like the sagas of the Norsemen. We have in fact in these American developments the work of Indians who were developing internally a civilisation in the same way as earlier races, but were conquered by Europeans before they had reached to the heights of the great races of antiquity.

The following description of the chief temple in the city of Mexico is drawn by Mr. Lewis Spence from an account given by one of the Spanish writers.

"This temple was erected by Ahuizotl in honour of the god Huitzilopochtli, in the centre of the city within an enclosure girt by walls 4800 feet in circumference. These were constructed of rubble-stone laid in mortar, coated with plaster, polished on both sides, and lavishly sculptured, serpents figuring most frequently; hence they were designated Coetpantli, or walls of serpents. On each side was a building, the lowest storey of which gave access to the enclosure. The great temple inside the court was a parallelogram in form, measuring 375 feet by 300 feet, and was built in six storeys, each smaller than the other, in a terrace-like formation. The walls were composed of a mixture of rubble, clay and earth, covered with large stone slabs carefully cemented and thickly coated with gypsum. The upper platform, reached by a flight of 340 steps which passed round each of the terraces, was surmounted by two three-storeyed towers, 56 feet high, the two upper storeys being of wood and only accessible by ladders.

"In the lower storey of the teocallis were situated the sanctuaries of the deities, their colossal statues being concealed by magnificent draperies, while at their feet stood the stone of sacrifice, made of green jasper. The walls and floor were bespattered with human blood. In all the temples a sacred fire was kept perpetually burning, as it was supposed that its extinction would entail national disaster. In Mexico alone six hundred braziers were kept burning night and day. Forty smaller temples surrounded the principal one, amongst which was that of Tlaloc, reached by a flight of fifty steps; that of Quetzalcoatl, which was circular and crowned by a dome, with a low door representing a serpent's mouth, through which worshippers had to pass; and that of Ilhuizatlican, dedicated to the planet Venus, at the very moment of whose appearance above the horizon a victim had to be sacrificed. In one of the teocallis an immense cage was placed for the reception of foreign gods, so that they could not succour their worshippers. The bones of the victims were collected in the Quauhzicalo, the skulls being deposited in the Tzompantli, an immense oblong pyramid, in which the Spaniards alleged that they discovered 136,000 heads.

"The court formed the largest portion of the enclosure, and within it immense crowds gathered to assist at the sacrifices, and in the gladiatorial combats. It was surrounded by the dwellings of thousands of priests, women, and children, charged with the care of the temples and their precincts, and was kept in a scrupulous condition of cleanliness."

The deities of these peoples of the New World in the main were personifications of the forces of nature, and were regarded with fear. Human sacrifice appears to have been extremely common, and its main object was to secure favour of the rain god, in whose honour perhaps gladiatorial combats were held.

We are fortunate in possessing some interesting accounts of the ceremonies connected with this worship, as they were observed by the Spanish invaders. It is true that the writer, as a pious Jesuit missionary, takes a delight in attributing the origin of these ceremonies to the devil himself, on account of the analogy between them and those of the Catholic church; and it may well be that his description is prejudiced, and that the actual ceremonies were not really so much like those of Catholic Spain as they were thought to be. Nevertheless the descriptions are so lively that they impress us as being those of a naïve and intelligent eye-witness. The reader may therefore be interested in some of the following extracts which are drawn from a delightful old English translation of the *Memoirs of Fr. Acosta*, made by Grimston.

The first is a general account of Peruvian sacrifice.

"Wee may draw all the sacrifices the Infidells vse into three kindes—one of insensible things, another of beasts, and the third of men. They did vse in Peru to sacrifice coca which is an hearb they esteeme much, of mays which is their wheate, of coloured feathers, and of chaquira which otherwise they call mollo, of shelles or oysters, and sometimes gold and silver being in figures of little beasts. Also of the fine stuffe of Cumbi, of carved and sweete wood, and most commonly tallow burnt. They made these offerings or sacrifices for a prosperous winde, and faire weather, or for their health, and to be delivered from some dangers and mishappes. Of the second kinde their ordinary sacrifice was of Cuyes, which are small beasts like rabbets, the which the Indians eate commonly. And in matters of importance, or when they were rich men, they did offer Pacos, or Indian sheepe bare or with wooll, observing curiously the numbers, colours, and times. The manner of killing their sacrifices, great or small, which the Indians did vse according to their ancient ceremonies, is the same the Moores vse at this day, the which they call Alquible, hanging the beast by the right fore legge, turning his eyes towards the sun, speaking certain wordes according to the qualitie of the sacrifice they slew; for, if it were of colour, their words were directed to Chuquilla and to the Thunder, that they might want no water; if it were white and smoothe they did offer it to the Sunne with certain words; if it had a fleece they did likewise offer it him with some others, that he might shine vpon them and favour their generation; if it were a Guanaco, which is gray, they directed their sacrifice to Viracocha. In Cusco they did every yeare kill and sacrifice with this ceremony a shorne sheepe to the Sunne, and did burne it, clad in a red waste-coate; and when they did burne it, they cast certaine small baskets of Coca into the fire, which they call Vilcaronca, for which sacrifice they have both men and beasts appointed which serve to no other vse. They did likewise sacrifice small birdes, although it were not so vsuall in Peru as in Mexico, where the sacrificing of quailes was very ordinarie. Those of Peru did sacrifice the birdes of the Puna, for so they call the desert, when they should go to the warres, for to weaken the forces of their adversaries Huacas. They called these sacrifices Cuzcovicsa, or Contevicsa, or Huallavicsa, or Sopavicsa, and they did it in this manner: they tooke many kindes of small birdes of the desert, and gathered a great deale of a thornie wood, which they called Yanlli, the which being kindled they gathered together these small birdes. This assembly they called Quiso. Then did they cast them into the fire, about the which the officers of the sacrifice went with certaine round stones carved, whereon were painted many snakes, lions, toades, and tigres, vttering this word Vsachum, which signifies, let the victorie be given vnto vs, with other wordes, whereby they sayed the forces of their enemies Huacas were confounded. And they drew forth certaine black sheepe, which had beene kept close some daies without meate, the which they called Vrcu, and in killing them they spake these words: 'As the hearts of these beasts be weakened, so let our enemies be weakened.' And if they found in these sheep that a certaine peece of flesh behind the heart were not consumed by fasting and close keeping, they then held it for an ill augure. They brought certaine black dogs, which they call Apurucos, and slew them, casting them into a plaine with certaine ceremonies, causing some kinde of men to eate this flesh, the which sacrifices they did lest the Ynca should be hurt by poison; and for this cause they fasted from morning vntill the stars were vp, and then they did glut and defile themselves like to the Moores. This sacrifice was most fit for them to withstand their enemies gods; and, although at this day a great part of these customes have ceased, the wars being ended, yet remaines there some relikes by reason of the private or generall quarrels of the Indians, or the Caciques, or in their citties. They did likewise offer and sacrifice shelles of the sea which they call Mollo, and they offered them to the fountaines and springs, saying that these shells were daughters of the sea, the mother of all waters. They gave vnto these shells sundrie names according to the color, and also they vse them to divers ends. They vsed them in a manner in all kinde of sacrifices, and yet to this day they put beaten shells in their Chicha for a superstition. Finally they thought it convenient to offer sacrifices of everything they did sow or raise vp. There were Indians appointed to doe these sacrifices to the fountaines, springs, and rivers, which passed through the townes, or by their Chacras, which are their farmes, which they did after seede time, that they might not cease running, but alwaies water their groundes. The sorcerers did coniure to know what time the sacrifices should be made, which, being ended, they did gather of the contribution of the people what should be sacrifices and delivered them to such as had the charge of these sacrifices. They made them in the beginning of winter, at such time as the fountaines, springs, and rivers did increase by the moistures of the weather, which they did attribute to their sacrifices. They did not sacrifice to the fountaines and springs of the desarts. To this day continues the respect they had to fountaines, springs, pooles, brookes, or rivers which passe by their citties or chacras, even vnto the fountaines and rivers of the desarts. They have a speciall regard and reverence to the meeting of two rivers, and there they wash themselves for their health, annointing themselves first with the flowers of mays, or some other things, adding therevnto divers ceremonies, the which they do likewise in their bathes.''

The second describes in great detail the sacrifice of human beings as practised among the Mexicans.

"Although they of Peru have surpassed the Mexicaines in the slaughter and sacrifice of their children (for I have not read nor vnderstood that the Mexicaines vsed any such sacrifices), yet they of Mexico have exceeded them, yea, all the nations of the worlde, in the great number of men which they had sacrificed, and in the horrible maner thereof. And to the end we may see the great miserie wherein the Divell holdes this blind Nation, I will relate particularly the custome and inhumane maner which they have observed. First, the men they did sacrifice were taken in the warres, neyther did they vse these solemne sacrifices but of Captives: so as it seemes therein they have followed the custome of the Ancients. For as some Authors say they called the sacrifice Victima, for this reason, because it was of a conquered thing: they also called it Hostia quasi ab hoste, for that it was an offering made of their enemies, although they have applied this word to all kindes of sacrifices. In truth the Mexicaines did not sacrifice to any of their idolls, but Captives, and the ordinarie warres they made was onely to have Captives for their sacrifices: and therefore when they did fight they laboured to take their enemies alive, and not to kill them, to inioy their sacrifices. And this was the reason which Motecuma gave to the Marquis del Valle, when he asked of him why being so mighty, and having conquered so many kingdomes, hee had not subdued the Province of Tlascalla, which was so neere: Motecuma answered him that for two reasons hee had not conquered that Province, although it had beene easir if he would have vndertaken it: the one was for the exercise of the youth of Mexico, lest they should fall into idlenes and delight: the other and the chiefe cause why he had reserved this Province was to have Captives for the sacrifices of their gods. The maner they vsed in these sacrifices was, they assembled within the palisado of dead mens sculles (as hath beene said), such as should be sacrificed, vsing a certaine ceremony at the foot of the palisado, placing a great guard about them. Presently there stept foorth a Priest, attyred with a shorte surplise full of tasselles beneath, who came from the top of the temple with an idoll made of paste, of wheate and mays mingled with hony, which had the eyes made of the graines of greene glasse, and the teeth of the graines of mays; hee descended the steppes of the temple with all the speede he could, and mounted on a great stone planted vpon a high terrasse in the midst of the court. This stone was called Quauxicalli, which is to say the stone of the Eagle, whereon he mounted by a little ladder, which was in the fore part of the terrasse, and descended by an another staire on the other side, still embracing his idoll. Then did he mount to the place where those were that should be sacrificed, shewing this idoll to every one in particular, saying vnto them this is your god. And having ended his shew, he descended by the other side of the staires, and all such as should die went in procession vnto the place where they should be sacrificed, where they found the Ministers ready for that office. The ordinary manner of sacrificing was to open the stomake of him that was sacrificed, and having pulled out his heart halfe alive, they tumbled the man downe the staires of the Temple, which were all imbrewed and defiled with blood. And to make it the more plaine, sixe sacrificers beeing appoynted to this dignitie, came into the place of sacrifice, foure to holde the hands and feete of him that should be sacrificed, the fift to holde his head, and the sixt to open his stomacke, and to pull out the heart of the sacrificed. They called them Chachalmua, which in our tong is as much as the ministers of holy things. It was a high dignitie, and much esteemed amongest them, wherein they did inherite and succede as in a fee simple. The minister who had the office to kill, which was the sixt amongest them, was esteemed and honoured as the soveraigne Priest and Bishop, whose name was different, according to the difference of time and solemnities. Their habites were likewise divers when they came foorth to the sacrifice, according to the diversitie of times. The name of their chiefe dignitie was Papa and Popilzin; their habite and robe was a red curtain, after the Dalmatica fashion, with tasselles belowe, a crowne of rich feathers, greene, white, and yellow vpon his head, and at his eares like pendants of golde, wherein were set greene stones, and vnder the lip, vpon the middest of the beard, hee had a peece like vnto a small canon of an azured stone. These sacrificers came with their faces and handes coloured with a shining blacke. The other five had their haire much curled, and tied vp with laces of leather bound about the middest of the head: vpon their forehead they carried small roundelets of paper, painted with diverse colours, and they were attired in a Dalmatica robe of white, wroght with blacke. With this attire they represented the very figure of the Divell, so as it did strike feare and terror into all the people to see them come forth with so horrible a representation. The soveraigne priest carried a great knife in his hand of a large and sharpe flint: another priest carried a coller of wood, wrought in forme of a snake: all sixe put themselves in order, ioyning to this Piramidall stone whereof I have spoken, being directly against the doore of the Chappell of their idoll. This stone was so pointed as the man which was to be sacrificed being laid thereon vpon his backe did bend in such sort as letting the knife but fall vpon his stomacke it opened very easily in the middest. When the sacrificers were thus in order they drew forth such as had beene taken in warre, which were to be sacrificed at that feaste, and being accompanied with a guard of men all naked they caused them to mount vp these large staires in ranke to the place where the Ministers were prepared: and as every one of them came in their order, the six sacrificers tooke the prisoner, one by one foote another by the other, and one by one hand another by the other, casting him on his backe vpon this pointed stone, where the fift of these Ministers put the coller of wood about his necke, and the High priest opened his stomacke with the knife, with a strange dexteritie and nimblenes, pulling out his heart with his hands, the which he shewed smoaking vnto the Sunne, to whom he did offer this heate and fume of the heart, and presently he turned towards the idoll, and did cast the heart at his face, then did they cast away the body of the sacrificed, tumbling it downe the staires of the Temple, the stone being set no neere the staires as there were not two foote space betwixt the stone and the first steepe, so as with one spurne with their foote they cast the

body from the toppe to the bottome.  In this sort one after one
they did sacrifice all those that were appointed.  Being thus slain,
and their bodies cast downe, their masters, or such as had taken
them, went to take them vp and carried them away: then having
divided them amongest them they did eate them, celebrating their
feast and solemnitie.  There were ever forty or fifty at the least
thus sacrificed, for that they had men very expert in taking them.
The neighbour Nations did the like, imitating the Mexicaines in
the customes and ceremonies of the service of their gods."

Two Peruvian Inca hymns are finally appended, as they
appeared in Dr. Mean's *Ancient Civilisations of the Andes*
(1929).  The first of these is taken from the Quechua
text (though whether Dr. Miguel Mossi's emendations of
it are such as to make it more Christian it is hard to
determine): the second is from the collections of Bishop
Ore (1547–1627) published at Lima in 1598.  They are
not addressed to the same deity.

(1)

Vira cocha, Lord of the Universe!
Whether male or female,
at any rate commander of heat and reproduction,
being one who,
even with His spittle, can work sorcery,
Where art Thou?
Would that Thou wert not hidden from this son of Thine!
He may be above;
He may be below;
or, perchance, abroad in space.
Where is His mighty judgment-seat?
Hear me!
He may be spread abroad among the upper waters;
or, among the lower waters and their sands
He may be dwelling
Creator of the world,
Creator of man,
Great among my ancestors
before Thee
my eyes fail me,
Though I long to see Thee

for, seeing thee,
knowing Thee,
learning from Thee
understanding Thee,
I shall be seen by Thee
and Thou wilt know me,
The Sun—the Moon;
the Day—the Night;
Summer—Winter;
not in vain
in orderly succession
do they march
to their destined place,
to their goal.
They arrive
wherever
Thy royal staff
Thou bearest
Oh! Harken to me,
listen to me,
let it not befall
that I grow weary
and die.

\*        \*        \*        \*

(2)    O Pacha camac!
Thou who hast existed from the beginning,
Thou who shalt exist until the end
powerful and merciful,
Who didst create man by saying,
"Let man be"
Who defendest man from evil,
and preservest our life and our health,
art Thou in the sky or upon the earth?
in the clouds or in the deeps?
Hear the voice of him who implores Thee,
and grant him his petitions.
Give us life everlasting,
preserve us, and accept this our sacrifice.

## Appendix B

## OF JAPANESE RELIGION

THE national life of Japan is strongly marked, owing no doubt to the fact that its people inhabit islands rather than the mainland. Racially the Japanese, though superficially resembling their neighbours on the continent, are a very distinctive people. The first inhabitants of the country were called "Earth-dwellers" or dwarfs, and little is known of them. They were displaced by the Ainu, a hairy people, greatly resembling the Russian mujik in appearance, who were an eastward movement of an ancient group of white folk. The Japanese proper, although they have now in their turn displaced the Ainu, have in places intermarried with them, and are in the main of two sorts (a) aristocratic or Daimyo type, resembling the Koreans and Manchurians, (b) plebeian or Proto-Malay type, who are Mongolians of the stock from which the true Malay is derived.

The religion of Japan prior to the year 522 A.D. had no special name, but was apparently a form of polydaemonism. From that date onwards Buddhism was introduced and developed from China by way of Korea, and the Chinese word Shinto was then also introduced to describe the non-Buddhist religion of Japan. It is not surprising to find that the two systems became gradually interwoven. Shinto means literally the way of the gods, and it was purely a nature-religion; but the Shinto deities came in time to be called reincarnations of the Buddha. This syncretism, however, was followed by a reaction, and during the period 1700 to 1841 Japanese national religion was purged of all Buddhist and Chinese influences, and for the time being reduced itself to a form of Mikado- or emperor-worship, and the inculcation of the duty to obey one's instincts. Nevertheless Shinto is really a polytheism evolving into a pantheism, influenced perhaps by the Mahayana Buddhism and also sometimes seeming to merge into monotheism, for we read in one Shinto writing "The earthly eternal divine being (the god Kuni-Tokotachi) is one and at the same time the eight hundred myriads of deities. It is the one great common root of heaven and earth; all things in the universe are in this one god; from the beginning of the universe to its very end the God Kuni-Tokotachi exists everlastingly." There can be no doubt that in later times not only Buddhism but also Christianity has exercised influence upon Japanese national religion, and hence there has come to pass a certain ethical transformation of the deities and of the rites connected with them, a tendency to iconoclasm and a movement towards the reinterpretation of the ancient myths, which were seen to be often self-contradictory and even foolish. Modern Shintoists who have become acquainted with western religion and philosophy have tried to defend Shintoism as being inseparably bound up with the life of the Japanese people, so that it is impossible, as long as the Japanese remain what they are, for it to cease to exist. They even say that it stands fundamentally upon the same truth as Christianity, and that though the latter may vary from it in form, yet both in essence are the same. It is difficult to agree with this so long as Mikadoism maintains its central place in modern Shinto. We may well believe that Shinto has been greatly purified and that little or nothing remains in its higher expression of the old nature-polytheism. Nevertheless it is impossible to identify Mikadoism with Christianity, just as in the past it was found impossible to identify the cultus of the Roman emperor with primitive Christianity. Christianity is essentially interracial and international, and cannot be identified with any purely national cultus. It allows a limited and restrained patriotism, but not one which is exclusive.

It is worth noting that one of the most interesting Japanese deities is Kwannon, the goddess of mercy. She appears often with a child on her knees, and evidently represents the Great Mother, a female deity of the same type as Isis or the Madonna. Among the peasantry there are plenty of survivals of religious practices connected with more primitive types of religion, differing only in detail from those to be found in other parts of the world. Thus we have traces of sun and fire worship, and the deification of trees, mountains, and animals, especially the fox, the crow, and the crocodile.

On the other hand there is a great, rich, and complex development of Buddhism in Japan. As we have already observed, Buddhism on entering a country readily received the various Shinto deities of both sexes into its scheme. They appear in multitudes in the Buddhist heaven, or are regarded as reincarnations of the original Buddha. Japanese Buddhism has split into a large number of sects varying greatly in thought and practice. Thus one group specially emphasises justification by faith. A particular incarnation of the Buddha called Amida postponed his attainment of Nirvana in order to show compassion to the rest of mankind. To trust in Amida is therefore a means of redemption. Works are not needed. All that is necessary is to lean upon Amida's promise. No one can fail to recognise the resemblance between this doctrine and that put forward by certain types of evangelical Christianity. There is no need to assume any connection between the two phenomena. Each is a separate and independent development, due to an insistence upon a certain aspect of piety. Another Japanese sect teaches the exact opposite, and insists that personal effort is essential to the attainment of perfection. A third type relies entirely upon meditation, with the object of realising that in one's self lies the true heart of Buddha, since it is held that once this has been grasped, the individual will have passed beyond good and evil and will have attained perfect peace and rest. These latter sects are on the whole more influenced by Indian and Chinese thought of a monistic character, and are less distinctively Japanese in expression.

It is difficult usefully to forecast the future of religion in Japan, since Christianity in its various forms has established a firm hold among the Japanese and is slowly forging ahead, and this is leading to modifications and reforms both among Shintoism and Buddhism. At the same time the developments of industrialism and modern scientific culture are complicating the situation. Marxist materialism and various other forms of unbelief are rampant, and the Japanese who have learnt to read English or German are fully versed in the speculative literature of the West, whether from Europe or the United States. No form of Christianity which fails to take account of the modern view of the universe or of modern studies in the origin and development of religion seems likely to have the least chance of winning its way among the educated Japanese or for the matter of that among the educated Chinese either. The influence of the evangelist Toyohiko Kagawa is leading to a widespread popular Christian movement, which is entirely under the control of Japanese, and aims not only at the conversion of individuals, but also at the regeneration of the social and industrial order, and at the building up of a society based upon co-operative methods.

## Appendix C

## OF MANICHAEISM

MANICHAEISM is now recognised as an independent religion, as independent as Islam. It arose in opposition, not to Christianity, but to later Zoroastrianism. In a sense it represents the more completely developed type of Gnosticism, *i.e.* the attempt on a large scale to set forth a pre-Christian universal religion of salvation and to connect the world to it. It was formed by Mani, the son of a noble Persian of Hamadan, who was born in Babylon in 215. Mani derived his cosmology from the ancient civilisations of the East, and he made Babylon to be his spiritual metropolis. He took from Parseeism cosmic and eschatological principles, and from Indian teaching the ascetic ordering of life. To these he added certain elements from Christianity which powerfully increased the effect of his system. He gave himself out to be the last and greatest prophet, the final teacher sent by God to Babylonia, just as Buddha had been sent to India, Zarathustra to Persia and Jesus to the West.

The basis of his teaching is the theory of the conflict between light and darkness. This is represented in the form of a myth, based no doubt upon elements which go back to the very earliest notions of cosmic happenings current in Mesopotamia. The king of the paradise of light has five spiritual and five corporeal elements. These surround the king of light and are the pleroma or body of the god of light. The light stretches in all directions, and strikes downwards to the realm of darkness, from which it is separated by no hard and fast barrier. Darkness also is a personal element, and is indeed a female spirit having five sub-divisions, and extending its sway in all directions as far as the confines of the realm of light. The origin of Satan is to be found in the mingling of elements of light and darkness when our visible earth was brought into existence.

From the elements of darkness through their imprisonment within them of certain elements of light arose Satan, the original devil, who, like the Babylonian Tiamat, is thought of as a dragon.

The god of light despatches to fight the devil certain elements of light known as the mother of life and the original human beings. Satan and his powers of evil are partially victorious and the primal man is captured. The god of light then throws his reserves into the battle and rescues the primal man; but in the interval a mingling of the elements has taken place, and out of this mingling has arisen our world consisting of ten heavens and eight earths, each heaven with twelve gates, each gate with six storeys (and so on), in which the elements of light have the preponderance. The creation of the world is the work of the god of light, and has for its purpose the freeing of the lost particles of light. Round the earth there is a kind of fortification to prevent the escape of particles of darkness into the realm of light. The heavenly bodies, known as the signs of the Zodiac, form a kind of machine into which the light, as it is extracted from the earth, is conveyed to the moon, and then, when it becomes full, into the sun. The moon represents the primal man, the sun the mother of life. The human race is on the bodily side darkness, on the spiritual side a fragment of the primal man.

Man was not created by God but by a lower being, the first archont or spirit of the power of darkness. In man, therefore, the two elements are at war, although in Eve there was a preponderance of light over darkness, in Adam the reverse. The god of light then sent Jesus and a second spirit of light in order to instruct Adam as to the nature of light and darkness. The interpretation of the Bible narrative proceeds on these lines. The principal writing in which the Manichaean cosmogony is set forth is called the Fihrist. The development of the world has for its

goal the freeing of the imprisoned light, and he who follows
the teaching of Mani co-operates in this work of liberation,
and when the process has been completed the visible world
will come to an end with the appearance of the third
Ancient (the first being the god of light himself, and the
second the primal man) and the latter will gather together
the perfect Manichaeans. Omophorus, who carries the
earth on his shoulders and who belongs to the world of
light, will let it fall, whereupon it will go headlong into the
depths, and all will be burned up in a conflagration lasting
for 1468 years. Meanwhile a new paradise will be created
in which will be collected all the light and all the perfect
Manichaeans. The devils will go back into their own realm
there to be imprisoned for ever.

So much space would not have been given to this curious
and fantastic cosmogony if it had not been for its wide
influence, and for the fact that it represents an honest
attempt at a complete world outlook, which has had no
small survival value. It has been remarked that there
are no Manichaeans to-day. This may be so, but there
are a great many people calling themselves Theosophists
who believe in a cosmogony which in its own way is quite
as peculiar. It needs to be remembered that the followers
of Mani in the fourth century A.D. were both numerous
and influential, and that they succeeded for a time in making
a disciple of Augustine of Hippo. Something very like
Manichaeism continued to exist in Eastern Europe for
many centuries, and there seems little doubt that a form
of it was embodied in the notorious Albigensian heresy.
Modern theosophy is in no sense a direct descendant of
these movements, but it undeniably belongs to the same
group of queer oriental religious philosophies, in which the
deity is stepped down to humanity by a series of inter-
mediaries or aeons; while great stress is laid upon the
practice of inducing peculiar states of consciousness in
which it is alleged that revelations as to the mysteries of the
universe may be obtained, those who attain to this occult
knowledge being called adepts, and corresponding to the
class of perfect persons in Manichaean gnosticism.

Mani divided humanity into three classes:

(1) Perfect or elect Manichaeans;

(2) The Hearers;

(3) Those who are not Manichaeans.

The perfect ones had three duties; they must live only on vegetable diet, since plants contain elements of light and are purified by being eaten by the elect; they must eschew marriage and all sexual intercourse; and they must employ the material elements only in accordance with the service and significance of the world of light.

The hearers were enjoined to reverence the elect and to minister to their needs. The elect had special feasts but no sacrifice. They fasted seven days in every month, and on Sundays with the hearers.

Four times of daily prayer were prescribed, mid-day, immediately before sunset, immediately after sunset and three hours after sunset. On praying the Manichee turned himself to the sun or the moon, or, if that was impossible, towards the north point of the heavens, as being the seat of the king of light.

There was an annual festival in memory of the founder, which was known as the Bema, in token of the empty seat or bema, which signified the invisible presence of Mani.

In controversy with Christians Mani claimed to be the Paraclete of the fourth Gospel, and attacked certain parts of the Pauline teaching. He gave the name of Jesus in his teaching to the saviour from the realm of light, but in reality the latter denoted a celestial being whose movements are determined by the moon. The historical Jesus in the teaching of Mani belongs to the unredeemed part of the light. In the West Manichaeism appropriated to itself a measure of trinitarian doctrine, and its adherents took part in Christian festivals.

N.B.—For further information the reader must be referred to Prof. F. C. Burkitt's Donnellan Lectures on this subject.

# POSTSCRIPT TO VOLUME V

THE descriptive accounts of various systems of thought and practice which this book contains may be regarded in two ways, either as static, or as a serial process. The tendency of the latest European thought with its revival of emphasis upon dialectic is to conceive of development as discontinuous, and the attempt is being made to try out this hypothesis of dialectic upon the various departments of human activity, as well as in the spheres of biology, chemistry, and so forth. This inductive method no doubt has its uses, but also its great dangers. It may lead to the wresting of facts to suit theories, and to hopeless rationalisation. British scholars still prefer what has been called "creeping empiricism," or the careful observation of the facts by field work, photography and experimental research. They like to look at the facts, and to let the facts teach them, without prejudice, and without prescribing the conclusions to be reached. I venture to think that if we pursue this method it will be possible to discern both continuity and discontinuity in the course of the history of religion.

No doubt it is possible to arrange the religious developments of mankind so as to make them into a pattern of our own devising. Is it not, however, better to let them fall into their own pattern? And is not that natural pattern one which puts the pivot and centre of religious development just where Christians have always put it? I invite the reader to consider this, and to bear it in mind as he passes on to the consideration of the next volume, in which the scheme is completed by a survey of Judaism and Christianity.

# BIBLIOGRAPHY

THE aim of this section is to provide students with some sort of working scheme. No attempt has been made at an exhaustive catalogue of books; but it is hoped that enough references have been given to enable the scholar to forge his way further for himself, and to indicate the directions in which fuller information may most swiftly be sought.

### GENERAL WORKS.

KEANE, A. H. *Man Past and Present,* new edition revised by A. H. QUIGGIN and A. C. HADDON (Camb. Univ. Press, 1920).
Deals with racial anthropology.

JEVONS, F. B. *Introduction to the Study of Comparative Religion* (Chicago, 1901).

TOY, C. H. *Introduction to the History of Religions* (Ginn & Co., Chicago, 1913).
*Introduction to the History of Religion* (Methuen, 1902).
Old books, but still useful.

MOORE, G. F. *The History of Religion* (Edin., 1913).

JEREMIAS, A. *Allgemeine Religionsgeschichte* (Münich, 1924).

FRAZER, Sir JAMES. *Collected Works, The Golden Bough,* etc. (Macmillan).

DE LA SAUSSAYE, CHANTEPIE. *Lehrbuch der Religionsgeschichte,* re-edited by BERTHOLET UND LEHMANN (Tübingen, 1925).

JORDAN, L. H. *Comparative Religion, its Adjuncts and Allies* (Oxf. Univ. Press, 1915).
Is merely a detailed and rather commonplace biography, but is nevertheless useful.

HEILER, F. *Das Gebet,* 1917. English Translation (abridged), *Prayer, a study in the history of psychology of Religion,* 1932. Trans. by Dr. Samuel McComb.
See especially the Bibliography. The original edition is immensely rich in detail.

DE LA BOULLAYE, PINARD, S.J. *L'Étude comparée des Religions* (2 vols. Paris, 1920).

HOPKINS, Prof. E. W. *Origin and Evolution of Religion* (Yale Univ. Press, 1923).

UNDERWOOD, A. C. *Conversion, Christian and Non-Christian* (Allen & Unwin, 1925).

JAMES, E. O. *The Emergence of Religion* (in "Essays Catholic and Critical, S.P.C.K., 1926).
The footnotes contain useful references.

CLEMEN, K., AND OTHERS. *The Religions of the World* (trans. into English). Bonn, 1930. Trans. pub. G. G. Harrap & Co., London, 1931.

SÖDERBLOM, Archbishop. *The Living God* (Gifford Lectures, 1931, Oxf. Univ. Press).

*Propyläenweltgeschichte*, Vol. I, first six chapters (Leipzig, 1931).

*Die Religion in Geschichte und Gegenwart* (Encycl., 2nd edition, 1931).

HASTINGS. *Encyclopædia of Religion and Ethics.*

HAAS, F. *Bilderatlas zur Religionsgeschichte* (in several volumes).
A useful series in studying the symbolism of the various ancient religions.

For general reference see the volumes of the *Archiv für Religionswissenschaft*, and *Annales du Musée Guimet*.

## FOR CHAPTER III.

The most recently and sympathetically written books upon this subject are the Gifford Lectures of Dr. R. R. MARETT, "Faith, Hope and Charity in Primitive Religion," and "The Sacraments of Simple Folk" (Oxf. Univ. Press), but they are not very useful to the student who has not first gained a grasp of the available data. Dr. MARETT'S small volume, *Anthropology*, in the Home University Library, forms a useful introduction. Consult also *Lehrbuch der Religionsgeschichte*, BERTHOLET UND LEHMANN, sections 1 and 2. E. TYLOR'S *Primitive Culture*, 1913, is still indispensable.

On individual peoples, in view of the hundreds of monographs available, it is difficult to make a selection. The series published by Seeley, Service & Co. should be consulted, and the records in *Man*, (the Journal of the Royal Anthropological Society), and in corresponding foreign journals.

The following are typical:

RIVERS, W. H. R. *The Todas.*

LANDTMANN, GUNNAR. *The Kiwai Papuans of New Guinea*, with Introduction by A. C. HADDON (Macmillan, 1927).

2 E*

TALBOT, P. A. *Nigerian Fertility Cults* (Oxf. Univ. Press, 1927).

SMITH, E. W., and DALE, A. M. *The Ba-ila of Northern Rhodesia* (Macmillan, 1920).

See also the works of Dr. ROSCOE on the peoples of Uganda; Prof. W. C. WILLOUGHBY, *The Soul of the Bantu* (Student Christian Movement, 1928); and RAOUL ALLIER, *The Mind of the Savage* (G. Bell & Sons, 1929).

On prehistoric man Mr. M. C. BURKITT's *The Old Stone Age* (Camb. Univ. Press, 1933), and especially its Bibliography, may be consulted. See also Mr. BURKITT's *Our Ancestors* (Home University Library, 1930).

The Bibliography at the end of Dr. A. C. HADDON's *Races of Man* (Camb. Univ. Press, new ed., 1924) is very complete.

Consult also the *Reallexikon der Vorgeschichte*, ed. MAX EBERT (Berlin, 1929, 15 vols., but not yet complete).

On the "High God" controversy the principal works are

SCHMIDT, Fr. W. *The Origin and Growth of Religion Facts and Theories*, trans. Prof. H. J. ROSE (Methuen, 1931). An abridgement of his large 4-vol. work published in German, *Der Ursprung der Gottesidee*.

RADIN, PAUL. The Arthur Davis Memorial Lecture, 1924.

LOWIE, R. H. *Primitive Religion* (London, 1925).

BETH, KARL. *Religion und Magie* (Teubner, Leipzig, 1917, 2nd edition).

COOK, Prof. S. A. 1. Review of Fr. Schmidt in the *Journal of Theological Studies*, 1932.
2. *Ethical Monotheism in the Light of Comparative Religion* (pubd. by the W. London Synagogue Association).

SÖDERBLOM, Archbishop. *Das Werden des Gottesglaubens* (Leipzig, 1926).

## FOR CHAPTER IV.

The *Cambridge Ancient History* (especially Vols. I–IV and the final volume of Plates) should be consulted. Cf. also BERTHOLET UND LEHMANN, Vol. I, pp. 423–644, and Prof. JASTROW, *Religious Beliefs in Assyria and Babylonia* (Putnams, 1911).

On SUMERIA the writings of Mr. C. L. WOOLLEY (Oxf. Univ. Press) give the latest information.

The works of Dr. C. H. W. JOHNS (Camb. Univ. Press) represent the position of study in pre-war days, but contain useful matter.

Texts may be studied

1. In ENGLISH from the S.P.C.K. Texts for Students, Nos. 24 and 25 (1921), and the publications of the British Museum Trustees (edited by Sir E. A. WALLIS BUDGE).
2. In GERMAN in the *Textbuch zur Religionsgeschichte*, LEHMANN UND HAAS (Leipzig, 1922); and in

HARPER'S *Assyrian and Babylonian Letters* (13 vols., Univ. of Chicago Press and Luzac & Co.).

The symbolism of both areas may be studied at the British Museum and in the Museum of the Louvre at Paris, and the British Museum official illustrated catalogues contain much useful matter.

On EGYPT consult

BREASTED, Prof. J. H. *The Development of Religious Thought in Ancient Egypt* (Hodder & Stoughton, 1912); and his references and translations of texts (see below); also

KEES, H. *Kulturgeschichte des Alten Orients. Egypt* (Münich, 1933).

See also Articles in the Supplementary Volume of HASTINGS' *Dictionary of the Bible*, and in his *Encyclopædia of Religion and Ethics*; also the Article in *Der Religion in Geschichte und Gegenwart* (new, 2nd edition, Tübingen, 1932).

Texts may be studied

1. In ENGLISH in the publications of the British Museum Trustees, which give most of what is required.
2. In GERMAN in LEHMANN UND HAAS, *op. cit.*, and in GÜNTHER ROEDER, *Urkunden zur Religion des Alten Aegypten* (Jena, 1923).

See also J. H. BREASTED, *op. cit.* ; also his series of Ancient Records of Egypt (5 vols. Univ. of Chicago Press, 1906) and the Collected Works of Sir E. A. WALLIS BUDGE, which comprise translations of nearly all the available texts (35 vols., Kegan Paul); also his *Gods of the Egyptians* (2 vols., Methuen, 1904).

Consult also A. ERMAN, *Aegypt und Aegyptisches Leben im Altertum* (Tübingen, 1923); A. S. GEDEN, *Studies in the Religions of the East*, Chaps. II and III (C. H. Kelly, 1913); also Articles in *Revue d'Assyriologie, Zeitschrift für Assyriologie*, and *Orientalische Litteraturzeitung*.

## FOR CHAPTER V.

For general use consult the *Encyclopædia of Religion and Ethics* and *Die Religion in Geschischte und Gegenwart* (2nd edition); also A. S. GEDEN, *op. cit.*, and S. CAVE, *Living Religions of the East* (Duckworth, 1929).

On ZOROASTRIANISM, apart from the previously published versions of sacred texts, the best works are those of the late Prof. J. H. MOULTON, *The Treasures of the Magi* (Oxf. Univ. Press, 1917), and *Early Zoroastrianism* (Williams & Norgate, 1913).

Consult also SCHEFTELOWITZ, *Die Altpersische Religion* (Giessen, 1920); M. N. DHALLA, Ph.D., *Zoroastrian Theology*—written by a Parsi High Priest—(New York, Luzac & Co., 1914); R. REITZEN-STEIN, *Iranische Erlösungsmysterium*, and O. G. VON WESENDONK, *Das Weltbild der Iranier* (Münich, 1933).

On INDIA a good introductory work with full references is that of Sir CHARLES ELIOT, *Hinduism and Buddhism*. With this the Introductory Section of the Report of the Simon Commission may be studied; also J. N. FARQUHAR, *A Primer of Hinduism* (Oxf. Univ. Press, 1912).

Consult carefully the Bibliography given by Dr. HADDON, *op. cit.*, pp. 167–8, and refer especially to the *Census Reports*, the introductions to which contain valuable matter.

In addition the following books are of value:—

PRATT, Prof. J. B.   *India and its Faiths* (Constable, 1916).

MACNICOL, N.   *Indian Theism, from the Vedic to the Mohammedan Period* (Oxf. Univ. Press, 1915).

STEVENSON, Mrs. SINCLAIR.   *Rites of the Twice-born* (Oxf. Univ. Press, 1920).

MACKENZIE, J.   *Hindu Ethics* (Oxf. Univ. Press, 1922).

GRISWOLD, Dr. H. G.   *The Religion of the Rigveda* (Oxf. Univ. Press, 1923).

RADAKRISHNAN, Prof.   *Indian Philosophy*, 2 vols.

URQUHART, Prof. W. S.   *The Vedanta and Modern Thought* (Oxf. Univ. Press, 1928).

OTTO, RUDOLF.   *Westöstliche Mystik* (Gotha, 1926), also translated into English (Macmillan).
    Deals with the comparison of Sankara with such western mystics as Eckhart.

For Texts the old edition, begun by Prof. MAX MÜLLER, of the SACRED BOOKS OF THE EAST, is still useful, but the *Bhagavadgita* has been translated by J. D. P. HILL (Oxf. Univ. Press) and by E. J. THOMAS (Wisdom of the East Series, John Murray). The most convenient translation of the *Upanishads* is that by R. E. HUME, *The Thirteen Principal Upanishads* (2nd edition, Oxf. Univ. Press, 1931). The Textbook of LEHMANN UND HAAS, again, of course, for those who read German, is to be consulted.

Consult also J. N. FARQUHAR, *Outline of the Religious Literature of India* (Oxf. Univ. Press, 1920); and also THE HARVARD ORIENTAL SERIES, edited by C. R. LANMAN.

On special features, the series "The Religions of India" (Oxf. Univ. Press) may be studied:—

WHITEHEAD, Bishop.  *The Village Gods of South India* (2nd edition, 1921).

UNDERHILL, M. M.  *The Hindu Religious Year* (1921).

KENNEDY, M. T.  *The Chaitanya Movement* (1925).

BRIGGS, G. W.  *The Chamars* (1920).

DEMING, W. S.  *Ramdas and the Ramdasis* (1928).

KEAY, F. E.  *Kabir and his Followers* (1931).

CARPENTER, J. ESTLIN.  *Theism in Medieval India* (Williams & Norgate, 1921).

CAVE, Principal S.  *Redemption, Hindu and Christian* (Oxf. Univ. Press, 1919),

OTTO, RUDOLF.  *India's Religion of Grace* (Student Christian Movement, 1931).

On BUDDHISM there is a rich literature. Apart from the previously cited work of Sir CHARLES ELIOT, who for diplomatic reasons omits all reference to Japanese Buddhism, the most readable general survey is

PRATT, Prof. J. B.  *The Pilgrimage of Buddhism* (Macmillan, 1925).

SAUNDERS, K. J.  *The Story of Buddhism* (Oxf. Univ. Press, 1916) may also be used.

It is, however, most important to take account of the work of Mrs. RHYS DAVIDS, and her intimate knowledge of the early texts renders her conclusions all the more weighty, even though debatable. The countless publications of the PALI TEXT SOCIETY, of which she is President, as well as the relevant volumes in the SACRED BOOKS OF THE EAST and TRÜBNER'S ORIENTAL SERIES, should be studied alongside of her *Manual of Buddhism for Advanced Students*, and especially the Bibliography contained in Chapter II, and her *Sakya* (Kegan Paul).

See also *The Sacred Books of the Buddhists*, several volumes, translated by Lord CHALMERS and others, under the patronage of the King of Siam (Oxf. Univ. Press, 1921).

In German we have a monograph, *Buddha*, by PAUL DAHLKE (trans. Macmillan, 1927), and also H. OLDENBERG, *Buddha, Sein Leben, Seine Lehre, Seine Gemeinde* (Berlin, 1921).

W. H. MCGOVERN, *An Introduction to Mahayana Buddhism* (Kegan Paul, 1922), by a Scotsman who has become a Buddhist, is of some interest.

The ASOKA EDICTS have been magnificently edited by E. HULTZSCH (Oxf. Univ. Press, 1925, Vol. I of *Corpus Inscriptionum Indicarum*).

The JATAKAS, or folk-tales of the various incarnations of the
Buddha, have been translated by a group of British Scholars
(Camb. Univ. Press).

M. B. MAW, *Buddhist Mysticism* (Bordeaux, 1924) compares the
latter with the mysticism of St. Teresa and of Lady Julian of
Norwich.

Prof. S. TACHIBANA, *The Ethics of Buddhism* (Oxf. Univ. Press,
1926), is an attempt to explain and justify these ethics in the face
of other systems.

On Japanese Buddhism consult

LLOYD, A. *The Creed of Half Japan* (Smith, Elder & Co.,
London, 1911).

REISCHAUER, J. K. *Japanese Buddhism*.

SUZUKI, Prof. *Essays in Zen Buddhism* (Kyoto, 1927).

STREETER, Provost. *The Buddha and the Christ* (Bampton Lectures,
1931, Macmillan).

On Tibetan Buddhism consult

BELL, Sir CHARLES. *The Religion of Tibet* (Oxf. Clar. Press, 1931).

On JAINISM the following recent works may be consulted:—

STEVENSON, Mrs. SINCLAIR. *The Heart of Jainism* (Oxf. Univ.
Press, 1915).

GUÉRINOT, Dr. A. *La Religion Djaïna* (Geuthner, Paris, 1926).

MARATHI HYMNS have been translated by MACNICOL.

The sacred literature of the SIKHS has been edited in translation
by M. A. MCAULIFFE, *The Sikh Religion* (6 vols., Oxf. Clarendon
Press, 1909).

A valuable commentary on BHAKTI, containing specimens of
lyrics, is D. J. ESTLIN CARPENTER'S work on *Indian Theism* (see
previous page).

The literature dealing with CHINA is again, of course, immense,
but for practical purposes the reader may consult THE CHINESE
CLASSICS (2nd edit. revised, trans. by Prof. JAMES LEGGE).

W. E. SOOTHILL, *The Three Religions of China* (3rd edition,
Oxf. Univ. Press, 1929) is indispensable.

A useful historical survey will be found in the *Propyläenweltgeschichte*, Vol. I, pp. 170 ff., by F. E. A. KRAUSE (richly illustrated).

Study should also be made of

BRUCE, Prof. PERCY. *Chu Hsi and his Masters* (Probsthain, 1923).

GILES, Prof. H. A. *Confucianism and its Rivals* (Hibbert Lectures,
Williams & Norgate, 1915).

MACLAGAN, P. J. *Chinese Religious Ideas* (Student Christian
Movement, 1926).

HARVEY, E. D. *The Mind of China* (Yale Univ. Press, 1933).
Especially the last chapter and Bibliography.

Nearly all the best literature upon China is in French. The
following list is a selection:—

WIEGER, L. *Histoire de croyances religieuses et des opinions
philosophiques en Chine, depuis l'origine jusque à nos
jours* (Paris, 1922).
Regarded by experts as a careful and trustworthy
compilation.

GRANET, MARCEL. *La Religion des Chinois.*
*La Civilisation Chinoise* (1929, English trans.,
1930).
*La Pensée Chinoise.*
*Fêtes et Chansons anciennes de la Chine.*
(Bibl. de l'école des hautes études, Sciences
religieuses, 34. Paris, 1919, trans. E. D.
EDWARDS, Broadway Library, London, 1932.)

CORDIER, HENRI. *Histoire générale de la Chine.*

COUVREUR, Fr. F. S., S.J. Translation of the Classics (very careful
and complete).

T'OUNG PAO. *Archives . . . de l'Asie orientale* (Leide, many
volumes still appearing).

*Variétés sinologiques* (Shanghai—a Roman Catholic series of studies,
in many volumes), contains useful matter.

Also the works of CHAVANNES on CHINESE ARCHAEOLOGY.

On Eastern religions in general a very suggestive commentary,
though not always a wise one, is Count HERMANN VON KEYSERLING'S
*Reisetagebuch Eines Philosophs* (1921, trans. into English and
published in 2 vols. by J. M. Dent & Co.).

On MEDITERRANEAN RELIGION it is well to set down first the
monumental work of Sir ARTHUR EVANS upon Crete—*The Palace
of Minos at Knossos* (4 vols., completed 1930, Macmillan). With
this may be taken the detailed but highly individualised studies by
Miss JANE ELLEN HARRISON:—

1. *Prolegomena to the Study of Greek Religion* (Camb. Univ. Press,
1903).

2. *Themis* (Camb. Univ. Press, 1912).

3. *Epilegomena to the Study of Greek Religion* (Camb. Univ. Press,
1913).

4. *Ancient Art and Ritual* (Williams & Norgate, Home Univ. Lib.).

Outline surveys are those of Prof. GILBERT MURRAY, *Five Stages
of Greek Religion*, and of Prof. M. P. NILSSON (Lund), *Greek Religion*

(a translation of the section written by him contained in BERTHOLET UND LEHMANN, *op. cit.*); also THADDEUS ZIELINSKI, *The Religion of Ancient Greece* (Oxf. Univ. Press, translated from the Polish).

Detailed study is given by WILAMOWITZ-MOELLENDORF, *Der Glaube der Hellenen* (Berlin, 1932).

Apart from the actual works of Plato, the following may be recorded:—

ADAM, Prof. JAMES. *The Religious Teachers of Greece* (Gifford Lectures, 1908).
*The Vitality of Platonism*, and Other Essays (1911).

BURNET, JOHN, LL.D. *Platonism* (Lectures, 1928).

MORE, P. ELMER. *The Religion of Plato* (Princeton, 1921).

TAYLOR, Prof. A. E. *Plato, the Man and his Work* (London, 1929).

For the symbolism of Greek Art see PFUHL, *Malerei und Zeichnung der Griechen* (3 vols. Münich, 1923), and the great *Corpus Antiquorum Vasorum*, being published internationally; also the Catalogue of Greek and Roman Sculpture in the British Museum, *Hesperia*, the Journal of the American School of Archæology at Athens (Harvard Univ. Press), and the works of Sir CHARLES WALSTON.

On GREEK RELIGION in general see

*Religiongeschichtliche Versuchen und Vorarbeitungen* (Giessen, in many volumes, still appearing).

COOK, A. B. *Zeus* (Vols. I and II, Vol. III in preparation. Camb. Univ. Press).
A perfect mine of information.

DEUBNER, LUDWIG. *Attische Feste* (Berlin, 1932).
Plates and most interesting calendar.

FARNELL, L. R. *Cults of the Greek States* (5 vols. Oxf., 1909).

On the MYSTERY RELIGIONS CONTROVERSY:

BEVAN, EDWYN. *Hellenism and Christianity* (Allen & Unwin, 1921).

REITZENSTEIN, R. *Der Hellenistischen Mysterienreligionen* (3rd edition. Teubner, Leipzig, 1927).

SCHULTZ, W. *Dokumente der Gnosis* (Eugen Diederichs, Jena, 1910).

ANGUS, S. *The Mystery Religions and Christianity* (John Murray, 1925, 1926).
*The Religious Quests of the Græco-Roman World* (John Murray, 1926).

On ROMAN RELIGION :

FOWLER, WILLIAM WARDE, LL.D.
    *The Religious Experience of the Roman People* (Gifford Lectures, 1909–10).
    *The Roman Festivals of the Period of the Republic* (1899).
    *Roman Ideas of Deity* (London, 1914).

FRAZER, SIR JAMES. *Ovid's Fasti* (edited in 5 vols., London, 1929).

FOR CHAPTER VI.

ISLAM.

The most convenient edition of the KORAN is that published by J. M. Dent & Sons, Everyman Library, Rodwell's translation, and with it should be read

SALE, GEORGE. *Preliminary Discourse to the Koran*, edited by Sir EDWARD DENISON ROSS (Warne & Co., 1921).

STANTON, H. U. W. *The Teaching of the Koran* (S.P.C.K., 1919).

Other recent works are:—

BUHL, FRANTS. *Das Leben Muhammeds* (German trans. H. SCHAEDER, Leipzig, 1930).

DERMENGHEM, EMILE. *The Life of Mohammed* (Routledge, 1930).
    The two best and most recent.

WENSINCK, Prof. A. J. *The Muslim Creed* (Camb. Univ. Press, 1932).
    A useful survey of Mohammedan theological development up to as-Senusi.

MARGOLIOUTH, Prof. D. S. *The Early Development of Mohammedanism* (Hibbert Lectures, Williams & Norgate, 1914).

BROWN, J. P., and ROSE, H. A. *The Darvishes* (Oxf. Univ. Press, 1927).

LAMMENS, Fr. H., S.J. *L'Islam. Croyances et Institutions* (Beyrouth, 1926). Hostile.

TITUS, M. T. *Indian Islam* (Oxf. Univ. Press, 1930).

NICHOLSON, Prof. R. A. *Islamic Mysticism* (Camb. Univ. Press, 1921).

On the modern situation:—

*The Report of the Jerusalem Conference of* 1924, Vol. I.

*Whither Islam?* Ed. Prof. H. A. R. GIBB (Gollancz, 1932). Especially the final chapter.

JONES, L. BEVAN. *The People of the Mosque* (Student Christian Movement, 1932).

FOR APPENDIX A.

JOYCE, T. A.   *South American Archaeology* (1912).
Prescott's *Conquest of Mexico* (2 vol. edit., 1922).
Reports on the British Museum Expedition to British Honduras, 1926 and 1928 (reprinted from the Jl. of the Royal Anthropological Institute).
Guide to the Maudslay collection of Maya Sculptures in the British Museum (1923), and especially its Bibliography, page 85.

SPENCE, L.   *The Civilisations of Ancient Mexico* (Camb. Univ. Press, 1913).   Note its Bibliography.

MEANS, P. A.   *Ancient Civilisations of the Andes* (Scribners, New York, 1931).

Richly illustrated and with a very full Bibliography; especially of the old Spanish writers such as Fr. Acosta.

Consult also some of the publications of the Hakluyt Society, and the American Journals of Ethnology, etc.

FOR APPENDIX B.

ANESAKI, Prof. MASAHARU.   *History of Japanese Religion* (Kegan Paul, 1930).

KATO, GENCHI.   *A Study of Shinto, the Religion of the Japanese Nation* (Meiji Japan Society, Tokyo, 1926).

See also BERTHOLET UND LEHMANN, Vol. I, pp. 262–421, and the texts given in HAAS.

FOR APPENDIX C.

ALFARIC.   *Les Écritures Manichéenes* (Paris, 1918).

BURKITT, Prof. F. C.   *The Religion of the Manichees* (Donnellan Lectures, Camb. Univ. Press, 1925), and the references therein given, especially LE COQ.

"New Manichaean Documents found in Egypt." Article by SCHMIDT AND POLOTSKY in the *Sitzungsberichten* of the Prussian Academy (Berlin, 1933).

(These and the other documents found near Turfan have revolutionised our knowledge of the Manichaean religious doctrine.)

# INDEX

445

PRINTED BY
W. HEFFER AND SONS, LTD.,
CAMBRIDGE, ENGLAND.